BEYOND PRISCILLA

One gay man, one gay truck, one big idea …

The Beyond 'That's So Gay' National Tour

DANIEL WITTHAUS

Clouds of Magellan | Melbourne

© 2014 Daniel Witthaus
First published 2014

ISBN: 9781742983929

Clouds of Magellan, Melbourne, Australia
www.cloudsofmagellan.net

Daniel Witthaus is the author of *Beyond 'That's So Gay!' – Challenging homophobia in Australian schools* and the *Pride & Prejudice* educational package. He continues to visit country communities to challenge homophobia one cuppa at a time, occasionally chatting with media outlets. In 2013 Daniel founded the National Institute for Challenging Homophobia Education (NICHE), which focuses on the needs of regional, rural and remote Australia. He likes to use Melbourne as a base, with occasional sojourns in Berlin.

For the women of my extended family who taught me the beauty, art and importance of the humble cuppa, especially Mum, who perfected it – *DW*

Contents

Introduction

ABC Studios, Melbourne, VIC

'So what are you drivin'? A bus with a shoe on top? Like Priscilla?'
Cue half-nervous laughter.

'No,' I reply, 'I'm driving my openly gay truck called Bruce. He's got an empty roof rack on top.'

I'm in at the studio of 774 ABC Melbourne for a live interview with Jon Faine. Jon is known (quoting his website) 'for his quick wit and willingness to ask the stickiest of questions'. I've been feeling nervous about my encounter with the firm but fair radio host I've listened to for years. Perhaps I shouldn't be so awed. It becomes clear in the moments before the interview that Jon is less than prepared.

'I have to admit that I have no idea why you're here. I guess you'll be able to explain it yourself ...?'

I nod, perhaps a little too vigorously in an attempt to hide my disappointment and increasing anxiety, assuring him it's 'no problem'. I quietly take my seat in the brightly coloured studio next to another author.

Although Jon tries himself to appear at ease and a little too casual, I wonder in the seconds before we go to air if he's actively avoided researching his second guest this morning. It leaves me with the feeling that I'm an inconvenient addition to his morning. And that I'm about to be reduced in the listeners' ears to the most familiar stereotype that mainstream Australia has for gays in the bush. Though I suspect it's inevitable. Tell most Australian people of a certain age that you are going to drive non-stop around the country to challenge homophobia in regional, rural and remote areas (and by homophobia I mean fear and hatred of anything that is not 100% heterosexual), and you'll cop some *Priscilla* reference.

'We're joined now by a man who is about to set off to do an almost Priscilla, Queen of the Desert road trip I suspect ... Good morning Daniel Witthaus.'

'Good morning Jon and I think it's more Leyland Brothers than Priscilla Queen of the Desert but we can go through the details later …'

Jon laughs. 'Are you going to walk into a crowded bar in an outback NSW pub dressed like Hugo Weaving was …?'

'I doubt that, I don't think my legs are as good as his, but I'll definitely be a little more low key about it …'

'What is the character of your trip then?'

My answer – 'more Leyland Brothers' – I believe, is accurate. Rather than an abbreviated personal quest to the centre of Australia with shades of provocation, entertainment and titillation, mine will be an extended, simple journey to engage and educate.

You couldn't get more simple and straightforward than Mal and Mike Leyland, the famous brothers who, through the power of television, took millions of Australians each week to every nook and cranny of their great country. Along the way they would uncover parts of Australia most had only ever heard about, and certainly were not expecting to visit anytime soon. When encouraging younger folk to imagine Mal and Mike I typically say, 'think of your most embarrassing, daggy uncles'.

*

The Beyond 'That's So Gay' Tour was a 266 day self-funded road trip that I took around Australia from February to November in 2010. And just as Mal and Mike in their journeyings answered the questions of everyday Australians about the land we inhabit, I too was looking for answers to everyday questions about life for lesbian, gay, bisexual and transgender (LGBT) people in regional, rural and remote Australia.

There are currently two 'camps' as to how to 'get along' as anything but straight in the bush: one says LGBT people need to entertain, provoke and cajole, almost forcing something approximating tolerance and acceptance; the other says LGBT people should hide, or assimilate, as well as we can, but at the expense of ourselves. I was planning to do neither. My secret 'challenging homophobia' weapon on my journey wasn't a party frock or a closet. It was a regular, everyday cup of tea: a 'cuppa'. My plan was to have a thousand conversations. I light-heartedly joked that I was going to challenge homophobia 'one cuppa at a time'. It was a strategy aimed at disarming and engaging the most hardened of opponents. And it worked. When I set out, most people feared I would be run out of town with pitchforks, that I or my openly gay truck Bruce would be harmed, or that, at best, I'd be met with deafening silence. But instead I had more cuppas than I ever dreamt possible in 38 weeks. In fact I never exhausted the invitations extended to me in towns big and small.

I'm indebted to the many who readily shared their everyday stories. Many of them are included in this book.

Enjoy the ride!

Daniel Witthaus

NOTE: LGBT *is a mouthful. But to LGBT you could also add Intersex (I), Queer (Q), Questioning (Q), Gender Questioning (GQ) and Allied (A). For the purposes of this project, the focus was on LGBT people with exploratory conversations with IQQGQA individuals and communities. This in no way represents my belief in their existence, legitimacy or right to visibility.*

Day 1

Monday, 22nd February – Geelong VIC

Bum, bugger, bastard.

I stop pacing my mum's kitchen to let the news sink in. *This* on the first day of my tour. My own hometown and I can't even get through the first day without a homophobia hurdle.

I'm on the phone to Jami, the relaxed, strategic and enthusiastic project worker with the City of Greater Geelong's 'GASP!' – 'Gay Adolescent Support Group', an LGBT young people's support project I worked on in the late 90s. Only months before, she secured a spot for me in a writer's festival as part of Geelong's multicultural festival, *Pako Festa*. The Polyglots Writers Festival aims to highlight German poetry and music, and Festival organiser, 'Bill', had seen my name, Witthaus, and assumed correctly that I was German. It was only now that Jami had sent through my author bio and the details of my book, *Beyond 'That's So Gay'*, that it became clear that it was not an 'appropriate' entry.

Yet it didn't end there. Rather than politely rescinding my inclusion on the basis of the Festival's criteria, Bill decided to give Jami a piece of his mind.

Bill commenced his tirade by outing himself as a Catholic who worked in a local private secondary school, declaring my work in schools to challenge homophobia was 'not culturally appropriate', especially for a festival reading 'with a multicultural audience' who couldn't handle such content. It seems Bill in his teaching work also decided for others what they could and couldn't handle. Describing recent Victorian Education Department policy efforts to support sexual diversity as 'imposed' and 'bullshit', Bill outlined how the government was out of touch with 'all the teachers' he know.

Jami had the calm and good sense to immediately call the *Pako Festa* organisers. They moved swiftly. Polyglots were contacted immediately and asked to explain why they should continue to be a part of *Pako Festa* after this incident. A review of the festival's policies has been launched to ensure that this won't happen again. Finally, the GASP! project and myself have been invited to march in the *Pako Festa* Parade: a first for Geelong.

Day 2

Tuesday, 23rd February – Geelong VIC

I'm sitting on the floor of a largely uninspiring training room at a local health centre. It's approaching late afternoon when I meet the current members of GASP! - the 'GASPers'. It's only been ten minutes and I feel like I'm transported back in time; roughly a decade earlier I had reluctantly left Geelong and GASP! behind to work on other projects. Now, in some ways, it feels like I've never left.

The young people clearly provide the colour and movement in this room of blues and greys. One young woman immediately begins to test me with her sarcasm and humour, yet softens when she realises I'm not going to bite or be particularly fazed. Five minutes later she is sitting next to me showing me a picture of her girlfriend on her mobile phone. When I ask what's best about having her as a girlfriend she says, 'She is like my best friend and my girlfriend at the same time'. Another young woman talks of having a very supportive, close-knit group of friends between the ages of 15 and 21.

This is my first opportunity to talk to LGBT young people about what life is like for them. It comes at the end of a long day of training locals and talking to the media. Morning tea sees me do an interview and get a photo taken for local newspaper, *The Geelong Advertiser*. It'll give my mum something else to stick on the fridge. Lunchtime and it's a phone interview with ABC Radio National's *Bush Telegraph*.

It is important that I provide training as part of the tour. On his own travels to regional Australia a decade ago, Rodney Croome found that teachers and health professionals were crying out for practical strategies and quality resources to challenge homophobia in everyday classrooms and workplaces. There simply were none. Pre-empting this I decided to provide training for those educators wanting to facilitate my challenging homophobia program, *Pride & Prejudice*, a step-by-step guide for teachers, health professionals and homophobia-curious others who want to challenge homophobia and support sexual diversity in everyday classrooms.

Whenever I ask locals to share the main issues for LGBT students in local schools the answers are: isolation, invisibility, bullying safety. It seems that Geelong is no different to any other regional area. When I ask what is available locally in Geelong to support these same students, again the answers are all too familiar. Apart from a local LGBT youth support project, Geelong's students have to cross their fingers and wish for a supportive school and staff. Too often supportive staff are thought to be an exception to the rule and seen as a breath of fresh air, not the status quo. As one educator said, there is a vast 'gap between [education] policy and practice'. Despite describing themselves after the training as 'inspired', 'motivated', 'enthusiastic', 'confident' and 'ready' with comments like 'I can't wait to get out there and try it', the gathered educators also add 'overwhelmed' and 'sad' when factoring in the broader education system.

Sitting on the floor with the current GASPers, I quietly watch and occasionally contribute to the busy preparations for the *Pako Festa* Parade. There is definitely a buzz. A number of placards are being put together for the annual march that will snake down one of Geelong's main commercial strips. Time and something practical, like placard making, helps them open up about their experiences. Soon it's apparent that although most young people here have found a better quality of life thanks to GASP!, most have arrived after an often harrowing journey. Many are still on it.

One young man says he has recently changed schools after being physically threatened and having his name with 'dirty faggot' written on a wall. Talking about her school's lack of awareness and support, a trans young person assures me she has been through enough to ensure she had three lifetimes worth of self-esteem. Each story encourages more and soon one young woman speaks of being regularly 'beaten up' over her early years of secondary school because other girls were scared she would 'hit on them'. Attending a religious private school, another young woman tells stories of being 'ranted at' in relation to the Bible and feeling unsupported by her teachers. Some gay and lesbian teachers were clear that they could not be open about their sexual identity or support her because they were fearful of losing their jobs under the Victorian Equal Opportunity exemptions for religious organisations.

Sadly, I hear resignation in most of their voices; a sense that this kind of treatment should not be so surprising, maybe that it's to be expected.

Day 3

Wednesday, 24th February – Geelong VIC

There are eight of us seated in the peaceful, idiosyncratic and cool courtyard of Go Café, the unofficial LGBT place to be in daylight hours. It's early evening, yet still warm enough for me to stick with shorts and a t-shirt. The dropping sun through the pergola overhead gives everything a green-ish tinge and somehow calms me. That and the fact that if I look over the terrarium in the middle of the large wooden table I can see my mum, my biggest supporter.

I needed a lot of calming after being shunned by the Polyglots Festival. It had left me without a book reading in my hometown. An assured audience of 70–80 people I would otherwise not ever have read to became an almost assured audience of zero. Luckily local owner of Go Café, Jason, a longtime supporter of local LGBT community efforts, has come to the rescue and offered his café for a dramatically reduced crowd. Warm and welcoming, Jason has joined this last minute crowd of locals for an intimate reading of *Beyond 'That's So Gay'*.

In amongst the mix of locals, most interestingly, is 'Noelene', a former primary school principal. Badgered into coming by Barb, the mother of my best friend from high school (hey we were desperate for numbers), Noelene seems tense and sceptical as I read three stories from my book that describe my coming out to a group of young men, my work in an all-boys Catholic school and a 'nightmare' parent scenario.

When I open for questions, Noelene dominates the initial discussion. In doing so she becomes a mouthpiece for typical concerns from teachers and parents, yet in an open and self-reflective way that can only result from experience and intelligence. She's clear she wouldn't be here had she not been 'hassled' into it.

Noelene's main concern as a parent is students making 'certain choices' after undertaking my challenging homophobia program, *Pride & Prejudice*. I gently challenge her underlying assumptions that sexual identity results from a sudden, reactive choice and bring the others in, encouraging a productive group discussion.

When I'm met with such resistance, I suspect there is probably more to the story and this is no exception. Noelene soon reveals to the group that she had been challenged as a young teacher when an older lesbian teacher came out to her in the staffroom. Previously happy to sit every lunchtime with the older woman to complete crosswords, Noelene would temporarily stop the cooperative completion until she realised that she was not going to be 'hit on'. Reflecting openly that she has some way to go, affirmed and supported by me, she resolves to go home and read *Beyond 'That's So Gay'* from cover to cover.

Mum and I stay behind with dusk soon to give way to night watching everyone filter out a side gate that has seen better days. I look over to mum who is quietly searching my face, although I'm not sure for what. I can tell she's dreading my departure.

Day 4

Thursday, 25ᵗʰ February – Geelong VIC

'And that's why I'm so proud to be here today launching David's national challenging homophobia tour.'

In the atmospheric surrounds of Geelong's National Wool Museum, complete with walls of brick and wool bales from years gone by, the seemingly improbable occurs. Against people's better judgment, Cr John Mitchell discards his speech notes, explaining that this only hampers his ability to speak with feeling. He then explains how vital supports are 'to young people questioning their sexuality'.

In a departure that surprises everyone he offers that he had done just that in his teenage years, adding that every man – no matter how macho – would have done the same thing: 'I've been in rooms full of some of the most macho blokes, and I can tell you right now, I know every single one of them would've questioned their sexuality.'

Perhaps then feeling the gravity of his words the Mayor says he hopes *The Geelong Advertiser* is not going to report that 'the Mayor thinks he is gay', adding a nervous laugh.

I'm not sure regional Australia has ever had such a high-profile individual reflecting so openly about sexual identity.

The fact that he called me 'David' for most of his speech is neither here nor there. By the third or fourth time I notice people shifting in their seats and nervously looking at me. I know they are feeling badly for me. I, on the other hand, am trying to contain my grin. If only a camera crew were here to capture it. It'd be great for the documentary. I chuckle.

As someone who has endured such introductions as Damien Williams, David Withers and Daniel Whitehouse over the years, it's more amusing than jarring.

In one lengthy passage, where the Mayor repeatedly says 'David' and thrusts his arm each time he does, pointing in my direction with an energetic yet polite outstretched hand, it feels like the audience of 60 people might start heckling. Suddenly he sees his advisor, who is becoming more and more physically twisted with embarrassment, and says, 'What's that?'. Being gently advised, 'It's Daniel, not David', he then realises his error and continues,

'See, I can't even say his real name I'm that excited about this tour …!'

Afterwards I have a brief but intense exchange with the Mayor.

'Anything we can do to support this tour Daniel, let me know.'

Perhaps he senses my sceptical reaction, hidden under a polite smiling nod, to his offer. He repeats, 'I'm absolutely serious, anything we can do'.

Later a number of people remark on how emotional the Mayor had been during his speech, some name it as a pleasant surprise and others a shock.

Day 5

Friday, 26th February – Geelong VIC

I hand over a copy of *Beyond 'That's So Gay'* to Ross, the principal of St Regional College. It feels like the least I can do, given that the book would not have been written had Ross not allowed me to pilot *Pride & Prejudice* with a class of Year 9 boys back in 1999. This successful pilot in a regional all-boys Catholic school kickstarted my career in challenging homophobia.

Ross, his wife and his deputy principal have invited me to dinner at an upmarket Indian restaurant. I'm hoping the food is good; I left my family at mum's where they were having fish and chips as a farewell party for me. It's not without some guilt that I take my first bite of warm naan bread; since the late 1990s my work has meant that I've missed so many milestones and other moments with my family. Now my own farewell.

Yet my family knows that if the upper echelons of Geelong's Catholic education system beckon for reasons of challenging homophobia, then I'll come running. All that they ask is that I don't rush back and that I drive safely.

When Marie, Paul's deputy e-mailed to suggest a dinner meeting to discuss the Catholic Education Office's silence around homophobia, I responded immediately:

'It's wonderful to hear from you. This in itself is some cause for reflection for me. I recall one of the main reasons that I first had the opportunity to work with [St Regional] was a letter from a former student who said that any correspondence from the school was not welcomed due to his experiences there. I feel grateful that I have a different feeling, confident that this would be a feeling of most, if not all, students. I was visiting a local gay and lesbian youth support project last night and asked one of your students if [Ross] was still Principal. The student said yes and described him, unsolicited, as a "good bloke". This was the same assessment from students I supported 12-13 years ago ...'

I'm reminded of Ross' warm, calm support when we all discuss the gravity of me driving around the country with no guarantees. I almost betray myself by sharing a great fear; semi-reformed workaholic and perfectionist that I am.

'The worst thing that could happen is that I'm sitting somewhere in regional or rural Australia and I'm left twiddling my thumbs because no-one knows that I'm there or no-one cares about the work that I'm doing.'

Ross responds the same way he's always done, including when I was a young and inexperienced gay atheist working in his school for the first time. With a manner that makes me feel respected, supported and believed in, he leans in.

'Of course you know that you will find yourself twiddling your thumbs ... which you know is OK.'

I wish he had been my teacher or principal growing up. I immediately feel a weight lift off my shoulders.

Day 6

I arrive late to find a familiar scenario. Having taken part in Pride marches and Mardi Gras in Australia and abroad I understand the long wait, delayed start, stop/start nature of any parade and how I mostly feel like I am in some kind of fishbowl. However this *Pako Festa* was anything but an LGBT celebration; more a regional, multicultural celebration with a small, yet significant, LGBT contingent of 15 people.

I chuckle to myself in the build-up. Some young people have sms'd to say they've slept in and are not coming, some change their minds, someone's arm is tired prompting a reshuffle of the flags and placards, and someone is bored. There is also a great deal of thought behind who will carry which colour of the rainbow flags, donated by Café Go's Jason. Then a young woman realises a nearby group's helium balloons can be used for pre-march entertainment …

We are wedged between the local Bosnia & Herzegovina contingent and a truck with drummers. The Bosnia & Herzogovina group numbers about 25 people, mostly women and girls. I like their *I Dream of Jeannie* pants and balloons in national colours. The truck of drummers gets more of my attention, not only for their tight-fitting black attire accessorised by real bunches of gum leaves, but for the young man with well-developed arms who can play a mean set of bongos.

After a long build up, with time to contemplate if the overcast sky might open up and drench us all, the parade starts. It moves slowly and, as with all other parades and marches I've been in, I'm looking forward to it being over. Not that I don't understand what this could mean for all things LGBT in Geelong, yet more immediately for the young people marching.

Did most people realise the LGBT nature of a banner with 'GASP! Geelong', some rainbow-coloured flags and umbrellas with placards saying 'Eat My Rainbow Shorts' and 'Pride NOT Prejudice'? Probably not. However some realise there is 'something about that group' that's different. A mother waves excitedly to her daughter and her female partner who are marching side by side. A young man from a local Catholic school marches with his boyfriend with whom he is celebrating a one-month anniversary.

By the time we finish the march it's clear to everyone that a page had been turned. GASP!'s participation in *Pako Festa* is not a tokenistic, one-time inclusion. It will happen again. A group of young African women run up excitedly to mix with the group, hold up their signs and get a combined group photo. There is no turning back.

Day 7

Sunday, 28th February – Geelong VIC to Mt Gambier SA = 370kms

Before the drive to Mt Gambier I spend some final moments with my family. They are pretty proud of a write up of my national tour in the *Geelong Advertiser*. Even my ordinarily non-demonstrative older brother gives the nod to the piece titled '38 weeks of busting homophobia'.

Twelve years before, myself and my GASP! colleagues had been accused on the *Geelong Advertiser's* front page of being pedophiles – and that was just the headline.

With all the attention of the tour and its Geelong launch, my sister decided she should sit my 15-year-old nephew down to clarify, if he didn't know already, that I was gay. Billy is my first nephew and single-handedly challenged my fear that I would make a terrible uncle. I was deep into studying for final year exams when we got the call he was born. I hid in the corner of my sister's hospital room, hoping she would not offer for me to hold him. When she did I was scared I would drop/hurt him or that he might start crying. Wisely my sister gently pushed. Remembering holding Billy in my hand (he was that small) for the first time still evokes powerful emotions to this day. Perhaps sensing my seriousness, he famously broke the ice by farting in my hand.

In this same manner Billy would unnerve his mother. When she 'broke the news' he rolled his eyes. 'Mum you are so stuck in the dark ages, I already knew that ... I worked that out fucking ages ago ...' Billy had observed me with male partners since he was born. Yet I'm told he still sometimes uses 'that's so gay' with his friends, although interestingly not as yet in front of his uncle.

Recounting the story my sister affirms what I had already known myself. 'He thinks the sun shines out of his uncle's arse ... He said he's so sorry he can't make it and to give you a big hug from him ...'

My niece Alannah had a completely different reaction to her older brother. When asked, 'What is the name of his book?' my sister replied, '*Beyond 'That's So Gay'*'. Alannah in her naturally curious way asked, 'What's gay?' My sister thought for a moment and said, 'It's when two girls love each other, or two boys love each other, just like mummies and daddies …' That was apparently all she needed. So excited was Alannah that week that she would race to the phone each time it rang and excitedly yell, 'I'm going to my uncle's book launch and it's called *Beyond 'That's So Gay'* and …'

Day 8

Monday, 1ˢᵗ March – Mt Gambier SA

Getting to Mt Gambier couldn't have been easier. I choose to bypass the scenic-yet-time-consuming Great Ocean Road. Admittedly having it on my doorstep means that I've seen it 'enough'. Four hours of relatively uneventful driving, via the middle of western Victoria (Colac, Camperdown Warrnambool, and Portland pass by in blur of cheese factories and cypress windbreaks), and I'm on Ben's doorstep.

I first met Ben, a local primary school teacher, 12 years earlier at the second national Health In Difference Conference in Melbourne which explored LGBT health. A wide-eyed volunteer with GASP!, I was excited that the City of Greater Geelong had invested in me by paying my conference registration. An eager sponge, I attended sessions with my GASP! co-facilitator and mentor, Elisa.

On the second day at lunch I was approached by a young man with the opening line, 'Excuse me, this might seem a little strange, but …' Ben then explained that his colleagues had spent the evening before talking excitedly about his 'twin' at the conference. Now emboldened by his giggling colleagues, Ben marched over to request a photo with me to prove he had a twin. A little taken aback I obliged Ben, and the photo was taken. When Ben departed Elisa showed great concern. 'You have no idea what could be done with that photo, he'll probably go home and say that he slept with you …'

As it was, Ben would show it to a colleague back in Adelaide, Dean, who would remarkably later become my boyfriend just over 18 months later. He was said to have marveled at the 'smiley boy' in the photo with Ben.

I now find Ben back in Mt Gambier after a 20-year absence. At 17, he left for Adelaide to study at university, eventually becoming a regular, devoted and adored volunteer in the LGBT community. Ben made the decision to move back to do what he loves most: teaching. He still possesses a storytelling ability and infectious laughter that is as potent as it was a decade before.

Ben revels in his new life as a rural primary school teacher. He relaxes and shares anecdotes about two 'camp' boys from higher grades who periodically seek refuge in his Grade 2 classroom; an unofficial, unspoken place of safety for boys who are not traditionally boisterous enough or full of bravado.

His class seems to have picked up on Ben's love of campness; one boy received a handout from Ben last week, only to respond with genuine affection, 'thank-you my Queen'.

Day 9

Tuesday, 2ⁿᵈ March – Mt Gambier SA

Well that experiment failed. I've been encouraged by many to provide 'open' workshops in every location I visit. I figure there isn't much to lose.

I sit calmly by myself at Mt Gambier Public Library, switching my gaze between the door which never opens and the wall, which is a wall-sized photo of a young family picnicking by what looks like the main drawcard of the region: the Blue Lake. To be fair it lives up to its coloured reputation. I stood looking over it yesterday and wondered if, like when I saw the rolling green plains of eastern Ireland, the myth had heightened my hue-seeking senses. It had certainly been a Blue Monday.

Although the newly finished library has everything you could want, the best thing from my tour-perspective is that I'm allowed to rent a space here for free. The last thing I want to do is outlay money for a venue that so far hosts only myself and the young family, all 2.4 of them, on the wall.

The clock on the wall confesses it's 1:09pm. With a start time of 1:00pm, I'm only willing to continue this delusion until 1:15pm. The only thing that could be worse right now is if one person arrives late expecting a room of people.

As well as the room, the wireless internet is also free and plentiful here. So, instead of workshopping with local teachers, health professionals and homophobia-curious others, I spend a few hours responding to e-mails, Facebook messages and updating my website. The free internet is appreciated, given an internet stick donated to the tour by a friend doesn't seem to work outside metropolitan centres; possibly not great when I'll be spending most of my time in regional, rural and remote areas. For now, at least, there is open wireless at Ben's thanks to one of his neighbours. Ordinarily I'd feel some guilt, however said neighbours' unknown contribution to LGBT young people across Australia assuages that somewhat.

Ben arrives home, enthusiastically asking how it all went. I try to mask my disappointment and, in turn, he tries to distract me with a story from his classroom.

'One boy told me he loves visiting his Nanna's small country town. He said, 'It's greater than lollies'.

Me: 'That's one impressive town. I've gotta go there.'

Day 10

Wednesday, 3rd March – Mt Gambier SA

I'd be lying if I said I expected to be driving up the tree-lined driveway to the local Catholic secondary school. I make a note to take a photo of the rusted, now unused mailbox out front.

Calling ahead to a Mt Gambier secondary school to discuss some teacher training I had planned, I was asked by a staff member to submit something in writing so that she could get it approved by the school authorities. Checking if this was just process or something more because of the subject matter, I asked her what it was that needed to be checked.

Staff member: 'It could be seen as controversial from a [education department] curriculum perspective.'

Me: 'Would you say that this training could be seen as controversial?'

Staff member: 'I'm not at liberty to say.'

Me: 'So challenging homophobia in a secondary school in South Australia is controversial?'

Staff member: 'Please, I'm really not at liberty to say. Just please send something through and ...'

I agreed to do this and the phone call was ended abruptly. For the record I didn't hear back.

Just as I had been urged to start my tour in Melbourne or Sydney with the LGBT-metropolitan mafia, so too I had been urged to call it something different.

'Call it 'Safety In Our Schools' or 'Bullying and Diversity'. You'll easily get funding for it and you'll pack your training sessions.'

Me: 'But people will find out what it's really about and get upset.'

'Do you want this to work or not? No-one will touch it if it's homophobia...'

Call me crazy but I call that deception and delusion. I was also mindful that resistant opponents to challenging homophobia will often accuse LGBT people of being deceptive and hiding their real agenda. The last thing I needed was such an accusation.

Yet where one government school stumbled, a local Catholic school was steady on its feet. The welfare staff at Tenison Woods College are very welcoming not only of me but also my ideas and questions. Starting, as I like to, by making a cuppa, I'm quickly given a school history lesson by Joe, head of a program supporting students who aren't quite fitting in at the school.

Julian Tenison Woods, the man you might guess the school was named after, was an influential man in Catholic education. It is said that on the day he rode to meet his fiancé to get married, he dramatically turned his horse at the last minute to ride to the local Bishop's lodgings where he begged to be accepted into the seminary. Between the lines Joe makes it fairly clear that Julian was thought to have been same-sex-attracted and conflicted. It is said he devoted himself thereafter to Catholic education for its betterment. It must also be noted that Julian is said to have had a hand in now-Saint Mary McKillop's excommunication.

With this as context, I hear about the work that Joe has undertaken with same-sex-attracted students at his school.

Me: 'Many people would be pleasantly surprised and a little shocked at how this could be happening in the Catholic education system. They would want to know why you are doing this work when so many others are not?'

Joe: 'I tell people who challenge or question me: you can say what you want, but when you stand at the gravesite of a young person watch the coffin go down and wonder what you could have done differently as a teacher, you'll know why. When you think, as I did, that as a teacher you were doing enough and you weren't (without me owning that death of course) and wanting to get better at what you do, you'll know why.'

Day 11

Thursday, 4th March – Mt Gambier SA

Holding her stock standard white mug with both hands and leaning forward, Ellen describes 'entrenched homophobic community attitudes' because of 'generational history in The Mount', as the locals call Mt Gambier.

A young local lesbian, her story echoes the LGBT folk who I've met this week in The Mount. All describe moving back for one of two reasons: work opportunities and/or a relationship.

Ellen is an example of someone who came to Mt Gambier to follow her partner, Olivia. Olivia 'won' a leadership position in education, a great opportunity for her career. Ellen, excited for Olivia, didn't think twice about following.

Ellen believed Mt Gambier must have been pretty backwards, based on the reaction of her friends and family, gathered from an upbringing in Canberra and early adulthood in Adelaide.

'They all asked, *Why would you go there?*'

Ellen laughs recounting these concerns because Canberra folk had said the same thing about Adelaide when she had first moved there; an assumption that Adelaide was a backward step.

The reality of Ellen's life in Mt Gambier might be described as private comfort and public concern. She is happily partnered, accepted and respected by her 'educated' colleagues and making a real, significant contribution in education. Ellen and Olivia go out with work colleagues for social drinks and meals, yet although their group knows they are together, those outside the group would not.

Upon arrival in Mt Gambier Ellen describes a role reversal in her relationship with Olivia. In Adelaide Olivia was the one more likely to show concern about their public displays of affection. In Mt Gambier, Ellen reflects that now it is her that shows the concern. Without the anonymity that

Adelaide's size provides, and concerned that local parents of their students might find out that they are a couple, Ellen and Olivia resort to one of two strategies.

'We don't go out together, or we need to have someone else with us when we do … to act as a shield …'

Listening to Ellen it's clear that this is a great cause of distress for both Ellen and Olivia as individuals, yet also a source of stress in their relationship.

When she looks around Mt Gambier, Ellen doesn't see any support services or groups for LGBT people, young or old.

Me: 'So what advice would you give LGBT young people in Mt Gambier?'

Ellen: 'The first thing that comes to mind, but it's not very nice, is 'be careful'. Be aware that not everyone will be as accepting as you'd like. Life is not easy, don't take it for granted. And tell them that gay conversion doesn't work, not that I've tried it!'

Ellen and Olivia's example was very similar to the experiences described by Matt and Carl. The difference is that Matt was born in The Mount. He has returned home to find a more conducive work-life balance whilst completing his post-graduate studies. Carl, a teacher, has moved to be with Matt and to find a better teaching environment.

Perhaps he has: Carl, a teacher at Tenison Woods College sat gobsmacked yesterday as I met with Joe. He tells me he found it hard to believe that challenging homophobia could happen in secondary schools, especially religious schools.

Matt and Carl have very different reasons for being privately 'out' (i.e. open with trusted colleagues and friends) and publicly 'in' (i.e. giving the impression of being single, asexual and/or not gay), yet the common theme is that being openly gay and a couple would cause irreparable damage to their careers, and most probably their quality of everyday life.

As with Ellen and Olivia, Carl and Matt don't have overwhelmingly positive tales to tell of family acceptance, although all report pockets of great support and signs of improvement over time.

Surprisingly for some, the foursome draw a significant amount of their support from behind the scenes at their places of work: education; secondary schools in particular.

Day 12

Friday, 5ᵗʰ March – Mt Gambier SA

I've spent the last few days passing in and out of consciousness, stealing as much sleep as I can between interviews and meetings.

Although not diagnosed until much later, I'm suffering a bad infection due to recurring tonsillitis. Passing out thanks to a migraine and waking up in pools of sweat have me thinking I have some freak flu.

Maintaining focus and not frowning during my everyday interactions has proven a challenge. I only woke up yesterday because my weekly Thursday morning interview with Melbourne LGBT media personality, Doug Pollard, awaited. Unable to eat due to the migraine, I could use a little more energy.

I receive some good news that I've made it into the Top 25 for the Vodafone Foundation's 'World of Difference' competition. That my application, to be paid around $75,000 to complete this self-funded tour, has caught the judging panel's eye lessens my weariness. The ensuing call with someone from the foundation quickly confirms that the Top 25 is as far as my application will go: I'm told that my project is too fully formed (and happening) for the foundation to have any input. Thanks but no thanks.

If I was looking for the locals to give me some sense of hope, I'm having a hard time finding it. The general assessment of life for LGBT young people in the region is bleak. The main reason for this dark outlook? 'Family'. The thinking in Mt Gambier is that young people will not come out 'because of their families'. Life in Mt Gambier is thought to centre on the family and family-related activities, particularly weekend sport.

Neil, a local gay man, believes the issue is not just about family, rather a case of 'everyone knowing everyone'. He describes the impact as very isolating for LGBT young people who therefore don't know other local LGBT people.

'You need to be discreet about your sexuality because everyone knows everyone … it could get spread around and you don't have control over who is told, when they are told and you don't know how they'll react.'

And it seems that bad reactions have cost this community young people. Betty, who holds a position high in the upper echelons of the region's Education Department office, puts it bluntly.

'Young people leave our community because there is nothing here for them. I know some of them and they feel they didn't have the opportunity to have any life here. The main reason they gave was community attitudes.'

My strength and appetite return around the same time. I can feel the difference as I devour a small bowl of pasta topped with some grated cheese; one of only a handful of items in Ben's old, noise-prone refrigerator.

Day 13

Saturday, 6th March – Mt Gambier

'So who is funding you for this?'

Keith pauses for the first time in about 20 minutes of discussion. His mind now begins to process the answers I've given to a barrage of questions delivered in classic Keith style: blunt, cheeky and brash. Suddenly his tone, uncharacteristically, becomes serious.

I explain that no-one is funding me. Now distracted from making his toast, Keith's head snaps in my direction. He studies me for a few moments, at first suspiciously, before concluding, 'Oh you are funding this through your book?'

I laugh, explaining that making money in Australian publishing, let alone educational publishing, is not really possible; especially with a book for teachers about 'gay stuff'.

Keith almost drops his coffee cup as he turns to me, this time slowly. The reality and gravity of what I am doing suddenly washes over his face. Given our history, Keith is one of the few people who can understand what this means.

The 20-year-old young man I had met in Sydney a decade earlier now stands as a 30-year-old man at his kitchen window in a northern suburb of Mt Gambier. As fate would have it, Keith is only one block away from Ben's, although the two don't know one another. In a moment void of his usual self-consciousness, Keith stares out that kitchen window at something in his mind. In my own mind I jump back a decade to that first Sydney meeting.

It was April 2000 and I was one of around a dozen people from around Australia selected to attend the inaugural meeting of *Outlink*, an ambitious undertaking by the then-Australian Human Rights and Equal Opportunity

Commission (HREOC). In part a response to alarming rates of suicide in north-west Tasmania, *Outlink* was to be a national network for LGBT young people in rural Australia.

Keith came as a representative for South Australia; a Mt Gambier resident. I attended both as a young person from regional Victoria and as a service provider.

The night before the meeting there was a distinct country-LGBT atmosphere in the air at Sydney's Hotel Y. I remember Keith bursting excitedly into the room. To me he was like an unexercised puppy: far too much energy, uncoordinated limbs yet somehow endearing. I, on the other hand, stood very still and observed. This was only my second time in Sydney and I was still trying to work out what was about to take place. I had never thought that I would be involved in anything remotely national or, in this case, national and remote.

Keith had come to Sydney as a key figure of Mt Gambier's LGBT group which in 2000 boasted around 50 members; no mean feat for a town with 25,000 inhabitants. The group was said to have a mix of ages, genders and identities.

In 2010 I found a very different LGBT climate in Mt Gambier. Although I had met with the local LGBT group earlier in the week, Keith was no longer a part of it. I had not even known he was again in town, given his stints living in Melbourne and Sydney, until I was alerted by his Facebook message: 'are you still in Mt Gambier? I'm living here now …'

'I guess I should have really paid attention to your schedule …', Keith offers, explaining that he had accidentally seen one of my Facebook status updates mentioning Mt Gambier. Given I was in the final hours before leaving Mt Gambier it was lucky he messaged when he did.

It seems, ten years after Keith and the local LGBT group were most active, no-one really knows quite where to start.

As I walk from Keith's door to get in my truck, Keith says, as only he could:

'And they really should have taken you to see someone when you were younger to fix your pigeon toes …'

Having been told off by my Pilates teacher in Berlin, I held onto my *very* slight pigeon-toe-ness knowing that it had worked for Steffi Graf and Andre Agassi (who, like me, are Olympic gold medalists in tennis, although my medals come from the Gay Olympics) and a handful of men in the last few years who have noticed it and said it was cute.

Keith is having none of it: 'It was cute when you were 4!'

I laugh walking slightly pigeon-toed, and wave goodbye as he gets distracted in his front yard.

Day 14

Sunday, 7ᵗʰ March – Mt Gambier SA to Adelaide SA = 434 kms

Thwack … thwack … … thwack!

The lean, athletic young dancer stands with his reddened back to the audience. Over and over again he strikes himself with a cat o' nine tails. Despite the dramatic start to this Fringe Festival performance there was a hint of apathy with each 'thwack'.

It's pure coincidence that I'm in Adelaide watching a dancer friend, newly returned from Berlin, debut a highly personal, experimental and energised one-man show. Despite what followed the performance's opening (including nudity and a large black sex toy), I fear the seemingly unconvincing 'thwacks' could follow me for my entire stay in Adelaide.

When I planned my 38-week national tour, I did so taking into consideration school holidays and Australia's varying seasons. I'd hoped that my tour might coincide with festivals and events in each place, yet little did I know that I would arrive in Adelaide in perhaps the biggest week of the year: Adelaide's Fringe Festival, Womad, and an event that almost every woman reluctantly named with a sickening shudder – the overly alcohol and testosterone-fuelled 'Clipsal car race' – all collided.

Not only that, but political calamity seems to be taking place in the lead-up to a state election. Adelaide appears to all to be at the height of her powers, and understandably a little distracted.

In what is to be the first metropolitan stop on my journey around Australia, competing for the attention of the inhabitants of Adelaide is going to be an uphill struggle.

Day 15

Monday, 8th March – Adelaide SA

'Dan, you don't need anyone's permission ...'

It was late on a hot, sticky night about two months ago when my ex-boyfriend, Dean, had suddenly called me out of the blue. Considering I hadn't heard from him since our break-up in 2000, I was taken aback. After he apologised for the extended pause in communications we 'caught up'.

Two months ago I was still a bundle of pre-tour nerves, and still second-guessing if I could complete the project with any success without the backing of many of the major LGBT organisations, especially those in Sydney. Dean was spot on when he said I'd spent too much time listening to people from Melbourne and Sydney, and not to everyone else around the country.

Tonight it's not so hot and sticky, but I'm seated having a delicious roast cooked by Dean's new housemate. It's refreshing to have my appetite back.

It's Dean who was Mt Gambier Ben's colleague in Adelaide who saw a picture of his 'twin': me, the 'smiley boy'. It's Dean who laughs when I recount Ben's answer when I asked him what's helped him overcome the challenges in his life. 'Madonna'. Classic Ben.

Funnily enough, I'm staying this week with Richard, my Melbourne housemate in 1999 and 2000 when I was dating Dean across the Victorian–South Australian border. Richard now lives in the Adelaide suburb of Semaphore. The house from the front has more than a passing resemblance to a small suburban church, complete with a weeping willow; the back, with its gently bubbling water feature and cement Buddha statue, could be the dark blue, corrugated fenced grounds of a suburban temple.

Day 16

Tuesday, 9th March – Adelaide SA

As far as scenic spots go, Adelaide certainly has more than the carpark beside 'that bridge' over the murky River Torrens. I'm shooting a video blog for my Adelaide leg of the tour to supplement the written materials I'm offering each week.

A local pointed out he remembered 'hearing about Dr Duncan when I was a kid, and that bridge used to scare the bejeebers out of me'.

This bridge is an infamous LGBT landmark; infamous because it was a known gathering place (i.e. a 'beat') for men who have sex with men and the setting for the murder of Dr George Duncan. George, then in his early 40s, and another man were thrown into the waters on a night in May 1972. Many believe it was a group of police officers. The other man survived, George didn't.

The outrage at Dr Duncan's murder is said to have swayed public opinion and turned the tide towards the decriminalisation of homosexuality a few years later. The fact that South Australia was the first state to decriminalise homosexuality leads many to believe that this laid the necessary foundations for Adelaide to be one of the most gay and lesbian friendly places in the country.

I take a break in shooting when I get a call from a trusted mentor. He makes the mistake of asking how it's all going in Adelaide. All my frustrations spill out about two cancelled meetings with key LGBTI organisations at the 11th hour. The camera keeps rolling:

' ... and they tell me, *something's just come up so let's not have that meeting, but good luck with your tour, it's really important and essential work you're doing but it's not convenient this week*. Convenient? I'm going out of my own fucking way to drive around the country for 38 weeks and they can't spare 15 to 20 fucking minutes for a cuppa?!'

If I'm honest I'm concerned that one of my greatest fears will come true. Many have said that they fear I'll be run out of some town, perhaps with pitchforks and shouting, and others have feared for my physical safety, or at least that of my truck, Bruce, in a Priscilla-esque 'AIDS FUCKERS GO HOME' moment. However my fear is that I'll drive around the country and have no-one to talk to. All this effort could count for very little.

Despite interviews yesterday, today and for the rest of the week, I'm not certain the cuppas will keep coming.

Day 17

'He's had to fight for years, so he's not interested. It's safer for me as a parent.'

I'm sitting with Marie at a café to hear about what it's like being the mother of a gay son in modern day Adelaide. She is one of a dozen people who attended a book reading at The Second Story, a state government youth health service that runs LGBT programs. Marie offered to share her personal experiences and her involvement with the local branch of international support group movement PFLAG, Parents and Friends of Lesbians and Gays.

Before starting we laugh about a young woman's reaction at the end of the reading. She shared with the group that she felt excited at the potential applications of my work in her life, and likened my signing of her recently purchased copy of *Beyond 'That's So Gay'* to getting her book signed by lesbian author extraordinaire Sarah Waters. That's a comparison I had never anticipated.

Marie drifts off, looking into the distance to recall her son's teenage years in her 'more curdled than blended' step family.

'[Brett] says he started questioning his sexuality at 13. I knew he was going through something challenging, I just didn't know what. I remember he took me to see the movie *The Sum Of Us* for 'a school project'. He then took me to Second Story for 'a school project'.'

It wasn't until his partner outed him as gay when Brett was 20 that Marie put everything together.

'To be honest it was just a relief.'

The last few years have been tough by her own admission – 'he's received death threats' – yet she's stayed positive throughout. I ask why she has always been able to demonstrate her support to Brett and, according to Brett, never said anything negative.

'It's who I am, who my family is, what my work is.'

Not that working in the health industry means Marie is immune to homophobia. Through her own contacts in the health industry she's heard about how some staff responded to working with her son: 'whenever I'm rostered on with [that person] it makes my skin crawl'.

Marie says she faces questions from her educated, social work colleagues that assume she has 'done something wrong' in raising her gay son and listens to them describe things as 'a bit poofy'.

Now Brett is thinking about moving interstate to escape Adelaide, which he describes as 'a hellhole'. Perhaps it's a post-relationship break-up decision.

'He was with this hyper-masculine partner for months. He moved in, but even though [Brett] was out as gay, this guy wasn't. He was so paranoid about his own family, friends and even the neighbours finding out about it that he forced Brett to soundproof the door and put extra padding on the windows to prevent any noise escaping.'

Day 18

Thursday, 11th March – Adelaide SA

'I spoke about this with my Principal and he was clear that if I was to attend, it would be on my personal time. I have to admit I was quite shocked.'

Last night a welfare teacher in a Catholic school, Janet, attended the book reading and painted a picture of how far off getting to beyond 'that's so gay' was at her school.

'The other teachers are happy as long as someone else is doing it. They all say they are too busy.'

In the main program room at The Second Story, I can only think of how much I want Janet to be with us. 'Us' is a dozen teachers, health professionals and homophobia-curious others for a Beyond 'That's So Gay' workshop. In a room this size, twelve people still feels like a small crowd. That's somehow strange because the high ceilings and painted brick walls in this converted factory from years gone by make for a space that is hard to 'fill'.

Everyone agrees that there are two certainties in local schools: homophobic language and teachers failing to challenge or interrupt it. Most doubt much can be done.

Kirsty, a project worker coordinating challenging homophobia in Adelaide's northern suburban schools, cites teacher apathy.

'They say they don't have time to challenge student homophobia.'

Experience tells me that, although they are as busy as anyone else, teachers' time management is rarely the barrier to them doing this work. So I ask Kirsty, is that all?

'Well teachers who don't think homophobia is an issue say they don't have a problem at their schools because they don't see any gay bashing. The teachers that do see it as an issue say it's too controversial.'

Once the workshop is done I ask a young woman in attendance if she is happy to have a cuppa at some stage before I leave. Venus accepts immediately and offers to meet as soon as I finish up.

Venus describes herself as 'gender blind'.

'I tell people I'm gay because it's just easier. I sometimes tell them I'm homoflexible, and if they're interested I'll expand.'

During the workshop Venus talked about life for her as a young 'gender blind' woman in the public service. I ask her to elaborate.

'At my job you're not allowed to discriminate, but you know it happens anyway. News flies so fast in that environment. I feel so powerless being young and new there. There was a young woman who was bi, and they all made disparaging remarks about her being *loose* and *taking everything she can get*. They tore her to pieces. They just picked at her and picked at her. And her supervisors were social workers I might add.'

If Venus needs any more incentive to remain in the closet, she talks about a director.

'Everyone at work describes her as *the fucking dyke* and *that man-hating bitch*. I'm scared about what would happen if they knew the truth. I recently got this [short] haircut and have been told *now you look like a dyke* and *that's a shame, you looked so pretty with long hair*. They assume I'm straight and I even give my female partner a masculine name. I'm scared of slipping up. I've been lying for so long now that I feel trapped, like I can't be myself. It's not only stressful; it's exhausting. If I don't hide who I am they'll say *I'm* being aggressive and out there and then *they* can respond by being aggressive. I know for a fact that some would stop talking to me and that it would start impacting on my relationships with clients. It sucks because I'm just being me, and that they can do that is frightening.'

Afterwards I can't help but wish Venus could find the high school equivalent of herself at work: at her Christian school she played the role of guardian angel.

'I always seemed to find the gay ones. They always seemed to gravitate towards me. I was aware that they were having a hard time. One guy was convinced that he was going to burn in hell. This other friend had his father physically abuse him. I always felt incredibly sad about that, so I would sit and listen to them. I was always advocating for gay rights, which got me into trouble a few times but I could always say, '*I'm not gay*', a great one-liner that I can't use any more.'

Venus leans forward, holding the chipped blue mug with both hands and looking into her instant coffee.

'I'd love straight people to know how good they've got it.'

Day 19

Friday, 12ᵗʰ March – Adelaide SA

'Adelaide is gay because the balls touch in Rundle Mall …'

The group laughs. Their welcoming, relaxed and skilled female worker cringes with embarrassment whilst checking to see how I'd react to this common reference to a local silver sculpture. For the record I chuckle.

I'm sitting with a group of young same-sex-attracted and trans women and I've just asked why Adelaide is as gay and lesbian friendly as it is said to be.

The laughing stops when I ask why these young women come to *The Girls' Lounge*, a program at The Second Story. They all agree it's because it's 'a safe space' where they can come every fortnight to be with other young women like themselves.

'It's the only safe space I have.'

Over this hour I get a small glimpse of what makes *The Girl's Lounge* a place that young women want to return to. For a split second I wish that I could come here every fortnight.

The communal dinner they've invited me to could be any other gathering of young people: gossip, laughter and catching up.

'I like coming here because there are rules to abide by. One of the big ones is that this is not a pick-up place.'

It's clear the structure encourages 'great friendships' to form and even 'learning'. Referring to a toilet paper comparison, one young woman offers an example, 'Like tonight I learnt the difference between scrunching and folding. I'd never heard that before.' For the record she doesn't share which side of the fence she 'sits' on.

As I expect it takes some time before I get a sense of the young women's experience of *The Girl's Lounge*. Some talk of 'mutual understanding', 'being on the same page' and appreciating that 'some things you don't have to say'. One young woman speaks of 'feeling united even though there is only one thing that brings us together'. Others describe a 'comfortable' environment free of judgment that allow them to 'be free to be' themselves and 'express [their] sexuality'.

When I ask about how things are outside of The Second Story's walls I hear more of the young women's lives in Adelaide's schools, homes and on its streets. It becomes clear that *The Girl's Lounge* is 'one of the few safe spaces' available to them.

A young woman talks of things being 'better' at her school only once she came out; her being lesbian was 'more of an issue when it was a rumour'. One young woman has been 'kicked out of church'. Another describes how her mother 'swore and stormed out' when she came out. Most agree that they monitor their behaviour unless they are walking the streets as a large group.

'I'm very careful with my girlfriend in public', explains a young woman who has real concerns of discrimination and violence. 'You have to know when to be public, and when not to be public.'

As they continue, Adelaide's walls seem to close in on these young women. Whilst being 'arty' and 'open', most young women agree that the city suffers from 'small town syndrome': 'in some ways it felt smaller and safer' and in others 'you feel unable to escape, worried about being 'outed'. Some explain that 'once you come out in Adelaide, then everyone knows' and that 'gossip travels at the speed of light'. This directly impacts on many of the young women's comfort in being themselves and being open about their identity. For example, one young woman shows concern about her reputation and safety.

'You hear about other people who are lesbian, even if you don't know them'.

Day 20

'My high school culture was really homophobic. Not just homophobic jokes, it was really deep-seated stuff. If other students were suspected as gay then they got even more overt physical and verbal stuff.'

I'm sitting at Adelaide's Central Markets waiting for a former colleague from Kids Help Line to arrive. As I do I think about and re-read notes from my interview with young bisexual man, Jesse, a few hours ago. He'd talked of getting through school and his family picking up the pieces post his 'violent, gay bashing dad'. He told me coming out as bisexual didn't help.

'Mostly it's been generally negative. I've been quite shocked by the gay scene, but also girls as well. They say things like 'it's just a phase', 'you're just experimenting', 'you're really just gay' or they ask 'are you confused?' It's boring to fit into boxes; people who fit into those boxes compromise parts of themselves to fit. If life was just black and white you'd miss out on all the pretty colors of the rainbow.'

I'm brought back to reality as Kerry, former State Manager for Kids Helpline in South Australia arrives and it seems like only yesterday I was sitting having a hot chocolate with her in 2004. I remember it so well and tell anyone who asks that Lucia's make the best hot chocolate I have ever tasted.

This time Kerry and I sit outside Lucia's, which has not changed one bit: their sign lettering reminiscent of a 19th century circus in North America; ergonomic wire-backed chairs; the chessboard tiles inside. Kerry hasn't changed either, and I don't realise how much I need to debrief with her until she's sitting before me: gently curious, brimming with enthusiasm and care.

It's the third week on the road and already I've heard plenty of tales of challenge from LGBT people. Purposefully I've been keeping my interviews constructive, focusing on what has helped people overcome challenges, feel connected and supported. To end I always ask, 'What are your hopes for the future?'

Time and again in Geelong, Mt Gambier and now Adelaide, the young people have all been unanimous: what they all hope for, without prompting, is to be able to hold the hand of their partners in public. Not only to hold hands, but to do so without fear, concern or anxiety of something happening to them or the one they love. After hearing for years about how LGBT people want special rights want to flaunt themselves and are asking for more than they should, to hear a chorus of young people hoping for one simple public display of their love hits me hard.

I guess what I hadn't expected to hear were so many in Adelaide echoing this.

As I report this to Kerry some tears flow. After several weeks of stories I finally realise how this simple fact has played over and over in my head, driving me to continue.

After two delicious, unmatchable hot chocolates, I bid Kerry farewell, somewhat lighter emotionally. For the rest of the day and into the evening Jesse's words repeat over and over in my head.

'I can't think of who said it, *Any man suffering diminishes me.* I think it was Voltaire? If that were the motto for our society, then I think the world will be a whole lot better.'

Day 21

Sunday, 14th March – Adelaide SA

'Adelaide is more lesbian-friendly than gay-friendly. Lesbian friends have said that Adelaide is for lesbians what Melbourne is for gay men. I cannot say I've ever seen two men holding hands in Adelaide, yet in the time that we've been sitting here three lesbian couples have walked by holding hands. Had you noticed?'

Despite sitting by a floor-to-ceiling window in a café down the progressive end of Rundle Street, I'm too busy writing interview notes to take in my surroundings, much less its inhabitants. I look up to catch a glimpse of a lesbian couple holding hands and vanishing down a sidestreet.

I ask Markus, a young gay man, whether he experiences Adelaide as 'arty', 'open' and 'OK' with gayness as young women had suggested.

'No. Look, OK we are doing better than Whyalla, but that's irrelevant.'

Markus had been a punctual and enthusiastic attendee at my book gathering earlier in the week. Given that he was recently an out young gay man in an Adelaide school, I wanted to hear more of his story. The pervasive theory at the moment is that if a student is 'out' in their school then everything is OK, fuelling the 'things are much better these days' assessments across the country.

According to Markus, the pivotal moment in his high school career was an assembly. In hindsight, he believes this could have made him or broken him. In the early years of high school, not too long ago, he explains he 'was the effeminate student who got chased … kicked' and targeted for other forms of intimidation. Yet in Year 10 he was one of two people required to make a presentation at an assembly to his entire year level, teachers and the principal.

'I was already shitting myself. I got up and was at the microphone. Everyone settled down and went quiet before I started to speak.'

As he did so, a voice broke the silence.

'Fag!'

Markus looked to his teachers wondering what to do. The principal and the teachers did nothing. With everyone's eyes upon him, Markus recalls he was 'forced to continue'.

As the assembly finished the Year Level Coordinator stood and asked the offending student who yelled out 'fag' to see him after. That student would eventually be given a suspension for disrupting proceedings rather than for what he'd said, something that still bugs Markus.

'But that assembly changed school forever. I started getting positive attention. Lots of people came up after to ask if I was alright and telling me that guy was an arsehole. And people started saying stuff like, *Hey you're actually a nice, funny guy and not a bad person.*'

Seemingly out at school from this point, Markus describes a life of spending a lot of time in the library for safety.

'I never hated school, I just hated the bullshit. I spent my lunchtimes in the library because no-one ever went there and I liked to read. But even though the staff were supportive, I didn't feel OK to read gay books as there was still 'shtick'. It just wasn't entirely safe for me.'

Despite this, some girls were supportive, sometimes dramatically so. One day a male student walked through a group of girls that Markus was in, purposefully bumping him. He laid the blame on Markus: 'Watch it fag'.

'He didn't realise that his girlfriend was in the group and saw the whole thing. She walked up to him and just said, *He's my friend. We're done.* You should have seen his face!'

If he was hoping for respite and support at home, Markus didn't find it in a strict Roman-Italian Catholic household. His father could not accept his effeminate son's ways and took to trying to improve his coordination for soccer. Not only that, from about the age of 10 Markus recalls his father didn't like the way he walked and tried to teach him a more masculine stride whenever they walked together.

'My stepmother stepped in and started mocking me as well. She'd only buy me masculine clothes. It meant I had to get really good at hiding all my tighter fitting t-shirts and bracelets in my bag. I'd then go around the corner after I left the house and get changed.'

Me: 'It sounds tough. Was it?'

Markus: 'Well from 5 to10 I was called a girl. From 10 I was called a fag. At school the pressure got worse. I had to be happy, to be flamboyant. I was known for singing and being funny, but if I came to school and I wasn't 'up' and 'out' on any given day, then it seemed intervention was required. They'd then be asking, 'Do you need to go and see the student counsellor?' Because I'm not entertaining people and brightening their day there's a problem? I can't have an off day?'

Markus is visibly frustrated and angry as he recounts this. Being out at school did not result in Markus feeling entirely safe and supported to be himself. Being out did not mean that he did not experience bouts of depression. Being out did not mean he fully embraced his sexual identity.

The impact that Markus' outness had on other students at his school became clearer much later. Whilst that defining moment of a very public and homophobic comment changed things for the better for Markus, an incident for a fellow student changed things for the worse.

'A guy in my class had *dirty fag* and his name graffitied on a wall at school. Everyone saw. He left school not long after and didn't come back. It turns out he was gay. But I was gayer than he was. Quite a few others from school have since come out to me, but they say it wasn't safe for them at school. They said they weren't like me; that they couldn't be like me.'

Day 22

It's 6am and Bruce is packed. But I'm ready to unpack everything again. Well, to be honest I could tear everything out until I find it.

It is a rainbow wristband consisting of a few pieces of coloured thread, gifted to me by The Dancer. Now on the road, this wristband has come to symbolise my connection with him.

The Dancer came into my life at both the best and worst possible time: 3 weeks before the tour began. Only a week before I had said goodbye to the most fulfilling, healthy and life-changing relationship of my life with The Circus Performer. In 2009 he and I spent 2 months out of 12 together, in 2010 it was 2 weeks out of 52. The fact that we both had traveled so much for our work (him: South-East Asia, New Zealand, Darwin, later Nepal; me: Europe, Asia, now the country) and that this would continue to separate us into the future was the main reason for us breaking up. It still feels incredibly strange for us both (and for so many of the people around us).

Looking ahead we reluctantly conceded the carnival was indeed over. Reeling from the loss of my greatest support and confidante, and feeling the sobering reality of my tour's start date, I crossed paths with The Dancer, who was himself reeling with the reality of coming home after years working on cruise ships. After traveling the globe many times over, it was time to come home and rest for health reasons.

Had I observed it happening with anyone else I would have seen it for what it was: a convenient rebound involving me groping in the dark metaphorically and literally. As coping strategies go I could have done much worse, such was the heady rush of passion that only a three-week affair, with two people in denial about their respective realities, can bring. I needed some security, and being in The Dancer's arms was a temporary shelter from the coming storm.

In the hour it takes to drive to Dublin, designated breakfast pitstop, I've calmed down. Part of me knows that my anxiety in finding the wristband is a realisation that my bond with The Dancer isn't as strong as his immediacy suggested. I know finding that wristband won't change it, yet on some irrational level I still think it could.

To keep the dancing theme going, the oversized sheep cup I eat my cornflakes from was gifted to me at an international LGBT conference in Vienna by a ballet dancer. The setting for my sunrise breakfast could not be more ideal: fields of knee-high wheat, simple lopsided gates from a farm from yesteryear and dirt road underfoot.

Unfortunately, the scenic vista is tainted by a pungent smell of unknown origin. Firing up for a video blog that would form an 'Out Take', I talk to the camera.

'You know when you go out to the country and you go in one of those makeshift dunnies where it's like the open [pits]? That's what it smells like now. It's fucking disgusting.'

If there was still a doubt going into Adelaide, now there's none: I'm on the road.

Day 23

Tuesday, 16ᵗʰ March – Port Lincoln SA

'Well if you go, don't tell them I had anything to do with it. No, I didn't say ANYTHING.'

Mary, a senior education department official for Port Lincoln and the surrounding region, the Eyre Peninsula, has spent most of our first 15 minutes together looking at me with suspicion. She displays with her body that she is, at the very least, slightly repulsed by my presence in her humble office. I assure Mary that I am merely asking a question: Did she have any contacts in the local Catholic school?

Another week, another assumption that Catholic education could not be beyond 'that's so gay'. Explaining my first weeks of the tour, I remind Mary that it was a myth that such matters could not be discussed with Catholic schools.

Mary came recommended by a colleague in Mt Gambier, in hindsight the only thing that gets me through the door that she probably wishes she'd never opened. When I explain my national project, she immediately assumed I was there to trip her up, judge her and get something from her that I really shouldn't. Whilst I inevitably encounter anxieties from most people along the way (e.g. 'I'm not sure I'm the right person', 'I don't think I'll have much to say' or 'I don't think it's my role'), these can be typically calmed, relatively quickly and easily.

Not so with Mary. At least 5 or 6 times in 15 minutes she physically recoils, leaning back further in her business chair, turning her body away from me and, unknowingly, screwing up her face at my questions. Her response each time is an almost hysterical, 'But what do you want from me?' Time and again I answer that I want to hear her observations of how schools are supporting lesbian, gay, bisexual and transgender students, if at all, and what is and isn't working in local schools to challenge homophobia. Yet I am selling an un-sellable idea. At one point I stop and think, 'I'm an Amway salesman. My whole life, all my work and everything I've done has come to this moment: I'm a door-to-door Amway salesman'.

'Look, schools are time-poor and are expected to do so much. Why do schools have to do this when it's up to individual families to do this with their own children?'

I ask Mary what she feels the typical LGBT student's experience in local schools might be and her face almost turns grey.

'I really wouldn't ... like to say. I just wouldn't. I mean, of course it's going to be diffi ... No I just wouldn't want to say.'

Mary is momentarily calmed when I mention my new book.

'Oh, I've heard about that somewhere.'

I mention my publisher and she confirms she subscribes to their mailing list. Thank the challenging homophobia deities that it was featured that very month. Maybe I have a slither of credibility after all.

Against all the odds, and thankfully so, the meeting ends with a win-win situation. Mary wants me out of her office as quickly as possible, or at least I assume that based on her squirming. I don't take this too personally, especially as I'm slightly amused by her lack of self-awareness in this situation. In order to get me out quickly, Mary offers up names of other people I should talk to in the region. I appreciate the shortcuts, thank Mary for her valuable time and leave her to squirm in peace.

Day 24

'Look there are no gays and lesbians here. They all fuck off to Adelaide.'

I had just asked the former Gay and Lesbian Liaison Officer (GLLO) for the Eyre Peninsula, Senior Constable 'Peter', if any LGBT people had come forward during his time as GLLO. Peter was frank.

'Not one.'

Having walked into the police station for this meeting, not being a victim of crime and getting the reception that I did at the counter, I find myself thinking that I'm not that surprised.

'Mate, I want to know where the association is for white heterosexual blokes.'

Certainly it isn't the first time I've spoken with an older, white heterosexual male who feel he's somehow missing out, whilst having little or no concept that the only thing he's missed out on was the point.

Peter has warned me he'll be frank. Almost 60 and intending to retire, he explains that homophobia has always been a part of police culture.

'I've lived with homophobia in the job for years, but I'm leaving so be prepared …'

Peter was acting as a GLLO while a colleague was on maternity leave. Now that his superiors in Adelaide have ruled that only police with a higher rank than him can take on the role of GLLO, he's pessimistic about it continuing. Recently Peter informed his boss that they'd be required to do an LGBT training course.

'Oh, what was the response again? I believe it was *fucking queers* or words to that effect. See? I told you I wasn't holding back mate.'

A known and hardworking identity amongst young people in the region, he makes it clear why he took on the role.

'I am here for the kids. I have my phone on 24/7, during holidays, but I don't care cos the kids are important to me.'

Rather than sit at the police station, Peter drives me to a Port Lincoln Roadhouse for the 'best coffee in Port Lincoln'. I appreciate his hospitality, frankness and, in some strange way, his swearing. After the briefest of phone calls to introduce myself and explain why I want to talk to him, we both get into a police car for a drive. I suspect he is as wary of me as I am him, both not exactly sure what will transpire.

Once in the car we both attempt to break the ice. I let him know that this is nothing special, given I grew up with a father as a policeman in Geelong. This entailed plenty of walks through, and time in, police stations, drives in police cars and socialising with policemen (given there were no policewomen who worked with my father when I was growing up). Heck, I had even mowed the lawns for one police station for extra pocket money.

Peter for his part attempts to make it clear that he is gay and lesbian friendly, which I believe he largely is, although occasionally he misses the mark.

'Oh, have I told you that I'm a lesbian? I have lesbian friends and I ask them what they do. When they tell me, I say *I'll have what you're having!* See? I told you, I'm a lesbian.'

But Peter's commitment is clear. He has proactively supported both lesbian and gay young people in the region. One he describes as young, gay and indigenous.

'He cops it from the kids at school. Then he goes home and cops it from his family.'

Me: 'Does 'copping it' mean that he experiences physical violence?'

'I honestly don't know mate, he won't tell me.'

Me: 'Many would say that being gay and indigenous don't go together. Is this your experience?'

'Yes, basically this is why this kid's head is fucked'.

The reason for Peter's support of LGBT young people is simple.

'I'm afraid they'll go into their own room and I'm afraid if we are not careful we'll lose 'em.'

Yet Peter openly questions whether there needs to be a GLLO role. Whilst he can acknowledge that all his colleagues were homophobic to the point of hostility, he fails to see that a 'gay and lesbian friendly' port of call at the local cop shop might therefore be important. Perhaps this reflects in his attitude to such an initiative in the police force.

'If you throw it down people's throats they'll choke it back up. You need to stop throwing it down people's throats …'

Peter describes how he has found greater value in meeting and befriending lesbian policewomen in recent years. Although he seems a little too preoccupied and titillated by examples of his lesbian colleagues lives (he's mentioned one couple and their outdoor spa three times already), Peter is enthusiastic about how they have had a positive impact on lesbians, at least, becoming more accepted amongst the male police force ranks.

Slightly amazed and taken aback that I will soon be driving through this lesbian couple's patch on my drive west from Port Lincoln, I'm encouraged by Peter to visit one such police station that is said to be 'manned by lesbians'.

Day 25

Thursday, 18th March – Port Lincoln SA

'You in the naughty books?'

An older female teacher has just waddled past in the administration area of one of Port Lincoln's secondary schools. I've been sitting feeling in some ways like I was back at high school. Perhaps I have that look on my face. She watches me break into a nervous grin and nod.

Me: 'I hope not.'

She giggles and continues waddling on.

It's not the first time in my challenging homophobia career I find myself sitting in the school administration area watching students and teachers going about their everyday school lives. I sit and admire the firm but fair women at the administration desk, who have a tough yet calm and caring approach with their students.

Sally, one of two student counsellors, breaks me out of a daze and welcomes me to the school. Within a few minutes we're walking into the staffroom. I stop to think about how many staffrooms I've been in during the last 13 years, quietly chuckling at its familiarity and atmosphere. Indeed this could be any staffroom in Australia: don't take the wrong mug or risk your life; don't bother hoping there'll be a clean teaspoon; and, expect coffee through the sugar, if there is any sugar at all.

A self-described proactive school in teaching sexual health and healthy relationships Sally tells me they made a conscious effort to challenge student's homophobic language 5 years ago. A male teacher, who had been subjected to student homophobia because he didn't match the traditional masculine stereotype, led staff in a discussion. He talked about the need to do something about it and asked teachers to discuss how they might respond to 'that's so gay'. This led to a significant change in the school climate.

'Look, five years ago we took a very disciplinary approach when students used 'that's so gay'. We felt united and strong to do something back then, but now? It's crept back in and, to be honest, it's pretty common. It worries me now that we talk about it, because many young boys still have a lot of homophobic attitude, and they are just scared. The junior and middle year boys are all trying to find a girlfriend just so they don't get called gay.'

It reminds me of a news story I've seen this very week of a 14-year-old boy in northwest Queensland who was forced to have sex with a female prostitute because his father feared he was gay.

I finish my cuppa with Sally and drive over to West Coast Youth Services, described to me by one Adelaide contact as 'a progressive youth service'. I'd called ahead to see if someone at the service had 20 to 30 minutes, yet I arrive at a converted family home to find six eager and attentive youth workers.

When we start talking they admit that 'you can be gay in Port Lincoln, but …' What follows are all the conditions: you must not be open to anyone but your close family and friends; you must not talk, dress or act in a certain way; you must be a part of the everyday workforce; and so on.

Yet no matter how progressive the workers at West Coast Youth Services are, they're still pessimistic about life for most LGBT young people in Port Lincoln.

'It's a huge taboo. They either believe or pretend it doesn't exist. Young people keep it very quiet and hide the fact that they are gay in school. It's probable rather than possible that they will experience abuse, harassment and discrimination.'

Echoing Mount Gambier folk, it seems relationships are kept very private.

'If two gay guys are in a relationship, they pretty much can't be seen to spend too much time together. Often they'll let everyone think they are just living with their good mate.'

Despite one worker saying she knows gay and lesbian people who reside here, they believe that most LGBT young people will leave town, head to Adelaide and come out. There have been, and are, exceptions to every rule.

'I know of one young gay guy, really effeminate. He lived not far from here and had this secret relationship with the macho footy star at high school. He went on to come out and stay in town.'

Talking about staying on, this 20 to 30 minute cuppa with one staff member has turned into almost 90 minutes with the six of them.

Day 26

Friday, 19ᵗʰ March – Port Lincoln SA

'I'm not gay but my boyfriend is.'

Jack laughs at his answer to my question of how he likes to be identified, admitting he doesn't have a boyfriend. When I ask him why he likes this label, he pauses and gets serious.

'I can't dress for shit, I drive cars and I'm messy. That's not how people personify gay. The gayest thing I do is wear pink, but every guy pretty much does that these days. My best mate, who is straight as they come, probably wears more pink than I do. I'm not attracted to females in the slightest. They sit on my lap, some try and touch me when they're drunk but nothing happens.'

We sit at a concrete picnic table on Port Lincoln's foreshore late afternoon. Too late I realise how impractical this is with the wind lifting my notebook pages and other notes off the table every time I move my arm. I make sure I face Port Lincoln so that Jack can look out across the choppy water.

Having left school and come out only recently, Jack feels he fits in here.

'Everyone says that Port Lincoln is one of the most homophobic towns in South Australia, but that's not how I find it. I am who I am, I'm not hiding myself. I've always stayed the same, I'm pretty much a regular guy.'

Jack's sister and friends discovered some 'evidence' in his room on New Years Eve (Jack later admits this was a series of gay erotic stories). He arrived home on New Years Day to admit that he was gay.

'One week later she told mum in the car, then mum told dad.'

Jack admits that his family is further along than others. His father has an openly gay brother, his mother is a well-known health professional, and is apparently well-liked amongst local younger people; she has completed 'some gay counselling course years ago'.

'I was teased at high school. There is always that kid that gets teased for being gay. I was that kid. I didn't always hang out with the guys and play sport. But I didn't get bullied and I didn't get bashed.'

He has many stories of young people who moved away without letting people know that they were gay or otherwise. Most have felt that they did not have the choice.

'I don't know. If I'd had bad reactions from my friends, then I probably would have moved. But most of my friends are modern.'

Jack is very clear on where he wants to be.

'I don't want to move away. I have my family, I have my friends and I have my dream job. I just wish I could find a boyfriend here … but that's harder than you would think in this town. But even though it's hard, I don't want to move. It's just a lot harder because there are no guys here, or at least guys here who like me. I just want to find someone nice. I just want to be happy.'

Notwithstanding the seriousness of Jack's love challenge, I have to contain a smile. As Jack briefly looked out over Lincoln's waterfront, he conceded his only probable chance of a relationship would be found in Adelaide. Only a week before in Adelaide, Markus had bemoaned the lack of beau-availability in Adelaide and conceded his only probable chance of a relationship would be found in Melbourne or Sydney.

'I can't say I have confidence in finding someone here …'

Day 27

Saturday, 20ᵗʰ March – Port Lincoln SA to SA/WA Border = 1595kms

I'm sitting with my head down in the very down-to-earth roadhouse at the South Australian-Western Australian border. In my hands is an exorbitantly over-priced burger which looks and taste like something I would have attempted in primary school. Even if I slightly hyper-ventilate about my budget with each bite, I look at it as a reward to acknowledge getting this far.

A feature of the famed, perhaps infamous, Nullabor is road trains that travel in both directions. The drivers of these intimidating, imposing and, at times, inconvenient vehicles are another feature. Now eating amongst these men at the diner, I observe their 'safe' interactions. Their conversations stay on safe topics: the road, the weather, the food.

Safe territory also appears to include winking, nudging and lewd gesturing every time the German waitress brings a meal, invariably a burger and chips ordered from a cracked, laminated menu with bad font, and walks away. From experience I conclude that homophobia would not be too far away. I'm unlikely to talk about my tour with anyone.

I've been surprised by what I found on the Nullabor: I expected blue skies and great expanses of sand. Instead I found the Nullabor in a dark, overcast mood with patches of rain across its surprisingly vegetated plains.

I have decided to break up the drive into two days, both of around 10 or 11 hours of driving, not including breaks. I figure if I start at 6am both mornings, both days would end around dusk. Wearing a long-sleeved shirt to prevent 'trucker's arm' (i.e. a sunburnt arm through the driver's window), I enjoy ABC radio when in range and my own thoughts when the radio goes dead (for the most part). With petrol stations anywhere between 100 and 150kms apart, there is a lot of time to reflect on what I have experienced so far on the tour.

I have Markus on my mind because he sent me a message this morning which moved me. Previously too self-conscious to pick up the local gay and lesbian newspaper or read gay-related material in public, Markus told me he sat on the train and calmly read my book after my book reading.

'It's the first gay book I have been able to read on the train, and I know it's 'big'. People sniggered at me and I don't give a fuck quite frankly. I have the right to read and know. Previously I would have put it away.'

With the heat, the lack of anything to do and perhaps the waft of masculinity from my sweating body, I find the drive remarkably peaceful, if you don't count foot cramps and concerns of hitting kangaroos, wombats, emus and camels.

I keep myself partly amused acknowledging those driving in the opposite direction. In regional Australia there is a custom of waving or lifting a finger or two off the driving wheel as a friendly 'hello'. Whilst not compulsory, I find myself feeling strangely more at peace when a fellow driver returns my wave or, as I got progressively tired, raised fingers. Equally I find myself feeling somewhat miffed when my friendly gesture is not returned. It becomes clear that drivers from Victoria and women are highly unlikely to raise, or give you, the finger. The most likely to raise their finger are those driving trucks and vans, or retirement villages on wheels, and of course my favourite: men in *really* big hats.

Day 28

Sunday, 21ˢᵗ March – SA/WA Border to Esperance WA = 923kms

I'm munching quietly on my third (sheep) cup of cornflakes at Caiguna petrol station, some 1100km east of Perth. For now I am savouring the fresh milk and trying to process what just happened. Here's the set-up.

I'd left the mosquito-infested 'cabin' I slept in on the SA-WA Border early. I woke to find a huge mosquito bite on my forehead, despite the evasive action I took. Noting the huge gap under the door that invited swarms of mosquitoes into the cabin overnight, I pulled a flimsy sheet over me, theorising that they'll bite everything but your face. Not so it seems. Mosquitoes 17, Daniel 0.

After about three and a half hours driving I stop at Caiguna for a necessary fuel stop. Walking into the roadhouse to pay for fuel I'm taken aback by the attractive young man behind the counter. After weeks on the road, a lot of time to think and a lack of physical affection he is a welcome sight. Waiting to pay I watch him politely and efficiently serve customers. Seeing a sign that says they sell fresh milk breaks my daydream about him, which is getting progressively intense, and I look around to find the fridge. I would give almost anything for something other than warm UHT milk.

To find that fridge I look down the roadhouse to the diner section, catching the gaze of two truckers talking at a cheap looking table. They are sitting in front of the fridge housing the fresh milk. One, Tweedle Dum, is motioning at me with his head whilst saying something to his breakfast companion, Tweedle Dee, a rather large unattractive man with many tattoos who could be cast in one of your nightmares as the cellmate you didn't want to have. Social etiquette would dictate that they stop talking about me now that I am looking directly at them. Instead Tweedle Dum keeps motioning, more aggressively now, and Tweedle Dee keeps looking and laughing.

Suddenly I become self-conscious. I immediately wonder if somehow they have guessed what my daydream about the young man at the counter has entailed. My reflex reaction is embarrassment, like I've been caught doing something I shouldn't. Then, realising they are unlikely to have read my mind, I check my stance, my clothes … My clothes. My last pair of clean shorts was a pair of black shorts with tiny white stars on them. In a sea of plain, dependable and safe Hard Yakka gear, here I am wearing some shorts with flair. Were they laughing about my shorts? Were they laughing at the mosquito bites?

Getting back to Bruce, my truck safely and in one piece is the next thing that pops into my brain. The laughter and motioning are not light-hearted. There is something in Tweedle Dum's head movements and laughter that is accusing and nasty. I decide I cannot now get fresh milk from the fridge in front of Tweedle Dum and Tweedle Dee. I hope I can walk out to my truck, close the door, start the engine and drive off without incident. It is a long way to Perth.

As I turn from the large counter to the door I glance briefly again to see what they might do as I exit. And then it begins. One look at Tweedle Dum confirms that he is still nastily laughing. Suddenly the way his face screws up and the way he looks at me seems cowardly. One look at Tweedle Dee confirms that he is still chuckling along for the ride. Suddenly the way his huge belly moves when he laughs made him look comical.

As my shaking hand hits the door to push it open, my reflex of fear becomes anger. I'm met with a rush of dry, outback heat; enough to wake me up from my fearful slumber. By the time I hit the truck I'm fuming. I might have muttered something to myself about 'fucking homophobic truckers' and that there was going to be 'a punch on in Caiguna'.

I know as soon as the door closes behind me that I'm going back in for milk. The walk to the truck is merely to gather my thoughts. Now with fear subsiding my stomach grumbles, reminding me that although this is a matter of principle, it still wants some cornflakes with milk. As I purposefully march back to the roadhouse it feels like a moment from a Tarantino movie, and I suddenly find myself going back to a conversation I had with my older brother when I was about 14 years old.

It had been clear from a young age that I was not able to 'handle myself' in fights. Sensing my high school experience was tough, to say the least, my older brother sat me down for some home truths. The toughest kid in the northern suburbs along with our cousin, my brother taught me some secrets that I would only use once or twice in my life.

'Dan, you don't even have to fight … It's all about the eyes … Look, you just have to look crazier than they do, like a fucking crazy cunt … Get those crazy Hulk Hogan eyes when he goes into a rage … Look at them like you are going to kill them … If you have to say 'let's fuckin' go cunt!', hold your arms out and get the violent shakes, do it … Look at them like that, and most people will call you crazy and walk the other way … No-one wants to fight a mad man …'

My first step in the roadhouse is met with the customary look by every set of eyes in the place, a symptom of boredom and the lack of change in an isolated place. Turning right with purpose I walk slowly towards the fresh milk fridge, immediately catching the attention of Tweedle Dum and Tweedle Dee. Yet instead of looking at the fridge, with every step I look at them more and more intently with a dash of crazy. Not expecting to see me again, let alone have me come anywhere near them, both do what I had not expected. Tweedle Dee is first, stopping his laugh instantaneously, his moving belly shortly after, and looking solemnly at the floor. Tweedle Dum is next, averting his gaze to his empty, food-smeared plate.

As I get closer and closer to them I keep looking, just waiting to catch their eye. Momentarily I pause, standing in the small space between their table and the fridge, both of them painfully aware that I am looking at them. They both now seem so much smaller than the intimidating men they were only minutes before. As I turn my back to them, slightly puzzled by their sudden silence, given they could both crush me, one of them literally, I suddenly feel it could have been almost comical if it was not so serious.

With fresh milk in hand I turn to look at them, still without them meeting my gaze or making a sound. I turn one final time after paying for the milk, incidentally possibly the most expensive milk I'll buy in my life, to see two men avoiding confrontation.

Now back at the truck I almost can't believe what just happened. The adrenaline is coursing through my veins screaming, 'Drive!', yet I don't.

Instead I open the back of the truck and prepare breakfast. I remove the decorative peg my mum gifted me to keep foodstuffs from going stale; I ignore the crust of cornflakes and sugar at the bottom of my not-so-sheepish mug and fill it for the first of three helpings. Perhaps after all this effort I should pause, yet I choose to dive right in with a plastic spoon as crusted as the bottom of the mug it digs into.

I slowly munch on my cornflakes, appreciating every crunch in a way I'd never done so before. Not that my quiet breakfast lasts that long.

'Can I please check this in your truck?'

It seems Caiguna Petrol Station has one more surprise left for me.

I notice a young backpacker approaching. He and his traveling companion are parked beside us at the petrol bowser. I notice him instantly because he is topless, athletic and has a million-dollar smile. You know how I said it had been a while?

After he politely asks to see if his transformer will work in my cigarette lighter, my bare-chested friend answers my standard on-the-road question of where he's from. After finding out he is German-Indonesian, I surprise him by breaking into conversation in German. Some light flirtation follows.

I'm struck how at one lonely petrol station I can be intimidated to (near) violence by a pair of homophobic truckers and disarmed by a flirtatious, topless (male) backpacker. I pack up breakfast, check the GPS, take a last look at the half-dozen roadtrains sitting on the gravel, and slowly accelerate.

Day 29

Monday, 22nd March – Esperance WA

'Everyone knows everyone here. That's why Esperance is called 'Incest-perance'!'

I'm at the only pub in Esperance worth frequenting according to the locals. The small, sun-soaked, seaside town in the south-east of Western Australia has provided a stark, welcome contrast to the barren plains of the Nullabor. It's known for being a getaway spot, surviving very much thanks to tourism from Kalgoorlie-based mining families.

Esperance was not an original destination for the tour. Originally I had planned to spend that entire week in the mining city of Kalgoorlie. Instead I took a chance and came here, knowing that my ex-boyfriend's best friend from high school, Lisa, knew some local LGBT young people who were interested in sharing their stories. With no firm plans in Kalgoorlie, I decided it was worth a detour.

Lisa and some friends, gathered at short notice after a few sms' from her phone, have asked me to join them to talk about local LGBT life. Soon after I arrive they tell me that the town, no different to any other that I've visited so far, is hamstrung by its size: less than 10,000 people.

Some stories stand out, and soon I'm drawn to Mini, a young lesbian. She shares treasured memories easily, recalling them with good humour and hilarious impressions.

When she was in primary school, Mini remembers vividly a dream about her female music teacher, who she admits she had a huge crush on.

'I had a dream I had her baby and I was breastfeeding it. That's some fucked up shit for a 6 year old! But I'd always known. When I was 15 I had a best friend and I was totally in love with her. We used to wag school, steal her mum's wine ...'

One day Mini remembers that both girls went to the beach and sat talking under the pier. Her friend was complaining about her boyfriend until Mini finally said, 'If you keep whinging about him I'm going to kiss you ...' The friend kept complaining, and Mini describes how passersby were soon watching two girls in school uniform kissing passionately on the beach beside a bottle of wine.

'That was freakin' awesome! I pretty much knew from that moment. That was it.'

Mini excitedly told everyone at school that she had shared her first kiss, but admits that fear led her to use a male name when asked who it was.

Quite drunk, Mini finally confessed to her concerned mother that she was a lesbian. Her mother reassured her, 'You know what love, I still love you ...' This is something Mini still clearly holds onto. Her father is a different story. He believes that Mini is going through some phase.

This is evident when Mini talks of coming out to her grandmother on social networking site, Facebook. Harangued to join Facebook by 'Nanny', when Nanny looked at Mini's page and saw that she had joined a gay group, she immediately rang Mini's mum.

Nanny: 'Is Mini gay?'

Mini's mum: 'Yes ...'

Mini's dad [yelling in the background]: 'She thinks she's gay!'

Nanny would send a Facebook message simply saying, 'I love you.' Mini would reply, 'I love you. I'm sorry Nanny.' Nanny responded one last time, 'You have nothing to be sorry about.'

Mini cried.

Mini theorises that grandparents are much more relaxed with their grandchildren whilst being 'more angry' with their own children. At least that is her experience, acknowledging some brewing anger with her father.

'I'm not a teenager, my frontal lobe is fully developed so pretty much nothing is going to change …'

With support from friends, family and work colleagues, Mini was clear that she would be staying in Esperance, bucking the stereotype that young LGBT people are destined to move away to a larger city the first chance they get.

Not that things aren't hard. She admits that constant homophobic comments and insults yelled at her, especially from young men, hurt. Mini says she tries to stay light and laugh things off, yet concedes it gets to her and leaves her feeling unsafe.

As opposed to the common view that lesbianism might be 'cool', and even welcomed, amongst young straight males, Mini has other stories of the boyfriends of female friends who won't speak to her.

'These small-minded, cowboy boys, they are so dumb.'

She gives an example of one young man who has banned her from visiting her friend in his home. When he found out Mini had visited his girlfriend in their shared home recently, he kicked out his girlfriend who then had to stay with her mother for two weeks.

'All his porn is lesbian porn, yet his biggest fantasy threatens him too much.'

Day 30

Tuesday 23rd March – Esperance WA

'Come on Pumpkin. Have you decided already how this week is going to be?'

I'm getting an attitude readjustment during lunch. The setting: the picturesque foreshore of Esperance, and the company couldn't be more delightful. Or insightful.

Had you told me 24 hours ago I'd be sitting here I'd have thought you mad.

I'd ducked into the local supermarket to get some food for lunch. The easiest and cheapest is usually simple sandwiches with fruit. If I'm not worried about money on that day I'll grab a flavoured milk.

I decided last minute to grab some muesli bars and walked purposefully down the back of the supermarket, skim-reading the aisles as I went.

Suddenly I found myself stopping, backtracking and shaking my head. I had just spied the last person I expected to see going about their everyday shopping.

That person was Berlin Mäth, or Matt to non-Germans. During my first time living in Berlin, to write my first book, I had befriended an employee of my then-landlord. Comfortably heterosexual, Berlin Mäth would come to the gym and ask advice on exercises, take me for drives to his favourite spots on the outskirts of Berlin and come early to my apartment to have breakfast with me. I received a long warm hug each morning and he branded me 'Sunshine'. And I gave him the ironic title of 'Pumpkin', or 'Kürbis' in German. Yes, it was a Mad Bromance that caused us great pain when I left for Australia. I would learn from Mäth a great deal about how to express deep affection for men who I loved and cared for, yet was not in a relationship with.

So when he floated his plans to come to Australia with his girlfriend, Ramona, I got excited. Assuming we might meet at best on the East Coast at the end of the year, I was taken aback when I walked through the local Esperance supermarket and spied Berlin Mäth with Ramona buying ingredients for a cake. That cake would be for his birthday the very next day. Rather than rushing up, I decided to give Mäth time to adjust. I walked into the aisle and casually leaned against the shelves and waited ...

Munching on some communal cake, post-Frisbee-throwing – my birthday gift – I confess to him that I have arrived in Esperance feeling heavy and flat. With few contacts I'm feeling pessimistic. It seems unlikely to change. With a small smile, a warm hand on my shoulder and a hopeful look Mäth replies,

'Come on Pumpkin. Have you decided already how this week is going to be?'

He then reminds me that hard work is what I do best.

'You know, you are the first person I met who worked on his work [my book] every day. That was incredible. Your focus.'

Another piece of rather moist poppyseed orange cake later I realise it's less about making a few contacts.

I didn't realise how concerned I've been about not making it across the Nullabor until I reached Norseman, the first sign of civilisation. As I drank a strawberry-flavoured milk to celebrate, I realised how emotionally exhausted I felt. Yet it's only now in Esperance I figure out it's not the emotional cost I'm considering as early as Week Five, it's the financial cost every time I look across at the fuel pump. $1.37 per litre of diesel is a bargain compared to what

I paid on the Nullabor; certainly a dream compared to what I'll be paying after Perth.

Now well and truly underway, the financial reality of the tour is sinking in. In Melbourne I left behind an income. Relying only on my savings, which I can only hope will sustain a tour that I find impossible to accurately budget for, I'm also benefiting from the generosity of others.

Having agreed to auspice my tour, Shepparton's Uniting Care Cutting Edge is receiving tax-deductible donations from community groups and individuals, keen to see myself and Bruce get around the country. A small-scale 'Fight Homophobia One Tank of Fuel at a Time' campaign was launched, immediately receiving support.

Indeed the first donation, from Motafrenz, a Melbourne-based car club for gay men, caught Jon Faine's interest when I mentioned it on 774 ABC Melbourne's Conversation Hour.

Jon: 'There's a gay car club? …'

The good news is that early fuel donations mean that I can get to Perth without having to dip into my own savings once. The bad news is that I'm then driving through the most remote locations of Australia, and therefore the most fuel-expensive areas, most likely using my own money.

For now I have cleared my first major driving hurdle. Nullabor Desert: tick. What waits on the other side is all that southern Western Australia has to offer. Mäth helps me see this.

Leaving Mäth and Ramona I jump into Bruce to escape the noisy sea winds and make some phone calls. In what's a pleasant surprise, they go well. Suddenly Esperance looks very different.

Day 31

Wednesday 24th March – Esperance WA

'It's just really frustrating that I didn't know about this before …'

I look across a relatively large school nurse's office to one of three school psychologists and ask, 'Can you tell me why?'

'I wish I'd known about all of this because we need it …'

I find myself at a local high school after a recommendation by a local worker. After meeting with local youth and mental health workers it seems I got the thumbs up. An endorsement by one of them has me seated in the school nurse's office on the very same day. Notoriously overworked and under resourced, that the support staff of this high school make time for me at such short notice says one thing: challenging homophobia is important to them.

To my surprise the lead psychologist, Tanya, has convinced two other psychologists from the regional office, the school nurse and the school chaplain to join us. But wait there's more. Tanya had immediately got off the phone to me and walked the school grounds asking health and physical education teachers if they addressed homosexuality. All those asked would say that yes they did look at homosexuality in relation to values and discrimination: 'Everyone has the right to be homosexual and if at any point we encroach on that, that's a problem.'

To cap it off the school principal, an older woman with a smile that could make your day, drops by, shakes my hand firmly and wishes me well with my travels.

Tanya and her colleagues are clear that they could support LGBT students and provide them with safe spaces within the school.

'For the [same-sex-attracted] girls they present most with self-harm. For the [same-sex-attracted] boys it's drug and alcohol. It's tough. All the students use *gay*. It's commonplace.'

The frustration that Tanya expresses is about the lack of knowledge, such as research on same-sex-attracted young people's experiences in schools, resources, such as the *Pride & Prejudice* educational package, and strategies, such as those outlined in *Beyond 'That's So Gay'*: how to challenge and interrupt homophobia in students without being disciplinarian.

After the fifth week of introducing my tour, talking to and sharing resources that teachers, health professionals and homophobia-curious others find useful, there is no doubt in my mind that most, if not all, lack training and resources outlining practical strategies they can use immediately in their everyday classrooms and workplaces.

Tanya and the school nurse, Betty, seemed quite focused on supporting 'out' students.

'We'd support them when they came to us and disclosed.'

Me: 'Is there a reason you'd wait until they did?'

'Well that's the most important time to support them. They'd be out and there'd be risk.'

I gently challenge this focus, referring to research that looked at young people's thoughts of suicide and their attempts. It found that not only were same-sex-attracted young people much more at risk than their heterosexual peers but that gay, lesbian and bisexual young people would attempt suicide in the months *before* they came out to anyone.

Me: 'So if we are waiting for young people to disclose before we offer support, we've missed their most at-risk time. The second most at-risk time is when they disclose and there is a bad reaction.'

Everyone in the room falls silent. I look across the large, imposing wooden desk that Betty sits behind. She looks ill. My aim is to motivate for small changes, not ruin their day.

Me: 'So the research evidence tells us the best strategy is to demonstrate our support *before* students come out to us. What are the things you can do to demonstrate that?'

Understandably without time to reflect, and the news that they might have, with the best of intent, missed some opportunities to support LGBT students, not much was forthcoming.

Me: 'Could you start challenging and interrupting homophobic language if given the tools to do it and send a clear message that it's not OK to use 'gay' as a putdown?'

All: 'Yes.'

Me: 'Do any of you do introductory talks, or chats in classrooms about the support you are giving?'

Betty: 'Yes, we go to all the home rooms and talk about what we do.'

Tanya: 'Sure and we also tell them if they are struggling with something or are confused that we are a great place to come.'

Me: 'Could you give some specific examples, and include as one of them, *And we've had some people talk to us because they think they might be gay* … or something similar?'

Pennies dropped quickly. Tanya and Betty look at one another, and then the others, in a sort of disbelief that they hadn't thought of this before. This soon gives way to excitement about other ways that they could demonstrate their support for LGBT students.

'You're right. *Come to us if you are feeling troubled or confused* is a bit broad.'

I'm in a good mood so I drive from Esperance's inland outskirts straight down to the windy waterfront. I take my time downing a strawberry-flavoured milk.

Day 32

'It's difficult because it's a mining town. You get that macho element around town. There is drinking and drugs. Everyone works long hours and shift work is really tough.'

Echoing *The Adventures of Priscilla: Queen of the Desert* character, Bob, local mental health worker, Donna, sums up Kalgoorlie.

As I arrive in Kalgoorlie I recall the various advice I'd been given from friends, family and colleagues, including:

Just drive in with your windows up, get your petrol – and a cup of coffee if you have to – and then just drive the fuck out ...'

On my Facebook status, for example, someone has written, 'Come back in one piece please!'

Almost everyone I spoke to, and not just my overly concerned mother, gave me a pre-Kalgoorlie warning. When I drive through the wide streets characteristic of an old-school mining town, my heart beats considerably faster. It certainly looks like any other country town I've been to: franchise-heavy on its periphery; one, or two main streets; huge iconic pubs screaming out at you from every corner, pedestrians with all the time in the world who would be mowed down on any city street.

Then when I find my bed at the local backpackers, it has Winnie The Pooh bed sheets. Surely this is a good sign?

Donna was recommended as a great person to have a cuppa with once I arrived in 'Kal'. She explains how challenging it is for local workers to overcome all the stereotypes. A former long-time resident of Kal, Donna grew up with very different views to now.

'I was racist, homophobic, you name it ...'

Formal education, learning and 'having fantastic friends' are credited for her more liberal stances in life now. Donna describes one friend who took time to 'gently challenge' her which led to change over time.

'I used to say things like, *they shouldn't have kids*. But you can change, and I feel free to admit that I was racist and homophobic. It all comes through fear. Like I used to be scared of Indigenous people, and laugh at them ...'

Despite some signs of LGBT life in town, Donna is pessimistic about what can be done for LGBT people in Kalgoorlie.

'There is a lot of bantering. It can be quite judgmental. They are pretty tough. Young people don't come out as gay or lesbian in school, and I find that cause for reflection in itself.'

Me: 'So what's the most challenging thing for you?'

'Mainly that the group who is homophobic would be too big and too strong. There is just enough of them that they can support their own views and drown you out …'

This fear of being an overwhelmed, solo voice is a common theme that I have heard time and again. It seems no-one puts up their hand to be the only gay-friendly voice in the village.

Day 33

Friday 26th March – Kalgoorlie WA

I park Bruce out the front of an unremarkable former high school and follow some signs to the reception area. The dusty, plain exterior that looks like some portable classrooms hides an internal courtyard. When I enter the small courtyard, I gasp. The old classrooms exit onto a dark, wooden internal verandah that gives way to lush green grass, lit by the mid-morning sun. It could hardly contrast with Kal more.

I'm here to have a cuppa with local school psychologist Sam, a colleague of Tanya in Esperance. Despite the fact that the tranquil seaside town and mining town could not be more different, they sit in the same 'Goldfields' region in WA.

With a general climate lacking any tangible LGBT-friendliness, it's understandable that teachers and health professionals describe to me not knowing where to start.

'Teachers don't know how to approach students saying *that's so gay*, let alone look at other ways to support sexual diversity.'

Sam gives an example of one young indigenous man caught by his friends 'in a sexual act with another boy'. His formerly close-knit group of friends has now ousted him.

'They've beaten him up a few times, and some others at school. His mother is worried he is going down the path of self-harm.'

Whilst Sam describes everyone scratching their heads about what to do, one mother's common sense might be making all the difference. The mother of a former friend of this boy is trying to intervene, telling her son and their friends that it is like their acceptance in the group of a disabled young man.

'You accept [the disabled young man] and he cannot change that, just like he cannot change the way he feels.'

Sam says there is a different experience for men and women.

'Kalgoorlie is harder for guys. It has this impression of a mining community: rough, manly and stuff. I think it would be harder because of blokey blokes. The fly-in, fly-out thing [of miners] means a lot of people are anonymous and keep to themselves.'

To add to local opinion, I employed a strategy suggested by Rodney Croome.

Dan, I make sure that I walk around the place that I'm in for at least an hour. How else am I going to get even the slightest idea of what it would be like to live there?

Having cut my LGBT support teeth in regional and rural Victoria, I would add to that a pivotal question as I take that walk.

What is there around here to give someone the idea, the hope or the challenge that not everything is necessarily heterosexual?

Taking this walk around Kalgoorlie yesterday, I did not get a sense that it was as hostile as some had led me to believe. I was surprised how my gaydar and lesdar were pulsating as I walked the streets. This was not only during the day but also the nights, when I was warned of men coming up from the mines to drink. For example, one seemingly same-sex-attracted young man jumped excitedly around with a group of young women outside one of the biggest watering holes in town, surrounded by apparent miners. I'd been told to be wary of that pub given that everyone had just been paid, meaning everyone would be out drinking. There were also plenty of women who looked like they could kickstart tractors.

I have to say Kalgoorlie was surprisingly, for me, one of the campest regional or rural places I can recall visiting.

Not that Sam and others experience Kalgoorlie that way. However they were no different to the 1000s of teachers and health professionals I've worked with for well over a decade: they want something straight forward, common sense and practical to be able to better support young people and challenge homophobia. With a relatively brief conversation, some resources and questions about what could make a difference locally, there are quickly signs of LGBT-friendly life in Kalgoorlie's teachers and health professionals.

Not for the first time, relief washes over someone's face at the end of a cuppa.

'It's about bloody time!'

Day 34

Saturday, 27ᵗʰ March – Kalgoorlie WA to Perth WA = 600kms

'Kalgoorlie has such a long history of brothels that no-one gives a fuck about what other people do sexually. I can understand that things seem camp here.'

This seems consistent with the experience of Drago, a young bisexual man from Kalgoorlie now living in Esperance. Drago, known to bikers as 'Nugget', described living in a Kalgoorlie bikie bar, documented as one of the most dangerous bars on Earth on a reality TV show, not so long ago.

'They all knew I was bi and they were OK with me. I was always 'Nugget' to them. They knew I was a strange young man, and they found out I was bi and they thought it fit. If I was gay I would have been an outcast, if I was straight I would have been accepted. But I was bi and it was OK ... I was accepted in a bar where people were punched in the face for saying *get fucked you fag.*'

*

Only now that I was driving to Perth did I stop and think about the last week – Esperance in particular.

In Esperance I was taken aback by the feedback of the young people, teachers and health professionals I spoke with. To be honest, feedback was what I needed to hear. Having spent so long planning what I would do on the road, I'm having some very human moments where I question if what I'm doing is: (a) even needed; and, (b) useful for people living in regional, rural and remote Australia.

Esperance mental health worker, Lil, was clear it was both.

'This really works, what you are doing … it's great! You are open, friendly, you have personality and energy and it just works. You just seem so familiar, but who do you remind me of?'

My familiarity and that I reminded people of someone was evident whilst talking with some of Esperance's LGBT young people. Mini again.

'You seem familiar, I'm not sure … It's not just how you look, it's your manner, your voice. It's almost like your voice is just comforting. I just feel really relaxed and comfortable talking to you. [Lisa] said it was going to be relaxed and it is … You're so clever … I have been coming here for years, yet suddenly tonight the [pub] feels different … For the first time the pub feels nice …'

This comfort seemed apparent when a group debrief happened.

'That's only the second, third, time I've ever told anyone that,'

Drago chimed in.

'This is freaky, I had a dream that this very conversation, this moment would happen …'

The group then talked about dreams, with Drago saying he never hits the ground in dreams where he is falling, citing the urban myth that one will die if they do hit the ground in their falling dreams.

Lisa would have none of it.

'That's bullshit … I always hit the ground in my dreams. Man, I hit that dream hard …'

I will also give Lisa the final word, given that she encapsulates the aspirations of this tour. As much as I can hope to talk to as many young people, teachers and health professionals as possible, it will be the ensuing conversations of locals with other locals that will mark the success of this national project.

Lisa would talk at a weekend taekwondo competition to a 13-year-old boy who admitted he'd had sexual experiences with another boy. Her being open about herself would mean he felt safe to talk about this for the first time in his life.

'You coming has started so many conversations. I've had conversations with people at work, with my housemate about my sexual identity and with my neighbour who said, *I didn't know you were queer.* It's been so good!'

Maybe I was some way to being on the right track.

Day 35

My first weekend in Perth and I'm lucky to be at Subiaco Oval watching the Fremantle Dockers play the Adelaide Crows in a home and away AFL match. It's been over 12 months since I was last at the footy, so I'm gladly soaking up the late afternoon atmosphere.

Subiaco had only ever been a stadium name for many years, yet now that I'm here I'm struck by how much it reminds me of Kardinia Park in my hometown of Geelong, where I spent many weekends thanks to cousins who barracked for the Geelong Cats.

I'm here because a local LGBT activist, The Swimmer, has invited me as my welcome to Perth. He's a one-eyed Dockers fan, and I now see how seriously he takes his football. Usually he comes to the footy with his dad, yet today he beams when he tells me he's bought us Premium Tickets for the occasion. I pretended to know what that means, however I now realise the great seating position in the afternoon sun as it drops is worth whatever money he paid.

Yet things got complicated when The Swimmer started making contact with me on Facebook a few weeks ago. The Swimmer admitted that without meeting me, he had developed a crush on me merely from looking at my photos, reading their captions watching my video blogs and reading through my blogs.

I mention this because I find that my work can evoke powerful emotions in people, be they good or bad. Time and again I experience a great deal of emotional force from people merely for the work that I do. At times exhausting, it is important for me to always remember that this has less to do with me and more about what this means for the person in question. Not taking it personally, even when it is overwhelmingly positive, is vital to me maintaining my emotional sanity.

The Swimmer has a vested interest in the tour's success, given his own experiences in secondary school that would not be wished upon any young person. Known for his own experiences in LGBT advocacy and contacts throughout the west, The Swimmer has offered to actively organise any number of cuppas with all manner of influential, interesting and everyday locals only too eager to engage with the tour because they trust his judgment.

Sitting here now it's clear that we have chemistry. And The Swimmer becomes even more publicly affectionate with me once the Dockers win the match.

I drive him home in Bruce, parking out front and make it a point to explain my 'Campsite Rule' for the tour.

Me: 'The Campsite Rule? On tour I have to leave everything better than the way in which I found it. Me coming into town, having an affair with someone I've only met because of this tour and then leaving is not likely to see that happen.'

The Swimmer isn't taking no for an answer, and senses I had thought about mixing business and pleasure.

'C'mon, we're both young and hot for each other. No-one's going to get hurt.'

'Sure,' I say to myself. 'Famous last words.'

Day 36

Monday, 29ᵗʰ March – Perth WA

Fuck! No, that can't be true. I re-read the text message again.

'Dear Daniel, the situation in Surabaya is not safe. I urge you to cancel your ticket because of the terrorist threat here. I will try to get back home today or tomorrow. Peter.'

It's just over 24 hours before I fly from Perth, Western Australia to Surabaya, Indonesia. I jump straight online in order to save my international organisation considerable expense. Yet my mind is really on the fact that I have built my time in Western Australia around this one week – the result of a professional commitment given in 2007.

Peter is Peter Dankmeijer, Executive Director of the Global Alliance of Lesbian, Gay, Bisexual and Transgender Education (GALE). Surabaya, Indonesia's second largest city, was to be the site for some project work with the Ardhanary Institute, an organisation for lesbian, bisexual and transgender (LBT) women throughout Indonesia.

I was lucky enough to visit a rural base of the Ardhanary Institute in October, 2007. What I found was a large, simple and open warehouse space filled with women working on huge sheets of butchers paper. It soon became clear that these women were from all over Indonesia, participating in a rural lesbian social mapping project. The task was to work together to create a visual representation of their communities, including the links between LBT women and opportunities for support.

Yet the magic seemed to come from the conversations that were taking place between the women.

The fact that this project encourages such storytelling from LBT women from all parts of Indonesia is something of great interest to GALE. The aim of this Dutch-government-funded organisation is to identify, enhance and share better LGBT education practices around the world. There is a focus particularly on developing countries, which is why the majority of my international work thus far has included such locations as Sri Lanka, Poland and Thailand.

I was to spend time in Surabaya working with groups like the Ardhanary Institute in attempts to skill LBT women to then go out and collect the stories of their LBT sisters. The learning from this project was then going to be made as close to universal as possible and shared with other projects around the world who are ready and waiting.

Although somewhat uncomfortable with leaving Australia during the tour, I understood the international ramifications of my time in Indonesia. I had also committed to following through with this very project years before. A few thousand dollars for my time were also going to come in handy for what is going to be the most expensive leg, fuel-wise, of the tour: the north-west of Australia. I decided that one week so close to Western Australia's school holidays, a time I'd be unable to talk to school staff, could work.

I'm left feeling anxious and confused. I text Peter back, and he reassures me that he is OK. I was concerned for the safety of the people I knew who I would have been meeting again, such as Sri and Poeji. Peter says that everyone is safe.

My time in Surabaya, Indonesia was to follow an international Asia-Pacific conference for ILGA, the International Lesbian, Gay, Bisexual, Transgender and Intersex Association (ILGA). Yet the arrival of groups of men 'from conservative and hard-line Islamic groups' the day of the conference led to the eventual break-up of the conference. I'm told that local police could guarantee the safety of international delegates from 16 countries only to the airport and out of the country. They were said not to have guaranteed delegates safety if they continued with the conference.

I calm down considerably when Peter tells me he is safe at the airport awaiting a flight to Bali where he'll spend the week working on a beach. I start to come to terms with the additional time and quickly become preoccupied with two pressing dilemmas: firstly, a sudden, gaping black hole in my plans and secondly, no injection of money from my international work, which right now I sorely need.

Whether I like it or not, money is the concern that follows me around the country and keeps me up at night, more than my own self-doubt or homophobia itself.

Day 37

Tuesday, 30ᵗʰ March – Perth WA

'You're a long way from fucking anywhere …'

Hope's definition of 'anywhere' is 'Sydney and Melbourne'. Not that Hope, an LGBT advocate and educator, believes that Sydney and Melbourne are necessarily the places to be, or else she would have recently returned there from Belfast, Northern Ireland, instead of to her hometown, Perth.

I accept her invitation to some of her hot chips as I write in my large purple notebook. I normally wouldn't accept food during an interview, however I know Hope well after a week spent in Belfast in 2007 on some international LGBT work.

We're sitting together at a table enclosed by a hedge at the largest pub I've seen so far: The Balmoral Hotel. This feeling of not 'being anywhere' is something that is playing itself out in almost every conversation that I've had so far in Perth – conversations starting with an anxious, somewhat hopeful question. 'So, are you from WA?'

I'm one to quietly observe, absorb and form impressions about anyone I meet or anywhere I visit, yet Perth isn't having any of that. With the best of intent, Perth's residents are set on convincing me how great it is. The economy is booming ('you can tell a city's wealth by the number of cranes you can see …'), the lifestyle is easy ('in Perth you can drive anywhere in 15 to 20 minutes, it's just so easy here, not like Sydney or Melbourne …') and there's an abundance of things to do ('we have museums, art galleries, cafes, shops, bars …').

All true. Yet as time goes by, I feel the need to gently challenge those eagerly and anxiously selling Perth and, more broadly, Western Australia.

Me: 'Let Perth be … If Perth is so great, then you don't need to sell it to me, it will sell itself …'

There is no doubt that there is a distinct energy in Western Australia's people at present that was lacking as I moved through Victoria and then South Australia. Yet this boom-related energy has its downside according to Hope.

'The boom has been bad in a way … All they want to talk about is their property, cars and their next holiday …'

This, Hope believes, has led to a more conservative climate that, combined with Perth's lack of proximity to the East Coast, ensures that the LGBT community adopts its own conservative approach.

'I notice it here with young lesbian and gay people. It's much more prescribed, there is no individuality. This is what you look like if you are a boy, this is what you look like if you are a girl. Just go out here. They all look the same Dan!'

Day 38

Wednesday, 31ˢᵗ March – Perth WA

'If you're a lesbian out in the open then you have to have as many credits to your name to make up for all the arrows they'll put in your back.'

I'm having lunch with Anita at The Swimmer's house. She explains her time at a prestigious, select-entry school in Perth. While Anita was out to her students and fellow staff, even (arguably) being the first teacher in Australia to take a high school banner in an LGBT Pride Parade, it became increasingly obvious that she was not supported by her colleagues and the school leadership, or as she likes to call them, 'fucking gutless pricks' or 'fucking heterosexist bastards'.

'I thought I could be openly lesbian but I couldn't. They said to themselves, *Let's totally fuck her over.* It absolutely killed me. My physical health suffers as a result of the trauma. When they saw that I saw an injustice and wouldn't be quiet about it, they had a problem.'

Yet the abuse and harassment of students was what concerned Anita the most.

'Until recently the school had a chaplain from the Church of Christ who handed out anti-gay leaflets, scared because he didn't want the Pride Parade going through Subiaco. He did not counsel a gay student who'd had a knife held to his throat. That same student came back to school the next day after his mum had taken it to the police who said they can't do anything about it. He headed back to school and was beaten up that day by the other students.'

When Anita suggested there be some measures put in place for LGBT students the chaplain said, 'Why don't you do something for left-handers?'

'I said that I would when he could tell me about left-handed people who are not allowed to be open about being left-handed, who are beaten up at school because of it, thrown out of their homes, labelled as pedophiles and rejected by their families.'

Some students saw Anita as a breath of fresh air.

'One student said, *Coming into your classroom is like walking out of hell.*'

Not that all students were supportive. One student in the school yard spat on the ground and called her a 'fat lesbian'.

'So I spat on the ground and said *I have a problem with being called fat …*'

Day 39

Thursday, 1ˢᵗ April – Perth WA

'I have difficulty [in talking with schools and organisations], whether it's because they really don't want to know about it or they are busy. You never know which one it is really.'

At Perth's The Freedom Centre, a space for young people with diverse sexualities and genders (DSG), coordinator Nina tells me she faces resistance from most schools. If she does get into a school it's because she works with school nurses, who are not employed by WA's Department of Education and Training (DET). It would be fair to say that DET is not thought of fondly in LGBT/DSG land.

Nina tells a story of one school psychologist who recently contacted her to send some LGBT-related material to his school.

'He asked me what would be on the envelope that I was sending the information in. He was legitimately concerned that he'd lose his job for being sent this information about a service for young people, funded by government. This is in Perth!?'

Whilst many in WA speak to me fondly of the law reforms for LGBT people, years later there is little change on the ground. There is clearly a lack of resources to educate the broader community about those changes. Most agree that there is still a long way to go. Nina says it best.

'There needs to an education campaign to understand current, contemporary climates for LGBT people. You have a wide range of views about what people think life is really like. All the key health indicators show that we are overrepresented, especially in terms of mental health, but also physical and sexual health.'

Me: 'Yet people still say that it's better these days. What would you say to them?'

'I can understand why people might think that, but it's not the case.'

This sentiment is echoed at Uniting Care West, my next stop. Tour-wise, I'm supported by Lois Lane, who incidentally relished the invitation to pick her own pseudonym. Lois Lane and the *'True Colours'* project, servicing both Albany and Bunbury, are a breath of fresh air. Perth-based Uniting Care West is the sister organisation of those auspicing the tour, Uniting Care Cutting Edge (Shepparton).

Without suspicion, doubt or defensiveness I'm warmly welcomed to Uniting Care West and offered a base to work from. Infrastructure like a phone, a photocopier, a desk and even another person to make small talk with at the tea station has been hard to come by. It is only when I experience it, after a few months without, that I realise how much I missed it.

Day 40

Friday, 2ⁿᵈ April (GOOD FRIDAY) – Perth WA

Although it's Good Friday, it doesn't turn out to be a holiday. The Swimmer and I get on the road early. This morning we meet with openly gay former politician, Brian, for a cuppa in Subiaco. He echoes Hope's sentiments in needing to escape Perth periodically to escape its 'mono-culture'.

'I used to fly out regularly. Now ...'

Not that this apparent mono-culture didn't throw up all manner of characters and individuals. On the contrary. Over a milkshake, The Swimmer and I hear from an older gay man who now splits his time between Perth and Albany, where I'll be next week on tour. We sit entertained and engaged by Larry's stories, typically from times gone by.

'In Albany they try and run you out of town. There was a Priscilla night a while ago at a local restaurant and the local church was picketing people coming through.'

On progress, Larry isn't too enthused.

'We've come a fair way but there is so much that needs to change. It requires major cultural and educational change. Especially in government and business.'

Me: 'So why has there been no change in government and business?'

'Because right wing gay men have everything they want.'

Brian was equally blunt, and perhaps more cynical.

'People will happily pay a few hundred dollars for dance party tickets and outfits, yet wouldn't give $20 to a human rights campaign ...'

When The Swimmer and I sit down later with Pride WA's 2006 Patron, gay Indigenous leader, Jim Morrison, gestures are examined.

'I felt me being Pride Patron was tokenistic, but felt a real bond between queer and Indigenous communities around inequality and discrimination. After that I formed Queers for Reconciliation. Now there is always a Welcome To Country and heaps of queer people attended National Sorry Day. I think there is an increased tolerance of the Indigenous community in metropolitan Perth. There are more out Indigenous young people in the LGBT community.'

Working with Aboriginal prisoners most days, Jim has also had the blessing of the region's Aboriginal elders to work with their young people on LGBT issues.

'Often they'll come to me and say, *We need you to talk to our boy*, or *we need you to talk to his family to help them become more understanding to their son.*'

Not that it's just young Aboriginal men.

'Indigenous communities are more willing to accept women than men. There is better acceptance of lesbians.'

And Jim has stories of Sistagals, Indigenous transgender people.

'Recently there was this boy going to school every day dressed as a girl who is now going to uni dressed as a woman.'

Day 41

Saturday, 3rd April – Perth WA

With a little more time up my sleeve in Perth, I give myself the weekend off, aside from culling an inbox that has exploded to unmanageable proportions.

I'm in good spirits after receiving a letter of support and a donation towards my tour from Australian LGBT Royalty, the Hon. Michael Kirby:

In one sense, Australia is still terra incognita – in regional and rural Australia it can sometimes be hard to grow up facing homophobia. Daniel Witthaus tackles this problem in a young, fresh & challenging way. I admire him and support him.
Hon. Michael Kirby AC CMG
Justice of the High Court of Australia, 1996 – 2009

That he calls me 'a strong, courageous and fine person' and signs off with 'Hang in there!' puts me in the right mood to head out to Perth's gay focal point, The Court Hotel.

The Court Hotel is on a busy thoroughfare a few minutes' walk from the centre of Perth. Walking in I'm greeted by an extended black marble bar with too many chandeliers, perhaps a reflection of the new money status that so many are describing here.

On warm nights like this the front section opens out onto the street, however the centerpiece is the open air courtyard out the back. Most people seem to be mingling out here waiting for a drag show to start that provides something to talk about and a convenient pause in any social proceedings. I like hanging further down the back on a raised area that is dominated by a large gum tree.

Without warning I'm surprised by Kris, a young woman I had supported 13 years ago in Geelong. She spotted me in the crowd and excitedly screamed, in her unmistakable half-mocking drawl, 'Dddaaannn!'

Maybe it's because of a few scotch and cokes, but it really feels like not so long ago that Kris came to GASP! as a 15 year old. Not out to anyone in her life and still questioning her sexual identity, Kris befriended an older, 'known lesbian' at her all-girls school. The school found out about this new friendship and called a meeting with her parents where they announced that Kris was a lesbian. Kris would be prevented from seeing her new friend again. She would also need to leave her family home, although she would occasionally go back when she lied and promised she would 'be straight', wear her hair longer and wear a dress.

We look at each other after a second hug. It becomes clear that we have both come so far since then. We laugh about stories long gone and try to work out what the old gang is doing now.

As Kris prepares to head back to her group, one of her friends approaches. A short blonde woman with a smile that could warm up your day, she wants to talk to me.

'Where do you come from?'

Me: 'Melbourne, originally Geelong, but Melbourne now.'

'I could just tell. Yep.'

Me: [half laughing] 'Can I ask how?'

'You are just classy, that's all.'

Me: 'Me, classy?'

'Yes, you're all classy in Melbourne.'

Day 42

Easter Sunday, 4th April – Perth WA

I'm sitting in a large, tiled lounge area in a home in Perth's outer suburb of Canning Vale. It's early morning and I'm enjoying the silence. With few chances to do nothing, I struggle to fully relax when moments like this present. I find I'm doubting myself. I'm sure there must be something I'm missing or need to do.

I have my customary cuppa double: Milo in my big mug and green tea in another. The green tea is usually just the right temperature once I've finished off my Milo. I slowly sip and look out onto the tree-lined fence through the sliding glass door.

From the moment I arrived in Perth I've been given nothing but the gold standard in hospitality, be it accommodation with exemplary hosts, access to practical and moral support from a sister organisation, or assistance with setting up interviews with key stakeholders from fellow activists. This has relaxed me in ways I couldn't have expected. I raise my mug in honour of Berlin Math and his calm reassurance.

I've quickly gone from cursing the fact that I couldn't be in Surabaya to feeling lucky to have such a productive pit-stop after almost 10,000km on the road. On that note, perhaps most relieved is Bruce, who was checked in for a major service and a 'sore foot' – they discovered he'd picked up a nail, most probably on the Nullabor, in his front, right-hand tyre. This explains why he's been losing air the whole way.

Day 43

Monday, 5ᵗʰ April – Perth WA to Albany WA = 417kms

I've stopped to get petrol about halfway between Perth and Albany. I enjoy the break as it's been a hectic morning. I woke early to attend a Greens breakfast featuring Bob Brown. The Swimmer, the official photographer for the event, managed to get a photo of Bob and I as I rushed out for a *very* early cross to gay and lesbian radio station, JOY94.9FM. Damn that time difference.

I park Bruce off to the side and devour some home-made banana cake. I had a cuppa with a young gay man I'd been talking with on Facebook for years. We'd never even thought we'd meet; it was more me responding to his messages every so often. Ryan is a perfect example of LGBT people who add me on Facebook after hearing about my work in the media. Despite the misgivings of my more social media prudish friends, I accept all their friendship requests and correspond accordingly.

Now eating this cake, I wish I'd met Ryan sooner. I laugh to myself thinking, 'Get that young man a husband!'

It's still mid-morning so I'm tuned into ABC radio. It's refreshing that I know I'll be able to complete a full drive without losing radio reception.

By chance I hear Giz, a sitting member in WA's upper house, being interviewed about parliamentary inquiries. The Swimmer had organised a cuppa with Giz who gave me the heads up on Albany.

'In Albany there are so many women who look like dykes, but aren't. You could swear they were, but they're not. It's so confusing.'

Amongst gay men, Larry explained on Friday that many gay men in Albany won't come out, and might even be part of the problem.

'They keep quiet or are very publicly homophobic, yet the next week you'll see them out in gay venues or saunas in Perth. It really gets up my nose. No-one really comes out to each other. You know there are gay people but you don't know who they are. You know not to put your head above water; you keep your head down. But there is a fairly strong lesbian community, especially in nearby Denmark where it seems to be tolerated.'

I arrive in Albany, a comfortable 5 hours drive from Perth, and it feels like I've driven into a town many more times its size, given the aesthetics, quality of retail outlets and 'traffic'. Perhaps not coincidentally, I get out of my truck on the main street and feel like I'm being sized up favourably by a passing giggly young man. Maybe I'll find some LGBT life here after all.

Day 44

Tuesday, 6ʰ April – Albany WA

'Once a week I go to an arthouse movie. Tonight I can go to one of 60 cafes or restaurants. There are so many art galleries here and a disproportionate amount of media for a town this size.' Albany has a population of around 30,000.

I'm at the Men's Resource Centre having an early morning cuppa with local LGBT ally, Nathan. A well-connected men's health advocate, he explains that Albany benefits from having such a wealthy population. Nathan hails from Sydney, with a background in film and television that's evident in his subtle, swashbuckling manner. He could have easily been in an American 80s cop drama.

'There is a higher than average number of gay people here, some of them in fairly significant positions. It's significantly healthy, but it's an underground gay and lesbian community. Albany's unique demographics means there's a plethora of health and social services. It's *highly serviced.*'

I feel like Nathan wants to say overserviced. He believes that locals aren't accessing all those services anywhere near as much as would be expected, one reason why he's so passionate about his role in linking, connecting and referring men in the region.

One issue might be that those people needing services might live outside of Albany's disproportionately wealthy borders. In 30 minutes you can be in Mt Barker, by all accounts a very small and challenging town to Albany's north, or Denmark, described by some as 'the Byron Bay of Western Australia'.

Our cuppa is interrupted by a short woman in her 40s with equally short hair. She tells Nathan she's just dropping off a pamphlet and apologises for interrupting. Ever the connector and gentleman, Nathan introduces me and Mandy does a double take.

'Are you Daniel Witthaus!?'

I can't go *anywhere*, I think to myself with a chuckle.

Me: 'Yes I am.'

Day 45

Wednesday, 7th April – Albany WA

The morning couldn't be going any better. Mandy and I are having a cuppa and sharing her thick, buttered fruit toast as she tells me about her LGBT work in and around Albany.

I'm feeling much more relaxed this morning after a great night's sleep. The night before I'd missed out on the extraordinarily early closing of reception at the local backpackers. I drove around unsure of what to do for a while before I finally settled on sleeping beside a footy oval overnight in Bruce. Not the comfiest of sleeps however one of the cheapest sleeps in Albany.

I started the day with a very early swim at the local aquatic centre, which had doubled as a chance to shower and freshen up.

Nestled in a suburban street corner, it was easy to see why Mandy and others adore the popular Vancouver Café & Store. A former family home with a verandah skirt, I feel like I'm back in primary school visiting a friend's place: everything has a meaning, the owner's individuality is apparent with a touch of class from yesteryear and you get the feeling there is just that little bit too much 'stuff'. Mandy and I find a large wooden table and soon I get her take on things.

'Albany is very intolerant of anyone who is not mainstream ...'

Mandy, like Nathan, believes that the local LGBT community is underground and informal. Yet she believes that this is only in adult communities over the age of 25 years.

'Everyone will tell you that when young people leave school they go to Perth. A lot of young people between 18 and 25 years are not getting their needs met.'

I'm reminded of what Larry told me in Perth when he said, 'You get out quickly'.

Mandy's clear that visibility was a problem.

'You don't walk around holding hands with someone of the same sex. I've never seen it happen. It would be huge for someone in Albany to stand up and say *I'm queer and proud of it*. What do you do with such a strongly heterosexist place?'

Yet Mandy, an ally educated later in life, is still enthusiastic even if unable to solve the problem immediately. She is a great example of what I've observed for well over a decade in teachers and health professionals: sometimes the best come from outside the sector. Some of the best youth workers I've met were originally trained as teachers, and vice versa. Some of the best LGBT workers I have met have come from mainstream organisations, and vice versa. As an ally, Mandy seems to be doing things that other LGBT workers around the country are not doing.

The secret is that Mandy is having everyday conversations with people who would previously have never been approached. The Chamber of Commerce in Albany, the local GPs network and others are all finding themselves in conversations about local LGBT people and how they might create a better quality of life for them. Excitingly, these new connections are starting to bear fruit.

The pin-striped, apron-wearing café owner, Alison, approaches the table soon after to say hi to Mandy and ask how we've found everything. Once Mandy introduces me and gives a brief on my tour, Alison asks immediately how she can help. Looking through her oversized glasses she offers her venue for anything that could help. She also offers to contact her gay friends in Broome to see if there is anyone who can put me up during my stay.

Ever opportunity savvy, Mandy asks Alison to join us in a photo with Mandy's purchased copies of *Beyond 'That's So Gay'* and a *Pride & Prejudice* educational package. Alison hands me her contact details, wishes me good luck and floats away to other customers.

Me: 'Why are you an ally to the LGBT cause?'

'I'm living here, I'm committed to this city and I want to see diversity.'

Day 46

Thursday, 8th April – Albany WA

In most regional, rural areas I visit around the country, *headspace*, a national youth mental health foundation, is mentioned often as making a very real difference.

headspace regularly head to nearby Mt Barker and Denmark, all part of the 'Great Southern' region, to make sure young people in more isolated communities get the support they need. For example, they collaborate with other local services to take a specially designed bus where hoards of young people can jump on board to learn more about the large number of services on offer to them.

headspace counsellor Cass sees these times on the buses as opportune times to challenge and interrupt homophobia. When I explain some of the strategies outlined in my book she quickly sees an opportunity.

'We could probably do more of that. Often on the bus there are groups of boys who are using *that's so gay*. We could probably pick up on that because it's just become a part of terminology, the way they talk.'

Cass, who tells me she used to work in Melbourne's western suburbs, explains that it is not only in group settings that she hears homophobic language.

'In every counselling session, *that's so gay* comes up at least once, if not more. It can be hard for them to share their feelings when they come from generations that think that gays are the scum of the Earth. These farm boys have grown up and been pumped with *gays are bad*. No wonder they make it tough on LGBT young people.'

The majority of young LGBT people that Cass works with at the moment are young, gay Indigenous men between the ages of 16 and 21 years.

'It's difficult because they think that it's only if you are white, have got it together and are comfortable with being gay. Of course we try and change that idea.'

As a lead youth agency in the region, Cass is very keen to get me back to Albany soon to train local educators and health professionals. From my time in south-west Australia's retirement capital it would appear that such training is sorely needed.

To be honest these requests leave me with mixed emotions. On the one hand I am excited knowing that most regions are eager to have me return to work with their schools and organisations. Yet on the other hand there is frustration given that I am not on this tour to market my wares; I simply cannot go back to many of these regions, given my itinerary is yet to take me through WA to Tasmania until November.

With that foundation, Albany gets one step closer to having a community eager to better support the young LGBT people it would otherwise lose to Perth, or worse suicide, each year.

Cass believes that there is hope.

'I really think Albany is progressing … It's starting to change …'

Day 47

Friday, 9ᵗʰ April – Albany WA

Echoing the sentiments of *headspace* is Young House, another lead agency, this time in youth housing, in Albany and its surrounds. For years Young House has been front and centre in putting LGBT issues on the local agenda. The organisation enjoys very positive reviews from workers not only from Albany but also Perth. Young House's great work and it being a finalist last year in the WA Youth Awards has resulted in it receiving additional funding. As I talk to Young House's Acting Manager, Mia, a representative for a State Minister comes through to organise the Minister's visit the following week.

I must admit that I've been given a reception fit for a State Minister by Mia, who proudly shows me around Young House's facilities. From the front you could miss Young House, but for its sign. It has the look of a well-kept suburban family home with green leaves spilling over the cream-coloured, head-high picket fence. Although I feel at times people afford me a better reception than is required (i.e. a simple cuppa and an informal chat), it does make a remarkable difference after the number of times I'm made to feel like an Amway salesman.

Young House led the way to make sure that LGBT young people had somewhere to go a few years ago. A lesbian worker at the service had been working with local police officers to provide support to at-risk young people on Albany's streets. A number of LGBT young people identified through this work needed something that Albany, at that stage, could not provide: 'they want a safe place to go, where they are not going to be judged, to talk.'

Hearing about a promising regional LGBT project in Bunbury, the Young House worker lobbied to get a local project happening. That project was, and is, *True Colours*, a project for LGBT young people run by Uniting Care West.

Not that it's all easy and fun, but *headspace* and Young House serve as examples where an organisation is doing its best, working with LGBT organisations and not hiding what they are doing.

Yet the presence of *True Colours* does not mean that all young people feel they can turn up. In the early days of the project, Mia explains that Young House gave important feedback to *True Colours* about how young people saw it. Young people who were being supported in temporary accommodation were not interested in going to a group for gays and lesbians 'because they were still trying to work out who they were'.

'For example one young woman had been in and out of our service for three and a half years. We'd always known she was questioning, hadn't pushed it, just supporting her and waiting for her to share it when she was ready. Eventually she was. That time was important for her.'

Day 48

Saturday, 10ᵗʰ April – Albany WA to Perth WA = 417kms

I wake up glad I made the drive back to Perth last night.

I'd driven back late, after attending Albany's *True Colours* young people's group. The whole drive I was conscious of animals jumping out and maiming Bruce beyond repair. With no real pattern or consistency the roos nibbled gently at the sides of the road; I slowed down, but it seemed to make no difference as they stared blankly and continued chewing. Unfortunately me slowing down means nothing as to whether they would choose to hop out spontaneously or not; it just means I'm less likely to have a roo through my window. I saw a movie once where a roo got hit by a 4WD, got stuck and scratched the driver to a bloody, screaming death.

Day 49

Sunday, 11th April – Perth WA

I'm on the courts of Alexander Park Tennis Club with kids coach and long-time Facebook friend Al. Another example of someone I chatted to every so often about tennis results yet never expected to meet, Al was lovely enough to invite me to have a hit at his club.

I'm both excited and nervous; I haven't hit a tennis ball in 4 months. Deciding to go on tour meant that I was not joining my tennis friends from around the world at the Cologne Gay Games. Realising that traveling won't allow me to be in the form to play at my best – I've won several gold medals over the last few years – I opt out with a heavy heart. There will be other tennis tournaments. But still.

We head to a pair of hardcourts, despite the fact that the whole place is a sea of grasscourts: I didn't have any grasscourt shoes. Heck I could be hitting on asphalt and I wouldn't care.

Like all good coaches Al suggests we warm up midcourt, standing on the service line. We hit up and chat as we do, trading halfcourt forehands and backhands. Before we retreat to the baseline to continue the warm-up Al has some feedback.

'I'm in awe man. I've never warmed up with anyone who didn't miss at least one or two shots. You haven't hit for four months and you didn't make one mistake.'

Me: 'That's why they call me the brick wall. But just wait, they'll happen.'

They do. I delight running around the court yet feel the four-month absence as I go down 6-1, 6-1. My ego is hurt because first impressions in tennis count, however I'm grateful that Al doesn't mind too much about my form. He generously says he can see what I'd be capable of with regular hitting.

We walk off towards the clubhouse which looks over the main court where the men's doubles final in the club championships is being played. Sitting on the balcony, feeling muscles I haven't used for a while and watching great tennis is the perfect way to end my Sunday afternoon.

Day 50

Monday, 12th April – Perth WA to Bunbury WA = 172kms

Everyone raves about the 'new road'. Now it's even quicker to get from Perth to the second largest town in Western Australia, and vice versa.

None of this hides the fact that Bunbury is 'a big country town', as Andy, a young gay man now living in Perth, describes it. 'Drive two hours and go back 20 years.' A young gay man who spent his high school and post-high schools years in Bunbury until recently, Andy and I enjoy a cuppa on a warm Perth morning ahead of my drive down.

Andy was born to a logger and a nurse in Bridgetown, about one hours' drive from Bunbury. Andy says that the only thing that Bridgetown, with its few hundred inhabitants, is known for is an annual blues festival which he describes as 'an excuse for a piss up with music'.

Whilst many would think that growing up in such a small community might be less than ideal, Andy sees it differently.

'I actually loved it. I would not change a thing about growing up there, be it my friends, the community, shooting rabbits and kangaroos on the farms … none of it …'

Andy's move to Bunbury with his family came at what he believes was an inopportune time: him starting high school.

'Things changed when we moved to Bunbury. It's never good to move to a new high school I guess. It was definitely a big shock; a new place, not knowing anyone and worrying about making friends. My sister made friends easily because she played netball at a regional and state level. I could only meet people through tennis, but they were sort of non-inclusive people.'

Indeed everyone I have spoken to across regional and rural Australia thus far has spoken of the importance of locals playing sport in order to become an accepted part of the social fabric.

Yet Andy's greatest concern was his experience at school.

'It was a public school full of bad people, most likely with bad parents … People who would say *I want to fight you* even though you didn't know them and that it made no logical sense. Like one time in Phys Ed we had a sport for the term: Jujitsu. Great, now they have an avenue to do this. OK, I have fuckwits in my class and they all want to fight me and each other. I faked a lot of asthma attacks … '

'In Year 9 I kept asking myself, why am I not even remotely attracted to girls and why am I finding guys so appealing? Not having been exposed to anything but my life, there was basically mass confusion. It's all about what was taught at school and what parents teach you . This *never* came up. I used to get upset, emotional and cry, *I don't want to be gay*. It didn't seem like an acceptable life, it seemed like a life of people's disgust at you … '

'I went into survival mode in high school, I made no efforts to socialise just in case. I went to school and basically hoped to get through the day, then I came home and was thankful I was at home and not there. I threw myself into work, lots of part-time jobs so that my family, no-one, asked questions.'

It isn't surprising then that Andy did not perform to his potential and looked to leave school earlier than many of his peers. This even though he won an English award.

'I wanted to get out of there as fast as I could, so possibly I didn't do as well as I could.'

Drawn to cooking, Andy's work experience placement would provide him with his ticket out of an everyday hell. Approaching the restaurant for an apprenticeship he was successful.

'Yippee, get the fuck out of my life … I never want to see anyone from [high school] again.'

Andy would soon join a mass migration out of Bunbury at 19.

Day 51

Tuesday, 13th April – Bunbury WA

I arrived in Bunbury yesterday and found a city that feels like it's gone through a recent major development. I get the impression that Bunbury is self-consciously showing off recent wealth in the form of streets lined with quickly assembled franchise buildings and housing developments. I sigh. This could be anywhere in suburban Australia. I'm disappointed there's an absence of any Bunbury flavour to it all (whatever that might be).

In contrast to Esperance and Albany, it seems that most, if not all, LGBT young people feel unable to stay in their own communities. The proximity to Perth combined with the new road might very well exacerbate the point made by local *True Colours* LGBT worker, Renee that 'there is no cohesive gay and lesbian community in Bunbury …'

'There's no queer nightclub, bar or café here. There's just not a place where you can meet people …'

When I worked in my hometown of Geelong in the mid to late 1990s, the fact that it was on Melbourne's doorstep was a barrier to anything LGBT happening. Most people thought it was easier to drive an hour up the road to have everything they could want and need relatively anonymously, rather than live their LGBT life in their own community. For many it just seemed too hard; in contrast, if they had the means, the drive to Melbourne was too easy.

On the surface, controversy that swirled around a suggestion that Bunbury needed a Pride Parade demonstrated how it might all just be 'too hard'. For example, a letter at the height of the furore.

' … the gay lifestyle promotes lavatory sex …'

If ever you are fortunate enough to receive hate mail, this is the kind of thing you can expect to read. I say fortunate because of an African-American advocate from the US who I sat with on a panel at a conference in Montreal. Accustomed to hate mail from the religious right, she referred to it instead as 'fan mail'. To Sylvia, 'fan mail' from the religious right meant she was on the right track.

A local advocate for LGBT rights started receiving such 'fan mail', including the above line, in the aftermath of the 'Bunbury Pride Parade controversy'.

A few years ago, following the 20th annual Pride Parade, a former Pride President questioned its modern day relevance in the heart of Perth. Blogging that perhaps the Pride Parade was preaching to the converted every year in Perth's gay heartland, Daniel Smith suggested that heading out of Perth might do more to advance gay rights.

Rather than encourage a dialogue, from all accounts it resembled more of a quick and heated debate. Renee summarises the response by Bunbury City Council's Mayor:

'He said Bunbury doesn't need a Pride Parade because we are beyond discrimination here. He is a privileged white man who has no idea ...'

Renee explains that one Bunbury Councilor attended a Council meeting soon thereafter and proposed that they conduct a cost analysis on the likely impact of the Pride Parade on Bunbury's local economy. Without debate, that Councilor was 'shut down'.

At Edith Cowan University, Tina, a vocal LGBT advocate and ally received a rather elegant, handwritten letter. That letter, as Renee paraphrases, suggested Tina 'should be so careful because [she] is around so many impressionable young people' and reminded her that 'the gay lifestyle promotes lavatory sex'.

Tina's response at the time?

'I'm a straight married woman and *I've* had lavatory sex.'

The untold story is that locally the suggestion, as it was never actually proposed, of a Bunbury-based Pride Parade created many unexpected conversations in everyday situations. Not only were there letters to the editor in the local newspapers for 10 weeks (!) after the first reports of the matter, the suggestion meant that Renee and others had been involved in unsolicited discussions with people they had not expected.

'I didn't bring it up most of the time ... most [discussions] were positive, apart from the people who ran the church service in a park right before the council meeting ... which was quite terrifying ...'

Day 52

Wednesday, 14th April – Bunbury WA

'Even though Bunbury is WA's second largest city, it's quite rural really and isolating, especially if you can't drive, as drinking and driving is the main way of socialising here ... It's a mass migration at 18 to Perth, which I know is a problem across rural Australia, especially for anyone who feels isolated and at-risk ... We do hear that from young people that they just want to go to Perth ...'

Renee sees it as part of her work to continue supporting LGBT young people who move to the big smoke, seeing transition from regional to metro as a potentially high-risk time. Often young people will move without any support around them. Once they arrive in the state or territory's capital, their experience could be best determined by the flip of a coin, which is why this was identified as a priority area by workers across the country in the original *Outlink* project way back in 2000.

Whatever the case, Renee feels that the broader 'tough' homophobic climate fuels depression in local LGBT young people.

'You can isolate yourself because the wrong words to someone could mean so much more. In a community where you are isolated because you can't talk to anyone or you'll face violence if you do talk to anyone or you hear people yelling *that's so gay*, where that stuff is everywhere, pervasive, it's tough. I recall one young local trans woman, she identified as a gay boy at school because she knew she would probably be beaten up, but if she came out as trans she thought there was a good chance she'd be killed in Bunbury.'

Day 53

Thursday, 15ᵗʰ April – Bunbury WA

Having a down day means I can catch up with my various e-mail inboxes and make some phone calls that are coming close to being overdue. My days off invariably include something work-related, and I think back to my conversations with Renee.

As a young bisexual woman she faces the dilemma that so many LGBT workers in regional and rural Australia face: how to separate one's personal and professional LGBT life in such a small community. Knowing from personal experience the toll this can take, I asked Renee what her own experience was.

'It bleeds a lot. I don't work 9-4 because I'm always aware of what I can do and what could be done at all times. Technically I'm supposed to think about this job for 14 hours a week, but I'm always conscious of the seeds that I can sow. I figure out how to do things at 11pm. We have such limited funding where we try to achieve so much with so little so our personal life becomes a part of it. I know I don't know when to back off. Some of these projects don't have anyone else. I don't think I'm irreplaceable, but if I do give slack I know there is no-one to pick up the slack.'

Similarly when I met a worker in the project that preceded *True Colours*, Kate described a feeling of the rural world on her shoulders.

'Trust in regional areas takes a very, very, very long time but can be overcome by having a regional-based worker. I did it because I was gay and living in the country. I really struggled, I made a lot of personal sacrifice, I didn't socialise with people my own age, they were all potential clients or volunteers. Everyone assumes you are the expert who can handle everything. I was limiting myself and it was too hard in the end. But who is going to do it if I don't? I've thought very long and hard on it. It's not an ego thing, it's finding people who can do it, training them, etc without tainting them with cynicism.'

Day 54

Friday, 16th April – Bunbury WA to Perth WA = 172kms

I leave Bunbury behind after my least busy tour week yet. Not that my lack of activity reflects on Bunbury's potential.

It seems that Renee is making some progress with the seeds she is sowing. The day I met her she was going to pick up robes for her graduation ceremony, having completed a social work degree. In Bunbury the local university organises an annual parade, not of the LGBT Pride kind, but one of academic pride. This march through Bunbury's streets, lined with friends and family, ends at the university where the formalities continue. This year Renee will be the first female student to hold the ceremonial mace.

It's moments like these that help keep Renee in her hometown. With her own thoughts that one day she might move to Perth, there are things that keep her at home.

'I want to be happy. I hope to live somewhere and be who I am, whatever that looks like and I guess it's something that is happening at the moment. I have a family and I have a little brother who I adore and would do anything for and a mother who I love. I want all that here.'

Sitting in a sunny suburban kitchen, young gay local Andy reflects on his time in Bridgetown, Bunbury, and later, Cairns, Sydney and now Perth.

'I feel qualified to talk about all this because I have lived in all these places, and most other people haven't. I don't want to ever go back to Bunbury, and I can't say I'd want to live in Sydney again either.'

He jokes about what happened when people asked where he was from, and how they knew nothing outside of Perth, except for Margaret River, 'because that's where all the wine that they drink comes from'.

Andy moved from Sydney to Perth to support his father who was diagnosed with cancer. Now that his dad's cancer is in remission, Andy spends four days every week driving between Perth and Karratha – 'basically a mining town full of cashed up bogans' – in a truck with his dad. Although his dad talks too much to the radio and wants his own version of talkback in the cabin, the time together is working out well.

The hopes Andy has for the future are modest.

'Probably the same as everyone: I want to meet someone, I want to be content with them, to build a life together … I want to build a house with him, have a good group of friends around me and basically do what I want.'

Part of Andy still craves life in Bridgetown. It seems that life has never really been the same for him since he moved. He questions why everyone else is not instilled with 'country ideals' like him.

'I just wish everyone was like that.'

Day 55

Saturday, 17th April – Perth WA

My second time here at The Court Hotel and the pattern is striking. We arrive around 10pm and make our way out to the courtyard. The place bubbles with an enthusiastic yet relaxed LGBT crowd enjoying their weekend, with the air still warm after a clear-skied day. I see The Swimmer and a few other people I've met through the tour so far. I start to daydream about what it might be like to live in Perth and come here every week with my friends.

That all changes almost immediately as the clock ticks over to midnight. At first it starts as a trickle: a straight couple here, a few straight guys there. Soon it's a steady flow, and an obvious heterosexual crowd has all but invaded. How do I know they're straight? The mostly young, grim-faced guys stand still and eye off everyone around them. Every now and then their girlfriends come to check if they're OK on their excursion to the LGBT Zoo. Many of the guys then glare in the direction of gay men as they hug, kiss or frottage with their female partners, making sure everyone knows who they'll be going home with. I know because at one stage I stare just a little 'too long' at one of them, less about him and more about him being in my line of vision. Their behaviour towards lesbians seems much more relaxed.

I realise that this is what happened last weekend too.

The atmosphere has changed, almost as if it's matching the temperature. Gone is the warm, friendly air, replaced now with a cool, indifferent breeze. The fun has stopped. Well that's not completely true, lots of straight girls seem to be having a great night, as I'm sure they would anywhere in Perth on a Saturday night. Yet that's the point, they could be anywhere. The gay men on the other hand are no longer having that kind of night. Although perhaps unnoticeable to them, they have now stiffened just that little bit and increased the distance they stand from one another ever so slightly. The easy, affectionate reaching distance for the occasional touch, hand-rest or energetic slap has widened and now no-one touches unless they do so self-consciously.

For the first time it clicks in my head: this is what everyone across the south of Australia is calling 'progress'; the integration of gay and straight. I feel like I'm caught in a failed social experiment. Progress means that the straights have yet another space to make their own; the gays have yet another space where they have to monitor and modify themselves. This is not progress, it's dressed-up compromise.

As if to punctuate the point, the most attractive gay man in the place walks by three times and bumps into me; part of a not-so-elaborate mating ritual in a now invaded pub wary of same-sex contact. Although shorter than me by about a head, his athletic body makes an immediate impression on me. His tan-coloured shorts show off the strong legs that help him make a physical impact. The first time he's subtle, and I let it go and ignore it. The second time he's a little more obvious, and again I ignore it, hoping that he'll instead say hi or just wave from his surveillance point across the boxed-in fernery that separates my collection of friends from his. The third time he virtually hip and shoulders me, annoyed that I am possibly the only gay man in the place not trying to get his attention. I acknowledge his football manoeuvre, turn, nod and then wave *hi* to him. He nervously smiles, which I'm certain has melted most hearts in Perth, and stops in a corner with a friend, staring in my direction yet not at me.

I shrug my shoulders with a smirk, offer both my hands to the cool night sky and turn my head to the side, gesturing, 'And now what?' He looks at his friend, says something and they walk off. A game I don't necessarily know how to play, or even want to, has begun. Maybe it's how good he wears his shorts, but I want to play the game and see where it ends up.

Alas the friends I'm with signal it's time to leave. I look around me, feel the atmosphere that Mr Shorts distracted me from and realise they're right. Time to leave.

Day 56

Sunday, 18th April – Perth WA

As the sun starts dropping on a Perth Sunday afternoon, I put the finishing touches on tidying up the place given that my Perth hosts, Nigel and Vince, are returning home today from Thailand. I'm looking forward to them being back. Despite having an ideal homestay, it has felt a bit strange doing so without the actual inhabitants here.

Vince is the first to burst through the door. Quite short and muscular, he has excess nervous energy to burn at the best of times. Nigel, taller and less energetic, lumbers in and offers his contagious, relaxed smile.

They both look 10 years younger thanks to some cosmetic surgery.

'Look, we've had our eyes done!'

Day 57

Sunday, 18th April – Perth WA

Yet again I find myself at Soto Café, a surprisingly sparsely furnished space along Mary Street in Perth suburb, Mt Lawley, which seems to be where LGBT locals like to gather.

I arrive knowing the dark polished concrete floors well and make my way to find Archie, 'a trans guy, kind of queer'. He sits, quietly and bespectacled, in a booth at the back of the bustling café.

Me: 'Can you tell me about your journey to becoming a 'kind of queer' trans guy?'

'When I hit puberty I thought, there is something really wrong and I don't know what it is. When I was 17 I accidentally came out to mum as a lesbian. It was a bit disastrous because it was the same day she found out my dad was gay. It came out as if I was trying to defend dad. She forced me back into the closet: *Don't tell your brothers, they've just found out your dad is gay.*'

Archie looks down into his cuppa as he goes back in his mind to high school.

'I s'pose I was dressing like a boy at that time and wearing Mohawks before they were in fashion. I heard so many times, *Is that a boy or a girl?* which I hated. It seemed to make them confused and that made me confused. With my female friends I would feel invisible. They were all relating to me as a girl which wasn't really who I was inside. I just felt jealous of the way they looked at other guys. I wanted them to look at me that way. And I was really uncomfortable with the way that the guys looked at me.'

Yet taking time to live in Sydney with his dad and attending a regular Wednesday Drag King night, where women dress as men and perform, made all the difference.

'I used to go out to this drag king night, and met a couple of trans guys. I would go out and dress up with facial hair and I really liked it. I got a lot of positive feedback. One friend said that I became this different person when I was in drag, more comfortable and confident, just happier and bubblier. It got to the point where after I'd been out I'd wake up and wouldn't want to take the facial hair off.

'I was talking to a friend about this book on trans people I found at the library. Pretty soon it all suddenly hit me, I was no longer in denial. On the one hand it was liberating; on the other the most terrifying moment of my life. I looked down at my body knowing my body didn't match what I felt inside, and realised I had a long road ahead of me, including telling my family. After the way mum treated me when I came out, I thought I'd be completely ostracised. But it was actually ok. She saw it as her chance to do it right this time. She said on the phone that she was really not surprised. She said I had to do what was right for me. I ended up moving back in with her and my two brothers.

'For me there was no doubt that I wanted hormones, surgery. When I accepted that I felt so much relief; I was really excited about my voice breaking and growing facial hair. Things changed so much after surgery, with issues from the past coming up one after the other. People think that when your physical body finally matches your inside that everything will be alright. But then it was the 25 years of living a life that was not my true identity. All the grief and pain that went with that, feeling that I'd been robbed of my birthright, that maybe my life had been a mistake.'

Now Archie has turned his attention to educating others. His face changes talking about this work, and a documentary project. Archie's message is ultimately one of hope, despite the struggles.

Day 58

Tuesday, 20th April – Perth WA

I sit in the waiting area of Fremantle *headspace*, located in a well-maintained redbrick house that's perched high on the edge of Fremantle, around 30 minutes drive from Perth. For all intents and purposes, Fremantle is like an outer suburb of Perth, although it fiercely maintains an identity of independence.

I know a great deal about Fremantle, given this is where The Swimmer resides. He had taken me for fish and chips on Cottesloe Beach, a remarkable place to watch the sunset at any time of year.

As I sit in the space where general counselling clients sit and wait I notice some LGBT-friendly materials lying around. Part of me imagines them running around madly placing such information before my arrival and I chuckle to myself. The reason I'm actually here is that this branch of the national youth mental health organisation has had a history of LGBT support work.

I contacted them, funnily enough, after seeing them quoted at a *beyondblue* GLBTI Roundtable, held, almost comically, at Melbourne Airport in 2009. A senior *headspace* staffer had said that Fremantle was doing some great work to support LGBT young people.

At very short notice a proud group of staff, including the manager, Joel, meet to discuss the work they're doing. It's important to note that with about 40 *headspace* locations around the country, each develops and evolves very differently. As Joel explains, 'We are focused on increasing help-seeking behaviour, we are somewhere else to go.'

Right from the start Joel and his team saw a need to engage the LGBT community. After considering the research evidence they were clear that LGBT young people should be a major focus of their resources. Not because of an LGBT staff member or an incident, just based on the facts and the need.

'The trauma that is created in a high school setting through bullying is amazing …'

headspace Fremantle is not just waiting around for young people to come out either. They recognise that LGBT young people 'have needs before they make that decision to come out to someone.' To them, 'in the meantime' is a vital part of their support.

Part of their work involves community engagement, such as participating in Pride events and collaborating with The Freedom Centre.

Me: 'Have you copped any flak for your involvement in LGBT events and support?'

'The staff have been having a real fun time. We use the photos from Pride as profile photos on the website. We haven't really had anything. Nothing at all.'

Day 59

Wednesday, 21ˢᵗ April – Fremantle WA

The sun has long gone down and I'm waiting for The Swimmer to arrive at Little Creatures Brewery in Fremantle. It's his final evening before he moves across to Melbourne to live, work and study. There is a Greens (political) party event here in about 30 minutes, his other passion next to LGBT issues and the Fremantle Dockers.

The table is on the mezzanine level of one of the most remarkable buildings in Australia. It makes me feel I'm in an aircraft hangar that happens to be full of people eating and drinking amidst brewery equipment. I'm taken with the enormous silvery vats, even if I'm not a beer fan.

It's loud, but not too noisy. I'm thankful for some time to breathe it all in, and daydream as I look down on people who are also unwinding from their days.

Today I trained the education team of the Equal Opportunity Commission of Western Australia. They wanted to see what more they could do in challenging and interrupting homophobia as part of the work they do across the state. It worked out well, given my experience in delivering sessions for its equivalent in Victoria for the last few years. I was running late thanks to Perth's morning traffic, and devoured a hot chocolate and a dry blueberry muffin as I took the lift to their floor.

The training only happened because the Equal Opportunity Commissioner had attended my book reading the week before, hosted by the B-LeGITs committee, an LGBT interest group with the State School Teachers Union of WA (SSTUWA). Opened by Upper House member for the Greens, Lynn MacLaren, a good friend of The Swimmer, there had been an exciting mix of senior DET staff, politicians, young people, LGBT community members, teachers, health professionals, parents and friends who braved a torrential Perth downpour to be there. The EO Commissioner said she was so impressed that she would go back and ensure her staff undertook professional development with me the very next week.

And thus we did. We even took a break for an interview and a photo with the *Sunday Times*.

I feel a mixture of sadness in my goodbye with The Swimmer, who has been nothing but supportive of my tour. Of my personal life, he could have done better. It all has to do with The Dancer, who I've mentioned previously.

When I commenced the tour The Dancer and I said our goodbyes in adult-like fashion: we'll meet up and see how things go after the tour … we'll go on a date if both of us have not met the man of our dreams, heck, we'll go for dinner anyway … if we keep contact, we keep contact when and if we can and desire to …

Many daily phone calls and messages later from The Dancer, because he feared I would forget him, he told me of his plans to come to Perth to see me. In his mind, this would be an emotional and physical 'pit-stop' and a contribution he could make to my tour. Believe me I was not complaining. My physical life on tour was as barren as the Nullabor.

However The Swimmer's admiration, in the weeks leading up to Perth, and since, spilled onto Facebook and that was when things with The Dancer turned sour. I would find out too late that The Dancer had been messaging The Swimmer, and vice versa, with the soap-drama theme of 'Keep Your Paws Offa My Man'. Friends started messaging me to ask if everything was OK after it became open warfare on my Facebook page.

The timing, for all involved, has turned out for the best. The Swimmer leaves tomorrow; The Dancer arrives the day after. Unfortunately both are promising to continue the feud when The Dancer returns to Melbourne.

Day 60

Thursday, 22ⁿᵈ April – Perth WA

If this tour is all about timing, today couldn't be better. I'm meeting with Gay and Lesbian Community Services (GLCS) WA on what turned out to be their 36ᵗʰ birthday (yes 36 years). Head of what used to be the Gay and Lesbian Counselling Service of WA, Denise, believes that GLCS is the oldest organisation of its kind in the Southern Hemisphere, and second only to one organisation in New York (go Perth!). Denise has been with GLCS for 10 of those.

We meet at City West Lotteries House, a pre-fabricated hub for community services. Denise and I share a cuppa in her office, down one-too-many white brick corridors that almost had me lost.

Me: 'Can you tell me why you believe that you and GLCS have had such longevity?'

'I think passion is obvious. And this job keeps evolving, so it never gets boring. They find new things for me to do. That change means I'm not stale from doing the same thing for 10 years. And working part-time is part of the secret. I'd never be able to do this full-time. I've always been working in other roles, which stops the isolation of the work. Much like having GLCS in this building, the networking has been vital for us. My other work supplements GLCS. I often think of it as supporting my GLCS habit.'

I'm keen to get Denise's thoughts on my plans to head north of Perth through more isolated parts of Western Australia. How LGBT-friendly WA is *depends*, according to Denise.

'It depends on where you live. Attitudes in the country are different; the north is a completely different world. It depends on if you are a white male professional in Perth versus an Aboriginal lesbian in Kununurra. It becomes the haves and the have nots. In Mt Lawley you can be as gay as you like. But really it's not that open. There is no street in Perth where two guys can hold hands.'

It hits me right then and there. *That* is what I'm trying to find out: on what does it *depend?*

Denise says that up north, trans people and their issues are largely ignored.

'It's where gay and lesbian politics was 10 years ago. When we headed north to do our training [with mainstream organisations] we realised we had to drop the trans component. We were coming across people who didn't even know what gay meant.'

Day 61

Friday, 23rd April – Perth WA

I'm in the guest bedroom at Nigel and Vince's and it's pitch black. I'm in bed with The Dancer. I'm lying behind him on my side, within easy reach, yet there is a gulf between us I can't fathom.

The Swimmer saga means that instead of arriving to provide me my promised 'pit-stop', I'm experiencing his Arctic, passive-aggressive blast.

The last time we were alone in the dark we were in my bedroom in Melbourne. After we'd had super hot sex we fell asleep, me holding him tightly from behind, my arm under his and clasping his soft, delicate hand in mine. There we stayed for a few hours before I woke up. I beamed: he can *never* sleep with my bedside lamp on, nor without his earplugs in, nor with me snuggling into his back; yet here he was, breathing heavily and at peace. He even fell asleep on 'my' side of the bed. I quietly turned the light off and sat with my back to the brick wall. The night was a hot and sticky one, so the painted brick wall helped cool me down. Perhaps he sensed I was no longer there, because he stirred and propped himself up to find me. I was a sucker for his slow, sleepy voice.

'You're awake? Are you OK? Oh my god, that was so beautiful to fall asleep like that.'

'I'm fine I just couldn't sleep. Just thinking about everything.'

'What are you thinking about? Tell me.'

'The book launch last night, the tour, moving out of here, you … everything really. I guess that every so often I find myself awake late at night, and you know I love my sleep so it's rare, and it's like the world goes quiet.'

In that silence I come as close as I'll get to contemplating the universe and world peace.

On that night in the dark in Melbourne he and I would talk for almost two hours about everything. I felt connected to him and that he understood. I was calm and ready to start the tour. We ended that talk and again I held him from behind until we drifted into a deep sleep …

Now all I want is to feel his warmth, to reconnect with him, and feel that calm again. Instead it's like he's a different person. It hurts and only exacerbates the feeling I have about my life right now. Having additional unscheduled breathing space in Perth has helped me conclude something that a few months of driving and a packed schedule – and myself – wouldn't allow: outside of the tour I'm not happy; my personal life is a shambles. Melodramatic or not, reality or not, right now things feel like they are falling apart. Outside of what I'm doing on tour, it feels like all I've done is made mistakes.

Tonight he'd walked up to greet me at the airport and gave me a reluctant hug. I felt like an idiot, like I do now: dependent on The Dancer's affirmation, even though he's unable to give it.

A sickness sits in the pit of my stomach and suddenly he breaks the silence.

'What are you thinking?'

Just as I had that hot night in February I don't censor myself. He quietly listens as I talk to his back. As I do he quietly inches his way backwards until he eventually has his body against mine. When I have nothing more to share I realise how much better I feel to have said it. At that moment I feel a tear fall that I can't catch in time. It must have hit The Dancer's back because he's turned on the light and turned around to face me.

I can feel I'm about to cry, so I close my eyes and suddenly feel the hot tears. At that moment The Dancer moves in and kisses me on the lips. I start crying from the relief of his warmth. I then nuzzle into his chest – which is furry at the moment and not waxed, just the way he knows I like it – and cry. I only come up for air, and then to get tissues for my tears and snot.

We look at each other and burst out laughing. God I needed that.

Day 62

Saturday, 24th April – Perth WA

I am enjoying the tour. *Really*. It was an accidental observation as I drove back to my base from an interview in Perth. I sat in Bruce driving down the highway, window down and radio loud. I sang at the top of my voice, rejoicing in the chance I had to talk to all the characters I'd met so far, pondering who I was yet to meet. Yet as soon as I thought about my temporary headquarters, and the characters who would meet me there, I felt sick. Literally sick.

The logical leap was not vast: whenever I was doing tour-related things I was joyous; everything else was making me miserable.

What I'm also clear about is I'm angry, mostly with myself, that the daytime soapie of me, The Swimmer and the Dancer have impacted on and complicated the tour; and this could have jeopardised it.

So now I resolve that if I'm to make it through the next 28 weeks of my 38-week tour, then I will have to be, whether I like it or not, ruthless in keeping myself as close to 100% in shape, physically and emotionally, as possible. LGBT people, their allies and their opponents around Australia care little for my own personal turmoil (except the ones following all the sordid details on Facebook). Instead they expect, quite rightly, that I only turn up on tour: share cuppas and collect their stories, do a book reading, speak to the media or deliver a workshop.

From now on it's just me and the tour.

Day 63

Sunday, 25th April – Perth WA

It's late afternoon beside a random lake The Dancer and I have found. He is picking at a pizza as I eat a fresh sandwich, determined to eat healthily and keep my weight down.

When it comes to eating The Dancer could not be fussier, and I watch him pick bits off the specifically ordered pizza that he can't eat until there is barely anything left. He starts carefully and purposefully feeding his picked-off pizza bits and crust to a progressively larger and larger gathering of hysterical ducks. I laugh, because as he does he talks to them as if they're kindergarten attendees.

'No, you've had some. Yes you, you've been patient. OK, who hasn't had any yet?'

On our first date we'd sat beside the Yarra River and talked for hours. I remember The Dancer talking in an American accent during a hilarious impression. Similarly one night he came over to tuck me in before a dancing gig. He'd read me some book on 'Wisdom', mocking the quotes and having me in stitches. Just like on those nights, I now laugh, captivated by him and realising I'm as crazily in love with him as I could be with such limited time together.

Just a few hours ago we were in bed together. I suddenly stopped and looked into his eyes.

'You know ... don't you?'

He nodded. He knew something had changed. He looked at me, no, he looked through me and observed I was overwhelmed. Perhaps as a parting gift, he let me know he understood.

'You feel like you're all alone and as if the world is on your shoulders. You feel like there is so much to do and there is no way you can possibly do it. Like everyone expects something from you and that you don't think you can give it. It will work out. Look at everything you've done. But it doesn't feel like it will.'

For him to understand is all I need. I myself understand, in this moment, why our three-week affair has turned my personal life upside down. Now that I feel yet again upended, it's time to face it all alone; not only alone on the road, but also now alone without a muse in the back of my mind keeping my grey matter warm, preoccupied and ever-colourful.

I drive The Dancer to the airport, and despite his promised intentions of seeing me after the tour, I know different. Despite him hating extended goodbyes I watch him walk down the windowless walkway that leads to the plane. I don't move as he walks around the corner, that final moment before you know you won't be able to see them again. Suddenly he walks back around the corner and sees me still there. He blows a kiss with a grin of delight and I fake getting knocked over. He laughs loudly and rolls his eyes.

Somehow as he once again disappears I know it's over. I don't want it to be.

Day 64

I'm lying on a squeaky double bed having just finished a Skype call with The Dancer. He'd wanted to check that I got to Geraldton OK. We're both surprised I even have internet access, given all I knew was that I was staying at a local backpacker's hostel. He likes the aqua wall and the painted, rustic furniture, which amounts to a wardrobe and a dresser.

I'm lucky enough to be staying here free for the week, and to have my own room and access to the owner's wireless internet.

I came to stay there because of my friend Pat. He doesn't remember our first meeting at a gay pub, nor does he want to. We met when he had consumed quite a bit of alcohol and had shown interest in getting to know me. Sensing that Pat was seeing me through 'beer goggles' and me wanting to be home in bed at a reasonable hour, I genuinely, yet possibly too shyly in hindsight, asked Pat for his number so I could call him in the coming days. Seeing this as a sign of rejection, Pat declined and said some things to let me know he was not happy.

Seven years later I would meet Pat again, for him like it was the first time. Pat looked white as a ghost when I recounted our meeting and what we talked about, including his name, regional WA past and my failed attempt to get his number. Not only did I remember this because I seem to recall such details vividly, I'd also been quite upset that my sincere attempt at a raincheck had been rebuffed. After all, I'd seen him modeling swimwear once and found him hot.

Pat apologised frantically, only imagining how he might have been so many years before and I apologised for not being clear in my interest at the time. Pat would go on to be someone who I would keep running into for the next few years, saying each time we should catch up rather than continually running into each other

So when I got to his hometown of Geraldton, he Facebooked me to ask if I had accommodation, offering that I should call his brother, the gentle, generous and patient Nate, who happens to run the local backpacker's. Nate could not have been more hospitable.

To get to Geraldton, or 'Gero' as the locals call it, you drive about 5 hours up the Brand Highway, or the 'Bland Highway' as most call it. I was lucky enough to have had morning tea with Ryan. Well-travelled between Perth and Karratha, to Geraldton's north, he gave me a printed A4 sheet outlining where he and his dad stopped for petrol and toilets, a freshly-baked batch of Anzac biscuits (marking the occasion of the Anzac Day public holiday) and a banana cake (an all-time favourite of mine) for my northward journey. For good measure he also gave me a huge container of vegetable soup for dinner the first few nights. He told me to keep the containers. Again: how this young man is single is beyond me.

For most that I spoke to, it seemed to be a wild concept that I was venturing north, perhaps even wilder than me going to Kalgoorlie.

'How ya getting' to Darwin from Perth then? You're what? Driving? Do you know how far that it? It's dangerous, why don't you just fly? You do know there are no gays in WA north of Perth, don't you?'

Day 65

Tuesday, 27ᵗʰ April – Geraldton WA

'There is always a component of homosexuality in my lectures. So therefore because I'm out other lecturers follow and ask me about what they can do in their lectures. For example I talk about what a massage student might do if they had a transgender person on the table. Would it change things for them?'

Annabelle, 'a gay lecturer' at a Geraldton TAFE campus, admits that this might be different outside of her areas of nursing, community services and beauty therapy.

'If LGBT young people went to apprenticeships and metals they'd not be out, I couldn't see anyone not being run out. But they're also sexist. There is a huge amount of issues with acceptance in those areas.'

Not that she only has students that accept her.

'I've had a couple of people pray for me in my class. I have one young woman who prays in my class every day for my soul. I say, *Keep it up love, I'll pray you'll become homosexual.'*

We're sitting having a cuppa in a common area at one of the campus' cafes. I find her energy, bluntness and laughter contagious. She takes a proactive approach in life to being open and out, as is evident in her interviewing of service providers for her and her partner.

'If I go to a GP and they ask, *Why are you here?* I reply, *I'm here to see if you're good enough to be my doctor.* I do the same for nutritionists and other service providers.'

Not that it's all good news for Annabelle, who cites a recent example of being discriminated against at the local hospital, so much so that she and her partner have now taken out private health insurance.

'You gotta live in a town. You've still gotta live here. It's a very discriminatory town in general. I don't know how a young gay couple would go trying to get a one bedroom flat.'

It's clear, in making her own seachange to Geraldton, that Anabelle brings her qualities and experiences as an older, experienced health professional with her. She made special note of how working in Sydney during the 1980s AIDS epidemic strengthened her resolve for life.

And as with every location I had visited, I found (and would continue to find) that whilst younger LGBT people tend to leave or disappear from their communities, older LGBT people were either moving to or moving back to regional, rural and remote communities. With them, they are bringing, as with Anabelle, their qualities and experiences that have been shaped, strengthened and incubated as only a metropolitan centre can allow, away from the pressure-cooker environment of a small community hypersensitive to difference.

'We're lucky because we have a publicly out lesbian policewoman who is pretty high profile and I wonder if that makes a difference. But there are not many men. I don't think gay women are as affected.

'There are certainly not as many young people as there used to be, but there's very few services for gay people out there. There is nowhere for them to go other than Perth.'

And it seems that there are many out and relatively visible community members, at least in her own circles, who are seen to contribute more broadly, and perhaps palatably. Annabelle gives a list of LGBT community members: local police, politicians, historians, museum and gallery curators, psychiatrists, wildlife carers and TAFE lecturers.

One anecdote goes that a lesbian couple who run the Post Office in Gero are frank about the consequences of homophobia from locals.

'Oh, you'd like to give us grief? How about you think about making that 4-hour drive to Perth to do your mail?'

Day 66

Wednesday, 28th April

'Most young lesbians come from broken homes with no fathers to pattern their lives ... so I let them know that men aren't all bad. That's what I think about 'em.'

That's what I thought the school chaplain was getting at, which is why I had asked him a question of clarification.

It was half chance that saw Rod, the school chaplain at this local high school, sitting in a meeting I had scheduled with Hayley, the head of student services. In what was a very impressive student welfare building, Hayley explains that Rod was 'a good bloke to talk to' for any one of 900 students. Rod explains his role further.

'A chaplain, as funded by the federal government, as I see it, is to bring a Christian influence into a government school. Keeping that in mind I don't have any problem with talking to kids about that. I'm certainly not going to condemn them. If I can help them, I will.'

Whilst Rod is clear that 'homosexuals and lesbians' are attending the school, he can only give one example of a young man coming to talk to him.

'He was going through a questioning time. But he was a young boy and his older brother was homosexual. Maybe there are more that way inclined and haven't said it. I don't ask any questions.'

Certainly by the end of my time here that was the point that came through: there were no questions being asked.

When I ask what would need to happen before the school supports sexual diversity and challenges homophobia, both Hayley and Rod opt for the 'let's wait and see' approach.

'Well for starters we'd need to see that there was a need for that. We have sexually abused kids, Muslim girls being abused, pregnant teens. The kids have to come to us if they need help. We need to see that there is a need, a sounding or a rumbling.'

At that point I pull out the latest in research evidence on same-sex-attracted young people's wellbeing that is now beyond debate. I imagine myself whacking him in the ear with them and asking him if that was rumbling enough. I don't.

I calmly sit and ask if they have seen the research evidence I held in my hands. Not surprisingly they haven't; although that is no indictment given that no-one on the non-East Coast reports having seen it. As in Esperance I run through the research basics and talk about the danger in 'waiting for disclosure'.

It would be safe to say that both Rod and Hayley's faces turn grey. Rod's especially.

'I don't think I've come across homophobia. I don't see people hammering homosexuals and making a big deal about it. The only thing I see, um, is *that's so gay*. It's just like a swear word.'

Hayley adds: 'They know it's not an appropriate word to use but know they are not going to get in trouble. As opposed to if they say *it's fucked*. I don't think it's homophobia.'

I take a deep breath as I leave, wondering if I have wasted my time. Hayley, unlike Rod, seems to be having doubts. They thank me for my visit, making a concession: 'They're probably not coming to us.'

Day 67

Thursday, 29th April – Geraldton WA

'I hear kids use all kinds of language. It's probably not helping but in the context of young people, it's the language they are using. At my old school everyone says *that's so gay*.'

Over a cuppa on Geraldton's picturesque waterfront, Adrian, former local school chaplain and predecessor to Rod, and now local government youth worker was unsure whether or not to see 'that's so gay' as an issue.

'Everything now is politically correct and it's hard to step outside of that. It's not just the homosexuals, it's everything.'

Between his burst of social commentary and sips of his cappuccino, Adrian explains his journey to Geraldton from his home country of Denmark. In a story that mirrors that of Tasmania's Princess Mary, and that momentarily captivated both the Danish and Geraldton press, Adrian met his now-wife, a Tasmanian, at a bar during the 2000 Sydney Olympics. Whilst Adrian and his wife became the subject of national television stories in Denmark, Geraldton ran a small story in the local newspaper. Adrian shows some minor annoyance that they failed to spell his name correctly. With every intention of returning to Denmark, Adrian was swayed by the school chaplaincy role in Geraldton. He now has three young daughters.

One of the reasons I use 'challenging homophobia' and not 'anti-homophobia' is because the latter can dramatically limit the opportunities I have for dialogue, challenge and change. Given that many fear they might be homophobic, yet remain hypersensitive and defensive about it, being 'anti' homophobia has the very real potential of ending a conversation before it even starts. This decision is highlighted when Adrian suggests there is no forum for him to develop his attitudes and practice.

'Everything comes back to understanding. Each and every person needs to know where they stand on the issue. The ability to talk freely without being judged. It's easy to be labelled as homophobic. It's all about an openness and a trust.'

One thing that seems to confuse Adrian is some gay people he knows use 'that's so gay'. What can be difficult to explain to teachers, health professionals and homophobia-curious others is that LGBT people can use homophobic language too. Yet it still doesn't make it OK. Often people will argue that if LGBT people use it, then it's fair game for everyone else too. It's not.

Despite his confusion, locally the bottom line for Adrian is clear.

'People have to realise that there is a need; that something needs to be done.'

I head to the local police station and meet Isabel. She's clear that something needs to be done. A number of key WA contacts had spoken highly of her doing great things for young LGBT people in Geraldton, and openly. Isabel has a diversity role with the police and came out very publicly in the local newspaper. Apart from talking in that article about supporting seniors, Indigenous and disabled locals, Isabel also came out as a lesbian.

'I'm lucky because I'm a police officer and I'm a parent whose kids have grown up here. I've got kids at high school. Being gay is a small part for me but maybe a big part for everyone else. My number one thing is being a parent.'

At the local TAFE Isabel regularly does guest lectures with the nursing and community services students, particularly around 'dealing with same-sex families'. Annabelle sings her praises.

Not that it's easy.

'Some know why I was going in and I'd have people with their arms crossed. The community is very judgmental; it's a big country town at the end of the day. Full of rednecks, homophobes and zealously religious people.'

Isabel is modest about anything that she has done.

'I've only supported a handful of young gay men, but they don't stay here. They all gravitate to Perth.'

Day 68

Friday, 30ᵗʰ April – Geraldton WA

The sun has set and I find myself seated next to a local media representative, Scott. We sit at a communal wooden table with 7 others as most move from finishing their dinner to drinking. I'm sticking to water after a week of attending the local gym.

It seems that my presence here has started lots of conversations.

On the first night I was invited down by Nate for some sunset beers with local friends. In between beers I headed to my room and returned to hear one of Nate's friends, Bill, talking about Bruce and the logo on the side, and in the backyard alongside all the other cars, mini-buses and campervans.

'That's so gay? Why does it have *beyond* written on it?'

I arrived back and we all looked at each other knowing that the pink elephant in the room was now under the spotlight. This was one of the moments many had feared would happen. A relatively run-of-the-mill heterosexual man in his 20s would spy my truck. Therefore I should consider where I park it.

Not so here in Gero. I take a deep breath, hoping Bill was not like the cheap stereotypes of men from fishing boats in my head and explained the basics of the project I was doing across the country. He and his other friend offered that it had happened at their school, admittedly many years before, then went on to ask questions about how things were and then the safe male territory of the tour logistics.

Later that week whilst eating a slowly-fried snapper fillet, care of Nate and these same friends – thanks for the cooking tip mum – I sat and talked with a temporary resident, Shelley, who has every intention of becoming a school teacher and said that seeing the truck parked everyday had her thinking a lot about homophobia. She said she imagined it would be tough in Geraldton. I even had a service station attendant politely interrogating me as I got a tank of diesel to leave Geraldton. She was genuinely interested and we only stopped when some other customers started clearing their throats wanting to pay for their own fuel.

At lunch yesterday I was in the communal kitchen cooking a meal when an attractive, athletic Korean guy joined me to cook his sausages. The smell drove me crazy, knowing I'd be having tuna. I sat quietly cursing myself when he suddenly offered me one. Goodbye tuna. We started talking and he said he'd heard I was doing some drive around Australia. He himself was the #4 800m runner in South Korea and was only on holiday due to an injury. Unfortunately he was leaving the next day: today.

Now Scott opens up more and more as he downs more and more beer. Maybe it's because I'm gay, maybe because I'm from out of town or maybe it's just because I'm there, but he is now confessing a run in with the law that possibly jeopardises his media posting.

'Man, I'm just gay, I'm not a lawyer. But here is how I'd play it.'

Day 69

Saturday, 1ˢᵗ May – Geraldton WA to Ashburton River WA = 836 km

As I set out from Geraldton for Broome I hit a milestone, 10,000 km driven so far on the tour, and almost hit two emus who decide they might try to cross the Great Northern Highway in front of me. The plan is that for almost four days I'll drive from sunrise to late afternoon, stopping before dusk: one of the most dangerous times to drive given the number of animals coming onto the road. Despite this caution I still see kangaroos, walllabies, cattle, oxen, a snake and even a wedgetail eagle.

As I drive through some of the most unfamiliar, unforgiving and relentless (and remote) of territory, I'm comforted by something that has grown familiar over the last three months on the road: the wave or gesture between passing drivers. Perhaps not coincidentally, I observe that as I get further away from any sign of civilisation, the number of people acknowledging my passing them on the road rises to almost 100%.

My first significant stop for the day is Carnarvon, where I have a late breakfast on a foreshore lined by wind-maimed palm trees. I call my mother to let her know I'm not dead if she doesn't hear from me for a few days; I'll most likely be out of mobile phone range. I call The Dancer who says he almost screamed his mother's ear off when he saw I was calling.

I head to the tourist stop toilet and wish I hadn't: the wall has 'GAY DOGS' scrawled on it.

At my second significant stop in Minilya, literally a petrol station and a telecommunications tower, I top up on fuel, as suggested by Andy on my A4 hints and tips sheet. Although he alerts me to the chance to have a Milo, a welcome change from just tea and instant coffee, I forego it and regret it about 10 minutes later as I drive further north.

My campsite for the night, Ashburton River, looks like a dried-out riverbed. It's my first real chance to experience the famed red dust of the outback. I sit on Bruce's tray, kick off my thongs and smile proudly at my dirty feet. In the absence of anything to cook on I have a dinner of pasta I'd made the night before, enjoying the company of cows with hides a deeper red than the dust they press their hooves into as they pass my truck. The green-winged birds are equally un-intimidated, meaning I can see their orange beaks picking at the crumbs in Bruce's tray and the few I throw around.

I celebrate a week since leaving Perth behind with a can of scotch and cola. I'm definitely in a calm spot after an emotional storm. It had hit in Perth with cyclone-esque force before leaving me to survey the damage, pick up the broken garden furniture and try to fathom where to start in the inevitable, lengthy clean-up.

The sun sets early and with nothing else to do I fall asleep at 7.00pm, hoping for a long sleep. A few hours later I get up for a toilet break behind a group of bushes and look up.

When I was a child my father, who I haven't spoken to in almost 15 years, used to point out stars and constellations whenever we camped in the bush. It was one of the reasons I was convinced until I was 12 that I would be an astronomer. At 12 my father told me there were no jobs in it and that I should instead become an airforce pilot, but that's another story.

As I look up I'm certain that I have never seen the sky so clear. I start to get dizzy looking up into the Milky Way. It's like a Magic Eye/3D picture: the longer I look at it, the more I see and the deeper I feel myself travelling. It all makes sense given the lack of light pollution and cloud.

I wish The Dancer was here with me to see it.

Day 70

Sunday, 2ⁿᵈ May – Ashburton River WA to Karratha WA = 276kms

Driving to Broome I get a sense of the dominance of mining in the north-
west of Australia, most obviously when I hit the Pilbara. Apart from its
tagline of, 'The Pilbara Region – It's ORESOME!' (which actually made me
laugh after too many days alone and driving), I discover that it accounts for
40% of Australia's exports. This is a point driven home by locals who feel
that despite their contribution to the Australian economy, they have been
forgotten by successive state and federal governments. This becomes even
more pointed because I drive through the weekend that Prime Minister Kevin
Rudd announces the new tax on mining companies' 'super profits'.

I roll into Karratha with about 10–20kms to spare in fuel – phew.

My own experiences of Port Hedland's little sister, Karratha, is limited
given the lack of affordable accommodation (I don't call a budget-style motel
at around $260-a-night affordable). Both towns are said to be severely lacking
in accommodation, and struggling to absorb the influx of people due to the
mining boom. Indeed I find that Karratha, the first of the two Pilbara sisters,
had just about everything you could want: except for shade.

I decided to move on. Somehow camping under the stars with large shady
trees in a dried up riverbed is much more appealing. Lucky for me there is a
campsite not far from town where all the truckers are said to stay. Bruce will
look just fine wedged between them.

Port Hedland is said to offer a more developed version of its little sister,
Karratha, yet little more shade (a new criterion for selecting potential stops on
my tour).

Anita, the award-winning teacher from Perth, had told me of her time in
Port Hedland whilst teaching at the secondary school a few years ago.

'Port Hedland has the reputation of beating the fuck out of gay boys and
putting them in ditches. Gay and lesbian students at the school would go out
with each other just for safety.'

Anita went on to talk about her experiences as a teacher at the school. She explained how for Christmas one year, she was paired in the equivalent of the Kris Kringle with the school chaplain.

'I received … a cactus in a little pot with a blue ribbon on it. A banana and two kiwi fruits. A cucumber with a red condom with a Father Christmas face on it. And a cheap shitty Christmas stocking. A progressive woman in the department took a photo of me, pasted the head on a picture of a skinny naked female, pulled the hair from her head and stuck it under her armpits and on her vagina and gave it to a senior school staff member.'

Day 71

Monday, 3rd May – Karratha WA to Nita Downs WA = 511kms

I've made quite good time today, thanks largely to the fact that I'm not stopping regularly to take photos. Post-Carnarvon I've been distracted by the red dust, something I haven't seen before. Driving at or above 100km/h isn't conducive to stopping suddenly when I see the perfect outback photo. Not that I haven't been trying.

I've heard it said before, and even seen it to some extent, that the landscape changes colour throughout the day, depending on the light. Early in the morning or late afternoon I find it impossible to drive 30 minutes without stopping for an impromptu photo session. I'm quite partial at the moment to a red dirt embankment with some shrubbery, which is handy because I can keep Bruce running and take it out the window.

The landscape feels relentless and unforgiving, yet there is beauty in that too. A friend has messaged to warn me that Chopper Read is up here at the moment, presumably capturing the landscapes on canvas. I tell them not to worry. For a year I lived around the corner from him in Collingwood (Melbourne) and sometimes saw him at the local milkbar.

I'm loving the heat, fully aware that this time of the year in Melbourne it's fast approaching wintry temperatures. I love that it's blue skies and days of 30C. My dream is to wear shorts and a t-shirt every day of my life.

I decide to drive a little further today, making tomorrow a shorter drive to Broome. Besides, I'd rather be driving and seeing this landscape in the late afternoon light.

I miscalculate a little and find myself pulling into a fuel stop with the sun fast going down. With the next camp area some 45 minutes away, I'll be breaking a tour rule and driving at night.

As I arrive at Sandfire Roadhouse and hop out to fill Bruce I notice a tourist with dreadlocks. I notice because he seems to notice me. As soon as he notices me he perches himself on one of the olive green picnic-style tables and lights a cigarette. There is no doubt he's watching me. Had I been in Melbourne I would be convinced he was cruising me.

After I pay for my tank of diesel I walk out and find him still there. I convince myself that I'm reading too much into his behaviour.

Nervous and out of practice, I decide not to use the picnic tables to sit and eat dinner and instead jump in Bruce to drive into the night to find my sleeping spot for the night. Around 2 or 3 kms later I realise how obvious he was. I kick myself. My friends will never forgive me for this missed opportunity and a great story. The feeling is exacerbated as I eat some cold minestrone soup.

Day 72

Tuesday, 4ᵗʰ May – Nita Downs WA to Broome WA = 321 kms

'Well there's white Broome and black Broome, not just Broome.'

Denise from GLCS WA had planted the seed in my head that I might find Broome to be a tale of two cities. Upon arrival I find myself in what must be white Broome.

I'm surrounded by enough Scandinavian-looking backpackers at this internet cafe to make me question whether I'm in Broome or at the Australian Open.

Theroetically Broome is part of a 'travel week'. When mapping this trip out I built in 'travel weeks' when the distance I had to travel between destinations was too great for two solid days of driving. If I couldn't spend a week at a said destination because of vast distances, I included a travel week. Given that 4000kms separated Geraldton and Darwin, I decided to give myself two weeks to get there.

Within a few hours of arriving in Broome I can understand how so many see it as an oasis in the desert, because it is like a mini-tropical paradise. Given its reputation as a popular tourist destination, I flirt with having some time off before quickly giving the idea away. I've never been good at sitting comfortably with free time. I quickly decide I'll make the most of a few days in Broome by talking with some locals. The way I see it, any interviews here will be a bonus.

Not long after leaving the internet café I get a phone call as I arrive at the backpacker's. It's Andy from Perth. He arrived back from a run to Karratha with his dad to find his place had been ransacked. Give the guy a break, sheesh. Paradise interrupted.

Day 73

Wednesday, 5th May – Broome WA

'Life in Broome for LGBT young people is a tough road. It can be, for many, not a very supportive place.'

At the local branch of *headspace*, the manager, 'Ariel', has lived most of her life here and has supported young LGBT people who have ultimately taken their life.

Part of the issue might be the very thing that attracts people, including LGBT holidaymakers, to Broome.

'It's a seasonal place that changes dramatically. It's a very transient town. In the wet season, no-one's in town. But it's very different in the dry season. Lots of people come to get away from the grey, as well as lots of foreigners, backpackers. You see visitors being gay, but not local young people.'

Broome swells from 15,000 inhabitants to around 40,000 during peak season. Whilst Broome benefits from the mining and tourism dollars, it could be causing local divisions.

'Broome is becoming more divided – local, not; white, Indigenous; affluent, not. There are a lot of Indigenous people who are struggling with housing, domestic violence, etc.'

It becomes apparent that if you move to Broome (or holiday here), are white, and have the money to participate, then it can be a very easy place to be LGBT.

Ariel describes some LGBT training she undertook years before whilst she worked with a housing service. GLCS WA had been involved. Five years on, Ariel recalls the outcomes of 'Opening Closets', and the reaction from other local services.

'For us it was never a drama. We put up a poster saying all young people are welcome, young people saw it and knew about it. But other services said it might be fine for you to do this, but we just don't have any gay young people that come here.'

That's not good enough for a member of *headspace*'s local youth advisory committee, Lily, who wants it talked about.

'There are similarities to the stigma around mental health. It's like some crazy person over there. So people say, *let's not talk about it.* I want to know what's OK, what's going to offend, what's not going to offend and how to educate young people so it's normalised.'

The feedback I tend to get is that my cuppas often provide the first professional, and too often personal, conversation that people have had around LGBT people. That so many are not doing something because they are scared they might 'offend' is both a frustration and an opportunity for progress.

'One cuppa at a time Daniel. One cuppa at a time,' I say to myself.

Day 74

Thursday, 6ᵗʰ May – Broome WA

'We would deal with those students on a needs basis. We haven't had anything surface. If we did, we'd deal with it.'

There are times when I feel my life is like Groundhog Day. Did I not just hear that from the school chaplain in Geraldton? Wait, should I be concerned that the above quote was from his equivalent in Broome, Joan?

I contacted the local secondary school and spoke with the Manager of Student Support Services. Noting that her team would be meeting the next day, she said she would e-mail her team to see if I could join in on that meeting and get back to me. When she did call back it was to say that I would only be able to have 5 minutes of their meeting time, asking if this was enough despite the fact that earlier we had spoken about a minimum time of 15–20 minutes. Instead she said she would meet with me personally after that meeting.

I arrive at the reception area where the school chaplain greets me. She immediately gives her manager's apologies. I realise straight away that this is less about something 'coming up suddenly' for the manager. I had been thrown the equivalent of student support service scraps.

Joan is pleasant and seems to search my face for any sign that I'm not impressed. I'm not sure how successful I am at hiding my momentary annoyance, but I am soon following her to her office to talk about school life for LGBT students.

Offered a seat on a colorfully adorned couch I sit amongst some Indian-inspired cushions and wait for a quick brush off. Indeed that is how it seems to start. I offer an introduction of my project – after doing this at least several times a day for the last three months I feel like I am almost on autopilot.

'It's not really an issue here. We did have an Aboriginal boy who used to sit by himself and used to sit with the girls sometimes. Oh wait, there is one boy at the moment that we have been asked to keep an eye on. He might be gay. That's very rare. It hasn't come up yet, but as soon as there is a hint of it, then Student Services would be very supportive.'

Again waiting for disclosure. Before I get to talk about research evidence or my own work in schools, Joan has watered down any thought of doing something proactive.

'But I can see that an education thing before that is not needed. To suddenly go into classes and talk about it … No. If something is not delivered properly kids could think, you know, there is something to try, if it was not done properly, if it was glorified. I know in our sex ed we tried something different once, but sometimes the wrong teacher can do a lot of harm. Because of their idea of what's OK. Especially when we are talking about Year 7s and 8s.'

Joan goes on to say that she imagines older students, such as Year 10s, might be 'more mature and able to handle it'.

'They are too messed up in Year 9, I think it would be really damaging. They are too experimental in Year 9. There are all the ramifications if you have boys experimenting with boys. I think it's important for kids to not feel free to do what they want before they have their heads together. They seem to act before they think.'

The damage and harm Joan fears is that young men will have sex together. The only way I could pilot my challenging homophobia program in an all-boys Catholic school in 1999 was to reassure everyone that it was 'not 6 weeks of anal sex education'. There have been no reports of any same-sex sexual intercourse as a result of the *Pride & Prejudice* program.

I finish by asking Joan questions and share with her the latest research evidence, including the perils of waiting for disclosure, some of the basics of my book and give a few examples of other schools I've worked with that are similar to hers.

I'm convinced that this is a waste of my time, and consider switching on my challenging homophobia auto-pilot of sorts, waiting for the 'thanks for coming; we don't want any, goodbye'.

Yet Joan's sudden enthusiasm for a school *Beyond 'That's So Gay'* shakes me violently from my pessimistic haze.

'The Beyond 'That's So Gay' message is something all the teachers could be open to. I can take that idea of challenging homophobic language to the next Student Support Services meeting. I'm confident they'll be supportive and it might even be something we do with all our teachers here.'

Despite being a little in disbelief, I leave with a smile on my face.

Day 75

Friday, 7th May – Broome WA

Steven moved here years ago with his family from southern, regional Western Australia. In his life Steven has mostly straight friends, something I get a glimpse of tonight at the local watering hole. It's the main destination in Broome on a Friday evening. I walk in and find it's more like an open-air arena lined with palm trees.

Tonight is the final in a swimsuit competition for a lowbrow men's magazine, so the stage is the main focal point. Up for grabs is a covershoot and spot in the national final. Uncomfortable with the whole concept given my recent years working in male family violence prevention, I'm not sure if I should be more disturbed that I'm here in the first place, or that I manage to predict Miss Congeniality, the People's Choice and the Top 3 place getters, in order.

I'm quickly accepted by all of Steven's straight, mostly female, friends, who like my T-shirt. In a slightly disconcerting moment, most of his friends tell Steven that they've seen me around town this week, including at the local gym. I was there each day, only to find myself as the only man in most group fitness classes. Apparently there are only two conclusions that fellow female class goers could draw: 1. He's gay; or, 2. New meat has arrived in town. I think my experiment to see how long my beard could grow between Perth and Darwin has confused some on which of the two conclusions to go with.

When they hear what I'm doing, Steven's friends start sharing their stories. The most entertaining comes from a local Catholic primary school teacher. Annie gives an example of one of her pupils who she adores. Jarred is said to always be dressing up for school costume days as The Little Mermaid or other Disney female characters. And it seems that it's not only just at school. Annie tells of a recent confession.

'Miss Annie. Tonight when I go home, I'm going to sneak into my mum's bedroom. I'm going to open up the jewellery box where her pearl necklace is and just *stare* at it.'

Jarred's mother, a fellow teacher at the school, doesn't believe Annie's account of this sneaking around and coveting, and dismisses it.

Even in the town's main bar, where Steven says the men come 'to get laid, or get into a fight because they can't get laid', he appears at ease and at home amongst his straight friends. He tells a story about the only time he felt unsafe there.

'I was with this guy I was dating, but you wouldn't have known that we were necessarily together. These two guys had obviously picked up on the fact that I was gay and started getting in my space, and talking about me so I could hear it. So I thought, *fuck that shit*, and walked over to the biggest friend I had. I pointed to them and he looked at them, pointed and went like this [Steven runs a finger across his throat]. He then walks to two of his big friends and points at these two guys who then do the same thing. They got out of my face and out of there.'

There are many other LGBT people I have interviewed who might have reacted differently.

After leaving the local watering hole I meet Steven's 'black sister', a charmingly down-to-earth Aboriginal woman called Selma. Steven and Selma have been very close friends since high school, and this fact means that her 10 brothers are protective.

'They'll always come up when we're out and ask if I'm OK. They're notorious, so believe me, I feel safe when I'm out.'

Day 76

Saturday, 8th May – Broome WA

Steven and I are sitting watching the sunset on the largely deserted beach at Broome's Gantheaume Point.

'It's just as beautiful as Cable Beach but without the tourists.'

Me: 'Or the camels!'

We laugh. I'd soaked up the famed Cable Beach sunset twice already. I took some local advice and perched myself on a stool, one of seemingly hundreds on a descending, manicured lawn to the beach. I sat for 60 seconds before heading down to the beach itself.

Sitting on a large piece of sandstone is the closest I can get to feeling that I am all alone on the tourist beach. I love the way the sky changes colour dozens of time. I'm obsessed with fruit cake at the moment and gobble too many pieces of it as I watch the ocean gobbled up by the sun. Perth and the turmoil couldn't be further away.

Steven and I get talking about Karratha and Port Hedland, and I recount my passing through, bemoaning the lack of shade.

'Well all the trees would have been ripped out by cyclones. Anything with shade cloth would be super dangerous to put up along the coast.'

Now, as the beach clears itself of some young local families Steven admits to me that he has 'not dealt well with the whole being gay thing …'

As the eldest of three children, Steven said family pressure meant he took longer to come out than most would suspect. But when he did come out to his entire extended family, he didn't hold back.

'It was at an aunty's 40th and I walked in with this hot boy who was 5 years younger than me and everyone just knew!'

Steven has made one close, long-term gay friend, Percy, a well-known gay man who he met through another friend, an older woman with a reputation for wearing lots of diamonds and having many gay friends. Percy actually helped Steven come out. They were all out to dinner with a visiting gay couple who wanted to know if Steven was gay. Percy didn't let Steven answer.

'Look Steven, you hang out with Broome's biggest fag and Broome's biggest fag-hag, you're gay and that's that.' He didn't argue.

109

The sun has completely dropped and more and more stars begin twinkling by the minute. Steven seems saddened by his lack of local connection.

'It's not even about finding people on the same page. It's about finding people in the same book.'

Day 77

Sunday, 9ᵗʰ May – Broome WA

'Bloody hell. What's that?'

Andrew, a local working in hospitality, stares off to the horizon, recalling a story from some two decades earlier. He momentarily closes his dark eyes and he's transported elsewhere: to the quiet, dusty main street of Broken Hill.

The moment Andrew goes to in his mind was anything but quiet. He slowly opens his eyes again, to recount one of Broken Hill's most defining moments in recent history. Certainly for Andrew it's one of the most defining moments of his life.

As he speaks, I can almost picture the very scene Andrew is describing. It isn't because I've been to Broken Hill. I haven't. I'm planning to drive there, but first I have 9000 kilometres ahead of me. I know my parents have been to Broken Hill for an anniversary one year, but that still isn't it.

'Mate, I remember everything. Mum and I were in the car. I was about 11. We were in Broken Hill, on the main street and she looked over and said, 'Bloody hell. What's that?"

'That' was a trio of three men dressed as women: Hugo Weaving, Terrence Stamp and Guy Pearce. Andrew saw the exact moment the actors got off a bus called *Priscilla, Queen of the Desert*, for the iconic scene in the movie of the same name. It's said that director Stephan Elliot wanted authentic reactions from locals to the three drag queens walking down the main street, and thus no-one in Broken Hill was forewarned.

It just so happened that on Argent Street, Broken Hill, a wide-eyed country boy, not yet assured of his gayness, was seated with his shocked mother in the parked family car that very afternoon. Andrew is convinced the director got the authentic reactions he craved.

Some time after Guy Pearce's character, Felicia, muttered 'C'mon girls. Let's go shopping', Andrew sat transfixed by more colour and movement than the remote mining town had seen for a long time; if at all.

I can't quite believe what I'm hearing, especially given I almost *didn't* hear it.

Andrew had just finished telling me about his move here. He moved from Broken Hill to Broome as soon as he could despite not having ever been there. A family friend would tell a young Andrew about Broome and thereafter he always knew where he wanted to be.

We sat drinking ice-cold milkshakes overlooking Cable Beach. I could look down and see where I was swimming about 45 minutes ago. I'm not a beach person yet it was actually warm in the water and I enjoyed myself.

Andrew insisted that he pay for my milkshake, amazed that I am self-funding this 38-week drive. I stopped protesting such offers after Perth. He returned from paying and stopped himself.

'I should tell you about. Aw, nah. Doesn't matter I guess.'

Me: 'No Andrew, tell me.'

'Well I guess you might find it interesting.'

And how!

Day 78

Monday, 10th May – Broome WA

The last thing I expect to do in Broome is to visit 'the Broome holiday estate' of one of Australia's few billionaires. Yet here I am slowly driving Bruce along Broome's most exclusive street.

As instructed I drive to the gate and am surprised at how casually I'm buzzed in. Concerned at first by how narrow the winding driveway is, I keep 'heading right' through a recreated rainforest, tended by several seemingly uninterested groundskeepers, until I find a modest cottage.

Before I know it I'm drinking tea and eating too many shortbreads that 'Percy' has purposefully fetched for my visit this morning. Looking much younger than his 64 years, Percy describes himself as 'totally gay … no half measures. I know you get that these days.' I laugh.

'It's just worked for me immeasurably ... Maybe because I'm not a threatening issue. Being gay is nothing but a plus. And also they all think I'm helpless so they just do everything for me.'

Talking with Percy I feel a sense of calm. His attitude is reassuring. I savor the shortbread.

While fishing for contacts in Perth, I had been told about a 'gay butler' for one of Australia's richest men who owned a holiday estate in Broome. I had laughed and said, 'Yeah right, I'm just going to walk up and knock on the door of all the estates up here and say I'm looking for a gay butler! ...'

But on mentioning this to Steven he had turned to me with a curious look. 'Oh, I wonder if that's Percy ... But he's not the butler at all ... Hang on, I'll call him ... That's so funny ...'

Rather than being a butler, Percy says he is referred to as 'the Ambassador', acting as a medium between the owners, the staff on the property, the neighbours and 'relevant' locals. For his trouble Percy gets to stay on the property and receives a generous allowance.

When The Billionaire purchased a property in Broome and required someone to be a set of eyes and ears on the ground, Percy was the first choice; partly because of a selfless deed to help The Billionaire's son and partly because of his top people skills. Percy is a bit laid back about all this, remarking,

'What you give out, you get back, that's the only reason I am here.'

Being 'totally gay' hasn't bothered the many people that Percy comes into contact with, now or throughout his long, distinguished career.

'I have never had a negative, anti-gay issue. Being gay has worked for me by a mile. None of the tradesmen or groundskeepers shake my hand. They always just say thanks and give me a hug.'

When I asked Percy to describe Broome, he gives some insight into why it might not be a place where anything formal and LGBT could happen.

'There are a lot of people in the tropics who are running away from something, wanting to hide or wanting to drop out. It's often a new start somewhere. It's hard to get any kind of group started in Broome, even the Country Women's Association and Rotary folded. It's a town that doesn't necessarily want to have normal groups. It's even hard to get people for the State Emergency Services. I do know a lot of gay people in Broome. There are more gay people than you think. A lot of them are here because they don't want to be a part of a group in Perth, Melbourne or Sydney.'

I drive out through the automated gate and note the manicured lawn that Percy says is regularly replaced, delivered to the site in refrigerated trucks to keep it lush.

Day 79

Tuesday, 11th May – Broome WA to Mary Pool Campsite WA = just under 600kms

Leaving super-early from what I now know to be the bed bug-infested backpackers in Broome, I drop my room key into a locked box designed for such early departures. It isn't until I get to Bruce and try to open the door with my room key that I realise I've dropped my car keys in instead.

With a heavy, sick feeling – and my ankles itching from bedbug bites – I slowly walk back to the plagued establishment and sit on the steps. 8am. It will be at least another hour before reception opens; if the rather relaxed staff even followed opening hours. However ten minutes later, as luck has it, the owner arrives and listens to my dilemma patiently before nonchalantly opening the key box. All he offers is a grumpy, *'Happens all the time.'*

As do the bed bugs it seems.

During my drive east to Fitzroy Crossing I'm struck once again, as I had been at the beginning of the Nullabor Plain, with the feeling that I'm experiencing my retirement years early. This drive was meant only for miners or those with too much time on their hands, a thought punctuated by the periodic whoosh of a two-wheeled Grey Nomad or caravan-pulling 4WD, accompanied by the customary one-finger salute.

After over 13,000kms of driving, the bridges over dried-up riverbeds have all begun to blur. Not so the extended bridge over the Fitzroy River. Local legend has it that once upon a time, during the height of the wet season floods, people would abandon the former low-lying bridge and take to a daring 200m-long flying fox to get to the other side.

I easily cross a river that has brought so many to a standstill, park Bruce and walk along the pedestrian-friendly footbridge that hugs the road. I say 'pedestrian-friendly', however when one has vertigo, seeing the dry riverbed far beneath your feet and feeling the structure shake as roadtrains speed unforgivingly across, it doesn't feel all that friendly.

Day 80

What I didn't count on are the distractions. The biggest casualty of this tour, apart from my bank balance and love life, has been my travel journal. As I originally mapped out my draft travel itinerary, sightseeing (I thought) would be a secondary concern.

Last night was the perfect example. Between Fitzroy Crossing and my final resting place, Mary Pool Campsite – only 180kms away – I got distracted by the distinct shift in the landscape, and even the cloud patterns. As the sun sleepily descended behind me, its light danced across the multi-coloured desert dust, across the scrub-covered rockfaces and the wildly broken up cloud. I lost count of the number of times I had to stop Bruce, get out and take photos, partially as a way for me to process the beauty flooding past me. Somehow I felt being able to look back objectively – through photos or journal – would sort out if I was having a particularly emotion-charged moment or not.

What that means is I've been breaking one of my driving rules: not to drive at dusk or after dark for fear of wildlife on the roads.

When I rolled into Mary Pool Campsite, I did so in utter darkness. I found a spot amongst the caravans and tents, surprised by the amount of people who seem to be there, and got out only once to quickly brush my teeth. I did so by mobile phone light – and with some anxiety after reading ahead to discover this campsite had been known for the odd wandering freshwater crocodile.

As I drive out of the campsite, intending to enjoy breakfast while in transit, away from the retirees who are already up, seated in foldout chairs and enjoying their first cuppa, I'm taken aback by the Mary Pool's early morning beauty. The 'pool' that these freshwater crocs live in is something else.

It proves to be a perfect setting for breakfast, albeit a quick one given the 460kms lying between me and Wyndham via Halls Creek, or Hell's Crack as some locals call it ... I enjoy a guilty bowl of muesli while staring across the gently lapping silver water.

My arrival in Halls Creek brings significant relief given that it marks the point where I had well and truly passed safely by Wolf Creek, of the infamous movie.

Meant as a mere pit stop for powdering my nose and grabbing fuel, I delay my departure thanks to two things. First, the Information Centre has, much to my disbelief, wireless internet that's cheap and remarkably decent in strength given our remote location. This and mobile phone coverage means I can let people know I'm alive – my mother takes some convincing without daily contact – and respond to pressing e-mails. Second, a street sweeper stops me, obviously eager to strike up a conversation. By now I'm used to this kind of interaction, typical of men in country Australia who are bored and in need of human interaction, however fleeting. After answering the standard questions of where I come from and where I'm going, the man highlights the importance of Halls Creek being the starting point for one of the toughest drives in the world, the Canning Stock Route. As I look up into this tall Indigenous man's eyes, he explains that Halls Creek and this once treacherous drive were the original reasons for steam engines and the Landrover coming to Australia.

Halls Creek falls away behind me. The Canning Stock Route lies in the opposite direction from the road to Wyndham. I put my foot down and arrive as the sun goes down.

Day 81

Thursday, 13th May – Wyndham WA to Camp (100kms from Katherine), via Kununurra, NT = 519kms

Stopping in Wyndham, the oldest town in the Kimberley in Western Australia's north-east, is the perfect opportunity, and frankly the only one, to see a friend I had made in my final year of high school. Shirley has spent all her years since university teaching in remote communities, both in Australia and Papua New Guinea, and subsequently has many tales to tell.

Wyndham, with its 800 or so inhabitants, is one of the larger communities Shirley has found herself in over the years. Working at the local Catholic Primary School, she was a welcome addition to the teaching staff, specialising in a program called 'Reading Recovery'. Far from feeling limited or isolated by the relative remoteness, Shirley finds that the pace, amount of people and proximity to others, suits her just fine.

I meet Shirley outside her home, on the edge of the Catholic Primary School grounds, and take her lead to not give her any welcome embrace or kiss (which is like second nature to me). Once inside her house she sighs loudly and tells me that there had been a lot of talk amongst her fellow teachers and the school principal about my visit. She had excitedly announced during a staff meeting that she had a friend coming to visit. This was of only passing interest until it was discovered that I was a male. Agreeing to follow the Catholic ethos as an employee of the school, Shirley was not meant to be having a male, non-marital partner staying under the same roof as her.

I laugh at her comment, meant to allay the fears of her colleagues and boss. She is not sure it worked.

'Oh don't worry about that, he's gay ...'

Her enthusiasm in discussing my reason for traveling the country also did not foster much excitement. Yet for all that I find myself staying on the school grounds themselves, which could be one small step for LGBT progress in Wyndham.

Wyndham has two distinct parts: the first, situated along a main road with a giant crocodile as its highlight; the second is the most important port in the Kimberley region. There is a lookout over this port area that is called Five Rivers, where I go to watch the sunset at the point where five rivers intersect.

Perhaps Wyndham has suffered because of its pretty, younger sister, Kununurra, which lies close to Western Australia's border with the Northern Territory. Shirley drives once a week to Kununurra, about 100km west of Wyndham, to go to a major supermarket chain that does not charge like a wounded bull. One highlight is that attached to one of the petrol stations in Kununurra is a major bakery chain where some creature comforts from the big smoke can be tasted. After a night at Shirley's I conduct my weekly radio interview with 'Freshly Doug' (JOY94.9FM). I do this on her landline because my mobile phone service provider does not work between Broome and Katherine. As it is, the landline service fades in and out rhythmically so that I hear only half of every question asked, but luckily my replies seemed to make sense.

Day 82

I'm fortunate that my ex-boyfriend, The Circus Performer (*aka.* Shaun) has recently moved to Darwin. A talented circus performer and trainer, Shaun is now the lead circus trainer with a local youth arts organisation.

As I half tumble out of Bruce, Shaun looks at me and says, 'Awww … You look exhausted. You need a nap!'

Given the energy-sapping humidity of suburban Darwin, I go beyond a nap and basically pass out early afternoon on top of some sheets to the quiet whirring of the overhead fan.

Perhaps sensing me stirring, I find Shaun hovering as I wake. An unknown amount of time has passed. Crossing from Western Australia to the Northern Territory had also meant losing 90 minutes from my day. Somehow channeling my mother from childhood days when I was unwell, Shaun sits on the bed, smiles lovingly and talks in a quiet, gentle manner. Shaun quickly works out that I'm hungry. And knowing that my protests that he really shouldn't get me something to eat are bullshit he soon returns from the bakery around the corner. Not only has he bought me a meat pie, he's also thought to get me my favourite drink: strawberry-flavoured milk.

As my eyes light up, Shaun laughs, 'How many times do I have to tell you? I know you better than you know yourself Daniel Edward Witthaus … A nap, something to eat and your strawberry milk and you're as happy as a pig in shit …'

Day 83

Despite being in a cocoon of sorts in Darwin, there are some unexpected challenges. During my week in Australia's northern-most capital I feel the impact of homophobia a little too close to home for my liking.

Shaun was so new to Darwin that yesterday I helped him move to his new place of residence. It's with some excitement that Shaun arrives, only to find that having me as a guest sours the situation: despite my staying being OK'd

117

by the household-to-be in the weeks before; despite us not being together. The thought that we once were is too much for one of Shaun's new housemates. Taking Shaun aside, The Housemate explains that he was abused as a child and that me being in the house makes him feel unsafe. This only after we've completed moving Shaun. At this stage The Housemate has not even met me.

Regardless of what I want to do, I stay out of the picture whilst Shaun discusses it with The Housemate. After all, Shaun is presumably staying here for some time.

When I finally meet The Housemate, he's had a revelation. He explains that I'm 'allowed to stay' if I pay for the privilege, setting a figure that he feels is 'reasonable'. This floors the other housemates who now have to pay extra rent every time they have a guest to stay. I'm floored that money can somehow change something that apparently affects him so deeply.

It's been sometime since I was accused of being, or likened to, a pedophile. The first time was when I worked supporting gay and lesbian young people for the City of Greater Geelong. In the mid-1990s my colleagues and I were effectively called pedophiles because of our work on the front page of Geelong's then-broadsheet, the *Geelong Advertiser*, which went ahead with accusations and threats from a disgruntled parent.

Now it's happening again, and under the roof of my former boyfriend. For Shaun's sake I keep the peace and go for a *very* long and vigorous workout at a local gym.

Fortunately by the time I arrive back Shaun has organised to move back with the housemate he was only supposed to be staying with temporarily in Fanny Bay. He concluded that this isn't the kind of household he can live in, regardless of the many benefits the new abode seemingly offered; amongst them a large garden to work in and a short trip to his workplace.

Later, Shaun reflects, as a young gay man (raised by a lesbian woman on a farm outside Adelaide who came out at high school) that this is the first time that he's experienced homophobia from others. Helped perhaps by the fact that he has spent much time in circus and other performing circles, he laughs that the only time he's experienced homophobia is because of me on my challenging homophobia tour.

Day 84

Sunday, 16th May – Darwin NT

Shaun and I are at Darwin's Mindil Beach Market, the most popular event up north during the dry season. Known for its second-to-none sunsets, the beach attracts many tourists and locals who sample a wide variety of international cuisines before settling on the pristine beach to watch the sun slowly disappear.

Seated ourselves, we do something I love to do: people watching. As I sip delightedly on my mango lassi, Shaun notes a tall young man walk by.

'Look, we are not the only gays in the village!'

I nod not thinking more of it. Moments later said young man approaches me and asks if I am Daniel Witthaus.

'Yes.'

I laugh, as did Shaun, who believes this kind of thing is always happening to me. Patrick, not the only other gay in the market village, confesses he recognises me from my tour video blogs.

'Someone other than my mother is watching them?!'

A German PhD student, Patrick is investigating programs for young men focusing on masculinity. It seems a little pre-destined that I run into him during his 3-month visit to Australia.

Before arriving, Patrick had been to a queer bingo night with a former lover of mine in his hometown of Berlin. My former lover recommended he talk to me on his travels. Now a Facebook friend, I note with curiosity that Patrick had even spent time in my hometown of Geelong.

'Daniel, how did you get started with your LGBT education work? And why this tour? Wow!'

I tell him that this tour is a logical, albeit a daring and bold, progression of my challenging homophobia journey. And in one sense it can appear amazing. In 1999 before I took my first step into a Year 9 all-boys Catholic school classroom I would have hyperventilated at the thought of driving around the country. Now of course it's different. But if people go 'wow' and that's all then I've failed. I want to make challenging homophobia seem less scary and more possible. Driving around the country is a logistical nightmare. Sharing cuppas with locals, is something very doable and different.

Day 85

Monday, 17th May – Darwin NT

As time goes by I notice the more comfortable the stay, the more surprisingly emotional I become at the thought of having to move on again. I know that leaving Darwin, and Shaun's emotional oasis (and catching up with old friends), is going to be the toughest moment on the tour yet. I reflect that I'm experiencing moving from place to place similarly to how I'd experienced backpacking through Europe in 2001.

In 2001 I arrived in Paris and experienced a mini panic attack. My first time overseas, I now had a few months to do as I wished and soak in the best that Western Europe had to offer. As I stood at Gare Du Nord train station watching the foreign hustle and bustle outside, I found it very difficult to catch my breath. I asked myself how my family could let me do something so crazy, and why I could not be safely at home with all the things I knew.

After sitting and catching my breath, I decided to put one foot in front of the other. I needed to find my accommodation (incidentally the Peace and Love Hostel) and then I would worry about food. Within a week I felt remarkably at home in Paris amongst it's famously arrogant people and laughed when thinking about how distressed I'd been for a few moments right at the start.

Yet at the end of a week I was due to leave for my next destination: Amsterdam. Once again I felt a sickness in my stomach at having to again work out a foreign city.

In some ways despite traveling for business and pleasure to almost 100 cities in almost 30 countries, this feeling has stayed with me. In Darwin I'm conscious for the first time that I have, albeit in a very subtle way, been experiencing the same feeling each time I move from tour location to tour location.

Day 86

Tuesday, 18th May – Darwin NT

'I had a pretty hard time at high school and faced a bit of discrimination. Some of it for being Indigenous, some of it for being gay, some of it for being overweight. My first day of high school, I came back from recess and someone had taped a sign to my desk which said something like *something smells, poof, poof*. I didn't even know what that meant, only that it was bad.'

It would continue this way for Edward until his final year. Five long years later he arrived for the first day of Year 12 to find something in his communal file.

'One of the boys had left something in there, a note with something like *we're going to get you poofta*. I then realised he must have left it in November for me to get it in February. So that was pretty calculated.'

This had an undoubted impact on his academic performance and school life.

'Most of the time I used to wag a lot. But I passed. The common theme through all of it was that I didn't know what those terms meant, only that they were bad. You become very secretive. I didn't really talk to anyone about anything. We all have the benefit of hindsight. It's not that I wasn't sure, but I wasn't out so to speak in terms of being able to stand up for myself, to the school, to other students.'

Edward's Presentation Ball was not a great end to his school career.

'That was difficult for me to have a date with someone that was female. I remember that all the girls had a photo together and then all the boys had that photo all together and they asked me not to be a part of it. Yep, school was pretty shit for me.'

Not that Edward didn't eventually thrive.

'Once I left school it was very much better. I didn't have the daily pressure. I s'pose it wasn't part of my life anymore and I had good people around me. I have a very strong internal dialogue. Coming out to myself and making sure that was the right thing for me was important. Most people decided for me before I really knew what that meant. I like to make up my own mind. I think maybe when I talk to other people, they know about themselves sooner and are perhaps able to challenge the system [and others] more.'

David, however, knew early who he was.

'I've always known I wasn't what the TV was showing me. I knew for certain, I was maybe 10 or 11 when I had my first erection. I was sitting in front of the TV watching weightlifters and something happened. I started to enjoy it a fair bit.'

David had a very different experience to other gay students in school.

'I guess I was lucky. I was the bully who picked on bullies. It was very hard to be gay at high school. If there was an effeminate boy at school, then I'd be friends with them. Nothing happened with them though. If I got picked on, I fought back, I belittled them.'

There are plenty of stories where he turned the tables.

'I walked on the oval one day and this boy walked over and started pushing me, saying, *So you're gay? What, you find me hot?* I just started humiliating him. I said, *Oh, please, my grandmother would hit harder than you.* And by the end of it, his group and my group were laughing at him, so he walked off humiliated. Then at boarding school this Year 11 boy kept saying, *You're gay, you faggot.* So one day I picked up the vacuum cleaner and chased after him. He ran off.'

Given that David's story was so different to most others that I had heard on this tour, I delve deeper, trying to understand why his experience is so wildly different.

'I felt like I was defending gay people, not just defending myself, that's where I got my power to fight back. I was always alone, I was always pushed aside. It was nothing I was taught. I was always told to be quiet, that I don't have a choice. Maybe that was it, maybe that's why. It was rebellion.'

Before my eyes David reflects for the first time on the link to his self-worth at the time.

'I guess deep down inside as much as I thought I was rubbish and I had nothing to offer the world, I knew I wasn't a bad person. I knew I was not wrong. I was told all gay people were pedophiles but I knew I wasn't attracted to children and I didn't want to hurt anyone, so I thought *Fuck you*, I'm not any of those people. I always thought of myself as an unimportant person. I stuck up for gay people, nerds, anyone. When I think about it now, I had no respect for my own life so I would stick up for everyone else. Now you've made me think about it.'

Both David and Edward have different stories of friends betraying their trust after they revealed their sexual identity.

David told of another gay student.

'He was the one that went out and told everyone I was gay, to take the attention off himself and put the focus onto me.'

Rather than getting upset, David sympathised.

'I thought, *How lonely must you feel inside to do that.*'

Edward was outed to other students after he told a female friend at school. Only recently this young woman approached him, relatively drunk at a Darwin nightclub.

'She said, *Edward, I've been in counselling since high school because of the mean things I did to people. And most of that was about what I did to you.*'

Stunned, Edward feels it gave him a sense of closure. He hadn't expected she would have really thought about it much once school was done. Edward on the other hand finished school differently.

'I stepped off the school ground and did the biggest exhale of my life and never looked back.'

Day 87

Wednesday, 19ᵗʰ May – Darwin NT

'I have all of your stuff, I went home and read it in one night because it was so relevant to our 13-year-old son. Some of the other kids found out about our family [two mums] and started giving him a hard time.'

It's refreshing that someone has read *Beyond 'That's So Gay'* before my arrival, rather than after my departure.

'I have to thank you for your book because we've been using it in our dealings with a right-wing teacher at our son's Christian school ... He was the typical example of a teacher saying we don't have any gay students at this school. I asked him, *Well what do they look like?*'

She takes her right hand and places it on her heart. As she closes her eyes she quietens her voice ever so slightly, 'Can I just say, thank you so much for writing about that Catholic school? It has helped so much with that teacher when he says *we can't, we are a Christian school.* He took the book and has since told us, *I can really work with this, this will work.*'

*

A local bookshop offers to host a book reading event at their store. Ever-excited at not having to organise something myself, my excitement disappears when I discover only two people have turned up: the manager of the bookstore and an NTAHC worker I've driven here.

Those two people decide that I should conduct the book reading as if there's a room full of people. Despite my bruised ego, I have a surprisingly fun hour. It allows for more in-depth discussion than the usual cursory question and answer session towards the end.

Day 88

Thursday, 20ᵗʰ May – Darwin NT

Rita, a student counsellor, is enjoying showing me around her secondary school in Darwin's north-east. I realise this visit is a win; every time I mention the visit I'm told by locals that the school is as rough as guts.

Once in the staffroom, Rita apologises that she can't immediately find a cup for my customary 'cuppa' and wondered if the one on the sink was OK. I laugh.

'I've been in too many staffrooms over the years and I understand that you can lose an arm for using the wrong cup, it's fine.'

As I contemplate taking my first sip I'm introduced to the head of Physical Education, who shakes my hand and apologises for being unable to stay for the meeting. He immediately tries to run away, yet has to stop when I ask what he'd want to know if he did attend. His response is immediate.

'What to do. Strategies about what to say when the kids say *that's so gay.*'

Out of the corner of my eye I see a gathering of teachers, mostly male, watching my every move. As he walks away over his shoulder I notice in the centre of the staffroom noticeboard a recent poster from the Parents and Friends of Lesbians and Gays (PFLAG), titled 'So Gay, So Yesterday'. Underneath is written 'Do you want to know how to respond to this and other homophobia? Come to the meeting room [date, time]'.

Rita explains that she'd gone to the IDAHO seminar thinking that challenging homophobia might be something the school could do more of.

'I left convinced it has to be a core part of what we do. It's essential.'

All the interested teachers are here now, during their recess break. I ask what they want to hear about most. This includes: new ideas for strategies to challenge homophobia; things that work; and, to get updated on what is 'politically correct'.

Part way through the meeting Rita gets up to collect something from the staffroom. She comes back fuming.

'I got in there and there were a group of guys [teachers] standing around looking sheepish. I asked them, *Why are you all being so coy and not joining the meeting?*. And you know what they said? It would be rude to walk in now. They are grown men Daniel!'

Day 89

Friday, 21ˢᵗ May – Darwin NT

Larissa and Jamie have very different coming out stories. Larissa got her first inkling through sport.

'I always knew I was different. I was heavily involved in rugby. It took me removing myself from rugby to realise that that was an aspect of myself. That I was gay. I didn't really understand until I got into that rugby environment, surrounded by a lot of openly gay people. I was very confused when I left. I was quite young and I wanted to make sure that I was not being swept up in the environment, the majority on that team. I wanted to go away and make sure that was how I felt, so I had to remove myself.'

For Larissa's partner Jamie it was different.

'[My story] is really boring. I just got fucking drunk. I had a boyfriend for 4 years. I dumped him because he was a dick. I got drunk one night, hooked up with this girl and she never left me alone. But I thought, *How much better is this!?*'

Meeting each other happened through work. Larissa was from out of town, in Jamie's town, and didn't know where she was going to stay.

Larissa: 'We met over skewers.'

Both: 'Crocodile kebabs.'

Larissa: 'She said, *We're going out for drinks, do you wanna come?*'

Jamie: 'She says she doesn't remember, I got up early the next morning.'

Larissa: I was not even awake. So I rang later. Because I didn't want you to feel cheap.'

Jamie: 'Then we met for breakfast a few days later.'

Me: 'So what drew you both to live in Darwin?'

Larissa: 'It's too expensive to visit. I find it frustrating that you can't swim anywhere.'

Jamie: 'You've met some fucking nutbag lesbians.'

Larissa: 'Psychos.'

Jamie: 'But we've met some of the nicest people. You usually find most people up here are running, from whatever's happened in their life. It's very laid back, it's not a race. Don't let anyone tell you Darwin is flat. It isn't. I ride a bike.'

Day 90

Saturday, 22nd May – Darwin NT

Noting that Perth and Darwin's gay nightspot(s) are tending towards a 'mixed' environment of gay and straight patrons, I ask some locals if this progressive combination is a model that works. Gay men are unanimous.

'If it's a model then it doesn't work. For the gays, there are no real opportunities to express themselves.'

On a typically warm, humid Darwin evening I join Shaun for a few drinks at the gay bar that doesn't believe in ambiguity: 'Throb'. Throb could have been any similar gay establishment in country Australia, save perhaps for the topless drink waiters and the pole that a teacher from the IDAHO seminar, earlier in the week, takes to with a flair and enthusiasm that suggests he's been here before. A young topless waiter called 'Josh' – all swimmer's shoulders and dreamy blue eyes – flirts with me outrageously, ultimately disappointed that I'm not going to get terribly drunk and tip him outrageously.

Shaun is not a fan of mixed gay/straight nightclubs. 'A bunch of insecure straight men make a point of hugging and kissing their girlfriends so that everyone knows they're not a poof. And a whole lot of straight women come to gawk and say, *ahhhh how cute.*'

Leaving relatively early after the drag show formalities are done, I ask Shaun with some concern about how it would be for the average gay man to leave the bar and walk out onto the busiest street in Darwin at night.

'Well, recently,' he said, 'on my way into the city I had a bottle thrown at my head from a moving car accompanied by *FAGGOT* ... Luckily my ninja-like reflexes or their crappy aim ensured my safety.'

Day 91

Sunday, 23rd May – Darwin NT

By the end of my week in Darwin I feel lean and energised thanks to sleep, warm hospitality – personally and professionally – and a consistent exercise regime.

I don't realise how familiar a face I've become at the gym until today. After a twelfth group fitness class for the week – my fourth of this specific class – the female instructor sheepishly approaches me. She'd spotted me as a new face earlier in the week, and soon found out I'd been taking classes around the country. To her credit, she smells an opportunity.

'Can I ask you a favour? You seem like you really know what you are doing. I'd like your feedback on how I'm doing as an instructor. How do I compare with the other instructors you've had?'

For the record she didn't compare favourably, so I give her what many of us call a shit sandwich: some good feedback, really honest feedback that is harder to stomach, followed quickly by some more good feedback.

We talk about my travel for work and the challenge of maintaining a fitness routine. Post-Perth I admit that I've become over-zealous with working out. With so much out of my control, working out has become a coping strategy to channel all of my anxiety and also an outlet, and one that I prefer to that of feeling fat and listless. The instructor and I both conclude that I'm coming close to over doing it, yet in the whole scheme of things, there are many worse things I could be doing.

Perhaps the talk helps convince me to not only consume a roast lamb sandwich at Mindil Beach Markets in the evening, but also wash it down with not one but *two* mango lassis. After all, I'm about to drive into the desert for some weeks.

But first, I need a good clippering. After a month of leaving my hair and beard I'm impressed with how bushy and disheveled I look. Part of me has enjoyed my weeks of 'Grrr': not shaving, hardly showering (I certainly had to get used to my own smell in Bruce's cabin), eating on my lap. It amuses me no end how much I've enjoyed these traditionally macho, blokey things, although really, it matched the isolation I felt (in a good way).

Yet with all this humid heat my hair and beard are now driving me crazy. Shaun delights in taking a pair of clippers to me; when we were together we'd often cut each other's hair. I always loved the look of anxious concentration whenever he did, and now is no different.

Day 92

Monday, 24th May – Darwin NT

During my first week here in the Northern Territory, NTAHC have acted as warm, enthusiastic hosts to me, much the same as Uniting Care West in Perth. One of the workers from the Aboriginal and Torres Strait Islander Team, Daniel, makes sure I have a desk during my stay and periodically, without prompting, brings me a cup of tea to my exact liking. With every subsequent cup of tea I become more and more emotional. 'Why are you getting so emotional?' I ask myself.

Not only do I get a desk, a cuppa and an everyday workplace atmosphere – to my delight Daniel blasts music that only includes black divas – but I get invitations to brunch as well.

On my final day an NTAHC worker invites me to his home, a recently built brick veneer with a distinct 70s feel, where his mother lays out a Greek feast for brunch. Chris' mother, who married into a Greek family and took on the role of Greek matriarch with great gusto, offers a feast of fried fish, salads, breads and roast chicken. I'm careful not to spill anything on the white laced tablecloth. Any delight that I express, and there's a great deal, is quickly dismissed. 'This is nothing, Daniel, just something quick …' Nothing, not even the dolmades were bought. Everything is hand-made and cooked from scratch.

Darwin's hospitality knows no bounds. Its people have quickly grown on me.

Before I leave NTAHC Darwin for the last time, I get the energy to complete the lengthy drive from Daniel, who reminds me of one of my reasons for driving around the country.

'Daniel you are brave to do what you are doing. I love it that you are going to all of these places where people say, *Don't go*. You just say, *Fuck it*. I love it.'

As I go to respond he pre-empts me.

Whack! I gasp at his sudden, back-handed slap on my arm.

'Just shut up and take the compliment.'

Day 93

Tuesday, 25th May – Darwin NT to Attack Creek NT (via Katherine NT) = 940kms

'Well you know that [high profile footballer] is gay, don't you?'

And the feeding frenzy begins. I sit and listen as everyone explodes with stories and gossip about aforementioned high-profile-footballer. For the record, I didn't know he was gay.

It's the last thing I expect when I arrive at a local high school in Katherine to chat with a school nurse, a local educator from a non-government organisation and a football program worker. Coincidentally today, former Australian Football League player and media commentator, Jason Ackermanis, has everyone talking about whether or not gay AFL players should come out. Emotively, he encourages gay AFL players to remain in the closet, offering that, in his opinion, most players would be uncomfortable to have a gay teammate in the locker room.

The way the educator Vicky, puts it, she thinks *everyone* knows of the high-profile footballer's sexual identity.

'Well *I've* been around to my good friend's house when he was with [another less well-known footballer] and let's just say they were *definitely* a couple then.'

At this stage, Adam, who heads up a program to keep budding Indigenous footballers in education, expresses as much surprise as me, but for different reasons.

'Him? Really? But he's six foot four. He's an absolute monster!'

129

It was everything I could do to wait until I could Google the less well-known footballer's name and image. The gossip comes at the end of an interview about what they thought life is like for non-heterosexual students.

With a 50% Indigenous and 50% non-Indigenous student population, they have conflicting ideas at first about what the school environment is really like. Like other schools in regional and rural Australia, there's an example of an 'out' student.

'He was gay before he was born. He just goes around telling everyone. He is pretty out there.'

This point was gently challenged by Sue, a school nurse.

'He actually gets bullied. Certainly things get on top of him.'

According to Adam, there might even be a degree of acceptance, perhaps because of this out Indigenous student, who does not care much for football but is happy to come along every so often to the football program.

'Amongst the Indigenous guys there is an acceptance of being gay and bisexual.'

That this might be due to an acceptance of this particular out Indigenous student rather than sexual diversity in general is something Adam suggests.

'Our footy boys won't wear number 8. There's this guy from a rival basketball team who's gay. He wears number 8 and none of our guys will wear it. If they did, there'd be a lot of teasing.'

It seems in this environment, young gay Indigenous footballers will get teased for doing something as small as bending over to pick up a pen on the ground.

Like every other school, 'that's so gay' is common language and staff are uncertain of whether they should or shouldn't challenge it.

'Gay is the flavour of the day. It's become a derogatory term. I feel uncomfortable with it.'

Adam walks me out part way, mentioning earlier that he had come from my hometown of Geelong. When I ask which school he had been to, he replies, 'Norlane High'. We laugh at the uncanny coincidence. 'Me too,' I say. I graduated almost a decade before him. Adam observes that if someone had come out as gay at Norlane High then 'you'd be dead.'

Perhaps then it's good news when my mum sms'd only a day later to inform me that Norlane High is going to be closed down next year.

Day 94

Wednesday, 26th May – Attack Creek NT to Alice Springs NT (via Tennant Creek NT) = 603kms

Getting to Alice Springs from Darwin requires one night sleeping in the outback, 1500kms and a handful of Devil's Marbles.

To get to Alice Springs I wake at 5.00am for the 4-hour drive on the Sturt Highway to Katherine for my 9.00am meeting at Katherine High. Whilst I delight in the sunrise, I dread having to dodge wedge-tailed eagles devouring road kill. I hear they don't move quickly for oncoming traffic.

I use the stop in Katherine to grab fuel and ice. The Katherine Visitor Information Centre, which looks like a restored homestead, provides the setting for an early lunch ahead of many hours driving. My only company on its shaded, airy terrace is an elderly couple who munch quietly on their pre-prepared sandwiches. They offer a polite smile and silent nod, possibly the lunch-spot equivalent of the finger-wave between drivers on isolated stretches of road. I return the gesture, feeling grumbly that they probably had time to do what I didn't: visit Katherine Gorge. It was bad enough that I wasn't able to see Kakadu, and that I'll probably miss Uluru.

I grumble to myself, complete my blog, then drive for hours towards Australia's Red Centre.

Leaving Darwin has been surprisingly emotional for me, not only for leaving Shaun's knowing, nurturing hospitality. Darwin has been a kind of milestone; reaching there meant I'd completed the most gruelling section of my tour. Not that I was over any LGBT hump after 13 of 39 weeks, more that I now have a fair indication of whether or not my ambitious plans were realistic.

If I continue to be hosted, personally as I was by Shaun and professionally as I was by NTAHC, then it is all very doable. But what might Alice Springs bring? And after that, Mt Isa then Townsville?

I contemplate such things as I drive hypnotic distances down the Sturt Highway where the skies seem to be clearer and bluer than any I can recall.

My overnight resting place is Attack Creek, an oddly shaped patch of gravel beside the road about an hour and a half before Tennant Creek. Being so close to the road is theoretically conducive to us weary drivers feeling safe, however sleeping easy is a challenge with thunderous road-trains careering by at speeds faster than nighttime driving should allow. My meal before bed is an average appetising cold pasta I'd cooked at Shaun's the night before. It's moments like this that make me regret, not for the first time, being self-funded and not investing in a portable stove.

Day 95

Thursday, 27th May – Alice Springs NT

While you could spend a week in Alice Springs alone, understanding the town itself requires knowing it's merely a capital, if not a white Australian one, for Central Australia, all its remote communities and the workers who service them. As far as challenging homophobia goes, remote communities are second only to mining towns on the 'Daniel Don't Go There' danger list.

That remote communities can defy city expectations of their levels of acceptance and understanding is something that Daniel in Darwin talked about. Working across the Northern Territory in sexual health, Daniel had some calming news for all the remote hysteria that can whip up.

'I think people have this skewed view of what it means to be in a community. Living in a community is like living in a large city, it's just on a smaller scale. Each community is different. Some are 'dry', some aren't. Some are really proactive, some are in that welfare state. It depends on that community and the LGBT people, if they are visible.'

Local counsellor, Phil, adds to this and gives an insight into the potential impact.

'My understanding is that the behaviour is accepted but the identity is not. So they go to the cities. They can be more anonymous, but then they can lose their sense of connection without their family.'

Some communities have also been influenced by Catholic missionaries. Examples of such communities are around Alice Springs and on some of the Torres Strait Islands. Coincidence or not, Darwin Daniel mentions challenges in these areas around Alice Springs.

'Anecdotally it's not so good around Alice. To the point where kids are so worried about coming out that they start harming or take it to the full conclusion and take their own life.'

Day 96

Friday, 28th May – Alice Springs, NT

My base for the week is NTAHC's very own Alice Springs base, a welcoming house in the heart of Central Australia's capital. Its coordinator, another Northern Territory Daniel, will play host to me for my week in Alice Springs. Well-connected and tireless, Daniel has made time to assist my professional and personal adjustment to Central Australia. Offering a desk, plenty of cuppas and a comfortable stay in his guest bedroom, Daniel ensures I have contact with any number of folk of interest.

Phil is a perfect example of many I meet in 'Alice'.

'I came to Alice Springs for two years, and I've been here 17.'

Phil's varied experiences in Alice Springs have included being the school counsellor at the local independent, religious school and one of *headspace's* counsellors.

Indeed when I contact *headspace* I'm told that rather than talking to them, I should talk to Phil. I'm surprised, my request for a cuppa is dismissed over the phone, given the welcome responses of other *headspace* locations.

'I haven't clinically come across those young people and haven't come across those issues. Neither of the girls [i.e. other *headspace* staff] have either. There is nothing I'd be able to give you. Talk to Phil. I'm sorry I couldn't be more of a help.'

I feel like saying, 'It's not me you should be apologising to, it's the local young people.'

Phil, an independent political candidate, is clear that challenging homophobia is 'about educating the educators … them getting more comfortable …' One of Phil's slogans is: It doesn't cost a cent to change the way you think. To get to Adelaide from Alice Springs you need to drive between a gap in these ranges. Known as 'the gap', one of Phil's well-known slogans is 'Phil The Gap', which amuses or annoys depending on who you talk to (although those annoyed will say it's only because they have heard it so many times).

Sharing his own history of interrupting homophobia with students as an out school counsellor, Phil's style focuses on a mixture of correcting language and personal rapport.

Student: 'That's so gay.'

Phil: 'What? That's so wonderful and fabulous?'
Student: 'No Phil, that's so gay.'
Phil: 'Yes, I understand. It's wonderful and fabulous.'
Student: 'No, we mean it's shit.'
Phil: 'Well if it's shit, say, *that's* so *shit*, it's not gay.'

Day 97

Saturday, 29ᵗʰ May – Alice Springs, NT

A Sydney-sider who chooses to call Alice Springs home, Chloe, compares the local LGBT 'scene'.

'I think it is a lot more conservative here in terms of the queer scene. I've been around queer people who are also activists, been on the edge of normal. There are a lot less people doing alternative relationships. Like there are a lot of longer term monogamous couples. There is definitely less gender diversity and probably a lot more women who identify as lesbian. There's not that much of an organised queer community.'

What exists are 'Girls Drinks' and 'Boys Drinks'. I managed to get to 'Boys Drinks', which consisted of no-one who could be described as anywhere near a 'boy'. Around 10 men gathered for a Friday evening drink and some conversation.

At these drinks Daniel spoke with a German man, 'Patrick', who had received an exciting letter from Germany. As a teenager, Patrick had a secret relationship with another young man from his school. Patrick still even had a photo of the two of them sunbaking from the time. Fifty years on, he had been contacted about a 50-year school anniversary. After some investigative work, Patrick made contact with his former teenage lover, 'dropping hints' in his letter that he was gay. His former lover would reply, 'dropping hints' in his own letter that he was gay. Now, Patrick is preparing to head to Germany.

Far less entertaining and romantic was my own conversation with a local man from the media. He spoke of how frustratingly resistant the Alice Springs community was to change.

Everyone I speak to tells me about 'the 6 month', or thereabouts, rule. This rule states that you must leave Alice Springs every 6 months in order to maintain your sanity. Chloe is a believer in this rule too.

'You have to go to the city often enough to get out of that small town network.'

After 'Girl's Drinks', a number of women debated about the name. Having heard about the wave of feminists and activist women who had fallen in love with Alice Springs in 1983 and stayed, I find it quite odd that a women's gathering would include the word 'girl'. Chloe describes the debate.

'We had a big debate over what it was called, how it was a bit exclusive and what it might be called instead. Some people were saying it doesn't matter what it's called, and it was the younger people there that were saying it does matter.'

Chloe and her peers feel the absence of a LGBT specific space in Alice Springs.

'We don't have a space in town that is a queer space. We spend a lot of time together informally doing other things like drinking and going out bush. I'd like to see a space created. Even if it was only occasional. I think maybe because it's so small, like when we called about putting on a night, it's likely to be all the people you are sitting around in your backyard with anyway.'

I get the sense that maybe this isn't what Alice Springs wanted.

'The pace in town is a lot slower and people do sit on verandahs and have cuppas and go camping. They are less likely to have the kind of busy lifestyle that you have in Sydney or Melbourne. And in the city there are all sections of the community that are focused on being queer and I think it's just about the number of people and that people have other things as their priorities.'

Day 98

Sunday, 30th May – Alice Springs, NT

Journal entry:

'But really, people's generosity has surprised me. Basically that's my lesson this year: accepting generosity, goodwill and assistance. At times it's been tough, but I'll get there.'

Staying with Alice Springs-based Daniel, his fun-loving housemate Rhonda and her sleepy golden retriever Lily, I feel like it's a home away from home. Home is a spacious 4-bedroom house not far from the city centre. I get to watch the French Open (tennis) on pay-TV and even get to enjoy the

Eurovision Final, complete with left-overs I'd cooked the night before for the household and some champagne I'd bought for the occasion.

Luckily for me, Daniel finds time to show me around locally. His love for Central Australia is obvious whilst watching a sunset on Alice Springs' Anzac Memorial Hill. I'm not exaggerating when I recommend to do this at least once in your life, and preferably with a local. Prone to hugging the odd tree, you can literally feel Daniel breathe in his surroundings and become nourished as a result. Observing the nuances in the sunset-filled sky, Daniel can distinguish the colour of the horizon based on the time of year. More than any place I have been to on this tour, people's relationship to (and love of) their place is evident.

The bonding of Daniel and I is complete after a drive to Standley Chasm. Leaving Alice Springs we drive alongside the dry Todd River and through Phil's beloved 'Gap'. Despite the bone-dry riverbed that is the Todd, Daniel assures me that Central Australia has been experiencing greater rainfall than it's used to. He explains that the green and shrubbery I see springing up from the red dust isn't a common occurrence.

Once at Standley Chasm, Daniel and I make our way to the enormous sandstone rift that dwarfs all that wander through it, littered with an occasional tree defying the dry, rocky odds. As we begin our ascent up a seldom-used walking track, I'm moved by two intermingled trees: one black, one white. Both have grown towards one another, the white tree spearing through the branches of the black. I pause not only to take in the trees themselves, but to remind myself of how rare it is for me to savour the detail of my surrounds.

A little drunk on having a day off to explore geography and not observe its inhabitants, I feel lighter and have a good-humoured time with Daniel. Our jokes about being like mountain goats quickly cease when Daniel comes perilously close, twice, to walking through a human-sized spider web; or at least a 'Daniel-sized' spider web, given he isn't the tallest of men. One has a large spider that I'm certain a person without arachnophobia would describe as elegant and beautiful. Not us.

The frightful shock and his hysterical, irrational reaction are familiar; had I almost walked into it, I would have responded in a similar fashion. The rest of the walk involves recounting formative horror stories involving spiders. It's safe to say that we don't fully appreciate the view of the surrounds once we reach the summit.

Day 99

Merryn originally contacted me early during the tour and offered to spread the word throughout her organisation, NTAHC, about how they might support my time in the Northern Territory. I'm indebted to her.

I'm sitting barefoot with Merryn, a young queer health professional on a patch of sunkissed green grass wondering aloud over my herbal tea if Alice Springs has a similar appeal to Broome – a popular holiday destination that attracts people who are 'escaping' or 'hiding'. Merryn offers an alternative view.

'I think people come to Alice Springs for other reasons. I guess this place attracts people with a missionary sense. They don't like to admit that a lot of the time.'

And this missionary zeal seems to be most directed from white Australians toward Indigenous communities. Yet not everyone ends up staying, often when they realise that being someone's Saviour is not what they're cut out for.

Merryn herself has surely had one of the most interesting journeys to Alice Springs. Whilst at university, she was part of The Global Solidarity Collective. When the 'Children Overboard' incident occurred, the group decided to do something about asylum seekers.

A trip to Woomera Detention Centre cemented an idea.

'The government was putting refugees away where no-one could see them. We got back and decided to make it into a bigger project.'

That project involved collecting people's stories and raising awareness.

'We decided to confront the untruths that were in the media. There was a documentary made, media and public forums. We had a 52-seater coach that someone donated to us that couldn't go faster than 80kms/h. We all had to get our truck licences.'

As a group of predominantly gay and lesbian people traveling to regional, rural and remote areas of Australia, being non-heterosexual was not what was most challenging to people.

'That was amazing. We were having more trouble for being [in communities] about asylum seekers than we were about being queer. The worst confrontation was in Port Hedland. I was quite nervous about that. We had a run in with a couple of bikies who were upset cos we had our bus painted with stuff about refugees.'

Merryn wonders if the lack of homophobia came from the focus of their tour.

'We went into a lot of church groups and a lot of schools and a lot of conservative places in each town and I found people didn't have a problem with us at all. I don't know if that's because the issue of asylum seekers was a lot more divisive at the time than queer stuff, or what.'

Yet the pace was punishing.

'We did the whole thing in about 8 weeks. We averaged 1000km a day.'

Clocking almost 100 days on the tour during my time in Alice Springs, I reflected on the comparison to my 150km average per day to this point.

For Merryn this pace, and a lack of results, was a challenge.

'Towards the end of that I was feeling really burnt out and really frustrated that change was not happening quickly enough.'

Day 100

Tuesday, 1ˢᵗ June – Alice Springs NT to Apertula/Finke NT and back = ~ 1000km roundtrip

Journal entry:

'I'm quite excited to be heading out to a remote community. They say, or Jim anyways, that as you move away from Alice Springs the communities get more traditional. There is one community he spoke of that had only had their first white contact something like 20 years ago. Of course he spoke about bureaucracy, corruption and so on and then he would head into an invite re going to a relatively remote community …'

From all accounts there is an obscene, and in some cases, sickening amount of money flying around Alice Springs and the surrounding communities. 'Obscene' and 'sickening' are terms I use because every local has a story or seven about mismanagement of money, embezzlement and corruption.

Sick is how I feel hearing them and not just because I was hearing some of them in the back of a 4WD driving on dirt roads to a remote community. Jim, a good friend of Alice Spring's Daniel, has kindly offered to take me for a drive out to one of the communities he works in. For Jim, an older gay man relishing the country around here, the invitation was simple and straightforward.

'If people don't go then how are they supposed to know what it's really like?'

My excitement to see a remote community firsthand is partially fuelled by a missed opportunity soon after my arrival in Darwin. When news of the IDAHO seminar spread through Arnhem Land, east of Darwin, NTAHC staff received requests for me to travel to Nhulunbuy, a remote community on the Gove Peninsula. Not having the time to drive almost two days along dirt roads or the significant amount of money to fly there, I had to decline the request. Yet it's food for thought for anyone thinking there are not challenging homophobia opportunities in remote Indigenous communities.

Although excited to see a remote community firsthand, I'm less excited at first by the drive down dirt roads that I would feel unsafe on at 60km/h. Especially given that I'm in the backseat. Throughout my childhood I suffered fairly severe motion sickness that magically disappeared once I learnt to take the wheel of a car or similar vehicle.

Now I'm traveling along these roads at 120km/h, and somehow I feel calm, knowing that Jim has been driving these roads for years and years. The one concern I have is from the stories I hear from both Daniel and him about wheels flying off at 100km/h and axles breaking. Now driving down these roads at this speed I can see how brutal they are on any vehicle. Bruce wouldn't make it.

The roads we drive on are in quite good condition, if what I am told is correct. Add that it's not wet season and I'm having a fairly quiet Sunday afternoon drive compared to what it could be. A real fact of life is that sometimes you just can't drive some places for weeks because roads become flooded overnight. Occasionally Jim will assess his chances and drive through, telling tales of water rushing over his rather high truck bonnet.

It's these kinds of conditions that Darwin Daniel says makes supporting people in remote communities most challenging.

'It's the distance. Up here in the wet season, forget it. In the dry, not a problem. If you want to do something in the wet, you have to charter a flight, unless it's well serviced because there is a mine there.'

Now that I have traveled through most of the most floodable parts of Australia (touch wood), I am thankful for my original plans. Not aware of how much the wet season in northern Australia could have disrupted my plans in a major way, I mostly planned to be in northern parts during 'colder months' and down south before and after said cold months. Driving through countless dry riverbeds across northern Australia signed as a 'floodway' and hearing the stories, I feel rather lucky.

Back on the road to remoteness, it's possible I'm distracted from a potential driving fatality by Jim's stories. For me, he is as comfortable a man in his own skin as anyone I have met for a long time. Jim has an easy, natural and un-self-conscious way of telling a good yarn. One minute it'll be about the mistletoe on the trees we are speeding by or the local budgies, the next it'll be about his encounters with creepy crawlies.

Loving his life on the land, Jim has a country getaway. He can laugh when telling of the bite he received from a white-tail spider out there: 'I wouldn't want to go through that again.' Apparently no limbs dropped off.

'Nah, I just waited two days for the swelling to go down.'

Patience in the bush when help is far, far away may be a virtue. Jim tells of a large, dangerous brown snake in his bedroom.

'I got to the bed and saw his tail going from the pillow under the sheets. I closed the door, got [the dog] and put her inside. But the bugger went up the doorframe. I tried everything to get it out, but the bastard wouldn't come out. So I closed the door and didn't go in there for the next few days. But I do have other bedrooms, it's a big place out there [laughs].'

Having driven for 17,000kms now myself, I'm particularly interested in Jim's relationship with the land as he drove across it. What's obvious is his deep affection for it, as well as his ability to notice subtle differences along the way at over 100km/h. Time and again he tells of how particular parts are now flush with wildflowers or there is a great photo opportunity around a certain bend.

Upon arrival in Finke (of the Desert Race fame), or Apertula as the locals prefer, Daniel and myself take a wander around. I'm conscious that I'm not here by invitation, only a tag along, so I merely play observer for the day.

Daniel and I grab a pie from the only store, microwaved and, it turns out when eaten, frozen in the middle. Taking bites around the frozen centre at the football oval, I have a moment of emotional reflection.

On this very day I've hit 100 days on the road. I hadn't expected to get to such a remote community (despite wanting to) and hadn't been able to fathom what Day 100 of my tour would be like (despite wanting it to happen). Perhaps to some it might seem strange, but reaching the 100ᵗʰ day really takes me by surprise. Time hasn't flown, by any means, yet the launch of my book and tour seem like only yesterday.

I quietly tell Daniel about the milestone as we walk around the dry, dusty football field half-expecting that he'll understand what it means to me. Of course he doesn't (and can't), and so my visions of sharing a delirious 'can you believe it really has come this far' moment of skipping and laughing across the dirt-covered football field is instead an almost silent meander.

As I walk it all builds and I shed a joyful, disbelieving and somewhat lonely tear to myself.

Walking around the small community doesn't take long, given that 'walking around the block' as a child in Geelong would have taken longer. Built around an old train station on the Old Ghan Railway Track, Apertula still has some interesting offerings.

Daniel was concerned how I might react to coming to a remote community. I'm grateful for the concern, yet also amused given my travel for work and pleasure through any number of developing countries. Be it the putrescent smells of Egypt or Sri Lanka, the dog population in Thailand or remote villages of Indonesia, I'd seen enough to prepare me for remote Australia. Yet as Jim points out, 'We are living in a developed country in 2010. Things should not be like this.'

'This' is a few short streets of rundown houses that do a remarkable impression of an abandoned town: cars and machinery left to rust in the unforgiving weather; the absence of windows; buildings that haven't had love in far too long.

Change is happening, especially where there is not a fast turnover of good people. It seems white people coming and going is expected. And when they do, invariably it's in white government 4WDs. In Darwin Shaun told of how one of his fellow workers arrived to run an Indigenous community program with his new personal vehicle: incidentally a white 4WD.

'All the kids got upset with him and said, *Noooo Mr [worker]. Not you. We want you to stay, not to go!*

Government initiatives are called 'snow storms' in Darwin. It's said that every now and then all these white people, interestingly for locals in white utes, blow in and then quickly go again.

Some encourage turnover. Daniel tells of some Indigenous locals calling white people 'white goods'.

'Ya get em in there, run em into the ground and then ya get a new one ...'

But some great people are staying. And they're loving it.

On the drive there, Jim told of how in this remote community, the locals have welcomed the introduction of letterboxes. Previously, each resident had their mail delivered to a large set of pigeonholes. Privacy was an issue, with locals opening their neighbour's mail to check on their bank balances and the like, then dropping the mail on the floor or quickly stuffing it back into the wrong pigeonhole.

Now with their own letterboxes, Jim smiles when he sees them decorated with dot paintings or their football team's colours.

Day 101

Wednesday, 2ⁿᵈ June – Alice Springs NT

Whilst there is a relatively strong LGBT adult community in Alice Springs that's fairly active in public life, the same can't be said for LGBT young people.

A number of people observe that most of the adult LGBT community isn't from Alice Springs. Chloe speaks for many in talking about the situation for young LGBT people growing up in town.

'I think if you grew up here, it would be a different place to come out in just because everyone sees you, knows your business and talks about it all the time.'

This is the verdict when I speak with staff from a senior high school in Alice Springs. Brigette, a student welfare coordinator, describes the general school climate.

'As a community, a school community, we are probably similar to the broader community here in that we are at an early stage. I'd say it's much easier for young women, but the real issue would be male homosexuality.'

Jodie, a school nurse, thinks males would also fare worse.

'It's a tough town for that.'

Both give one example of a female student couple at the school, who are 'openly gay'. Brigette admits that one of the female students is a very strong and popular personality, and that this is important in their acceptance.

'In the school it was OK. But they were copping a hard time out of school a bit. But they've now dropped out of school. It was very complex in the end.'

One young man had been outed in recent years after a friend could not keep the news of his friend being gay to himself.

'That was very difficult for him. There was awful graffiti at the local shops that we had removed. They left town, his family, but not because he was gay. He actually e-mailed me from WA and was quite suicidal.'

Brigette worked hard to link that young man in with local services in WA.

'We're quite inclusive around race. We have 40% Indigenous student population. And around disability too, we are inclusive. I think our challenge is around sexuality, around inclusion.'

Jodie believes teachers are a logical start.

'We need to know where teachers are at. It would be great to have some tangible, non-threatening tools for teachers to use.'

Brigette adds to that.

'How to challenge *that's so gay* and the attitudes behind it. We already have some teachers doing that.'

Day 102

Thursday, 3rd June – Alice Springs NT

Whilst some speak of 'mainstreaming' LGBT issues through campaigns and services, in Alice Springs I once again see how one extraordinary individual, through her warmth, personality and courage can single-handedly mainstream LGBT issues. This time it's in a remote, Central Australian community.

'They don't give a fuck what you look like, just who you are and if you have a good heart. Out here I think the desert is so isolating so people are just themselves, and all the pretense of the city drops away.'

'They' are the Indigenous people in remote communities in Central Australia. And Star Lady certainly knows what she is talking about. As a transgender lady ('... I call myself a *lady* and not a woman ...') self-described as 'towards feminine', Star Lady has been working with success for some time in remote communities that are closer to Alice Springs than anywhere else.

Star Lady's journey to Alice Springs from Melbourne started when she was a child, which included a family holiday to Alice Springs. Years later she would participate in the Peace Walk, a reconciliation walk between Lake Eyre and Sydney spanning some 3000kms. Despite concerns from friends, Star Lady found a great deal of belonging, a spiritual feeling and acceptance.

Finding herself coming more and more often to Alice Springs, Star Lady noticed something important after three months of work in remote communities.

'I came off one of the communities and started crying, and I thought, *Why am I crying?* Then I realised that when I was in Melbourne I was getting abused. I was nearly getting into fights almost every day on public transport just for who I was.'

What Star Lady describes was a dropping of her defenses because, on remote communities, they were no longer necessary.

'I was crying and asking myself, *Had you closed yourself up this much?*'

Due to her appearance, Star Lady felt that seemingly progressive Melbourne was closing her in.

'In Melbourne people were trying to put you in this box, and that never worked for me. Most people thought because of the way I look I am a crazy, drug party person and I'm not. I'm really straight. I hate going to parties.'

Committing herself to remote community life, Star Lady decided to find out what skills she could develop to bring back to the people that had welcomed her so warmly.

When it became apparent that it was hairdressing and beauty therapy, Star Lady hopped onto a plane to return to Melbourne to learn just that. Now that's what Star Lady takes to remote communities, along with her background in youth work. From all accounts the locals cannot get enough of the lively, energetic and entertaining white 'lady' who comes in to give them small doses of 'feeling special'. Much of Star Lady's charm, apparent during my time with her, is her ability to relate easily and naturally quite quickly.

'If you can't relate to the people out here, nothing is going to be successful.'

Star Lady, fluent in local dialects, has been given a title that is given to women in the communities. Not that the locals don't like to play on it.

'Sometimes you see it, the women set up one of the old ladies. They send her up and she says, 'Hi [local dialect word for a male community member]'. And I tell her, in her dialect, that she must be blind, or that something is wrong with her eyes because I'm a lady. And I do it in a playful way and I can see all the other women laughing because they love to see me do it.'

What Star Lady sees in the communities she works in, she loves.

'It's a playful culture. They really like teasing.'

This certainly defies the expectations of most of Star Lady's friends in Melbourne who expect to hear tales of her being abused and harassed. But Star Lady says that this happened to her more in inner city Melbourne than in remote communities.

Communities working out what being transgender means to their everyday lives is something that excites Star Lady.

'Sistagal [an Indigenous term for transgender people] has a different meaning in different communities. Here they dress as a woman, they cook, they clean and they take one of the kids. I think if you look to Northern Queensland it's different again. Sistagal can mean that you are just a gay boy.'

Recently Star Lady has been showered with praise from the people who fund her important work. She describes a recent meeting with the head honchos in a government department. Star Lady walked in for a well-attended meeting with lots of men in suits.

'There I was, turning up in my pink hot pants and no-one raised an eyebrow. That would never happen in Melbourne. They said they loved my program and that the Department wanted to get behind it. They took me seriously and didn't care what I looked like.'

Star Lady laughs and says that she is now seen as someone with experience.

'But that's not hard in Alice. You just have to be around longer than 6 months. No-one stays longer than that.'

Day 103

Friday, 4ᵗʰ June – Alice Springs NT to Unknown Campsite QLD = 619kms

Leaving Alice, I find myself saying in my head the words that Daniel has used in response to spectacular sunsets, breathtaking landscapes and views from high places around Alice Springs. These were the words I uttered to myself as Brigette walked me out to the sunsoaked school carpark, brimming with enthusiasm; as I hugged Star Lady after a relaxed, hilarious and fascinating dinner; and when I found myself left alone in a remote community reflecting on my first 100 days. These words again seem appropriate.

'Now that's the shit.'

Day 104

Saturday, 5ᵗʰ June – Unknown Campsite QLD to Mt Isa QLD = 550kms

Heading to Mt Isa from Alice Springs requires quite a backtrack. At 533kms, this backtrack gets me to Three Ways, where you pick up the Barkly Highway that takes travellers through Mt Isa and all the way to Townsville.

Just as the drive to Mt Isa takes two days, it also takes the landscape about the same time to gradually turn from all shades of red to all manner of brown. The heavier-than-usual rains in Central Australia clearly haven't reached Central Queensland, with vegetation sparser than ever.

To save a night's accommodation in Mt Isa, I camp just outside town at the World War II Memorial Site. After dinner, cold pepper steak in a can, and rearranging Bruce, whose interior looks like a dog's breakfast, I meet what I first took to be an elderly couple.

Early in the conversation, in the shadow of their over-sized campervan, they make it clear they are actually brother and sister. Whilst I love my own sister, I reimagine the fights we had on family holidays as children and don't want to think about the challenge of doing so later in our lives.

Seeing that I had a very 'basic' set-up for traveling, they make my week when they nonchalantly offer a hot cup of tea. I gasp when I'm offered a dry biscuit as well. We have a great yarn, including giving each other the heads up on where to stop for fuel on the way through; they are headed west, me, obviously, east.

Their generosity extends to contacts too, with them offering up a friend's phone number who had been a former social worker with The Royal Flying Doctor Service.

I appreciate any assistance at this stage. Although Mt Isa is the most pressing, immediate concern, I'd be lying if I said I wasn't already concerned about the weeks beyond: Townsville, Cairns, rural Queensland and Brisbane.

Day 105

Despite Mt Isa's reputation, I'm still taken aback when I ask a local young gay man, Andrew, what life is like in Mt Isa for LGBT people.

'I can summarise it in one word for you: shit. You can write that 100 times, and that would be accurate.'

I could be forgiven if this was the impression I had of Mt Isa before I arrive on yet another leg of my 'oh my god, you are not seriously going there, you'll be run out of town' national tour of regional, rural and remote Australia.

Yet some clarification.

'It's hard being one of the only city-oriented gay guys in a rural area.'

Me: 'So what brings a Brisbane-born and bred gay man to a rural mining town area where there are so many bad stories of homophobia and LGBT life?'

'I really wasn't thinking at the time. I probably wanted to get out of Brisbane more than anything. I thought working in a rural town might be fun and I wanted to keep a friend company.'

Not only was he swayed by the offer to spend 12 months with his good (straight) friend in Mt Isa, Andrew also held a curiosity for rural Australian life.

'I'd never really been out to a rural area before. I'd always been fascinated with rural areas and how they operate. Just from watching the Royal Flying Doctor Service on TV and the way that emergency services differ from the city.'

Working as a local medical health professional, Andrew had an interesting journey to that role. Raised in a military family that included significant time spent in South East Asian countries, he decided at 19 to follow in his father's footsteps and joined the army. When I asked if he'd been concerned beforehand that being gay might not be compatible with military life, Andrew was clear.

'The fact that I grew up in a military family, I knew a lot about the workings of the army and knew that wouldn't be a problem. Not in the Australian army anyway. You're not encouraged to talk about your sex life, but ... They'd ask if I had a girlfriend, then I'd say no, then they'd ask if I had a boyfriend. There are quite a few gays in the army.'

Before long Andrew felt a need to change career paths.

'I got sick of the discipline and strategic planning side of things and felt I'd done all I could do in the military.'

So whilst there seems to be non-heterosexual life in 'The Isa', as locals call it, it differs to Andrew's experiences in metropolitan Australia.

'They are very underground and sheltered and they don't need to be. I can't go out and socialise like I used to, like I did in Brisbane. There's less opportunities to make friends because it's kind of integrated into the straight scene. So you might say they lose their identity.'

Socialising *per se* was not Andrew's biggest initial concern about coming to Mt Isa. He expressed concern about whether he might be the only gay in the village.

'It was probably my biggest worry. I actually talked to my friend about it. He assured me there were plenty of gays in The Isa. He said that yes, I would get sex from somewhere.'

Day 106

Monday, 7th June – Mt Isa QLD

'Why the fuck would you go to Mt Isa, Dan? ... There's nothing fuckin' there! ...'

Those words played over and over in my mind, not only as I rolled into Mt Isa with my fuel light flashing, given a head wind that had taken close to 100kms off Bruce's usual fuel capacity.

Out of practice given the great support of my hosts, NTAHC, in Darwin, Alice Springs and Katherine, I once again make the customary calls to the local schools: one Catholic, one government.

Typically I do whatever is required to bypass the administration team – exclusively women – that answer the school's phone calls. In 99% of cases it is very easy to speak to someone in student welfare who is invariably open to a cuppa-inspired interview.

This doesn't happen. Feeling a little relaxed after such good experiences recently, I suddenly find myself explaining the project to one of the school's administration team. When it becomes clear that she is freaking out I react and agree to speak to the school principal. I know better than most how school principals, as fear management experts, are often the last people you want to talk to in a school; I regularly talk with welfare staff who are opposed to their principal's stance on all things affirming LGBT people and challenging homophobia.

The Mt Isa school principal in question politely listens before telling me off as my Grade 2 teacher used to.

'Well you certainly haven't given us much time, have you? I mean, we are incredibly busy.'

I agree with her, thinking, 'You and the rest of the free world …' I explain the logistics of the tour and how the majority of schools had cooperated thus far. That cheeky bit of leverage doesn't seem to work.

I thought that calling on the Monday and asking if anyone, including herself, might have 15 to 20 minutes that week to talk about what life is like for LGBT students might be a reasonable request – most student welfare staff have agreed to meet within the next 24–48 hours!

'Well I'll talk to some of my staff and get them to call you back if they have time.'

Again, out of practice, I thank her without asking if I should call back or wait to hear. No-one called back.

When I manage to pick up the phone and do exactly the same thing with the local Catholic school, a Deputy Principal who will also never get back to me, I get grumpy with the rest of the world, and then eventually myself. After such a refreshingly straightforward time in the Northern Territory, it all suddenly feels too hard. Maybe people are right about Mt Isa. Maybe I'll end the week not talking to anyone.

I decide to take the rest of the day to blog and to respond to some overdue e-mails. As I write and calm down, my mind turns to that pivotal conversation months before as I sat on the picturesque foreshore of Esperance, Western Australia. Again I hear Mäth's words.

'Come on Pumpkin. Have you decided already how this week is going to be?'

Just as his words made a difference in Esperance, so too they do in Mt Isa. I tell myself that Tuesday would see me getting back on that challenging homophobia tour horse and trying again. I resolve to make a series of phone calls that, if I am honest, I do not completely have my heart in. Expecting the worst, I call the Police & Citizen's Youth Centre (PCYC) and am pleasantly surprised.

'What are you doing Wednesday for lunch?'

Me: 'Um, nothing yet, I don't have any plans.'

'Do you like home-made pea & ham soup? We're making some and you would be welcome to come have a bowl. Or two.'

Me: 'It sounds delicious, I'll be there.'

Day 107

Tuesday, 8ᵗʰ June – Mt Isa QLD

Someone else who spent her first days in Mt Isa feeling lost was Jill. In fact, Jill almost didn't get to Mt Isa in the first place.

Standing at the bus station watching the bus to Mt Isa filling up, Jill called her friend in hysterical tears.

'I said, I'm not coming. I've seen the people getting on that bus … I'm not getting on the bus if they are the type of people in Mt Isa!'

Describing herself as 'lost' in metropolitan Sydney after a break-up, Jill answered the call of a friend who had broken her collarbone.

'She said, Come up and stay here for a few weeks and get away from it all…'

Jill was the first person I talked to at the gym this week, the staff member that day on the reception counter. I looked into Jill's eyes on the first day and saw something familiar: a haunted look. In Jill's eyes I saw a depth that most could never know with a story that most would never hear. I noticed this because it is something I see in the eyes of many LGBT people: there was a 'story'.

Two days later I'm sitting on the stage with Jill after a group fitness class. Everyone is gone, and, our conversation turns into a long debrief about Jill's time with the gym, some ongoing dissatisfaction and not knowing how she really feels about life in Mt Isa.

Only knowing the basics of my tour, Jill asks for details of a radio interview I had given just before the class began – it saw me miss the warm-up song. How did it go? Which station? I mention it was Melbourne's JOY94.9FM and she nods almost knowingly and smiling. Still I don't click.

'So is this something you are doing off your own bat?'

Me: 'Yes, it's a national challenging homophobia tour ...'

'Homophobia? I didn't know you were here for that.'

I talk a little about trying to explode some of the myths about LGBT life in regional, rural and remote Australia, including trying to highlight all the positive stories.

'Yeah. Everyone was worried when I came up here and I thought I'd have to be really quiet about sexuality.'

Oh. Then I realised. Again I half-laugh to myself. My 'lesdar' must be temporarily broken. I'm also relieved. After being approached by brazen, heterosexual women at gyms in Geraldton, Karratha, Broome, Darwin, Alice Springs and now here, I'm feeling quite the failure as a gay man.

Jill tells me that when she first arrived in Mt Isa she was surprised that there was an openly gay instructor.

'He was really very confident. It surprised me that he was so accepted by everyone.'

Certainly Jill came to Mt Isa less confident about what it might hold for her. Nine months later, she is not leaving anytime soon.

'Mt Isa is like a half-way town for people who are lost or running away from something.'

I've heard that somewhere before.

Day 108

Wednesday, 9th June – Mt Isa QLD

It's just after midday when I pull up to the Mt Isa PCYC for lunch. Ominously in the shadows of The Isa's three imposing smoke stacks, I wander in looking for the head of the PCYC, Queensland Police's Gina.

Her welcome is as warm as the pea & ham soup I've been promised. Gina talks between slurps, whilst I write between grateful gulps.

Having worked in a role with local schools recently, Gina immediately gives me some context for the cold shoulder from the local government school principal.

'Last year the situation with homophobic language and behaviour at the school got pretty ugly and I think that the principal was very non-challenging of it. I'm very frustrated out here. I think they are neglecting it.'

Parents also seem to be a barrier for progress.

'The parents here are special. They're resistant to introducing anything – for example, getting a simple international day up and running was like pulling teeth.'

The locals, who are concerned about me directly quoting them, had a number of blunt assessments of the 'Rodeo Capital of Australia' as a place to live and the people who inhabit it. A selection of quotes include:

'I don't think they promote anything in this town unless it's a cow, a horse or a mine. You're either a miner or a cowboy. They really need to sit and watch *Brokeback Mountain* a few times.'

'It's a small town. It's like, *Oh, you got 6 rolls of toilet paper. Last week it was only 4. Is everything OK?* You couldn't buy a condom here without 27 people knowing.'

'It's hard to find people for everyday jobs here. If you are born and bred here you know you'll get a $90,000 job driving a truck at the mines, so why would you work for Woolies or Hungry Jacks? There's just too many jobs here.'

Back at the PCYC with Gina, I've finished my second bowl of soup. She explains that life would be tough for local LGBT young people, yet the adult community might have different experiences.

'There's still so much stigma attached to stepping forward about being gay. At the same time they have good representation of gay and lesbian people here. But they could do better at being open and visible [laughs]. I've just come from Cloncurry [small community east of Mt Isa] so it doesn't feel that bad at the moment.'

I explain my project and discuss the response from schools. Gina makes it all seem very easy.

'Who would you like to talk to?'

One phone call later – 'What are you up to now? Come down for some soup, there is someone I want you to meet.' – and within 5 minutes a school liaison officer has made her way down. Admittedly this is partially about lunch for her too. That officer offers to put me in direct contact with the school chaplain from the local government high school.

Gina is very positive about the possibilities for Mt Isa.

'In the big cities, PCYC's are businesses, but in this town I'm hoping to make it cater to all groups in the community. Someone people can come down to have a chat with. We would definitely be open to having someone based here to do LGBT work.'

Not that there is currently much around.

'There's no resources whatsoever to be honest. To see a counsellor you are looking at a 6 week wait. It's so difficult to get someone to get back to you.'

Gina admits she'd tried to find some LGBT resources for young people before I'd arrived, merely as an exercise.

'I put *gay youth* into Google and all these porn sites came up; pages and pages of them! It wouldn't have been a minute before I had [Queensland Police] HQ calling me and demanding to know why I was looking up porn on my computer. I was just madly scrolling through pages and pages trying to find something appropriate. It was an eye opener.'

Day 109

Thursday, 10th June – Mt Isa

There is a memory of 'some training a few years ago' on how to support same-sex youth.

At Young People Ahead, a youth organisation in Mt Isa, Trish and Leigh recall the training well.

'There has only been training offered once in my three years here. We sent staff and the feedback was really good. They got a lot out of that. But training is very limited because we're so isolated. Mt Isa lacks good quality training. Usually there is a waiting list for training when it actually comes to us.'

But LGBT young people tend not to be open at Trish and Leigh's service.

'It's not something that comes up on the radar. Young people don't identify any of their sexual stuff with us. Sometimes we employ staff who are gay. Some staff are comfortable with young people knowing about that, and some not.'

It was an incident with staff that forced Leigh to reflect on her own practice. With rumours amongst young people that some of the staff might be gay, she decided that it was time to address it at a staff meeting.

'I know I had to have a conversation with staff and I was shaking. I was shitting myself. I think it's cos I didn't know how they were going to respond. I was just really open in saying I wasn't exactly sure how to say it. But I worked out I was the one with the issue. Everyone else was OK; I was the one who was a mess. The feedback was great. They said I handled it really well. Now it's OK. I've done it once and I can do it again. If I was to have that conversation again it would be easy.'

Day 110

Friday, 11ᵗʰ June – Mt Isa QLD

A young gay man born and bred in The Isa, Jon, has invited me for drinks at the two main watering holes in the town. I go somewhat reluctantly, mainly because a member of the local police force had said of one of them:

'We send a van to sit out the front of that pub because we know that brawls are going to happen. It's actually a very violent town. Gay men do get bashed but they are not reporting it. If they are coming to the police counter, the only gay male officer is often sent to deal with it. We really need to have a Queensland Police GLLO here.'

I'm introduced to one of Jon's friends, a teacher at the local government high school. I want to talk to her, being mindful not to hijack her downtime at the end of a working week. Yet I don't. She stares off into space and gives a polite smile with a hint of sneer when Jon talks about the work I'm doing. It feels too much like work tonight.

Over a drink Jon tells me he's been working on a cattle station until only recently. Deciding to do this soon after finishing high school, his parents were unsure if it would be a good idea. Yet for Jon, out as gay to family and friends in high school, it was essential.

'I really needed that time away to get my head together and work out that I was actually gay. It was just what I needed even though my parents were worried that a male-dominated environment like that would not be the best place for me to work it all out.'

Refreshingly Australian with his accent and at ease amongst other local drinkers, Jon tells me how he came out to everyone on the remote cattle station after 6 months. By all accounts it was taken well. Jon knew it was 'all good' after an incident where all the cattle station workers headed into Camooweal (west of Mt Isa on the Barkly Highway) one Saturday night.

'I didn't even hear it, but apparently some guy walked past our table and said, *There's that faggot that works on [said cattle station]*. If I'd heard it I would've said, *Just leave it, it doesn't matter*, but they asked this guy if he had a problem and he went away. I said to 'em later, *Thanks for sticking up for me guys*, and they said, *Nah, you've done your time, you've worked hard, you're one of us. What you do in the bedroom doesn't matter to us mate.*'

On Facebook a friend had posted a similar story about a country pub:

'I heard a story I heard about a country pub where some out-of-towners were hassling a gay man at the bar. After a short time a group of local men (brutes, if you will) sidled over and bluntly commanded *oi, hands off our poof* – and that was the end of that!'

Day 111

Saturday, 12th June – Mt Isa QLD to Unknown Campsite QLD = 641 kms

Coming to Mt Isa I was mindful that it was infamous for its Mayor, whipmaker John Molony, who put out an invitation to 'ugly girls' or 'beauty-disadvantaged' women to come to the town. His rationale was that men outnumber women in the town five to one, and that this would mean they could find happiness with a local man.

Locals have been blunt when discussing their 'beloved' Mayor.

'[Groans] He is straight from the 1950s: racist, sexist and homophobic. In his mind he's still in the 1950s. He grew up in Camooweal where they probably were chaining up Aboriginals by the ankles. It's unfortunate that the people who vote in local elections here are the locals that are born and bred.'

If you believe popular opinion, then it's difficult for men to meet single women in The Isa. Yet this isn't my experience going to one of the local gyms. Standing waiting for a group fitness class to commence, I had the attractive young female instructor approach me and proceed to flirt with me outrageously. Only the week before I'd had a similar experience in Alice Springs. When approached by anyone and subjected to flirting I typically start blushing and respond to any question very nervously and invariably with one-word mumbles. I fear that this does nothing to communicate very clearly that

I'm gay (I thought my long soccer socks and attendance at a group fitness class might trigger it). Maybe I'm making the situation even worse.

Message to straight men in The Isa wanting to meet fit young women: go to group fitness classes at the gym and just stand there waiting!

Day 112

Sunday, 13th June – Unknown Campsite to Cairns QLD = 608kms

Not for the first time, I feel like a 'bad gay'; I'm the only gay person I know who hasn't been to Turtle Cove before. I pull up in the parking area with a head full of tales of nude romps on private beaches, attractive staff, visiting locals, visiting internationals and hedonistic parties.

I walk in to find the atmosphere unexpectedly subdued. I find out quickly that the whole resort is recovering from the (Saturday) night before to celebrate the Queen's Birthday Weekend. Who did what was yet to be determined.

I admit I'm uncomfortable. Until now I've only been hosted by individuals and couples. Now that it's a gay business I feel out of place. What are the expectations of my stay? Do I now have to rebrand my tour? Do they know that no-one reads my blog? What I do know is that it is a unique institution that has been around for 18 years in Far North Queensland and I want to find out more about it.

I leave Bruce under iconic palm trees interspersed with rainbow coloured flags. I follow the chatter of voices and intermittent cackles of laughter to find a literal oasis. If you're not careful you could walk straight into the pool, distracted by a vista of palm trees framing a beach.

At the bar I meet my contact, Ken, the barman on duty. He invites me to sit at the bar for a drink and to meet the new owners. Waiting to do so, he asks me to explain my project again. Having spent the last four and a half months talking about it, I almost go into auto-pilot. Yet I re-assess quickly when I turn back from the sun setting on the horizon to Ken who is now in tears.

'I'm sorry.'

Ken explains that he'd recently known two young men in love. Both living on farms on the opposite ends of Greater Cairns, one of them decided that he could not handle it all and had suicided. When his young partner heard about this he too took his own life.

Day 113

Monday, 14th June – Cairns QLD

It's just after 7am and I'm sitting in the breakfast area beside the pool. One of the staff tends to the breakfast arrangement, and one other person is at breakfast. I'm surprised anyone is awake so early after last night.

After the sun had gone down, a friendly post-dinner gathering around a bonfire (that flirted with being out of control), morphed into a drag performance and 'party games'. After four and a half months of being in what has felt like an LGBT desert, I was almost overwhelmed at times by three men dressed as sailor girls, best bare butt competitions and races to find Tic Tacs in the underwear of your partner (if indeed your partner was wearing any).

There were the 'gay cowboys' who were said to have broken resort records on the Saturday night. There were gay couples who were 'regulars' to the resort for their annual getaway. There were gay single internationals who could be a different version of themselves 1000s of miles from home.

Whilst it took me some time to become re-accustomed to such an intense concentration of gay energy, others found it a little too much. At dinner I'd spoken with a gay jackaroo, Gary, who I later found out was at his very first gay thing ever. Having never been to a pub, event or other venue, this man of the land decided that Turtle Cove would be his very first foray into all things gay.

He spent a large part of the night gripping my arm and asking all manner of questions about gay culture, the role of drag queens and other things that did not yet make sense to him (and to be fair may never make sense).

Jack, my fellow early breakfast companion has some news.

'Gary checked out really early this morning. He decided to head back to the cattle station. It was a bit too much for him.'

Day 114

Tuesday, 15th June – Cairns QLD

'It's a good school for cultivating creative students.'

Grant, a local student welfare coordinator, explains that students are selected to come to his school, with an emphasis on arts, music and other pursuits. As with other creative selected-entry schools in regional Australia, there were some more obvious examples of LGBT students.

'We have one male student who has made no secret of the fact that he's gay. In fact, he celebrates it.'

Coming out during Year 9, this male student had started actively pursuing other, usually younger, male students. This bucks the general trend of young gay men remaining romantically isolated in school environments. The school became concerned that he was 'soliciting younger students inappropriately'.

'I think he was just looking for a partner.'

Now in his final year, this student recently wowed his fellow classmates at the recent school camp.

'He had his kinky boots on. He got up and did Lady Gaga stuff with an entourage of girls behind him. He's got a fairly confident type of personality. He'd be out there if he wasn't gay. He always looks like he could deal with people putting him down. Gay is a kind of put-down they use regardless of sexuality. They know it pushes people's buttons.'

Grant believes adjustment as an LGBT student in a school environment very much 'depends on the individual student'.

'We've got kids like one girl here. She's pretty out there. She's copped a fair bit of negative comments. Her style tends to be pretty aggressive, she's a bigger girl, she plays AFL at a very high level. I don't think she has handled it particularly well. But I think that there is more going on for her than just her sexuality.'

He admits that he's learnt from his students' journeys.

'There was a transgender student that I supported for a while. The way she talked about it, the more we did, you got the feeling she was definitely on the right track. She was pretty comfortable with it, although others weren't.'

Prue, new to the school welfare team, has been quiet up until now. She appears a bit nervous. She sits stiffly.

'I don't know of any students personally, but in my son's small [mechanics] workshop there is a young guy. He's supported by his family and his friends at school. He seems happy within himself and he's really supported, you can tell. Obviously there is a little banter, but it seems to really work. It's not put-down stuff, it's more jokey. My son says he's a really lovely person to work with.'

Having spoken for the first time, Prue seems to relax into her grey lounge chair. Even her face relaxes and some colour returns to it. Grant has been relaxed from the start.

'I think it's about young people feeling accepted and respected themselves before they'll accept others. We did consider setting up a more visible support group in the school but that was not supported by admin. The preference there was that they would want it to be out of school. There tends to be a fair bit of conservatism around sexuality.'

Prue is keen to know what else could be done. She realises not everyone is going to have a kinky boots moment.

'It's the quiet ones I guess you worry about. The ones who can't share what is going on in their life.'

Day 115

Wednesday, 16th June

I've been nominated for a major LGBT Community Award. And I'm chuffed that I just got a Facebook post from a young woman I supported some 12 years earlier in Geelong:

'I like that you are caring, that you give of yourself to anyone in need. I like that you are sensitive, and gentle and fun. I like that you are making the world a better place, that you are going above and beyond the call for all these people who need your help that you haven't even met yet. I like how you went out of your way to do special research and reassure a frightened teenage girl. I like that when you listen, you *really* listen. I like that you can do a little thing for someone, and have a huge (positive) impact on their life. I like that you've been nominated for all these awards, because I can't think of a more caring, wonderful person who could possibly deserve any of them more than you!'

Day 116

Thursday, 17th June

'There is this perception here that young people cope better now. That things are better than they used to be. Whereas we get the stories of young people who are coming out in schools or post-school who are feeling quite isolated.'

Tony from the Queensland Association for Healthy Communities (QAHC), the new version of the Queensland Aids Council, isn't buying the good press on the modern experience of LGBT young people. Tony is eager to get a copy of *Beyond 'That's So Gay'*.

'I talk with all the school based nurses – we are actually meeting next week – and they get told to do all that stuff that schools don't want to do anymore. They are not supposed to run classes but often they are asked to anyway. This will be perfect for them.'

Like their other state and territory counterparts, QAHC struggles to meet a range of LGBT community needs given a tenuous relationship between what it's funded to do, what it has to do and what it needs to do.

'QAHC has brought to Cairns the first LGBT organisation, whereas the Queensland Aids Council was more support and care. Now we are, although our bosses don't like it, a one-stop shop. Ageing, lesbian, youth, transgender, you name it, we've got it.

'Sexual behaviour up here is no different to what happens anywhere else. We have the same lust and juices. Except perhaps for identity. There are barriers to people identifying up here. A lot of people, especially in the HIV-positive community – there is this fear of being identified. That is a real big issue up here: *I don't want to be known as that*. So they want to keep it hidden. There is a secrecy to it. Because the community is so small, there is a fear that it will be known that you are positive. But I think a lot of that stuff is long-term stuff that the sector has to face about stigma and discrimination and to put it on the LGBT community to see them as a valuable part of our community.'

'Community' is a concept that started getting a mention in Central Australia, and has since followed me to Far North Queensland. What they've said echoes the voices of LGBT people so far: living outside metropolitan Australia offers a different opportunity for 'community', albeit one that is not as visible, constant, commercialised or passively entertaining.

'I suppose there's this perception that there isn't enough to do. But I think a lot of people come here for that purpose, they want a change in lifestyle. So the social life is more about BBQs and the beach. So I feel more connected to LGBT community than I did in the city.'

Day 117

Friday, 18th June

'Sorry Daniel ...'

Damn.

So close yet so far. When the text message came through on my phone at the start of this week I realise that I might have to wait another 12 years to meet this man. He explained that whilst walking his dogs north of Port Douglas he was almost run over by a speeding local on a dirt road. All escape mostly unharmed, yet now Kent is laid up with a broken foot.

If I had a gold coin for every 'near miss' chat in a town or city, my self-funded tour would be sorted.

However Kent was someone I didn't want to be a 'near miss'.

I first knew Kent existed in 1998. In that year I was a baby LGBT worker from Geelong. With barely 12 months experience under my belt I attended the Health in Difference 2 conference (yes the one where I met Mt Gambier's Ben). Having just driven 20,000km in the last four months of this tour, I can laugh at how 'big' the 76km drive from Geelong to Melbourne felt each day back then.

Perhaps I was spoilt, because this conference would become my benchmark for all LGBT gatherings to follow. Whilst it lacked what we get now in corporate beige-ing and anxious mainstream envy, the conference was alive with a raw emotional energy. For example I recall one plenary that had three speakers: the first Victorian Police GLLO, a man living with HIV and an Indigenous man. I cannot recall if it was the GLLO or the man living with HIV who went first, but remember clearly what happened: they talked openly about their lives in ways I had never heard before.

The atmosphere was strangely intimate, so much so that each speaker would end up crying openly to a room full of people. Somehow it felt right, and I was not alone in joining them. There was no concern about professionalism or appropriateness, just about connecting over the sharing of our experience. Whether it was just a romantic memory of the time or not I cannot be sure, but for me there was an uncompromising honesty that I've never seen captured again in the same way.

With a backdrop of grief, celebration, sadness, beauty and healing, it was probably inevitable that I would be vulnerable to fall in LGBT-activist-love for the first time. Taking copious notes throughout the conference, I was taken aback when Kent stood to give his presentation on his research. It was not the first time I had seen an attractive, somewhat feisty, brunette who was also young and gay, yet it was the first time one had opened his mouth and had something to say that had me transfixed. I knew straight away that I wanted to be just like him: intelligent, articulate, confident, although I didn't know how.

What Kent presented were the findings of his thesis, 'Sexuality & Suicide – An Investigation of Health compromising and Suicidal Behaviours among Gay and Bisexual Male Youth in Tasmania'. I even remember an often lost point from this research about the relationship between self-identity, self-labeling, first same-sex sexual experience and suicidal ideation that I still talk to teachers and health professionals about to this day.

It would be Kent's research that would lead to *Outlink*, already described as this tour's predecessor. Just over two years after sitting to hear Kent speak I would be working on that very national project.

Now in Cairns, so very close to Port Douglas, I just had to finally meet him, broken foot or not.

Thankfully, for me, Kent calls.

'I have to come down to Cairns for the doctor's. Are you free for lunch?'

Me: 'You bet, just say where and when.'

We meet at a sushi outlet in a local shopping centre. We greet and it's like how I've imagined; not surprisingly I feel like I'm meeting an old friend.

Day 118

Saturday, 19ᵗʰ June – Cairns QLD

The waiting room at this medical clinic is half full, which is the last thing I expect or want on a Saturday night. It could be a medical centre anywhere else in regional Australia: plain, sterile, conservative. I slink into a grey-blue plastic chair that is probably teeming with a dozen people's bacteria. Two seats away a young mother in her late 20s negotiates two small children, one obviously distressed. I think how cute the small girl in tap shoes is, but then she starts squealing at her imp-ish little brother and I wish her ill.

A migraine that started yesterday is now blinding me in my right eye. My neck is on fire and I find it hard to stay awake between bouts of passing out and sweating.

It is diagnosed as severe tonsillitis.

Me: 'So what should I do?'

'Nothing,' says the doctor.

I think. 'Not happening.'

I arrive back ready to plonk on the bed, only to realise I've lost my wallet. I search everywhere inside my room and then head out to Bruce. Still can't find a thing. Distressed and confused, I eventually put my hand in my back pocket and find my wallet.

'OK Doc. You win.'

Day 119

Sunday, 20ᵗʰ June – Cairns QLD

I spend the day in bed, in and out of consciousness. When I wake it's brief, usually to find myself in pools of my own sweat. I can't eat; even the thought of drinking water makes my migraine worse.

My drive to Townsville is delayed.

Day 120

Monday, 21ˢᵗ June – Cairns QLD to Townsville QLD = 348kms

'It's not uncommon to see two people, although they are never locals, holding hands here in Cairns but you would never see that in Townsville. Unless it was two massive dykes who had tatts down their arms and were like, *If you come near us we're gonna smack you in the mouth.* Townsville is a funny place because it's different to Cairns. Cairns has a big international and domestic tourist market. It has two women to every man, whereas Townsville is the opposite. Townsville has the military.'

Tony from QAHC prepared me for my drive down to Townsville. The reputation of Queensland's second biggest city precedes it, and that reputation is of a dangerous city that is dominated by miners and military folk. Few have a good word to say about Townsville, with the exception of people in Mt Isa.

For Mt Isa, Townsville is at the end of a 10-hour drive east down the Barkly Highway and is considered 'the big smoke'. Mt Isa residents roll their eyes when describing how most people from The Isa have aspirations to one day live in Townsville.

I meet Jodie at a café on The Strand, which shoulders the beachfront and offers views of Magentic Island on a clear day. Today Magnetic is shy, hiding behind some mist. We have our cuppa at a table almost within touching distance of a huge old Moreton Bay Fig tree, whose roots fall around its trunk, making it look like the abandoned temples I'd marveled at when I visited Angkor Wat.

Far from being a 'massive dyke' with tattoos up and down her arms, Jodie is long-haired and traditionally pretty and an example of a young local lesbian who walks Townsville's streets holding her partner's hand.

'It's definitely more accepting in society for two women to be together. I wouldn't say there are a lot of people who are comfortably out. You see some girls together but not the guys.'

Jodie admits that there was a different set of rules in Townsville for gay men.

'There is still a stigma associated with men being together. It's stupid, it's ridiculous but until people choose to educate themselves that it's not the 70s, it will be that way.'

Yet despite two women having less societal pressure not to show public displays of affection, Jodie still doesn't experience holding hands as an easy task.

'I'm a Taurus, I'm quite stubborn, I'm me and if people don't like it then they can fuck right off. I don't have time for it. At home with my family is the one place where I can't and I don't. Dad's OK but my mum is actually a part of a very religious cult. It's only a recent thing, she joined about 10 years ago.

And it's really freaky in Townsville because they are all related and I don't think it's a good thing.'

Jodie describes begrudgingly making concessions.

'It's caused a lot of problems in my family. It's just easier if mum doesn't see it. It was all about compromise. She didn't lecture me and we don't hold hands or touch. It shits my partner to tears, but that's it. She's the only mother I've got.'

Not that abuse, harassment and extreme examples of violence don't happen in Townsville.

'I think the community is very tolerant. I wouldn't say it's a homophobic city. I don't think it's as bad as it could be. We don't have any problems, but I know others do.'

Day 121

Tuesday, 22ⁿᵈ June – Townsville QLD

Not only has a local gay man offered his B&B as a venue for me to meet local LGBT people, Trevor's also thrown on a spread. I'm having some biscuits with my cuppa, whilst others are delighting in an impromptu antipasto tray.

We all sit out the back of the property on a shaded patio. I'm disappointed that the local Queensland Police GLLO hasn't yet returned my call. Rose explains why.

'She had an accident. She was playing touch football and she had her nose smashed in so she's laying very low'.

Rose is a member of the LGBT Anti-Violence Committee (AVC) along with Madge. Both are pivotal in running the local transgender support, Transbridge. Madge, a local transgender woman, realised that there was very little for people like herself. Since starting a decade ago, Transbridge has seen little change in transgender people's experience in Townsville.

'One young woman, in this day and age, was thrown out of home. Imagine, to throw out your own daughter and reject her so vehemently? There was another young woman who went to a local GP. He said, *You're not transsexual, you're just weird.* She's not with us anymore. She committed suicide.'

Rose elaborates.

'He physically got her by the back of the neck, even though she's 6 foot. He pushed her into the waiting room and screamed, *You filthy bitch, don't you dare come back here.* She'd been transgender for many years. She was devastated.'

Madge believes that people automatically believe that she is going to be different.

'Nothing's changed for me, I'm basically the same nutcase I always was. They seem to think that I only wear a dress in order to pick up men. I don't. People also think that transgender people are pedophiles. They have no idea what being transgender is about. It's the cruelest, wickedest thing you could do to yourself [laughs].'

With no resources except for the time of people like Madge, Transbridge receives calls at all hours.

'They say, *I'm in a motel, I'm alone and I think I might be transsexual. Can you come down and talk to me?* So of course I do. You need an environment when you come out where you are safe and where you can talk to people.'

Transbridge also take local transgender people to other places where they can experience life as their affirmed gender. One recent drive to Cairns for the group presented some challenges when two transgender women were 'going out' for the very first time dressed as women.

'You have to go somewhere, you have to go and spend the whole day, go somewhere else where they don't know you. We had one woman who walked out of a department store with a security tag on. That set off the alarms and it drew attention from security and the other customers which was very tough for her. Then driving back the other woman had to drive through a police roadblock. It turns out she knew this copper personally. But he didn't recognise her. Thank god.'

Madge and others at Transbridge see the need to educate locals, and do so through talks such as to Queensland Police recruits, although the time they're given is often 20 minutes as part of a full day. Yet they make the absolute most of it.

'When we started they were slouched in their chairs and were halfway through the session. By the end, everyone was sitting up and full of attention.'

Day 122

Even though he's worked a full day Rob makes time to share a cuppa at a café just around the corner from where I'm staying. I arrive early and see him pull up in a dark blue ute, looking every bit the tradie as he finds his way inside.

Rob wanted to meet to tell me about a time he was working with a friend at a block of units.

'I was rewiring a unit. It was rough units. We'd finished the second day. [His co-worker on the job] was an ex-drag queen and had camped it up. He would have done it in the carpark. They might have thought I was gay by association.'

Truth is, Rob doesn't remember much. It's said he was set upon by a group of men.

'The next door neighbour had heard the noise and came to our defence. Everyone was chanting, *Kill the fags, kill the fags.* She heard it and ran down and got the guy with a baseball bat. Otherwise I'd be dead.'

The first successful prosecution in Queensland of a hate crime was small comfort.

'At the trial they said, *We thought he might have been a fag so we thought we'd kill him anyway. We hate fags, but he deserves to die.*'

Rob describes it as dark thereafter.

'I became suicidal, I was hating the fact that I was gay. I didn't so much come out, I was forced out. I went to work one day as an apprentice, I got home that day and dad came home and said we need to talk. And he went through and locked all the doors. He said, *We got a phone call today.* Some guy had called up and said, *Is he there?* And when dad said no he said, *Well just tell him he was the best fuck I ever had.* Dad took my phone, my car, my keys. He dropped me off at work and picked me up. For five months that happened. Then I decided I had enough.'

After moving away to Melbourne and finally coming home again under duress, Rob's father would have a change of heart.

'He said, *I don't really give a shit about the gay thing. I don't care what you do.* The attack and me moving away, it changed dad, it changed the whole family. It probably made mum clingier.'

Rob wonders sometimes if he wants to continue.

'I have no desire to continue to put up with this shit. I have to pull my socks up and get on with it. I ask myself why I keep going. Why don't I pack up? Why am I still in Townsville? Why am I single? I guess it's easier to keep going than to stop.'

'So what keeps you going?'

'I keep going for my nephew. He's got leukemia. If he can fight through everything he's going through, then so can I.'

Day 123

Thursday, 24ʰ June – Townsville QLD

I'm cross-legged on a big brown couch, notebook ready and cuppa within reach. I'm trying to be productive, although I've spent the whole morning unable to take my eyes off the TV: Prime Minister Kevin Rudd has just been rolled by his deputy, Julia Gillard. It has interrupted and altered the time of my weekly Thursday radio interview with JOY94.9FM back in Melbourne.

I'm hearing from Guy, who has been out for a decade, about the experiences of gay men and lesbians in Townsville. Most report a distinct change.

'I think there are a few things. One is a lot of Southerners have come up here and that's changed things. And the other is there are a lot of TV shows. They might be your stereotypical gay characters, but it's still in your face. The army has also worked a lot on equality and stressed that a lot. I know we are nowhere near having it yet, but still it's helped.'

Guy came to Townsville after growing up on the Sunshine Coast. His journey to realising he was gay had a few twists and turns.

'I knew by 15 or 16 that having sex with men was a homosexual thing, but I didn't want to be it. I didn't want to be abused and harassed. I was overweight already and I didn't want to add to the fire. High school can be a very traumatising experience for a lot of people. I knew I was different.

'When I was younger I always heard that a guy loses his virginity twice. Once to a girl and once to a boy. I wondered if I was only experimenting.'

Once in Townsville, Guy started a three-year relationship with a young woman and also joined the Mormon church.

'Part of it was soul searching, a part of it was denial. I couldn't understand why anyone would choose to be abused, harassed. I'd met a couple of gay people and seen quite a promiscuous lifestyle, and I didn't believe that was who I was. I believed I was very old fashioned. I was described once by someone as being an old soul.'

When it came to a decision to be baptised, Guy went ahead merely because of a new 'elder'.

'I was already contemplating it, and then a new elder came along. He was probably one of the most stunning men I've seen in my life. He sealed the deal for me. The baptism was in a large bath, warm water. Both of us wore white gowns and nothing underneath. I clung onto him, I latched onto him and yes I was massively attracted to him. Majorly I guess is the word.'

Yet this life caught up with him.

'I went through a time of feeling quite repressed, feeling depressed and contemplating suicide. In some regards I didn't feel complete. Within the church community I felt very accepted, but they weren't accepting me, they were accepting the heterosexual me. It was not long after that that I decided that I was gay and that I needed to identify with it in some regards.'

Watching a movie, a gay perennial favourite, *Beautiful Thing*, helped. He did so in his share house which just so happened to be full of lesbian housemates.

'They all kept telling me I was gay. I finished watching the movie and rang my mum. I didn't even get the word hello out before I started crying. She responded [to me coming out] with, *Don't tell your father*. I thought, *Crap, obviously this is the wrong thing I'm doing, this is going to disappoint people*. So I went back into my shell.'

A close gay friend he met on an online gay dating site helped Guy see there was nothing wrong with him being gay. This encouraged Guy to come out to the rest of his family.

'I was at my mum's birthday. I was working away at the BBQ and called dad over. I basically came out and said that I was gay. He said, *I already knew, here, you should have a beer*. When I told grandma later it was the first time I heard her swear. She said, *I know that. I still fucking love you.*'

Day 124

Friday, 25th June – Townsville QLD

As I prepare to head out to the local gay institution, The Sovereign Hotel, I think about what the locals have had to say about the spaces where they can gather as an LGBT community.

'I think it's the community fighting against itself which is the issue.'

Guy amongst others acknowledges that Townsville, like other regional centres, struggles with the community coming together for a common goal. Talks with locals revealed that there is a fragmented LGBT community. One gay business owner believes this is due in part to a gender divide in Townsville.

'A lot of women in this town don't like men, oh there are a few that do. It's the same with gay guys that can't stand lesbians. They just think lesbians are pushy, get drunk and take over. The lesbians think that the gay guys are too girly and bitchy.'

In recent times with the demise of a group that organised successful parties for women who love women, Jodie and her partner have started running parties to fill the void. In a move welcomed by many, the events now include those who are not strictly lesbian. A recent LGBT party with a Spice Girls theme saw over 400 people attend.

'For a while they had the women-only parties. There was this whole segregation thing. You had to be a lesbian. If you were transgender, then you weren't allowed. We never want it to be segregated. The history was that the girls were really organised but separatist. They wouldn't even have a male barman. And the boys. Well, they were totally disorganised.'

Disorganised except for a gay bar that has been running for 18 years. As with other regional and rural Australian places, Townsville has a love-hate relationship with the main jewel in the small local gay crown: The Sovereign Hotel. The owners were the subject of every conversation I had in Townsville, with just about everyone feeling that they are not open to anything else LGBT being run locally. Stories of sabotage and propaganda were in plentiful supply with common statements like, 'I've never known them to do anything for the local community …'

One local described a rite of passage.

'If you're banned from The Sovereign then you're considered a local.'

Interestingly The Sovereign Hotel has survived as a gay institution to this day, yet locals say that a decade ago there were a handful of gay bars. With locals describing Townsville as becoming more and more tolerant in recent years, it's almost counterintuitive that there would now be fewer gay establishments. But this mirrors international observations that the more hostile an environment, the greater lengths gay men will go to in order to meet. The theory is that when you limit gay men's opportunities to meet, socialise and have sex, then their creative and activist energy goes into overdrive. As one commentator remarked, some of the greatest examples of activism have come from the most unlikely places (e.g. Africa, the Middle East). These observers would say that Townsville's apparent drop in hostility has led to the demise of former gay gathering spots in the city.

A gathering of gay men of varying ages, a gaggle of gays as some might say, has taken over Guy's lounge room for pre-going out beverages. Drinks are flowing. I'm surprised at the main topic of conversation: straight men.

With so many men flying in and out for mining and so many men in the military, Townsville has a high incidence of men who have sex with men where men are not necessarily gay or single. All in attendance seemed to have aspirations to have sex with a heterosexual man, usually married and/or in the army. Boasting about having done so recently immediately boosts one gay man's standing in the group.

I can only take so much.

'OK guys, let's go out.'

Day 125

Saturday, 26th June – Townsville QLD

It's the third time I've been up Townsville's dominant landmark, Castle Hill, yet this is the first time I'm here alone.

It's mid-morning and I've walked a longer track to get to the summit. It's a clear day so I can see the city and Magnetic Island in the distance. This morning life feels clearer too. With my journey south from here tomorrow, northern Australia will be ticked off distance-wise. I'm feeling almost 100% after the infection; and I've been through some of the supposedly toughest locations of the tour.

This morning my mind is on The Dancer. A few months ago he excitedly messaged me before he got on a plane for London. I hadn't heard from him since. This week he came back.

I've heard people say that it hurts more when something is suddenly taken away. The Dancer was the sweetest of tastes, but then, suddenly, without warning, he disappeared. I guess he had his reasons, it's just I would have appreciated knowing them. I feel pathetic that I can't even listen to a Billy Joel song, because one night he showed me the moves he did to 'You May Be Right' on a cruise ship.

Atop Castle Hill I realise The Dancer is gone. My head knows it, but my body will take months to let him go.

I make a decision and walk back down feeling lighter. Once I'm back to my laptop I log onto Facebook and remove The Dancer as a friend. I don't want any further contact or reminders of what was.

Day 126

Sunday, 27th June – Townsville QLD to Mackay QLD = 390kms

I chuckle as I drive past the blue Townsville sign that welcomes anyone and everyone to the 'Capital of North Queensland'. Last night I momentarily silenced the gaggle of gays who had just asked me about my travels and what I thought of the local tourist hotspots.

'So many places I've been to have been overrated. Except Townsville.'

The locals all went silent and looked at me, steeling themselves for yet another anti-Townsville comment.

'Townsville is clearly underestimated in many ways. Seriously.'

Smiles and nods broke out across the room. Perhaps they felt that someone finally got it. At the local gay B&B, Trevor thinks it's happening slowly.

'We get people coming here to town. Usually they've been in Cairns and they've heard about here on the grapevine. They realise it's not the hick town they thought we were. They think at first it's Brownsville, you stop for a cuppa and you keep going. When people come here that all changes.'

Day 127

Monday, 28th June – Mackay QLD

'I lost two friends, male friends, to suicide a few years back when I was at school. One came out to his family and was disowned. The other came out and had such a hard time of it.'

Feeling unable to come out and live in Mackay, Mark moved to Sydney, then Melbourne to study.

'It took until the end of my degree before I could admit I was gay. Everyone was like, *It's great you are comfortable enough now to tell us.*'

Mark is a perfect example of a young gay man who left a regional or rural area to come out, and who then returned home for family reasons.

Mark was asked by his dad to move back to Mackay to take over the family business. Interestingly his father didn't want either of his two (straight) brothers to take over the business. Not that this doesn't involve some risk to the business that has been running locally for over 20 years. Mark is concerned that his father's older, more conservative clients might find out he is gay and that this might impact on business.

'I'd like to think that it wouldn't matter, but a lot of dad's clients are older, more conservative and it could.'

While Mark is openly gay with his immediate family and friends, he is more careful with his grandparents, extended family and the broader community. Yet Mark feels his grandmother is onto him.

'Gran tries to fish it out every time she comes up here. I was doing the ironing, as gay men do, and she said, *Mark, we have a homosexual in Gunadah.* I said, *Really gran, that's nice.* And she said, *But he's not a practising homosexual Mark.* I nearly burnt a hole in the shirt. Practising? What's that about?'

'My mum got so angry the last time she saw Gran. Gran was really getting stuck into gays and mum came back saying if she said anything else about gays then that would be it, the end of it.'

Day 128

Tuesday, 29th June – Mackay QLD

'Well it's funny because I went to Melbourne from Mackay to come out and get a boyfriend. I ended up having a boyfriend for the first month, then I was there for three years without one.'

Although Darren got a great deal from his time in Melbourne, he felt the need to return to his country Queensland roots.

'Well my grandmother is not well and my sister just had a baby. I have a connection to the land. I just feel very strongly about being here right now.'

Living west of Mackay on his parent's sugarcane farm, Darren and his brother are about to undertake a major fencing project on the property. Here, Darren gets to be on the land he grew up on, as well as pursue his passion in life: arts therapy.

'I just do it because I have a real affinity with self-expression.'

Not only is Darren using arts therapy with local disabled people, he is looking at trialing coming out workshops with an arts therapy focus. In many ways this is a way for him to step back into active LGBT community life.

'I just got burnt out.'

Darren is certainly not alone. On my travels in regional and rural Australia, most people say they leave LGBT community organisations and groups due to burn out, bad experiences and/or a lack of recognition.

One of the ways Darren has dipped his toe in the LGBT waters of Mackay is through the local Rainbow Youth Mackay (RYM) group. I sat for a morning tea of sorts with him at Pioneer River, the setting for gatherings of RYM. It's here that an impressive public space project has recently been completed, and I joked with Darren that this would be the most stunning setting for an LGBT youth group in Australia.

We're seated at a stainless steel picnic table on a wooden platform by the slowly moving Pioneer River. Although the massive space is covered, the morning sun warms us both. But I would have been wrong to think LGBT groups like RYM were relatively recent in Mackay.

'Have you heard about the Cyclonic Sisters? You have to watch it on YouTube. It's lesbians in the 1990s in Mackay.'

Later I sit down and watch a fascinating Youtube clip documenting the history of lesbian women gathering in Mackay from 1991. This two-part video charts the beginnings of organised lesbian activity in Mackay to a newspaper ad in the Saturday paper that set local women who love women ablaze.

Day 129

Wednesday, 30ᵗʰ June – Mackay QLD to Biggenden QLD = 668kms

By the time I reach Biggenden, some eight hours drive from Mackay, it's dark and I'm starving. Lucky for me my host, Jono, has been tracking my progress to coordinate a hot meal on arrival.

'Oh please, that's what we do in the country.'

Even though we've never met face to face, I feel like I know Jono. In his capacity as a journalist in LGBT media, Jono and I have spoken a few times for articles that he has written, which I have to thank for many responses from Queenslanders.

Jono was actually one of the first people to contact me about my tour after it was announced. Eager to share the story of himself and his partner Vinny, I was invited to stay with them months before I even arrived in Queensland. For my part, I was eager to hear their story in order to share some good news – we don't hear often enough the stories of LGBT people thriving outside of the metropolitan east coast.

Sitting at his big dining room table with twin Labradors Sappho and Hedwig, lying at our feet, Jono admits he'd thought that he was on a unique odyssey when he and Vinny moved to rural Queensland.

'I couldn't believe it when I heard about what you were doing. I seriously thought we were the only gay couple ever to have moved from the city to country Queensland.'

He and Vinny, then a young medical student, met 5 years ago at a street art performance on a bridge in Brisbane.

Taking advantage of a scholarship whilst finishing his studies, reality kicked in with the fine print: by taking up the scholarship, Vinny had agreed to work as a doctor in a rural location for two years.

A talented photographer and filmmaker, Jono decided that he would document his journey into rural Queensland with Vinny. And so the documentary, *The Doctor's Wife*, was born.

Watching trailers for the documentary you get a sense of the original journey that Jono and Vinny undertook to nearby Munduberra (about 45 minutes from Biggenden), five hours drive from Brisbane and home to about 2000 people.

'What makes you nervous?' Jono asked in the trailer.

'I've never been to Munduberra,' Vinny responded. 'What makes you nervous?'

'Uh, we're gay and we're going to rural Queensland …'

Being an openly gay couple was not the only challenge that Jono and Vinny faced when they arrived in Munduberra. What they found was a community who had not been overly happy with their doctors in the past and felt that those doctors and their wives were reluctant to get involved in the community.

For Vinny I suspect it was arguably 'easier' than it was for Jono. Vinny's challenge was to be a great doctor, and this was something he is said to have done incredibly well. In rural Australia, good doctors are few and far between, and news soon spread about Vinny.

I see first hand the very long hours that Vinny works with precious few breaks; he drops in for dinner before returning to the practice. Jono tells me a 10-minute lunch break in a 12 hour day is commonplace.

Yet for Jono the challenge was to find a role as the partner of the local doctor. Stories abound of doctor's wives who spent as much time away from Munduberra as possible and a vibe that they were 'too good' for the locals rubbed everyone the wrong way.

'Usually doctors and their wives come to town and they'll separate themselves.'

Somehow Jono knew that this was not going to be his approach. As down-to-earth as they come, he decided to jump right in and get his hands dirty. The locals noticed straight away.

A small yet significant social earthquake went through the town the first week when Jono and Vinny turned up at the local pub for a meal on the Friday night. One local café owner shared her first impression.

'We thought, *What are you doing here?* The doctor and his wife haven't eaten here in 20 years.'

In addition to supporting Vinny's local medical centre as business practice manager, Jono set about a plan to immerse himself in all things Munduberra, taking great care to shop locally and buy locally. 'And I made sure I was seen by as many locals as possible buying local produce and products.'

If there was an event, an opening, a wedding or a funeral, Jono turned up, even if Vinny was unable to attend because of his incredibly punishing hours as the local doctor.

Day 130

Thursday, 1ˢᵗ July – Biggenden QLD (day trip to Munduberra QLD)

Local hairdresser Sally, explains how she first met Jono.

'He was a little more nervous than me, maybe because he'd had a hairdresser in Brisbane for a very long time and he was a little bit worried about what I might do to him. But yeah, after the first do, it was all good.'

We're in a café on Munduberra's main drag, Lyon Street, that Sally and her four sisters are about to open. Relaxed, funny and warm, it wasn't long before Jono formed friendships with them all, thanks to many wines on the back porch I'm told.

When I arrived to stay with Jono and Vinny, the move from Munduberra to Biggenden (45 minutes drive east and a population of 500) is still fresh. It would be fair to say that both Jono and Vinny are still grieving the Queensland Health-orchestrated move from a community they had become a part of. Being forced to leave their newfound Munduberran home to Biggenden hurts more than they're letting on.

Today I get a glimpse into why the move has shaken their worlds, and how much the locals miss them. As we walk Lyon Street, the first words to pass everyone's lips are hopeful.

'Are you back now?'

Stoically, and repeatedly, a saddened Jono tells them, 'No'.

Jono explained to me yesterday that he was going down the street but he might take a while.

'Everyone loves stopping for a chat. I went to check the Post Office box and came back with a bed. It should have taken ten minutes and I didn't even end up checking the Post Office box.'

Local Munduberran, Doreen, as rough as hessian underpants and as lovely as anyone I've met on my tour so far, tells me the impact of Jono and Vinny on Munduberra and why they are held with such genuine affection.

'They don't judge you here on who you are, they judge you here on how you treat people. We're a town of 2000 people, so we all need to get along. And because of that, we are probably more tolerant here than you would find in larger places.'

Repeating a pattern that I've observed time and again, the number one thing that makes a difference is contribution to the local community.

As soon as the locals found out that Jono had multimedia talents, funding was found for him to run a school holiday program for young people interested in making films. Every young person had a DVD at the end of their time and a positive stir happened throughout Munduberra and led to requests from other nearby locales. So much so that Jono is now seriously considering setting up a company to work in rural Queensland on various multimedia projects (in his 'spare time'?).

Although they contributed differently, both Jono and Vinny became real people to the town of Munduberra. Materialising into flesh and blood, Jono and Vinny weren't the gay couple that no-one sees or knows because they were scared of the locals or thought they were better than them. As real people, it is impossible for the locals not to like this couple, gay or not.

'We know them, we like them. These two boys, I just love 'em. Just like my sons.'

Day 131

Friday, 2ⁿᵈ July – Biggenden QLD to Brisbane QLD = 286 kms

Jono has driven me about 10 minutes outside of Biggenden to a spot on a dirt track. It's a country Queensland landscape that Jono believes is perfect for what he has in mind: a photo shoot.

When he floated this idea, I explained that I have this uncanny ability to stiffen and be completely unnatural when a camera is on me. Jono quickly negates this concern.

'When I do a shoot it's all about me. I'll tell you exactly what you'll be doing and you have to do exactly as I say.'

Eventually I loosen up and respond to Jono's direction, a Hamlet-inspired portrayal of me.

'I want to bring out all these things I see in you that your work doesn't allow: the funny, shy and everyday side of Dan.'

Spending a few days with Jono has left me feeling both fortunate and disappointed; fortunate that I've met someone who I could imagine being lifelong friends with and disappointed that I have to move on. I explain this to Jono, observing that it's rare that I get a chance to talk about things other than the basics about my tour.

Last night, I stayed up until 2.30am talking with Jono and a friend about the moment I first knew it was OK to be gay. Asked whether or not I had a man in my life, I answered, 'I am in a relationship with my tour. And occasionally he allows me to see other people.'

'But Daniel,' Jono said. 'You can't spoon a tour!'

Day 132

Saturday, 3rd July – Brisbane QLD to Laidley QLD = 84kms

Josh's mum Nerida is fussing over me. She gets up from her chair to fetch me a blanket to keep me warm; it's dropped to around 1 degree Celcius according to news reports. With the blanket over my legs and Wimbledon on the TV, I melt a little: it looks exactly like the patchwork blanket my older brother, older sister and I all successively owned growing up.

Next, a hot beverage.

'How do you have your Milo love? What? Water and milk!? You can't have that. I couldn't have that. I have all milk.'

Josh had an immediately supportive response from his parents after coming out at school as a 16 year old. Now 22, Josh is back at home with his parents, about 90 minutes drive west from Brisbane, after a stint in metropolitan Queensland.

I met Josh in Copenhagen, Denmark during the 2nd World Out Games. He'd been excited for months about my arrival. His parents had no choice but to be excited too, because I drove to Laidley knowing that I was to join them all for an old-fashioned roast meal.

In yet another display of the hospitality with which I've been 'blessed' on this tour, I was warmly welcomed to Josh's family home by his parents and family pets, Boof and Muffy. I'm invited to sit by Josh's father, Kevin, who talks to me about his life in the military with a proud, reassuring warmth. He also talks about Josh's coming out.

'I remember the afternoon well. He had already told his mum. I wasn't sure if he was going to tell me. I don't know if he knew how to approach me on that. His mum told me when we were sitting out the front. I thought I was pretty calm and collected, so when Josh walked out I told him that I knew. He broke down a bit, but I told him we would work through it whichever way it goes. But I'm very proud of Josh. Always have been, always will be.'

Soon, Nerida, serves up a delectable roast that takes me back to my mum's in Geelong. I chuckle as I watch Nerida smack Josh for picking at the food before everything is served up.

'Joshua!'

Tired from two days of work and top-level softball (Josh has represented Australia internationally in softball), Josh retires for a nap ahead of watching the Wimbledon women's final with me. Kevin heads to bed at his customary early hour which leaves Nerida and I to talk while she cross-stitches a teddy bear image, occasionally handing me newspaper clippings of her son with pride.

Nerida explains how things have changed for Josh in his small hometown over the years.

'You know he lost his first job when the boss found out he was gay. He was still at school. He was just working in the local little supermarket. But everyone knows he's gay down there now and they love him.'

Intelligent, attractive, athletically gifted and with a down-to-earth charm that is obviously thanks to his parents, Josh was encouraged to enter the 2008 Mr Gay Brisbane competition and Nerida and Kevin proudly attended the final at Brisbane's Wickham Hotel. It was their first time in a gay bar.

'We were the first parents ever to go to the competition and support their kid. We supported our kids in softball, why wouldn't we support him in that?'

To everyone's surprise, Josh won. And family support was what Josh acknowledged right away after the announcement.

In an interview with *QNews*, Nerida said, 'We are really proud of him. His granddad would be really proud of him too. He passed away on this day twelve months ago. I know Josh dedicated his win tonight to his granddad.'

But a piece in the local newspaper celebrating the achievement was not welcomed by everyone in town. An anonymous letter was written to the editor not one, not two but three weeks later. With religious overtones, the letter made Kevin furious, as Nerida explains.

'I've never seen Kevin so fired up. He went straight to the computer. I said to Josh, *You know what your father is like with you kids.*'

One heartfelt, considered and moving letter later, Kevin sparked off a predominantly positive flood of local support for Josh and other non-heterosexual young men and women. Some other parents even felt encouraged to write about their own experiences as the parent of a gay or lesbian child.

Even though most have moved on, Nerida still thinks there are some locals whose attitude won't change.

'I've never told Josh, but when it all came out, I was walking down the street with him. There was this father and mother with their little girl, and I actually saw them grab her and take her to the other side of the street. Can you believe that?'

Day 133

Sunday, 4th July – Brisbane QLD

There is a fortnightly gay night in Brisbane called Fluffy. Comically, the venue is called 'Family'. It's still early here at Fluffy@Family, so we get in quickly and head upstairs.

I'm here with two new friends, Ed and his partner Sean, both from Hawaii. Ed had been eager to meet me once he'd heard about my tour.

'So how long have you been going for now?'

'133 days. I only know that because today is officially half way.'

'Wow! It's decided then, we have to take you out to celebrate.'

I'm talking with Ed when I see him. As soon as The Model turns at the bar and looks in our direction I've stopped listening to Ed. Soon I'm hyperventilating as he makes his way over. Who is that forward?

Phew, he knows Ed.

'How have you been Ed?'

As Ed starts his second sentence The Model stops paying attention and turns to me.

'And who are you?'

At first I was taken with his eyebrows, now it's his cheekiness and energy. Ed's not stupid and quietly slips away. The banter continues as he works out who I am.

'So let me get this right; you've written a book, so you're intelligent, you're driving around the country, so you do fascinating work, and you're hot *and* single? Please tell me what's wrong with this picture. Hello Daddy!'

Can he see me blush in the dark?

The Model reluctantly departs to find his best friend and says, 'find me later'. I guess when you are young and hot you can get away with that.

When I find him later before I leave, he's defensive. All I do is ask for his number so that I could ask him out for a cuppa whilst I'm here. After all, I'm in Brisbane for two weeks.

'Look, there are plenty of other guys here who'd love to go home with you.'

'I haven't met them and I'm not interested in them. I'm just seeing if you're interested in a cuppa at some stage or not. It's OK if you're not interested.'

We swap numbers.

'I'm sorry. I've just met some dicks lately. I'll call you.'

Unexpectedly The Model leans in and kisses me goodbye. I grab his arm so that the kiss softly lingers.

Day 134

Monday, 5th July – Brisbane QLD

'Hi, this might sound strange but I found this mobile phone last night and wanted to find out how to return it to the owner ...'

Luckily the mobile phone I found outside Fluffy@Family has 'Home' saved as a number. A woman with a morning croak in her voice answers.

'Aw, thank god. He got up this morning and needs it for work. He'll be rapt.'

Around 45 minutes later a sheepish older straight man turns up and thankfully picks up the phone. Others would suggest a man losing his mobile out the front of Fluffy@Family is unlikely to be straight, but I'll give him the benefit of the doubt.

Up early, despite a late-ish night, I start planning my fortnight in Brisbane and work through a backlog. I'm drowning in correspondence: follow-ups from where I've been; people to contact and schedule meetings with in Brisbane; and contacts for all that is to come in the second half of the tour.

I contemplate this and start making a 'to-do' list at the blue, laminated bench in Denis' kitchen. Denis is my incredibly generous and hospitable host for the fortnight. I'm lucky enough to have a comfortable bed in the guest room of his and his partner's spacious home in the inner northern suburbs of Brisbane. Their small yet significant Puggles, Yogi and Alba, provide background noise at all times.

Denis had contacted Rodney Croome to ask how he could help the LGBT cause. Rodney immediately recommended he investigate and consider my tour. An e-mail followed:

'We're both mighty impressed with the work you are all doing and have contributed to your tour through Uniting Care. If the tour takes you to Brisbane and you need accommodation while here, we have plenty of room in our house.'

I take up his offer of freshly cooked bread, munch and make notes in front of my laptop. Denis plays a radio podcast in the background. I couldn't feel more ready to play catch-up.

Day 135

Tuesday, 6th July – Brisbane QLD

'This year we've had young people coming out at 13, 14 and 15.'

It took me about 25 minutes to ride my bike from Denis' in Lutwyche down to Fortitude Valley, or 'The Valley' as locals call it. I brought my 1970s Toyosha (Toyota Auto Company) racer along in the hope of riding as much as I could around the various locales I visit. Brisbane is perfect for this with a range of bike paths to and from the city.

I'm now having a cuppa with Steph, who runs Open Doors Youth Services, a Brisbane-based service providing support for LGBT young people.

Open Doors did just that recently, Steph explains, with 45 young people coming along, 17 of them for the very first time. Steph, other workers and Open Doors regulars were on hand to make everyone feel as welcome as possible. To the surprise of some, there were parents in attendance.

'Recently a dad turned up to the Open Day with his 15-year-old son … He didn't come out to them, tthey actually found out he was gay, because there was porn on the computer at home … They said to him, *We don't mind if you're gay, it's really OK, but please don't look at porn on the computer because it means there will be [computer] viruses. But you need to meet some other young people and get some information.* I was like, *Oh my god, I love you guys. You are amazing.* I told them that usually parents are the last people to know. They said, *Yeah, we love our kid, but we see he's struggling.*'

Yet for all the great work that they do, Open Doors struggles like so many LGBT organisations to maintain funding and services. Despite the fact that they are not funded to do so, Open Doors feels pressure as the peak LGBT Youth organisation for Queensland. Between direct support, advocacy, research, community development and requests for professional development there is a lot of need that cannot be met.

'We're not funded to do that, but … we struggle to get any funding. There is currently no LGBT service funded at a state level. There is a lack of recognition of LGBT young people's needs, and that this should be recognised with significant funding. Sometimes mainstream organisations are more successful when they have their brand behind them, such as Relationships Australia and *headspace*. We are a gay organisation so we struggle for legitimacy a bit and are thought to have an agenda.'

Still, Steph pinches herself sometimes.

'I love being out in every aspect of my life with young people because I couldn't do that in other organisations in my other roles. I sort of fell into the work, but I love it. You start to see them becoming the adult they are going to be. I think a lot of adults forget how tough it can be to be a teenager. I love their energy and want to see them get through their 'shit' years. Knowing how hard the world is out there, seeing how we can make that easier.'

And reminding me of describing myself in *Beyond 'That's So Gay'*, as a 'professional poofta' and 'palatable poofta', I hear Steph refer to herself similarly.

'I call myself a professional gay. I'm a member of the community but I work in the community. We talk about boundaries a lot here, that it is a potential blurring. I have to think about what's work and what's not. It always takes a while to learn that. But seriously, it's great to be gay.'

Day 136

Wednesday, 7ᵗʰ July – Brisbane QLD

It's the second time I've seen The Model since we swapped numbers at Fluffy. Yesterday we had a hot chocolate and vanilla slice down on the shore at New Farm. I found out he doesn't 'do marshmallows'.

Today is his final night before he flies out for uni holidays, which sees him head to Sydney and Melbourne. Although bummed, The Model has my attention. Sometimes I look into his eyes and get a glimpse of his story; although his eyes are big and bright, there's a sadness I don't yet understand. It only makes me want to know more.

We meet at the Museum of Brisbane, after I suggest we see the 'Prejudice and Pride' exhibition. It's been put together to commemorate the 20th anniversary of homosexuality's decriminalisation in Queensland. Although there are audio-visual displays, I'm all for the black and white photos that show life of LGBT people for over 100 years.

I'm pretty sure Brisbane's immediate LGBT future looks bright. Walking here, I and other men were set upon by a group of flirtatious young men in their late teens offering 'Free Hugs'. They were not fooling anyone, or at least me. It wouldn't end in a simple hug; I'd have been lucky to have escaped with my dignity. I chuckled, blushed at their advances and wondered why I hadn't thought of the same thing when I was their age.

I'm pleasantly surprised The Model accepted my invitation, a prelude to dinner at the Barracks. Perhaps because it's his last night, he lowers his deflector shield and we talk for so long, with still so much to say, that we continue at Three Monkeys in West End.

'Just as long as you know, this is not a date.'

Me: 'Whatever you need to tell yourself …'

The night comes to an end and, with it, our platonic affair.

Day 137

Thursday, 8th July – Brisbane QLD

Steph has invited me to attend the Open Doors 'drop-in', a space where young people between 12 and 18 years are free to attend, talk to a handful of support workers, catch up with their friends and just 'chill out'.

A lively, energetic atmosphere greets me and every other person who comes through the door.

I sit amongst young Ls, Gs, Bs and Ts and we talk about coming out, their experiences at school and why they came to Open Doors. On this afternoon many of the young people are relatively new. The 'drop-in' is usually a stepping stone to one of Open Doors' other programs for LGBT young people.

Steph explains what young people typically coming to Open Doors are seeking.

'What they are most looking for is connection, meeting other young people. They want to know that they are not on their own, to not feel so alone whether that be a relationship or friends.'

I get talking to a young Aboriginal gay man, Blake, after Steph has introduced me to the crowd of young people gathered around a large table on all manner of couches and chairs. As you would expect, it's colourful furniture.

I explain I'd been through Mt Isa and Townsville on my way here and Blake stops as he walks across the room. He turns.

'There's gay kids in Townsville?'

Blake has recently moved to Brisbane on a scholarship to study performing arts with an elite Indigenous program.

I ask him what auditions were like.

'I sang 'Words' by the Bee Gees. But not like them. I sang it like Jessica Mauboy on *Australian Idol.* You have to YouTube it. I did it just like her.'

186

Day 138

Friday, 9th July – Brisbane QLD

I regret being here. I was invited, kindly, by the President of a Gay and
Lesbian Business Network to one of their first gatherings. If there is anything
I'm uncomfortable doing, it's small talk with people in suits, especially if I am
in shorts and a t-shirt.

About 20 of us gather on the first floor of The Wickham Hotel, one of
three LGBT venues in Brisbane. The safest place for me is at the bar and I
lean against it and watch people eagerly swap business cards. Every so often
someone comes up to get a drink, looks over and gives me a business card
after a pity-inspired pitch about their business.

I'm still not clear on why I'm here and tell myself I'll wait it out 30
minutes and then leave.

'So what do you do?'

Great, now the cute barman is pitying me as well. I'm sick of my own
voice and repeating myself tonight, so I decide to be ambiguous.

'I'm driving around Australia at the moment. I'm just here in Brisbane for
a bit and then I'll continue on.'

'Oh, really? Are you the guy that's driving around doing the homophobia
thing in the bush?'

I laugh.

'Yes, that's me. How do you know that?'

'I'm a barman, lots of down time and I like to read the gay press. I liked
the article they did on you.'

Between The Barman serving customers and going to collect glasses I
answer his questions about my work. I watch him, thinking he looks like one
of those teenage skateboarders who still skate in their early 20s. His lean,
athletic frame moves effortlessly like he's on wheels. He's easy to talk to. He
has soft dark eyes, lightly freckled skin and an easy, toothy grin. I've always
had a little thing for redheads. At one stage I think I see The Barman
checking me out, but I remind myself it's his job to flirt.

Even so, I'm done with awkwardly standing at the bar.

Me: 'Hey, it's been a pleasure chatting with you. Thanks for the company.'

'No problem, I really enjoyed it. I could have kept chatting to be honest.'

Me: 'Well we could always grab a cuppa or a drink if you'd like.'

He physically stiffens and hops back with his hands up.

'I'm really sorry, I have a boyfriend, I, I, um, can't.'

Me: 'Relax, relax. I said a cuppa or a drink. I didn't ask for anything else.'

I smile to show I'm OK with the rejection, yet immediately regret asking. 'Awkward Dan' strikes again.

'Look, I don't normally do this but …'

I watch The Barman write his number down on a small piece of paper with his left hand. He hands it to me with his right.

'We can meet for a coffee if you want.'

Me: 'Are you sure …?'

'Yes.'

Day 139

Saturday, 10th July – Brisbane QLD

It's now the third time this week I've ridden into The Valley to head to Open Doors. This afternoon it's to attend Jelly Beans, a regular gathering for gender questioning young people.

'The workers and managers here at Open Doors knew there were young people slipping through the cracks. Before Jelly Beans, you'd be hard pressed to find a trans young person coming to drop-in …'

Joan tells me that young trans people were also not going to transgender support organisations.

'The services that are around are more geared towards older trans people. They also focus on a medical model of transition. They'd say, *This is your ultimate goal. Your ultimate goal is surgery.* We wanted to give young people a safe place. It's not an automatic referral to the gender service. It's about talking, networking, communicating and giving young people a space where they fit in. It's basically a social group. Let 'em come, let 'em talk. I'll be there if they need anything.'

It's warm so we all head into Open Doors' courtyard to sit around a table with a layer of dust and a few well-used ashtrays. One young trans person excitedly tells everyone of coming out.

'I just came out to my step-mother on Wednesday night. We had, like, this hour and a half conversation and it was really good.'

Joan points out that this is a rare situation.

'The main thing [for trans young people] is usually coming out to parents, and parental reactions. Far too many end up with nowhere to live. Finding homeless accommodation for trans young people can be a nightmare. An absolute nightmare.'

The same trans young person tells us about coming out on Facebook.

'Everyone was really cool about it. All except for, like, one person.'

Joan says this is common.

'When they come out to their friends, their friends are mostly OK with it. It's usually interacting with the adults where young people have the troubles. That's also reflected with agencies when I've been advocating for trans young people.'

One agency, for example, refused service unless that young person stayed with their previous gender and went to church. Joan explained that this would be a problem given that young person had been raised in the Pagan faith.

'Interestingly in the trans community there are a high number of practicing Pagans. It's about the acceptance. The basic thing of the Pagan faith is that you do what you do and don't harm others. You're not hurting anyone so it's all OK.'

Advocating for trans young people is something that Joan takes seriously, yet she can also see the humorous side occasionally.

'When I'm supporting young people and I'm out and about, in a number of places I've been asked if I'm their mother or if I'm related.'

I chuckle thinking about just that as I ride the hilly route back to Dennis' in the quiet streets of Ludwyche. I ponder what it might be like if this was my daily commute and realise I'm here for another week of freshly homemade sourdough bread each morning with butter and vegemite. That taste in my mouth gives me just enough energy to tackle those hills one more time on my way 'home'.

Day 140

Sunday, 11ᵗʰ July – Brisbane QLD

I'm seated at a trendy, inner city café sitting across from The Barman. He's on a hamburger stool, me a corn stool. It's a little pocket hidden behind one of two major roads that cut through Fortitude Valley, with lots of rustic brick and earnest wall art.

'Breakfast is on me. Order whatever you want.'

Me: 'That's OK, I can get mine.'

'I got lots of tips last night and you are self-funded. I'm getting you breakfast.'

I got to know this little inner-city nook, Flamingos Café, thanks to a cuppa I had with Michelle, a young lesbian studying journalism. Michelle contacted me to share her story but also ask about how she might go with a posting to Mt Isa.

Originally from Townsville, Michelle came out to her family after some intense questioning from her mother. Unlike the majority of LGBT young people I have spoken with so far, Michelle successfully evaded her mother's question of 'Are you gay?' three times (most have told of coming out after the first or second time).

Undeterred, Michelle's mother struck a fourth time when she least expected it.

'I was woken at 3am by mum. She said, *I'll be really disappointed if you are, but are you gay?*'

After telling her mum, Michelle planned to come out to her father when she was ready and her mother agreed. At first.

'A few nights later mum couldn't sleep so she woke him up during the night and said, *She's gay!* Dad said, *No she's not, don't be stupid*, rolled over and went back to sleep. Mum wakes up people a lot.'

Fully awake, Michelle's dad absorbed his wife's news the next day. Having come out to her parents, it was now time for Michelle to come out to her brothers.

'Mum rang ahead and said to my brothers, *Your sister is coming around to tell you something.* They thought, *Cool, she's finally going to come out.* My younger brother said, *That's great, but just make sure that when you go buy your motorbike that I come because I know a thing or two about motorbikes* [laughs]. The next day my older brother e-mailed me a link about biker boots and wrote, *I thought you might be interested.* So they were totally OK about it.'

As The Barman and I both devour toasted sandwiches he seems a lot more relaxed than Friday evening. He explains that his boyfriend has been overseas for quite a while. Without a bar between us I now watch him more closely and see his hand shaking every time he drinks his glass of water. The (cute) Barman is nervous? Other times he talks to my arms when he talks to me and not my face.

The Barman is an absolute delight, a charmer, a dream. No wonder he was snapped up. I'm just happy to have had a chance to connect with someone, albeit briefly and platonically. After all, I'm becoming an expert on platonic affairs.

We are headed in the same direction so I offer to walk my racer with him until his gym.

'I'm trying to put on some weight,' he confesses.

As we walk he gets curious.

'So do you meet any guys as you drive around?'

I tell him my standard lines: I'm in a relationship with my tour and occasionally he lets me see other people; the campsite rule of leaving things better than the way in which I found them; and, I'm never in town long enough to form any lasting connection. He hugs me goodbye, and stays in my arms a little longer than I expect.

'That's a shame, you're such a handsome man. Shall we catch up again?'

Day 141

Monday, 12th July – Brisbane QLD (day trip to Maroochydore QLD)

'There is a little community in Rockhampton but it's not very big. I think it's hard to be gay in a small community. I thought, *I can't do this. I can't be here. I have to move to Brisbane. I have to see what it's all about.* I found it challenging. You lose your family, friends. And living in a big city for the first time. There are 3 or 4 gay places and they are open every night. In Rockhampton you had one small gay bar. You had to hide around the corner and run in, because it was around the corner from a heavy metal bar.'

Kerry, an Aboriginal lesbian woman, found it difficult to adjust to life in Brisbane without her support networks after moving from Rockhampton. 'It was hard not to have my family and friends here. So the way I got around that was to play sport. I found women's sport, it was great having team members who are gay.'

Yet despite her first steps into lesbian culture, Kerry felt that her own culture was being lost.

'Because you don't have your own culture around you, you adapt into the mainstream. So it becomes about the gay culture because there is no Indigenous culture around.'

I'm eager to talk to Kerry because whilst teachers and workers talk about the presence of young Indigenous men who identify as gay, bisexual or transgender (Sistagal), they haven't yet talked about the presence of young Indigenous women who identify as lesbian or bisexual.

'The [Indigenous] cultural expectations are that women are the lookerafterers of families, to be child bearers.'

Through her involvement with Open Doors the service has seen an increase of young Indigenous LGBT people accessing things like drop-ins and other programs.

One of Kerry's successes was getting a group of LGBT young people to play in a local football competition: Oztag (tag rugby). The team is a mixture of Indigenous and non-Indigenous LGBT young people, and the combination was challenging at first.

'After an Indigenous retreat we brought the group back to Open Doors for a BBQ with the other young people. There were some really racist comments about the group coming back. But after they'd played footy together that stopped. Perhaps they'd only had bad experiences before with Indigenous people.'

The result was clear.

'So these young people who were making those racist comments were now playing footy with the Indigenous kids and making friends. I think it brought the Indigenous kids out of their shell to be able to mix with the kids.

'The young people at first copped a lot of shit and homophobia. We had it all through the competition. I think it was like the stereotype like gays can't pass a football.'

Before the competition started the team had sat down and discussed the possibility of homophobic reactions.

'We said, *We have our own code of conduct, if players experience abuse, we don't give it back. We talk to the organisers if we experience it.*'

To everyone's surprise, the team played well and made it to the Grand Final.

'Then it all changed and there was none of that *faggot* stuff. They were all friends and then mixing in. We were a good team and we could play football, and they didn't expect that.'

And it was not just sporting prowess that did it. Kerry observed changing attitudes and behaviour.

'The way that the young people handled the homophobia and handled themselves – they would still talk to people, play football and turn up each week. I think they got to know us as individuals and people, rather than gays.'

'But we're the minority within the minority. There is still a lot of discrimination with the gay community. Hopefully that will change one day. That's really frustrating to me. I just hope we work together instead of fighting each other. I think we'd get a lot further. In Queensland we have a long way to go.'

Day 142

Tuesday, 13th July – Brisbane QLD

The day has ended well with news on Facebook from a Japanese friend, Azusa.

'Hi Daniel! I was informed that the second edition of *School Education and Support regarding Sexual Minorities* (in Japanese) will be published soon. I revised my translation of your 'Shadows of Homophobia in Sunny Down Under' for the new edition.'

This comes as a pleasant, somewhat overdue, surprise given that I gave up a weekend and a Melbourne Cup holiday in 2008 to complete a chapter for this groundbreaking textbook for Japanese universities; the first of its kind. Almost two years later here it is in print.

The Barman and I are seated at Three Monkeys Café. We've found ourselves in a section inspired, busily so, by a cross between Turkey and South-East Asia. There are plenty of references to the three monkeys in questions: see, hear and speak no evil. His reaction to the news is characteristically him: low-key, polite and genuine.

'That's great news, Daniel.'

I'm keen to see him, yet even I'm surprised to see him again so soon.

'Are you hungry? Great, I want to take you somewhere for dinner. No arguments, I had a great weekend in tips.'

After dinner at his favourite Chinese restaurant on Southbank, he admits he has something to tell me.

Me: 'I'm all ears.'

'You know how I said my boyfriend is overseas? That's only partly true. We actually broke up before he left. It's been all too messy and it's just easier to tell guys I have a boyfriend so I don't have to deal with it all. Sorry, I hate lying, it's just ...'

Me: 'No apologies necessary, you didn't even know me when you said it.'

We walk back to Bruce, and I realise now that it's all too soon for him. We walk under the streetlight and I look up surprised at how orange the light is. I look down and The Barman is looking serious.

'Can I ask you a question?'

Me: 'Of course you can. You don't even have to ask that.'

'Can I kiss you?'

Gobsmacked. Figuratively and literally.

After dropping him home and a prolonged goodnight kiss I anticipate the text message I'll get as I jump into bed on the other side of town.

'I'm in bed here asking why I didn't invite you to stay the night. Good night handsome.'

Day 143

Wednesday, 14th July – Brisbane QLD

I arrive at the training room of the Queensland Association for Healthy Communities (QAHC) on a cool Brisbane evening. Immediately I'm offered some food provided for the trainees, a hot cuppa and a warm introduction.

I've been asked in as guest speaker for trainee telephone counsellors for Queensland's Gay and Lesbian Welfare Association (GLWA).

One of the trainers, Vic, explains that telephone counsellors are often stepping stones to other services, projects and organisations, with sometimes their most important role being to just check in with callers.

I spend just under an hour sharing what I'd found in the first 20 weeks of my 38 weeks on the road. I focus on what teachers and health professionals had found useful, and what 'thriving' LGBT people in regional and rural Australia seem to have in common.

It's clear that the GLWA team has worked hard because the atmosphere is warm, welcoming and conversational. I feel relaxed, which unfortunately for them means I'm even more verbose than usual. I appreciate their questions which are more than: 'So what are you driving?'

I leave the evening feeling slightly guilty after having a meal, two cuppas, countless toffees and then being loaded up with pens, badges and a generous donation towards my fuel for the tour (especially given how organisations like GLWA often run on the smell of an oily rag).

I'm excited as I leave because I'm off to see The Barman. He wants to head up to the Mt Coot-tha Lookout. Driving up he finds a natural break in the conversation and drops in this remark.

'Did you want to stay over tonight?'

Day 144

Thursday, 15ᵗʰ July – Brisbane QLD

Feeling more content than I have in months, The Barman's goodbye kiss still fresh on my lips, I speak to Connor at QAHC's Brisbane offices along with three other workers. The time and expertise they share at such short notice are very much appreciated. I notice Connor for two reasons. One, I wonder if he's the real 'Condoman', an Indigenous sexual health superhero that I'd seen when I first started LGBT work in the summer of 1996-7. Two, he is almost falling asleep as I talk about my project and what I've found so far. To be fair I sometimes send myself to sleep when I'm talking.

This changes when he finally asks, 'If you don't mind Brother, can you tell me if you have spoken to any Indigenous communities?'

I explain my time with the ATSI workers in the Northern Territory, recounting my trip to a remote Indigenous community (and an invite to another) and the conversations I'd had with various workers. Suddenly his body language changes, as he sits forward and starts looking at me rather than my general direction. Clearly I'm not a white gay boy driving around the country just talking to other gay white boys. Not that I don't feel it is a fair enough question.

Whereas it seems easier to be gay or lesbian than transgender in metropolitan Australia, Connor believes the opposite might be true for remote Indigenous communities.

'Sistagals are clouding gay men in the community. It is easier to be Sistagal in many communities. I'm one of the few guys who'll stand up and say, *I'm gay.* When I go home to the islands I take on the woman's role. I have 42 nieces and nephews.'

This 'clouding' of the gay identity that Connor talks about becomes clearer when Sistagals arrive in metropolitan Australia.

'They drop the Sistagal identity when they come to the city.'

The QAHC workers refer to this as men having a 'Transitional Suitcase', where they have one identity that they carry back to their communities and another that they take to the city.

Despite it being a challenge, Connor still mixes it with the men in his community.

'I'll go hunting with the boys and stuff. They might slip in the odd joke, but it's hard for them too.'

Connor believes he is being pushed into an identity that doesn't fit.

'They are trying to put people into boxes. Brother, I'm struggling to fit into my own clothes, let alone other people's expectations.'

Someone who doesn't have expectations is The Barman. I arrive back at his place to find him busily preparing dinner.

Me: 'Can I help?'

'No handsome. I'm happy to. Seeing you happy makes me happy.'

Day 145

Friday, 16th July – Brisbane QLD

It's a short ride in from The Barman's place to my meeting in the CBD with Stephen Page, a lawyer who has been working with LGBT clients and community groups for the last 18 years. We meet at a café in the foyer of his building.

'I think probably the biggest change that you can identify is that the legal system is much more accepting of gay and lesbian relationships than it has ever been. Going back 20 years in custody disputes, if you were gay or lesbian it was thought that you were putting the child at risk.'

Whilst the legal system advances, there is some way to go.

'There is still discrimination … It's largely gone but there is some still some there. It's still an issue for clients, and for me as a lawyer, that you go before a judge who might be homophobic. You live in hope that they are going to be OK, but ultimately you don't know. Too often gay and lesbian clients worry about whether the lawyer they see will be homophobic.'

With changes in federal and state laws over the years, the legal fraternity have been exposed to greater numbers of LGBT clients than ever before, and Stephen believes this has helped effect change.

'I've had many lawyers come up who have also worked with gay and lesbian clients and say, *They're just like everyone else!* Or virgin lawyers. They ask, *What's it like working with gay clients?*

Nowadays Stephen finds himself mainly looking at relationship break-ups ('arguing over property … money … about kids …'), surrogacy and lesbian couples having a baby together ('the simple answer is: don't have sex with a bloke …').

One area that still has a long way to go, according to Stephen, is transgender people and the discrimination they face.

'It's difficult for transgender people. It shouldn't be.'

By the time I leave Stephen's building it's a warm Brisbane afternoon, despite being the middle of winter.

The Barman recommends we meet for lunch along Southbank, a focal point for tourists, arts and local folk, and then a visit to the Queensland Art Gallery. It's a part of the world you want to be in on a day like today. It's clear that romance has blossomed and here I am walking hand in hand with, arguably, Brisbane's most loved barman.

With my beloved vintage racer in one hand and The (beloved) Barman in the other, we walk by a bench where a father and his two sons are seated. As tends to happen with homophobes, they wait until we're a few metres past them with our backs turned before it comes: an audible wolf whistle.

I immediately stiffen, let go of The Barman's hand, swing my bike around and start to walk back. The Barman appeals, 'Daniel! Leave it, please.'

Within a few seconds I'm standing in front of three seated people. The father and his youngest son, around 10 or 11 years, both look away and down the river away from me. The eldest son, perhaps 17 or 18 years, looks up with a pleading look for mercy. I ask with what I hope is an urgent, curious tone.

Me: 'Is there a problem?'

'No mate, no. No problem at all.'

Me: 'No problem? You sure?'

'Yes. No problem.'

Me: 'That's great, I'm glad.'

I walk back to The Barman, find his hand and continue walking.

Me: 'He was wolf whistling you because he thought you're hot.'

The Barman laughs.

Later, pausing at his periodically clunky-sounding fridge, he explains how he'd objected to me approaching the whistler and had sincerely wanted me to leave it be. Now he remembers the young man's face and response.

'You know you have probably changed the way he'll think about this for the rest of his life. Really.'

I look at him with a slight smile and cross my upheld fingers.

And then I go in for a much needed hug.

Day 146

Saturday, 17th July – Brisbane QLD

After shaking my hand, Jo/e sits back down at an outdoor table. We've decided to meet on such a clear warm day along Southbank, at a café almost in the shadows of Brisbane's answer to the London Eye: The Wheel of Brisbane.

'I always knew I was different, I never fit in with the other boys. I never really fit in with the girls either. When I was a teenager I started questioning all the stuff that teenagers go through. I never felt like a straight guy, but I never felt attracted to males either. So it was a very confusing time.'

Finding out he had a brain tumour at 15 provided only temporary relief.

'It was almost a case of, *This is why I've always felt different*'. But talking to other people with different forms of brain tumour and cancer, I was still very different.'

It wasn't about sexual orientation for Jo/e.

'Knowing I wasn't straight, but not being gay, I thought, *What the fuck am I?* I thought I might be bi but that didn't fit either. And for a little while there I thought I was a male lesbian, but that didn't go down well with anyone I told. So I basically just tried to keep it to myself. I tried to fit in with a lot of different groups, and whilst some were accepting, I never felt I was really part of the group.'

Unfortunately school did not provide a safe and supportive environment.

'I changed school twice because I didn't fit. I was constantly picked on. I changed from a co-ed school to an all-boys Catholic school. That was a bad move for me. They tried to toughen me up. Then when I changed to a co-ed Catholic high school, I didn't fit, but I wasn't … let's just say the shit wasn't as thick. At the all-boys school it wasn't just the students that made it clear that I didn't belong by what they said and their attitudes. And when dad went to the school to complain about bullying, it was a case of, *We need to toughen him up.*'

Jo/e has strong ideas about teachers.

'There's a big thing at the moment with bullying. Young people who are gender diverse cop a lot of aggression in schools. That's something where teachers should be more proactive. With teachers I think sometimes they can get lazy. I know through talking to kids now, you'll get some really great teachers who really care about their kids and look after them. Then you get some who have probably been in the profession for a little too long and are just punching their time cards.'

Jo/e looks down for most of the interview, focusing mostly on his can of cola. He describes hours of *going almost crazy* on the internet to find out who and what he might be. This led Jo/e to Brisbane-based support groups for transgender people. Yet this still didn't fit.

'I'm someone who is neither male or female exclusively. Some things about me are male, some things about me are female. I don't switch between both, I'm in the middle.'

'For a long time they just assumed I was in the confused section. Basically [the group] is for males transitioning to females and all gender queer people are seen to be confused. Things were said to me that were rather nasty. Most of the people in the group were reasonably fine with me. They'd be pleasant, but wouldn't engage in normal conversations with me. One of the ladies running the group sort of said a lot of things about gender queer people. I don't want to get into what it was, a lot of it was very hurtful.'

For Jo/e the choice was simple when he heard about Freedom, a Gold Coast-based support group for transgender people. Although not Gender Queer-specific, Jo/e attended and hasn't looked back.

'I immediately felt at home. I'm accepted there. I've basically been trying to be me. It took a while for me to accept it.'

Day 147

Sunday, 18th July

'Students tell me about some gay in their family. One young guy recently tried to hook me up with his uncle. I told him it was not going to work. There were two reasons, one because I've seen your uncle, and two because I have a partner.'

Charlie is seated at Three Monkeys café, where I need loyalty points, recounting his experiences as a teacher at a school in Brisbane's outer south.

I meet Charlie for the first time, months after receiving his first e-mail. As a teacher he had shown interest in the Melbourne launch of my book back in February. He wanted to attend but also to assist in any way that he could in Brisbane. He's since jumped in the deep end.

'I joined the business network because I was looking for something to do and to meet new people. I stupidly said I'd help out and six years later I'm running it.'

As an openly gay teacher, with students, staff and parents, Charlie enjoys a position that most LGBT teachers who are partially or not out don't: he is a supported, valued member of staff.

'My first school was a Lutheran school, so I was not out with students, but I was with staff. I wasn't the only one there. Then the next two schools it wasn't a problem.'

Living locally where he worked, Charlie found his personal and professional lives blurred.

'At the time I was living in the area and I would be seen out with my partner, like at the supermarket. Then the question at school would be, *Who was that guy you were with?* I'd say, *My partner.* Other people, students, would just ask, *Hey, I heard you were gay. Is it true?* I'd say, *Yes.*'

Charlie remains at the same secondary school ever since he finished his teaching degree.

'Five years on,' I ask, 'do you ever get concerned about negative parental reactions?'

'That's difficult because it's not something I have experienced. I think what helps is it's a lower socio-economic area with a few more minority groups, so perhaps they are more open-minded to start with. I think [being openly gay] has made it easier. A lot of what I teach is based on experience. To be able to talk about it honestly makes it a lot easier. There's a lot of respect because I'm honest with the kids, and I get a lot of respect for that. I get a lot back about things that they're going through.

'I guess my character has a lot to do with it. I've proven myself as a professional person. I have some credibility with all the work I've done with the middle school. I'm not some 30-year-old weird guy working with kids, I'm with my partner of 10 years, we have property together, it puts a bit of stability onto it. Even with working on boys programs, we go away for a few days. There has never been a problem. All of the kids know, all of the parents know.'

Not that Charlie doesn't still face everyday comments and jokes.

'There are comments, but having a sense of humour, a laugh and joke with them about it has helped. They might say, *Are you going Mardi Gras?* and I'll say, *No, are you?* or *I missed it, did you enjoy it?*. There might be a kid every now and then that [reacts negatively] but when they look around and see the other 27 kids who are saying, *Whatever*, there is not a massive weight about what they've said.'

Me: 'Do you think you decided to be out first, or was it the result of the school environment?'

'The latter. The three principals I've had have been fine with it. They actually saved me once when a 12-year-old girl stood up and accused me of staring at her breasts. They actually had a laugh about it later.'

Day 148

Monday, 19th July – Brisbane QLD to (Robina) Gold Coast QLD = 83kms

Given the short distance to the Gold Coast, about an hour's drive, I decide to delay my drive for as long as possible.

We're in The Barman's king-sized bed and although my body clock has me awake, he's still asleep after a late shift at The Wickham. I move in behind him, slowly wrap myself around him and kiss the nape of his soft neck. He moves back so that we fit together even more tightly and then starts breathing heavier in his sleep. Now that's husband material.

Later in the morning I make an excuse and head out to do a tour of florists in the surrounding suburbs. I'm on a mission to find his favourite flowers, jonquils – whatever they are. Some florists don't even know what they are, others just don't have them.

I arrive back at The Barman's for our brunch empty handed and do a bad job of hiding my disappointment.

'You OK?'

I confess my plan, apologising because I'd lied and said I had to head out for something else. I'd just wanted to do something small for his hospitality warmth and company. His favourite line, 'It makes me happy that you're happy, Handsome', repeats in my head. I want to do the same for him.

Leaving him behind seems cruel, yet I have the perfect saying for the situation.

Me: 'The Germans say that you see everyone important in your life twice. I can't wait until I see you again.'

'I hope so handsome.'

My heart melts as much as he does when I take him into my arms, the ones he says over and over again that he loves so much, one final time.

My drive down south from Brisbane to the Gold Coast is not quite long enough for me. The consolation of saying goodbye to The Barman is that I'll be saying hello to a familiar face.

'Wow, you are SO gorgeous!'

Of all the greetings, this was perhaps the most positive I've received on tour. Lorraine, my Gold Coast hostess, invited me to one of her best friends' house for a roast dinner. For the record it's turkey I can smell and my hostess' friend, Sarah, seems quite pleased to meet me when she opens her front door.

'Which one are you? Gay or married?' And then over her shoulder. 'You didn't tell me he was so gorgeous.'

I walk in to greet Lorraine, then Sarah's husband, Laurie.

'Don't mind him,' she says.

I can tell I'm in for an entertaining evening, which is just what I need. Originally from the UK, Sarah, Laurie and son had purposefully moved to the suburbs of the Gold Coast rather than Sydney or Melbourne where the lure of higher paying jobs had beckoned.

'You can decide to go for the money or the lifestyle. We chose the lifestyle.'

As Laurie explains, 'You are 20 minutes from everything here. You have the beach that way and the hinterland out the back.'

Day 149

Tuesday, 20th July

'Almost every young person has been bullied in school at some stage. The drop-out rate from school at QSPACE is pretty high. A lot of them have done alternative education programs like TAFE.'

Lesley from QSPACE, a Gold Coast based support group for LGBT young people, describes a few recent stories.

'One of the young people was on the phone the other day and a boy came out of nowhere, knocked it out of his hand and into the gutter and kicked it down to some water and called him a faggot.

'Another young person was in class and a teacher was present and a boy said she should just take a pill to cure her homosexuality because it was wrong, a disease and a sickness. The teacher heard it and didn't say anything.

'Another young person was suspended from school for kissing his boyfriend even though his straight friends kiss all the time. He was told that same-sex relationships were not allowed at school. And this was a state school.'

There are examples outside of school as well.

'One trans young person, his mum is very unsupportive of him and saying it's just a phase. He's even had a letter from the Gender Centre and been to Medicare. He's even had people in the LGBT community say to him, *You don't belong here*, and: *You're just a freak.*'

Not all parents are unsupportive.

'Some parents will drive their kids. There are some that have been really supported. One mother even came to Gold Coast's Gay Day. When they drop off and pick up their kids they'll come in and say hello. But then there have been other parents who have been pretty horrific.'

Transport to QSPACE poses a huge barrier to young people attending the drop-ins. Stretched out along 70km of Queensland's southern coast, the

Gold Coast is inconveniently spread out for anyone without a car. A parent bringing a young person to QSPACE from Palm Beach takes 30 minutes each way. One young lesbian describes it as, 'Ridiculous. It takes about one and a half hours to get from one side of the Gold Coast to the other on a bus.'

Like Brisbane, if you want to go anywhere on the Gold Coast, invariably you have to jump into a car and go on a highway.

Harking back to my days running Mental Health Promotion Short Courses for VicHealth I remembered a study that said you can tell people's quality of life and state of mind by the time and distance it takes to get 1 litre of milk. It's said that if you can walk to the local shops to get some milk then life is best. If you have to jump into the car, get on a highway, fight for parking at a shopping mall and walk past lots of other shops in crowds then it is less than best. Bruce is certainly racking up kilometres quickly.

Lesley believes that this spread of the Gold Coast makes a difference on how connected people feel.

'There's no real sense of community here. People come in and go out, even in the straight community. There is no real central hub for the Gold Coast and for young people it's so hard. People move in and move out every two years so it's hard to build up solid friendships. Maybe it's that sense of community that is missing and that's why people move.

'The main thing is that they want to meet other people like them. There is a lot of social isolation here. Most people don't feel safe about being out. It's a bit of an escape from school and their families. They don't have to worry about what other people are gonna think or say. Oh and fun of course. Last night we had Guitar Hero Night, that's their favourite.'

Partnering with QAHC, Lesley has trained local teachers and health professionals on the rare occasion they are open to it.

'A lot of young people say they have teachers who won't say or do anything when other students say fag, dyke or whatever. A lot of people have that misconception that you need to be gay or lesbian to do work with the LGBT community. All you need is an open heart, a bit of knowledge, and to be non-judgmental.'

Day 150

Wednesday 21 July

I got to know my host for the week, Lorraine, through her sister, Kath. Kath was my former manager at Kids Help Line, where I spent a few years training teachers and health professionals across regional and rural Victoria and Tasmania.

At my book launch in February, Kath had brought along Lorraine. At some stage during that whirlwind evening, Lorraine had given me her business card and told me in no uncertain terms that I would be staying with her on the Gold Coast.

After so many weeks on the road I'm feeling dizzy from all the good hosting I've received, and this week is no exception. The good people of Queensland are looking after me as if they were taking part in a reality TV Show called 'MasterHost' where they're competing to make a traveling challenging-homophobia-educator's stay as easy, comfortable and productive as possible.

With Lorraine my week has involved invitations to dinners as well as free lunches at one of her growing empire of Subway stores. On the first night I found a hot water bottle with a teddy bear, complete with love heart, in my bed.

From the moment I arrive Lorraine is admirably open, reflective and candid. It'd be too easy to find out that Lorraine's youngest daughter is a lesbian and conclude that this was her motivation behind welcoming me into her home and life for a week, as well as to donate generously to my fuel campaign. But Lorraine has a history well before her daughter came out to the family.

She shares that as the kids grew up she had an open house policy, featuring her two daughters and their friends, both male and female, a consistent group of 12 or so young people. Lorraine is very clear why she had a house full of teenagers, possibly more than she would have liked.

'It was a deliberate strategy. I wanted to know where both of them were. One of the young guys, he was gorgeous. He asked to sit and have a coffee with me one day when everyone else was not there. I can't remember if it was the second or the third cup of coffee, but finally he came out and told me he thought he might be gay.'

And after talking it through and supporting him through coming out to his family, Lorraine's warm haven proved important.

'He spent quite a few nights on our couch.'

This isn't to say that Lorraine, from a strong and practising Catholic family, was not challenged by her own daughter's coming out.

'It was tough because I had all these pictures in my head as she grew up. Then they were gone and I had to build new pictures. Then I had to relax and let her do it herself.'

To this day, as a fast food magnate where the majority of employees are teenagers in their first job, Lorraine continues this LGBT-friendly support.

Recently there had been a young man, Matt, who worked in one of her stores. Taking time to get to know these young people, Lorraine became concerned when Matt took some time off work and came back with one of his arms heavily bandaged. He told everyone that it was 'a bad burn'.

When the bandages came off it was apparent that Matt had been self-harming. He clearly hadn't been 'mucking around'.

After much nonchalant loitering on her part and gentle conversation, Matt shared that he was questioning his sexual identity and his life in a strictly Mormon home. It was only a matter of time before he headed off overseas for his 2-year mission.

His parents' response to his self-harming?

'Oh you are just being silly.'

Not sure of what to do, Lorraine did what she and her friends often do: solved it over a walk and a coffee. Each morning Lorraine rises at 6am to walk with her friends, following this up with a coffee.

'We call ourselves The Brains Trust because we often solve the world's problems.'

Another member of her walking group told her that her husband, recently incapacitated, was looking for help around the yard. A light bulb went off for Lorraine and soon Matt was assisting the couple who became, she describes, 'like surrogate grandparents for him.'

Day 151

Thursday, 22nd July – Gold Coast QLD

'There is no homophobia in this part of the building. Our principal is – I have great respect for him, but he is pretty ignorant. He says things like, *He is too effeminate, he's asking for trouble.* There is no option for girls to wear anything other than skirts. But there will always be people who are homophobic. 80% of students couldn't give a rats, but 20% will always be yobbos. But they hassle everyone. I suppose they're a mirror of society.'

Jodie is an openly lesbian school-based nurse in a Gold Coast school of 1800 or so students. Given two days a week to support all those students and staff, Jodie has made a difference. Despite many years in LGBT and mainstream organisations she remains energised, motivated and upbeat about homophobia and transphobia in schools.

We sit in Jodie's office, a small space adorned with countless rainbows and LGBT-friendly posters. She recognises that not every student will understand what the rainbow means so she tells every student who comes into this space, and refers young people to QSPACE.

I sit across from Jodie and enjoy scribbling notes madly in a new notebook. My 450-page orange notebook has no space left, so now I've taken to this purple one.

'I challenge students when I hear them say *That's so gay.* I ask, *So gay people aren't nice?* and they say, *No, that's not what I mean.* Well, don't say it then.'

I ask Jodie if other teachers do the same.

'I'd say 50% would be fine, 50% that wouldn't. I'd say some of it would be about gender, more of the women would and some of that would be their own level of comfort, knowledge and understanding in challenging it.'

She points out that there is room for improvement.

'They tell them it's not OK, but not why it's not OK.'

Yet based on my conversations across the country, this school is ahead of the pack. Still, Jodie snaps up a copy of *Beyond 'That's So Gay'.* She also wants to know how she might run a professional development session for teachers.

'I don't know exactly whether they integrate anything into their presentations as a rule, I'm not sure. I think the barrier is that they are straight. It's not malicious, it's not on purpose, it's just that [they are straight].'

Jodie is soon on the phone with a heterosexual colleague, Tanya.

'It's all very well for me to talk about it being a dyke, but I thought it'd be better for you to talk to someone who is straight and also gay and lesbian friendly.'

It's not been 25 minutes and Jodie grills me about how I'm funding my tour and where I'm staying.

'So where are you off to after here?'

Me: 'Ahhh, Lismore, Newcastle, Sydney, Bathurst, Canberra, Brok ...'

'Who are you staying with in Canberra?'

Me: 'To be honest that is so far away I hadn't given it a thought.'

'Give me a few minutes. What are the dates?'

A few minutes later it seems it's sorted.

'Right, that's settled. You're staying with my sister and my brother-in-law in Canberra. I'll e-mail you their contact details but they're expecting you.'

Day 152

Friday, 23rd July – Gold Coast QLD

I meet with Tanya at short notice because her school is in the throes of an athletics carnival. We sit in a medium-sized meeting room that had been recently vacated. There were leftover treats, tea and coffee. Helping ourselves, we start our conversation.

'In the state school system, we support LGBT young people well. They've actually got somewhere to go, whereas other schools I've worked in, which weren't state schools, didn't.'

Tanya had recently moved from a smaller rural school to this full-time position in a school of almost 2000 students.

'The two schools are very different. In the rural school everyone knows everyone. But here there are about 2000 people and it's easier for a student to identify 1 or 2 others like themselves. In the little schools I think they'd be struggling, the culture is different. I think it's so small out there that anyone perceived as not normal would be targeted.'

As Tanya and I warmed up, me sipping my tea, the Deputy Principal interrupts us. Nora is sneaking a bite to eat on her way out to the athletics.

Tanya tells her that I'm there to talk about what they're doing for GLBT students in the school.

'Oh, that's great,' Nora says. 'Pleased to meet you. GL, what? Which ones are they again?'

Tanya explains, and I continue about my project thereafter. With her mouth still full Nora sits down.

'I know that particularly with the boys, the biggest insult that you can chuck at a boy is *faggot*. For girls it's *slut*. *Faggot* I find is the one. *Gay* they'll accept, but *faggot* they won't.'

'Do staff tend to respond?'

'Of course there are some that won't, but they will walk past anything. *Gay*? No, they probably throw it around themselves. *Fuck*? No, they throw that around too. Most teachers will draw a line in the sand and work on what crosses their own line. Ten years ago *fuck* was on the other side of the line. Not now.'

A theme that comes up is parents, or to be specific, parents who practice particular religions. It seems that parents can trigger mass hysteria.

'You would still find pockets of fundamentalist Christians, not the Catholics, I find them quite open. But fundamentalist Christians drive the agenda. But boy oh boy if you get that word homosexuality home, then wow, they come straight in. They frighten the system like crazy. *You're teaching my kid to be gay. I don't want my children hearing about those things.*'

Tanya does get the odd word in.

'As a non-Education Queensland staff member I'm constantly fighting to get things on the agenda. If it's not mainstream, it's even more difficult. I consider it mainstream, but other people don't. So while I would see it as justified to talk about GLBT, the powers that be would not think that.'

Another teacher pops their head in to collect Nora for a curriculum meeting. She leaves reluctantly.

'This is much more interesting than what we are going to be doing.'

With Nora gone, Tanya leans in, concerned.

'Was that OK? Sorry. Usually on a typical day that wouldn't happen, they'd be walking past. You know I was sitting there thinking about you while all that was going on. You must get that every day in schools. I was thinking, *How do you sit there and listen to that day in, day out?*'

I rested my hand after 90 minutes of writing down 'gold'.

'To be honest, that was perfect. She is a huge part of the demographic in schools across Australia. What she said in a few sentences sums up what so many others are thinking and feeling. I need to be talking to the Noras in schools. She sat engaged for that long, is thinking about how to start more conversations in the school and now she'll be reading my book. I couldn't have hoped for much more.'

Day 153

Saturday, 24ᵗʰ July – Gold Coast QLD to Brisbane QLD = 83kms

Joan from Jelly Beans in Brisbane has invited me to join her at her home in the north of the Gold Coast, nestled in the shadows of Mt Tambourine. On an overcast afternoon with the temperature dropping I sit on Joan's back verandah and share a cuppa. Only the night before the verandah had been full of people celebrating her birthday.

I was surprised to find that one of the most progressive transgender support groups seems to be thriving here on the Gold Coast, attracting folk from as far north as Brisbane and as far south as the Northern Rivers region of NSW. It's called *Freedom*.

'A bit over a year ago,' Joan explains, 'I had a longtime friend, a trans woman, who had been saying continually that we needed an alternative to Brisbane. We both felt that the local trans groups were not fitting the needs of all the community, that a lot of people were being left out. We also felt there were a lot of girls on the Gold Coast who were not wanting or able to get to Brisbane. There was a big gap on the Coast and a lot of us had been burnt by the Brisbane groups. She kept saying, *If I win lotto, I'd start an alternative support group on the Gold Coast*. One day I just said, *We don't need to win lotto to do this*.'

With 'advice and moral support' from Open Doors Youth Service and many trans hours, *Freedom* began.

'For trans people there is usually a period, a transition period, where you don't fit into either gender, and that's usually where people cop it. We decided we are just going to be open to everyone outside of the gender binary. For the most part, people find an accepting atmosphere. We don't care how you identify, as long as you're under the [trans] umbrella. The appeal of *Freedom* is if you don't really feel like a girl or a boy, you can be in between.'

The key to a great atmosphere is straightforward.

'We're not big on rules. It's a very easygoing atmosphere. The only rules we have are basic commonsense. We have a code of conduct, but we've never had to use it.'

Friends, family and other supporters of trans people are also welcome to attend and do.

'It's the opportunity to meet other people who are on the same track or meet friends and family who are in the same boat.'

In a short time *Freedom* has seen people's everyday lives changing.

'We've had young trans women who live only a mile apart and now they meet a few times a week for coffee. We've had young trans men who have been chatting online for 12 months and they come to *Freedom* and finally meet. That's the biggest thing that people get out of it. The building of community. I think that aspect is why I think we get people from so far afield.'

Day 154

Sunday, 25ᵗʰ July – Brisbane QLD to East Ballina NSW = 193kms

Arriving on the Gold Coast I had been eager to explore its depths because I was led to believe that it didn't have any. With no exceptions, when I told people where I was headed, I was met with: *What Plasticville?* and, invariably, giggles.

Over a post-roast cuppa I asked Lorraine, Sarah and Laurie about this perception. All of them were quick to point out that although the tourist centre of Surfers Paradise is all plastic, bling and polish, in the suburbs it is a different story (which is no different to many other parts of Australia). In many ways it seems to me a place where people come to chase or follow a dream. All had found it hard to find true locals.

'It took us 3 months to find someone who was born here!'

Mariah, a volunteer at Open Doors in Brisbane explains to me a bit more about the Gold Coast, incidentally on a road trip to the Sunshine Coast.

'It's very conservative, but *strangely* conservative. Like glam and gross, trying to be like LA – but at the same time it's very right wing.'

Tanya finds obvious differences between country kids and those on the Gold Coast.

'I'm like, *Sunscreen. Sunscreen anyone.* The students will all be there and cold but they still want everyone to see their bodies. It's so different here; so materialistic. I came from country Queensland and the kids there couldn't give a shit. But the kids here – it's all about the car you drive, the clothes you wear and even who you hang out with. It's so cliquey here.'

In a way that seems even more heightened than elsewhere, this focus on outer layers impacts on young people like Mariah.

'I feel very stared at and very uncomfortable when I walk around there. I feel like I have a wall around me. There's quite a substantial gay and lesbian community there, but it's pretty superficial. There's not enough subculture there within the Gold Coast.'

Mariah pauses.

'It's a special place,' she says, and laughs.'

I still haven't completely worked out how a tourist hot spot, which in any other part of regional Australia is a guarantee of LGBT friendliness, is not entirely that here. Mariah perhaps sums up how some, yet not all, feel about the Gold Coast.

'I don't know what's wrong with the Gold Coast. Maybe it's trying to be too many things.'

As I left the Gold Coast's borders yesterday afternoon, I was pretty excited. I didn't head south as planned. Well, not yet anyway. Another first for my tour: I backtracked. I drove north, back towards Brisbane after a plea from The Barman.

'My brothers are up from the country to play a gig in Brisbane with their band. I know you have a tour and money's tight, so I want to donate a tank of petrol to Bruce and buy you dinner in Brisbane if you drive back for the night? And before you say anything, I had a great week of tips …'

Day 155

Monday, 26ᵗʰ July – Brisbane QLD to East Ballina NSW = 193kms

The apartment is completely silent, except for a stylish, modern clock ticking. There are floor to ceiling windows that boast views of Richmond River moments before it meets the ocean. The sun is still climbing slowly to midday, blocked occasionally by grey puffs of cloud. It helps that Ben's apartment is on the fourth floor.

Ben and his partner, Joe, have headed out to work for the day, leaving me with unlimited wifi and space on a huge laminated table to spread out. I'm attempting to be productive. I'm half-succeeding.

I doubt I could have had a warmer welcome last night. Ben had kept in close contact with me about my arrival time; it altered numerous times as I delayed the painful, inevitable goodbye to The Barman: first thing in the morning became late morning, after lunch and finally late afternoon following final displays of passion, naps and new deep and meaningfuls. I understood a little more why Ben had tracked me carefully all the way from Brisbane when I walked through the door; I was greeted with a warm hug from Ben about the same time I got a nose-full of the almost-ready-to-serve apricot chicken. This would be followed closely by apple crumble made from scratch. Perhaps not coincidentally, the final of Masterchef came on right after a televised leadership debate between Julia Gillard and Tony Abbott.

It's great seeing Ben again. When he called me out of the blue, I was stretching in the gym in Mt Isa. Normally I wouldn't have my phone with me, but that night I was waiting on a call about a radio interview.

'I'm sorry I disappeared and didn't keep in contact,' he said.

New to Melbourne, Ben and I had a brief affair before he moved away. At the time I didn't take it personally.

'I was thinking about all the people I met, and how you are just this great guy. I felt bad that I had to leave so quickly and thought if there was a way, I want to have you in my life.'

When the inevitable, *So what have you been up to?* came around, I talked about the tour. He got excited when I mentioned I'd be in Lismore.

'You're definitely staying with us!'

Day 156

'Granny Gayle, why are they here? It's disgusting!'

At her recent 65th birthday party, Gayle, one of Australia's most progressive grandmothers, was confronted by her distressed grandson, Jake, a 20-year-old surfie from the Gold Coast.

Unlike her own children, of which she has four, Gayle explains that having around 20 gay male friends at the celebration was something her grandson wasn't expecting.

'I had to get my son and a gay friend and say, *Look, go and sort Jake out.*'

At the end of the night Jake would return to Gayle a different grandson.

'Wow Granny Gayle. They're so cool. Like really cool.'

Observing that her grandson is often concerned with what his friends think, she gave her grandson a huge Ottoman for his 21st birthday. She made sure it was in front of all of his friends.

'Here Jake. I bought you a bloody big poof for your birthday.'

His friends, and Jake, were said to have fallen about with laughter.

It's an 'accident' that I meet Gayle at all. We've just finished a group fitness class at a Lismore gym, which is more shed than gym. Gayle passed me and noticed my ankh necklace.

'I go to Egypt every year.'

Excited that someone knew what an ankh is and had actually been to Egypt, I dig deeper.

Me: 'Can you tell me why you go there every year and not somewhere else?'

Her annual pilgrimages invariably involve her joining impromptu 'digs' at any number of locations. We compare notes and I hear of her discovering her past lives whilst sleeping inside one of the Great Pyramids; after bribing one of the caretakers of course.

Then, out of nowhere, it came.

'Oh I miss my gay friends in Sydney.'

Well that was random. Was Gayle telling me this because she thought I was gay? Or was this something she dropped into conversations to anyone?

My jaw drops when Gayle tells me she's 65, because she could clearly pass for 15-20 years younger, despite having lost 10 kilos recently whilst sick. (She doesn't have 10 kilos to lose.) An ex-aerobics instructor, Gayle began to tell me stories of her time leading aerobics classes in the heart of Sydney.

'I lived in gay Sydney through the 1970s and 1980s. Believe me I saw it all. I used to go out dressed up like a drag queen. Guys would come up to me and I had to keep saying, *No love, I'm not a drag queen, I'm a mother of four from the suburbs*. They loved it, I had the muscled arms and everything.'

Day 157

Wednesday, 28th July – Lismore NSW

'I came up with a boyfriend. Part of the reason was that there was a fairly prominent social group. I came up and experienced Tropical Fruits. I wouldn't have considered coming to any other regional area.'

Known primarily for a dance party it runs each and every New Year's Eve at the Lismore Showgrounds, Tropical Fruits is an impressive regional institution. Former driving force of Tropical Fruits, Chris, now a youth worker, explains that Tropical Fruits wasn't thriving at that stage.

'[Tropical Fruits] was basically falling over when I arrived. For the first couple of years we worked our guts out to build it up and get people involved again. We focused on creating opportunities beyond the dance parties and the drugs and the alcohol. Since then, Tropical Fruits has been a perfect example of community development.'

Tropical Fruits has spawned an LGBT young people's group, Fresh Fruits, as well as a family day, Fruitopia. In recent years, Tropical Fruits has returned to its glory days, yet it has done so without assistance from local or state government. Myths are part of the problem according to Chris.

'One year we got a $5000 net profit, but it's a big turnover, and we're turning over half a million. There is a misconception that we are a low priority area. That pink dollar myth. I think it has worked against us.'

Despite the flow of dollars, for people like Chris it's more about the coming together of community.

'We have 300 volunteers for a week before Tropical Fruits. I stand back sometimes, look around and think, *I don't believe this*.'

This sense of community is something that Chris felt hard to find in Sydney.

'It's quite good. I'm quite lucky that I get to flit between Sydney and here. It gives me a good sense of the difference between the two. It's much better here. I have a very strong network of people that I can turn back on.'

Marcus, a health promotion worker with ACON, formally the Aids Council of New South Wales, agrees for the most part, yet still laments the challenges of regional and rural life for LGBT people. For this reason, Marcus is working to make non-metro life better for LGBT people.

'Just putting it on the fucking agenda really. I'm quite passionate about keeping people in the places that they want to be. Lismore is an alternative to the city, which is a few pubs and some greedy promoters really.'

When I ask Marcus about his background, he shows his humour, wit and modesty.

'I'm originally from Sydney, but don't hold that against me. Prior to this I was just a public loud mouth.'

It's clear that Marcus is proud of the work of ACON locally, as well as Tropical Fruits.

'It's the only perennial gay organisation that's not a pub.'

Part of Marcus' role, which for him is quite new, is to engage local schools.

'My job is basically just trying to get every school in the fucking region on board.'

I tell Marcus about the seminar for local teachers I'll be doing later in the week, and get the thumbs up.

'It sounds like a great way to penetrate the Department of Education. So to speak.'

Coincidentally, the week that I was in Lismore, Tropical Fruits received local government funding for the first time, along with a Roller Derby group heavily populated by lesbian women.

Day 158

Thursday, 29th July – Lismore NSW

I've made my way down the back of the Lismore branch of the NSW Teachers Federation (NSWTF). Simultaneously Tropical Fruits' Fresh Fruits, the young LGBT people's group, is meeting down the road. It's an unfortunate clash given Rob, the group founder, invited me to attend and collect some local stories. Still, I feel the need to be here.

Quite early on I was contacted by the NSWTF to discuss how they could help my tour through New South Wales. They agreed to host events at each NSW location I was visiting, with me reading from *Beyond 'That's So Gay'*, discussing my tour and using this as a conversation starter for the NSWTF's review and update of their LGBT policies (by their own admission last updated in 1994).

I'm still thinking about a cuppa I had with a woman who heads up a working group of local services and organisations working with young people.

'In the Northern Rivers region we've had a couple of deaths because of bullying. So the schools and the Department were like, *Whoa*. When it comes down to it, we don't have the resources to respond to this.'

Who knows if it's this or something else that draws a crowd? For a regional area, the NSWTF and myself are pleasantly surprised to see 15 local teachers from a mix of primary and secondary schools in attendance.

After the reading, Bob approaches me to check how his school is going. He's grateful that his school, arguably the region's most LGBT-friendly school, is taking leadership on the issue, yet feels like there is no real way of measuring whether their efforts are making a difference.

'I'm interested in that model you talked about, the one about a school's readiness to do this stuff.'

Rather than doing things in the absence of a framework, Bob's excited that there might be a way to see where his school currently sits and what the next best step is for its LGBT students.

During the reading of my book, another teacher, Ron, expressed great concern about how he was being supported by the NSW Department of Education & Training (DET).

'DET doesn't recognise or understand the impact of homophobic vilification on teachers. It's perhaps the most confronting thing for a teacher. I had students writing on walls, *Mr [X] is gay* and *Mr [X] sucks cocks*. My boss, a wonderful, wonderful man, just didn't know what to do and didn't do anything.'

A colleague chimed in.

'Actually some of your kids in class were the best at dealing with it.'

Ron is an example of a teacher who is adored by most of his students, who don't really care much about whether he is gay or not. The same can be said for another gay teacher who couldn't attend the reading. Instead all his colleagues attended for him. In a school where there are only 5 teachers, one also a principal, this was a big effort.

'We are four teachers from a rural school of five teachers. The fifth teacher is a colleague who is openly gay. He's an asset to the team, and unfortunately he couldn't be here. We are here to see how we can support him better, just in case something happens. Well, we know there will be no problems with the kids because they love him. It's the parents and maybe the community that we are worried about. We've had no problems so far.'

In this informal gathering, this led to a small round of spontaneous applause. Yet the principal continued.

'I'm a bit embarrassed to say this, and I've been a teacher for 17 years, but I've just had a light bulb moment. I'd never thought how important this really is. My whole career I've always felt secure, like the Department has my back, just as long as I follow policies and procedures. This makes me realise that there are no policies and procedures, and that I'm exposed, and I don't like it. The fact that we're avoiding this sends a clear message.'

Day 159

Friday, 30th July – Lismore NSW

'I left Sydney 10 years ago. I just had to get out, it got crazy. Literally not a day goes by when I don't think how lucky I am to be here. I feel blessed.'

Marg, a lesbian mother of two with her partner, Teri, loves Lismore.

'This is a fantastic place to live. The thing I love about Lismore is that it has all the diversity of a big city. When I was in Sydney, I lived in the north, and I was kind of protected.'

Without the cultural precincts of Sydney, Lismore's diversity is not to everyone's tastes.

'Here it's all in your face, and that's what a lot of people hate about it. It's not Pleasantville.'

Lismore, or as the local LGBT folk say, Lesmore, is the capital of the Northern Rivers Region that includes Byron Bay, Nimbin and Ballina, where I was staying for the week. It's said, by everyone in Lismore, to have the largest concentration of gay and lesbian people in rural New South Wales.'

For Marg, Lismore is mostly a safe and supportive place.

'If you are just coming to Dragonfly Café or coming to Tropical Fruits, you'll have no problems. But if you are out there, it can be pretty difficult at times.'

Whilst Marg and Teri have encountered more than their share of homophobia from adults and institutions as parents, the same cannot be said for the children who go to kindergarten and school with their own children.

'Kids will ask, *So why do you have two mums?* We say, *All families are different, and isn't that interesting?* The pre-school that both our kids have gone to have been great and framed it in difference. A lot of kids go, *I wish I had two mums.*'

Not that everyone's listening.

'I tend to over-talk things, and one of our daughter's friends asked the question and I said the usual spiel. I was doing the whole big blah blah and he was more interested in his tiny teddy that he'd been given. He'd zoned out.' She laughed.

I had the pleasure of meeting Marg and Teri's two children earlier. Invited to join them for a roast, I was treated to an impromptu concert and acrobatics display by Marg and Teri's son and daughter. There was much energy and laughter.

'I love my beautiful children and I'm proud of them and what we've all achieved to get here.'

Dinner with Marg and Teri proves a refreshing pit stop on my tour. I thank them on behalf of my mother who calms considerably when I share how warm and welcoming people are with me as I travel.

'Every time I eat a roast on this tour my mother sheds a tear in Geelong.'

I leave Marg and Teri's to drive home, with a container full of delicious roasted leftovers, then a text message: 'Daniel, you've left your notebook behind.'

I return to get my notebook and leave once more for my home for the week. Before bed I think of something I have to write down. As I open my notebook I discover that during the 10 minutes I'd first left Marg's, she had got to work and left me a surprise. It is yet another example of the lengths that people go to in order to make me feel as lucky as I do.

The text says:

'To the lovely Daniel. For a writer, you need a bookmark. Here's one I made earlier. You are a wonderful lesson and an inspiration. P.S. The kids thought you were pretty cool too.

I think back to my second departure from Marg's place. After a second kiss and hug Marg paused. Not for the first time I felt what was unspoken: both of us wished that I could stay a little longer and that my goodbye was a reluctant one.

'You must have a lot of goodbyes in you …'

Day 160

Saturday, 31ˢᵗ July

'I was attracted to one of my male friends. I thought it was just normal. Then at high school it became apparent that that wasn't so widespread. I used the classic bi as a segue thing, *I can't be attracted to males, it's just not right.* I got to the point in Year8/9 where I said, *Who am I fooling?* and came out to myself. I pretty much copped it every day for being same-sex-attracted.'

Relatively fresh from high school, Rob admits that despite Lesmore, ACON and Tropical Fruits, he didn't believe that other people felt like he did.

'It was kind of the only gay in the village thing. I thought all gay porn was 'gay for pay'. I thought no-one was actually gay, it was just a higher pay rate for the porn stars.'

Rob would eventually find stories like his own on the internet.

'I found a website called mogenic, and I actually found a media story where this guy in a rural American town who basically said he felt like he was the only one in the world and actually broke down in the interview about it. So that basically reinforced that I wasn't the only one.'

Despite this, depression became Rob's reality.

'I felt like I was the only person around who was same-sex-attracted and the feeling that I couldn't tell anyone about it. Then I told two friends. One spread it around the school, the guy, but the other, a girl, was very supportive, and she was actually a die-hard Christian. The teachers didn't really react in any way, but the students were kind of like, *We've heard you are gay or bi or whatever, is it true?* and I'd be like, *Yeah.* The boys would be like, *Oh that's gross, get away from me.* The girls would be like, *That's cool, you're still the same person.*'

Coming out to his family came next.

'I was watching TV and my parents were on computer and I started asking dad if he cared about gay rights and if he cared about it being in the

220

family, like nephews, nieces. It got to the point where my dad sounded frustrated and I turned around and said, *OK, I'm gay.* They didn't care. My dad literally said, *Who cares, do you want a badge?* Mum shrugged and says, *It happens.*'

Through getting his first boyfriend, Rob got involved in an ACON peer education course and was asked to help run a new LGBT youth group. For Rob it's about helping provide an alternative to Tropical Fruits, cheekily titled 'Fresh Fruits'.

'An organisation like Tropical Fruits is seen by young people as an older gay men's dance party, so they are reluctant to go to it. There is nothing for young people to do in the area except Fresh Fruits.'

Now Fresh Fruits, in it's ninth month, is going from strength to strength and looking to create an under 30s dance space at this New Years Eve's Tropical Fruits dance party. When Rob recently asked the LGBT young people attending Fresh Fruits what they got out of their time there, they gave similar reasons to other young people across the country.

'Support, socialising, something to do, making friends, building courage, somewhere to feel secure, getting more involved, understand what's happening in the area.'

Rob wants to stay put and rejects the notion that he should head for Sydney, or nearby Brisbane.

'I don't want to and I don't have to move away.'

Day 161

Sunday, 1ˢᵗ August – Lismore NSW to Sydney NSW = 737kms

There is no doubt that Sydney is the measuring stick for most folk around the country when it comes to matters of LGBTness. And now, here I am driving there after 23 weeks on the road.

Arriving in Sydney is, to me at least, like climbing an LGBT Mt Everest. When I first talked to people about going on my tour, I was urged to check if this was OK with particular individuals and organisations. One Sydney colleague warned me.

'They won't like it ...'

Another long-time LGBT mentor also warned me that if I didn't get permission I'd find it tough.

'Just be prepared for the backlash.'

Although not the primary reason for the logistics of my tour, this played a part in me deciding to cover ground in SA WA, NT and QLD before coming to the east coast with 'fresh eyes'. I figured rather than starting in Sydney or Melbourne and speculating on what I'd find, I'd instead listen to the non-east coast of Australia and then share this with east coast folk. If they'd be interested.

My landing in Sydney couldn't be closer to the LGBT bubble, some 150m from Oxford Street, Darlinghurst. Yet my landing could not be softer given my hosts.

Peter and Jai moved to Sydney late last year. I've known Peter since he was a 'baby gay' in Geelong. Peter came to watch the then-televised Sydney Mardi Gras with my mother and some other friends before he'd come out to his own family. Peter not only swore my mum to secrecy about his gayness, but also asked that my mum not talk about me being gay; my mum worked with Peter's mum at a nursing home and they often had a cuppa together during breaks. Peter feared 'gay guilt by association'. Later, my mum 'came out' as having a gay son once Peter had come out to his family. I even took Peter on his first Melbourne excursions to gay establishments.

Now it seems the shoe is on the other foot. Peter has run downstairs to let me in to rest Bruce in the underground carpark, a god-send given parking in Sydney's inner-city is as bad as it gets in metropolitan Australia. It's a remarkably tight squeeze, but worth it to have Bruce parked in the 'Tradesman's Carpark'. I'm actually planning to not use him again until I go, relying on walking, cycling and public transport.

Peter excitedly encourages me to load him up with whatever I need to carry upstairs. He smiles his trademark smile, big and bright, framed by a Chesty Bonds chin.

After dumping my bags in the guest bedroom I ascend the stairs to find Jai in the kitchen. He's talking to his two Burmilla cats, Sanchez and Miguel, and preparing dinner; yet another host coordinating dinner around my arrival.

Whilst cooking for others has always made me a nervous wreck, Jai is a natural, channeling his Eastern European upbringing into showing his love through food, amongst other gestures. I'm surprised not only by a roast chicken meal, with an inner-city gay twist, but also the mother of all debriefs about my previous 6 months. Knowing Peter since the mid-1990s and them both for over the decade they've been together, it was my first chance to have a typical and frank conversation with people who knew me well.

Although a Sunday, living right off Oxford Street means we all like the idea of going around the corner for a quick drink on the famous gay strip. As we turn the corner I'm caught off guard by a wave of emotion as I look over to Peter; our journey from Geelong's suburbs to Sydney's inner gay ghetto couldn't be more real. Peter senses the moment when he looks back at me.

Me: 'Do you sometimes …'

'Absolutely,' he laughs.

Day 162

Monday, 2nd August – Sydney NSW

In Week 24 things are no different: I'll take my cuppas wherever and whenever I can get them. I'm travelling out to Sydney Airport to see an old friend and mentor before he flies out on some international human rights work. I'm just thankful it's a train and not a bus like it would be in Melbourne.

I first met former Australian Human Rights Commissioner, the generous, golden skinned and especially golden-voiced Chris Sidoti in 2000 when I first travelled to Sydney as part of the *Outlink* Project. Remarkably at ease, Chris would offer his time and his wisdom readily to young people from across the states and territories.

At the time there had been a great deal of media interest, everyone was assigned a journalist and a corner of the Pitt Street offices. At that point I had only ever been the subject of one interview, as *The Geelong Advertiser's* subject for a Volunteer's Day feature on Page 3 (yes I was a Page 3 gay).

I made a play for the tea station for a cuppa, hoping I'd get missed in the flurry. Unfortunately Chris noted my reluctance. Wisely giving me little choice, Chris made his move.

'Daniel, the *Sydney Star Observer* wants an interview. Would you like to join me?'

I immediately protested. Going through a media interview *and* sitting beside the most eloquent person I'd shaken hands with? Surely he didn't need me getting in the way?

'I need you with me, you'll be fine. I'll help you.'

As we sat beside each other, our backs to the wood-panelled wall, Chris leaned in as the reporter readied his equipment. The message, and the warmth with which it was delivered, rings in my ears every single time I deal with the media.

'The trick is, Daniel, to not think about who will be reading this. Your job is to have a conversation with one person, them, and to convince them of your message. If you do that, you have succeeded. The same goes for when you are speaking on radio. Pretend that the audience does not exist and speak only to the interviewer. Convince them and only them.'

Our meeting is as bittersweet as the hot chocolate Chris shouts me. Today the Cologne Gay Games commence, and I won't be playing tennis against people from around the world.

Seeing Chris reminds me of when he hosted a dinner during the 1st World Out Games in Montreal. At the dinner I got to sit with Chris and other human rights heavies such as Justice Michael Kirby. Somehow I was left a spot next to Andrea, an employee at Chris' Geneva-based human rights organisation. He shook my hand warmly and broke into a huge, goofy and gorgeous Italian grin. Our conversation was engaging, given Andrea's intelligence, immediacy and genuine interest in everyone with whom he spoke. I also blushed when my fortune cookie proclaimed 'Be spontaneous.'

'Arrr, Denyerl uh, what does yours say, uh?'

I would win two tennis gold medals, only after slightly spraining my ankle on a date the night before my semi-final matches in singles and doubles. After he kissed me by moonlight on his porch, I mocked falling down the stairs twirling, and was not as Fred Astaire as I'd hoped. Andrea was beside himself for his 'beautiful little champion'. Having my ankle blow up to the size of a small football after winning both my finals was worth it.

This Italian Human Rights lawyer would turn my world upside down for the next two years, whenever we met in Melbourne, Geneva and Berlin.

'You know what you say about Chris? That he has this voice of pure gold? I think the same about you my beautiful little champion.'

Day 163

Tuesday, 3rd August – Sydney NSW

A wintery Sydney evening. I find myself sitting amongst about 30 people in the basement of ACON, or 'the bowels' as some call it. Each week people from Pentecostal, Charismatic and Evangelical faith backgrounds gather for Freedom 2 b[e] meetings. I've been invited along by religious pioneer Anthony Venn Brown to share my tour experiences so far.

Every person I spoke to about Anthony and/or Freedom 2 b[e] talked openly about the impact of Anthony and his work. One guy said, 'It saved my life. It's the reason I am alive today.'

I wanted to meet with a man who many believe is not only an Australian leader in bridging faith and sexual identity, but also a world leader. In his bestseller, *A Life Of Unlearning*, Anthony outlines in great detail his own journey.

His website sets the scene:

'Formerly a high profile preacher in mega-churches throughout Australia and overseas, for 22 years Anthony tried every possible means to change his homosexuality through psychiatric treatment, ex-gay programs, counselling etc. Although a happily married father of two for 16 years, he eventually had to admit that nothing had changed and since 1991 has been living as an openly gay man.'

Anthony is clear why Freedom 2 b[e] is having such an impact.

'It's a chance for people who have a faith background to come together and open up. You can't have those conversations in a gay bar.'

In an age where so many LGBT young people find solace on the internet, Freedom 2 b[e]'s website, freedom2b.org, boasts countless stories shared by young people from Pentecostal, Charismatic and Evangelical faith backgrounds.

Anthony points out that LGBT people from these faith backgrounds have a point of difference.

'LGBT people experience a range of negative life experiences but we experience it with greater intensity, because it has eternal consequences. That's pretty heavy.'

Perhaps fittingly, I arrive to find a group of people politely seated and ready for the meeting to commence. Anthony observes this.

'Ooo, it's like a little congregation actually, isn't it?' he laughs.

Soon he's in full flight, and it's easy to imagine Anthony, as he once did, preaching to a huge congregation at a mega-church. He recalls his dress sense in years gone by.

'I was the trendiest preacher in the Assemblies of God. But there were limits.'

Although frequently drawing laughs from the audience, this is much more than a comedy routine. Stories are told of LGBT people, such as someone involved in the 'ex-gay' movement.

'He said, *I realised I lost my 20s.*'

Anthony's message is that, in our own time of course, we must come out.

'When we choose to live authentically, we chip away at others' prisons of pretend.'

Day 164

Wednesday, 4th August – Sydney NSW

It's about 90 minutes before my Sydney book reading with the NSWTF. I'm sitting in a modern café called Toast – it's like many other places in Sydney for cuppas, except that it boasts indoor climbing vines.

Unfortunately Dorothy, head of The Federation of Parents and Citizens' Associations of NSW, can't make it due to travel commitments. Many people, including Dorothy, think P&Cs might be an under-utilised force in supporting LGBT young people given its infrastructure across the state.

'Parents and Citzens Associations are different to school councils in that schools run school councils that have some parents and citizens as representatives; P&Cs are a representative body where there are some school representatives. There are 2200 schools in NSW and 1900 schools have P&Cs.'

More recently the P&Cs' stance on challenging homophobia in schools came to a head during its annual conference.

'It was the same weekend as Mardi Gras. We left it too late so we went in under the auspice of PFLAG. There was a group who walked, a dozen or so, and the response from our Council was, *This is fantastic.* If we are going to do something about discrimination, it's no good just saying it. This is putting our money where our mouth is.'

Not that everyone from across NSW was supportive.

'What we found out was, there were people who were really offended and wrote offensive e-mails … Disgusted would be the best word … I think some of them were country people … I think the notion is that it doesn't happen in the country, it happens only in the city … The actual reaction from the Mardi Gras crowd and people on the sidewalk, we had kids say, *Oh my god, the P&C is here!*

Giving a preview of the book reading that she'll miss, I update Dorothy on the Lismore book reading. When I tell her about a Principal's reflection on the lack of policy support, she agrees.

'I think a lot of Principals think Department policy is strong, and it's not. When you actually read them, there is not a lot of depth to it. They think it's covered under the Anti-Discrimination Policy. Until something arises, people don't often think about these things.'

Day 165

Thursday, 5ᵗʰ August – Sydney NSW

I want to get a sense of Sydney's outer suburbs, so I spend an hour on a train, then a car ride to get to a Campbelltown school. The decision to come here was not a difficult one after receiving the following email.

'My name is Mel. I'm a secondary teacher (fresh out of university) and I'm gay. The university and the schools I have worked in are still riddled with homophobia from teachers and students. My current school in Sydney's south west has a huge population of gay students who are not only not being supported but are being bullied and traumatised. The school has no system or real policy in place to support and protect these students. I have personal concern for these students – I was lucky to survive school, my first girlfriend committed suicide at 16. I understand this may be too late to organise during this tour perhaps we could meet the next time you are in Sydney or through another means? We are ready, willing and eager to create change and would love your input.'

Mel picks me up from the train station, half-laughing, admitting that she expected not to hear back for months.

'I thought I'd get some standard, *Thanks for your e-mail, but …*'

This explains in part the energy that surrounds my arrival, which includes four teachers, one Deputy Principal and Mel's lecturer from university. I was asked for my hot beverage preference so that the tea ladies could have it waiting – for the record it was a hot chocolate. Mel has also brought home-made chocolate cupcakes.

Like many outer metropolitan schools, this secondary school claims a diverse student population that includes Aboriginal and Islander students. The school's reputation precedes it, as a younger female teacher explains.

'A lot of people told me not to come here to teach because it's housing commission, there's lots of Aboriginal kids, etc. There was just this stigma attached to working here.'

Insults such as 'faggot' and comments such as 'that's so gay' are commonplace. Encouraged by a gay male friend, another female teacher had found some success in challenging homophobia in her classrooms.

'I say, *My friend is gay and when you say that you hurt him and you hurt me*, and then they say, *Awww, sorry miss.*'

Mel herself finds an interesting dynamic in her own classroom as an arts teacher.

'I have one class where there are a few gay boys and some straight macho boys. It seems that the gay boys sit up the back and as far away as possible from the others. When we do group activities they get very conscious of physical space. Like the other day, no-one would stand behind the gay boy. Thank goodness he was oblivious to it, to the drama going on behind him.'

For Mel it's about small, everyday wins.

'It's about what's appropriate and what's not. We can talk about being gay or bisexual or lesbian, but we can't use inappropriate words. It drives me to distraction some days. Last class we only said faggot twice. *Well done guys.* And I'm only with them 6 periods each week.'

'Ria', the deputy principal approaches this meeting with some caution.

'I'm here to make sure no big decisions are made and that the school is not committed to doing anything major.'

Me: 'You don't have to sign up for anything, and to be honest, I don't have anything for you to sign up to.'

Cue some sighs and smiles. Any change seems to be in the 'too-hard' basket.

'But we have, like, 50 staff,' one of the teacher's says. 'And we could only get five people here from staff.'

Me: 'Think about what has happened here so far today. We have spoken for 90 minutes, and we could keep going. With only a simple framework and some simple questions, you have all come up with stories, experiences and ideas. Right?'

'Yes.'

Me: 'Imagine if you multiply these 5 people by 10. Do you think you would have plenty of other stories, experiences and ideas?'

'Yes.'

Me: 'Would it be possible to set aside an hour or two in the next 3-6 months where you start a conversation as a whole staff group, where you ask teachers to think about how ready the school is and what could happen next?'

'Yes.'

Me: 'Could you get someone to come in and start that conversation if you didn't feel confident yourselves?'

Now it's relaxed, excited smiles. The biggest smile is on Mel's face. This has been on Mel's agenda even before she stepped into her current school, which is all the more remarkable given this was only her third (yes THIRD!) week in the school; her first school.

On the way back to the train station, on my fourth or fifth chocolate cupcake by this stage, Mel shares some of her own story.

'The first time I came out my dad said, *No you're not, eat your dinner* ... The second time I was kicked out when I was in the first year of uni ... I was in wet bathers and shorts and that night I slept in the park ...'

Day 166

Friday, 6th August – Sydney NSW

I'm munching on my cornflakes, relaxing on Peter and Jai's couch. There are 100 days to go on tour. After a bitterly cold few days I'm grateful to look out across the balcony and see patches of blue sky.

Checking Facebook I get an update from Marg in Lismore.

'Hey Daniel. Here's the link to the great story Lina did of your visit to Lismore – love the t-shirt pic! When my daughter saw your photo in the newspaper she laughed out loud and couldn't figure out why there was a picture of you!'

Following up from my book reading earlier in the week, some ACON staff are keen for a cuppa, including the head of the Anti-Violence Project. I arrive with my notebook.

The ACON crew have different ideas. I don't get to write a single word as they turn the tables and interview me about the tour.

'We've been thinking about what to do with a large donation. At first we thought of doing some kind of LGBT conference, but then we thought, why not do a *Beyond 'That's So Gay'* conference and invite all your contacts from around the country? We could build on those networks.'

It's with a heavy heart that I pour cold water on the idea.

'If you have a conference, then most of my contacts won't be able to make it. Just about every one of them is over-capacity, stretched and under threat. They aren't funded to do the work, they're expected to do it over and above what they're already doing. If we hold a conference we'll get the same faces and perhaps new ones who are within driving distance.'

Before they boxed me as a Debbie Downer, I gave another idea.

'Instead I would love to see something like a weekend summit that involves key LGBT stakeholders from around the country *but* we also invite key allies within mainstream and philanthropic organisations. The goal would be to look at how mainstream and philanthropic organisations could incorporate more LGBT and challenging homophobia education into their existing work and look at ways for key LGBT stakeholders to work with mainstream and philanthropic organisations, both immediately and in the longer-term. Get a mainstream organisation to host it and use the funds to fly LGBT people in and get a great facilitator.'

I leave the table of warm, welcoming men of varying ages and walk the short walk 'home' through the alleyways and streets of Darlinghurst, reflecting on how my fears of Sydney's rejection of regional, rural and remote engagement have been unfounded. I realise some people I listened to before the tour were very wrong.

Day 167

'Based on our funding, we are functioning about 164% of our capacity.'

Arriving to meet a Twenty10 Coordinator, Alex, I find a 'busy' organisation. Arguably the leading LGBT youth organisation in the country, Twenty10 has been leading the way in supporting LGBT young people since the 1990s. Many LGBT projects around the country consider Twenty10 to be the benchmark.

Whilst unsurprised by how busy it is, given my experience with every LGBT organisation I have met and worked with, I'm pleasantly surprised that Twenty10 have been documenting their actual vs funded capacity.

'It's new and partly about awareness-raising with staff around burnout. We ask, *What is your capacity. What is Twenty10 here for?* Because burnout has an impact on the service, the young people and yourself.'

Before the NSW Teachers Federation generously agreed to host book readings at all five of my NSW locations, Twenty10 had offered their support when the tour was a fledgling idea. It was support of organisations like Twenty10, and in particular friend and colleague Sydney Louis, which made that fledgling idea soon become a reality.

Now I get to see Twenty10's main functions: direct support for LGBT young people. We are all upstairs in an impressive space at Twenty10's Newtown headquarters. I'm distracted by the view out the modestly-sized windows to the rooftops of suburban Newtown, wondering if I'll ever own my own warehouse. I'm here to spend time with those attending the Saturday drop-in. They introduce themselves and it's a mix of young people born in Sydney and some who have come from other places.

I tell them a little about my travels.

'Many LGBT young people around Australia are excited when they talk about Sydney. They all say they wish things in their towns were like Sydney. What would you say to them?'

Like Alex, the young people watered down these fantasies.

'Sydney is not magical. It's actually just a small portion.'

However that small portion is loved by most.

'I walk up Oxford Street and I'm home. It's ours.' He smiled.

Two young men from regional and rural NSW remind everyone of non-Sydney life.

'I wasn't openly gay in in my small town. If someone was known to be gay then the local gangs took it upon themselves to re-educate the gay person. And I mean bashings. My only understanding was that gay people were hunted down.'

The second young man found local support in a coastal town in the form of an LGBT youth group, yet still felt different at school.

'My boyfriend and I were watching heterosexual couples growing up in a country high school. I used to think, *Why can't I do that?* We were in love, but we couldn't show it. And that had a serious impact on our relationship; when your boyfriend denies you in public because of what people might say.'

In Sydney, examples of same-sex couples and public displays of affection seem more common and visible, at least in certain pockets. It's the knowledge and accessibility of these 'certain pockets' of LGBT-ness and LGBT friendliness that distinguishes Sydney from most other locations, but doesn't automatically grant it LGBT-utopia status.

I put it to the participants of Twenty10's Saturday drop-in that many LGBT young people across the country would be surprised that a service like Twenty10 would be needed in Sydney.

'Why do you come along?' I ask, and everyone has a slightly different answer.

'Everyone was treating me differently – my parents, my friends. I just needed someone to understand and treat me as normal.'

'Being more active. To just feel like you're contributing, whether it be in conversation or whatever.'

'I don't fit in … in the suburbs. I like friends.'

'To meet other young people who are going through similar things.'

'Coming from a country town; the amount of people that come here; coming from no gayness to faggotry; going from nothing to Carnivale. It's interesting to go from nothing to everything.'

'Kind of like a lottery.'

There is general laughter at this comment.

'It's easy to become friends with people, get people's experiences and stuff. It's fun!'

'I like the idea that if I come here, that there are other people like me. I think I feel different where I come from and I don't feel that here.'

'For most of my life I was the only gay in the village.'

Before I end my time with Twenty10, I ask them all what their hopes are for the future, which ranged from the delightfully ambitious through to the simple things in life.

'I hope for utopia. I'm a dreamer. I'm a writer.'

'Super powers!'

'Meet someone, settle down, get a house and a cat, keep my job.'

'I want a boyfriend and I would be happy.'

Day 168

Sunday, 8th August – Sydney NSW

I head out to a major gym chain. It's only a quick ride down in an elevator, one that changes colour as you descend and ascend, and then a short walk to the end of Peter and Jai's street.

Back home after my workout, I share my observations.

'I have been to gyms all over Australia for the last 24 weeks, and it's guaranteed that all the hot guys are straight. Here at said gym chain I can safely say that it's the opposite: ALL the hot guys are gay. I'm not coping.'

If I needed an antidote to months of relative LGBT deprivation, inner Sydney provides an overdose. With such a comfortable base, it could be easy for me to not venture out of Surry Hills and Darlinghurst.

During my time in Sydney I've had to challenge some of my own misconceptions. It would be fair to say that until now Sydney and I have had a relatively uneasy relationship. Try as I might, I've always been left feeling like I don't fit in, that after a few days I needed to get home and shower (and not in a good way).

For the first few days I looked around and thought about removing significant amounts of my body hair (and those who know me would know that therein lies a big challenge), actually thinking about what I wear and sucking in my stomach, before relaxing.

Last night I got great feedback. After Jai's specialty silverside soup we ventured out. At one of Sydney's main gay bars I was mistaken for a rugby player. The guy was specific, saying I look like a fullback for the Canterbury Bulldogs side. I was thinking about going home to bed when suddenly it all happened. Walking by a group of four men I was stopped. More specifically I was grabbed.

'You've just won the 10 second game.'

Me: 'And the 10 second game is … ?'

'Someone says, '10 seconds!' and we all have 10 seconds to choose the guy we most want to shag. We all picked you!'

'Awww, look, he's blushing.'

I returned to Peter and Jai laughing, and probably blushing.

Within minutes a young man is bumping into me, pretending it's by accident. As usual I pretend not to notice until he makes it so obvious I have to laugh and say, 'Hi'.

His name is Marco, an Italian student here for a year to do design. Maybe he is new to this, or perhaps it's me who is new to how forward young Italian gay men are. When he asks if we can spend the night together I check in with Peter. It's obvious he approves – his eyes are almost popping out of his head.

'Oh my god he's *hot!*' he says to me in a whisper.

Me: 'I know, that just happened, right?'

Day 169

Monday, 9ᵗʰ August – Sydney NSW

My facebook status: Daniel Witthaus:

Wakes to the annoying news that his Newcastle accommodation has fallen through … And Sydney rain … And I don't care if we need it …

Spoiled beyond my expectations during my stay with Peter and Jai meant that what would normally be nothing more than a logistical blip takes on more annoying proportions. My annoyance and frustration gives me a clue to what I'm really feeling: dog tired. In Sydney I'd merely pressed *pause* on the inevitable for a few days.

I'd met a gay couple from Newcastle during my stay at Turtle Cove in Cairns. Over dinner one night they asked about my tour experiences and relayed their own story of having a commitment ceremony. Both had endured a great deal of rejection and hostility from their parents, yet after a decade together both their mothers would proudly attend their sons' commitment ceremony.

I still remember one of the men crying as he spoke of the vast change that happened within his own family and him asking for a long hug. Both men implored me to stay with them on my long trek down the east coast.

What none of us planned was a family medical emergency exactly as I was due to travel there. Suddenly I'm looking for somewhere else to stay. Ordinarily perspective would remind me that I've been hosted every night for the last two months, yet with this rain bucketing down in Sydney, in this moment I don't care. I want to just stay still, not drive, not meet new hosts or book into a backpackers. I just want to be a blob on the couch.

Day 170

Tuesday, 10th August – Sydney NSW to Newcastle NSW = 159kms

My week in Newcastle doesn't fill me with excitement until one of my Facebook friends comes to the rescue. It had been 'Nick' who had approached me following my book launch to give me feedback on the event.

'I used to work on the Central Coast of NSW and had to leave. I realise that I've not felt a sense of community since I left. Tonight I felt like I was a part of something again. I want to thank you for that.'

Although busy at work, Nick has organised for me to stay with his parents, who he adds 'love a guest'. I'm pleasantly surprised when I call Nick's dad, Clark. He has a warm, almost playful voice.

'We Googled you and we have some questions.'

Me: 'You Googled me? Really?'

'Yes, we know all about you. It's very interesting. Of course we wanted to know who was coming to stay at our place.'

I'm welcomed by Clark who makes dinner and we sit and eat together. This gives us a chance to discuss my tour and to get to know each other. I certainly feel better for the 'dad energy', reflecting with Clark that I haven't spoken with my own father for over 16 years.

Soon Nick's mum, Ellen is home and I get the chance to get to know her over a freshly made mug of Milo that she insists she makes so that I can finish my blog. Despite my disappointment at my original hosts falling through, I'm left thinking how lucky I am to experience the hospitality of Clark and Ellen.

Day 171

Wednesday, 11th August – Newcastle NSW

It seems appropriate, and brings me great delight as I travel around the country challenging homophobia one cuppa at a time, that tonight's venue for the Newcastle NSWTF book reading is Devonshire House. I've been warmly welcomed by local organiser, Barnie, I have a cuppa, now all I need are some scones.

'I'm sorry Daniel, but there are only four RSVPs for tonight.'

I'd been warned earlier today by Gina from NSWTF not to expect big numbers. It was Gina who first contacted me in March about the five NSW events that are currently taking place. She'd driven from Tamworth to attend the third of five NSWTF book readings, and we were enjoying a cuppa only hours before it was set to kick off. Gina said she'd received positive feedback so far from both the Lismore and Sydney events.

I could tell Gina was concerned at how I might take this, so I assured her I'd read to two people before, so the four who RSVP'd would feel like a significant crowd. I knew that Gina and her organising counterparts in NSW locales had worked hard to ensure teachers knew the event was taking place. I knew to wait and see who actually turned up.

Rather than feel anxious at how many people might turn up, I instead take in the surroundings that include an impressive painted banner by a local artist. Barnie tells me that until recently they could name the teachers and every student in the painting that was essentially a visual time capsule from the 80s. Something about that captivates and charms me.

Hunter Valley and its capital, Newcastle, have a rich educational history. For example, I find out that Newcastle East Public School is said to be 'the longest running public school in the Southern Hemisphere' (i.e. since 1816).

With 30 minutes until the reading there are four people. Barnie suggests we wait until the advertised kick-off time. Then a few more arrive, then a few more. As the reading starts, two other local teachers arrive, swelling the small audience to 13, only two off the 15 that 'Gay Nirvana' Lismore attracted and five off the 18 arrivals for 'Gay Nirvana Squared' Sydney. At short notice with teachers under great time pressures, this is a win.

In starting my book readings, I attempt to role model what the national tour is about. I immediately get people talking to one another, rather than focusing on me. It sets a more intimate, conversational mood for the evening.

Me: 'What I'd like you to do with the person beside you or the people around you is to talk about the main reason or reasons for coming tonight. I'll give you a few moments and then bring you back.'

'It's a giant gap in the curriculum.'

'The school is very much, *We have out kids, we'll deal with it when they come out.*'

'It's funny this is called *That's So Gay* because young people are saying it all the time.'

'My kids attend the local primary school and I'm a gay dad.'

Even if I had heard it many times over, it does not lessen the importance of it being said here and now. For these people, it's the first time.

Question time comes around later.

'So who is funding this tour? Is it federally funded, or Victorian?'

Me: 'It's self-funded.'

Cue the sound of 13 jaws hitting the floor.

Day 172

Thursday, 12ᵗʰ August – Newcastle NSW

'You've delivered the *Pride & Prejudice* program?!' I'm amazed.

'Well, we run things that work, and it does.'

Marie and I are having warm, buttered banana bread at a little café not far from her office at ACON's Hunter Valley branch.

'When I'm at work I just assume people will just think, *This is her work, so she must be a lesbian.* I expect that and that's OK. If people ask me, I'll tell them.'

When we get to ACON after our cuppa, staff are quick to welcome me. The manager of ACON Newcastle invites me to use desk space and other facilities, allowing me to potter in a semi-organised space for the afternoon.

Marie admits it has taken a while to understand that not everyone thinks and feels the way that she does, and gets surprised at times.

'I see things how I would like them to be. I get surprised when people don't see things like I do, that they can be done. Sometimes you do get surprised, remembering that people are different and come with different experiences and won't always come along with you. Sometimes when you are constantly surrounded by like-minded people everyday it's easy to think it's all OK, until you are confronted by people. It's a reminder of why you do what you are doing.'

For Marie a big gap is something for those aged 18-25 years.

'There's not a lot of organised things outside of the pub.'

Later I finally get to experience 'the pub', the only gay establishment in the Hunter Valley. Tonight it's Gay Trivia Night, a weekly institution and a chance to get some cheap pub meals. I arrive with an extra skip in my step after being propositioned by a prostitute on the way in.

Apparently the pub is also in the red light district. Perhaps she was thrown by my hopping out of Bruce, a rather butch 2007 Ford Ranger.

Day 173

Friday, 13th August – Newcastle NSW

From a prominent LGBT community member, mover and shaker at the University of Newcastle, and recent author of a book on homophobic violence in Queensland, via email:

'The timing is unfortunately not good because I am leaving the country on long service leave.'

OK, so how about a colleague who has had considerable involvement in LGBT-ifying university life and curriculum? Via email:

'I've heard about your work from [said colleague], and it's great that you're coming to NSW, but unfortunately I can't connect with you this time, because I'm on study leave too, and will be in Adelaide at the time of your visit.'

Fair enough.

Her colleague, prominent in university equity and diversity management? Voicemails after e-mail contact.

'…' [sound of silence on my mobile]

Local teachers, lecturers and prominent lesbian couple? Via SMS:

'Sorry for the short notice but we have a bit of a family crisis here and I'm going to have to cancel …'

How about the local LGBT support group? Via SMS:

'Unfortunately due to a recent tragedy in our group of friends. So sorry for the late notice.'

Ordinarily I find myself having missed connections and cancellations; however, rarely has it happened more than once in the same location. It takes a phone conversation with The Barman to understand why it's all hitting so hard. I'm taking all the missed connections, cancellations and other hiccups personally. I'm feeling like it's my fault that everything is 'going wrong'.

'If only I'd picked a different week or scheduled the meeting earlier or later or …'

I decide on an early night and potter on my laptop. I sit on the couch after dinner, watching a Rugby League match with Clark and Ellen. Clark eventually nods off in his chair, reminding me of my mum's with a blue, black and white handmade quilt thrown over the back. Ellen gets lost in a game of online Scrabble, explaining earlier that she is quite the formidable competitor.

This is exactly what I need. After carefully placing my half-slurped mug of Milo on the doily-covered side table I follow Clark's lead and close my eyes. The Rugby League commentary in the background quickly fades away.

Day 174

Saturday, 14th August – Newcastle NSW

'Dad found an article at the bottom of my drawer about gay and lesbian services. He came to pick me up from the gym and posed the question. I guess that's how I came out to my parents.'

Simon attended my book reading then invited me for a walk along Merewether Beach. He notes it's not my preferred method of a cuppa with a laugh, but concedes 'I feel better talking and walking'. I'm more than OK with the change-up.

'It all ended up messy. My grandmother spent about two days on the phone trying to find support for my parents and finally found PFLAG [Parents and Friends of Lesbians and Gays] and they started to go down to Sydney for meetings. When I was 15 I ended up going down to PFLAG meetings with them. I definitely knew I was gay. That's when I started dating guys.'

Emboldened by everything that was happening, Simon decided to tell a few friends at his school.

'It seemed to blow out a bit that I was gay. That's when the trouble really began.'

'Blow out a bit' is an understatement.

'I guess the students were pretty bad. I had homophobic teachers, but the students were relentless. It was being pushed down stairs or my bag being stolen, fruit being thrown or lunches being stolen.'

Teachers provided some safe haven, but only some.

'There was one who was a hippy and an English teacher. Every Wednesday we had journal where we wrote for a period. She asked me to start writing about what was happening and what I was doing with my life. So I would. I wish I had the journal, just to see what I'd written at the time. Beyond her I had, on my side, the Work Experience Coordinator, her son was gay and the same age as me, and I also had a Geography teacher who taught my sister. He was very protective over me. He used to pull me aside, have chats and make sure I was doing OK.'

There were also safe places to hide.

'I can remember going down to the Ag farm because it meant that I didn't have to be on the playground. I used to spend my time with a rough kind of farm assistant, and he was good because he kind of knew it was giving me a break. So he used to let me work with the animals and run around on the tractor.' He laughs at the memory.

Several teachers were as homophobic as others were supportive.

'One Ag teacher would say each time I walked in, she'd go, *Simon get out!* When I asked, *Why?* she'd say, *Because I'm not having a faggot like you in the classroom.*'

With such open hostility from several of his teachers, it was perhaps inevitable that it would all come to a head.

'I remember being in a year 10 assembly and there were a few boys who were always the ring leaders. They started throwing the fruit at me, and started with *Poofta* and *Faggot, faggot, faggot* and there was a year level teacher up the front announcing something. I remember a piece of fruit hit a girl beside me. I remember throwing it back in frustration and screaming, *I may be a faggot but I can get more women than you!*

There was a clear difference with how boys and girls responded. The boys sat and stared.

'All the females stood up and clapped me. It even went in the Year Book as a Most Memorable Moment.'

It's moments like these that can turn an entire school experience. Many times I have heard of these moments changing LGBT student experiences for the better. But for Simon it didn't.

'So after that the physical stuff started to escalate from being just kicked, having fruit thrown at me or pushed down the stairs.'

Me: 'Escalated to that?'

'It went from being singled out to it being a group of boys coming up and giving me a hiding. It ended up I had to make sure that I had my girlfriends around me or that I was in the art room or up in the staff room. Mum had taken me to hospital a few times because I'd been punched or kicked.'

Understandably, Simon wanted out. His mum said she wanted him to first hand-deliver a letter to the Principal.

'The letter said, *I'm sick of taking him to the hospital and to the doctor. I'm sick of the level of violence and I don't think you're dealing with it.* He denied that there was a problem.'

Yet Simon was not leaving without challenging this. It was not that he was not bright.

'I managed to stay a straight A student, despite everything, apart from the few homophobic teachers that marked me down. I reminded him that there were two formal complaints made about the violence by two teachers who'd had enough. It was then that he recoiled and realised I was actually being serious.'

Going to another school wasn't an option.

'I couldn't stay here, I couldn't go to any other school on the Central Coast because it would be known that a gay guy was moved.'

Shortly after that, Simon decided he needed to go to the big smoke. His older gay friends organised a place for him with their friends in Sydney.

'When I was 17, I decided the Central Coast was probably a little too small and that I should move to Sydney. From there life became a hell of a lot easier. I met a lot of people and found my little spot in the world.'

Day 175

'Fuck!'

A short man who looks to be in his late 20s grabs his chest, in gay speak 'clutches', and breathes a sigh of relief. We're in a local gym change room and I have come in to get changed.

'You move so silently, you should think about being a Ninja!'

I laugh and apologise. I hadn't thought about being quiet, only quick. I'm due for my very first Roller Derby, which Simon says has to be seen to be believed.

'Women of all shapes and sizes going at it on roller skates,' he laughs.

We arrive at an ageing sports hall that has 80s graphics of stick figures playing things like basketball and squash. It's now early evening and a cold day just became an even colder night. After finding our seats in the bleachers, I grab us hotdogs and tea, more for the heat than the sustenance.

Soon Michelle, a local lesbian born and bred in Newcastle, joins us. It doesn't take long before she announces that she's unimpressed.

'Someone just said to me that once you know the strategy of Roller Derby it's really interesting and you can get into it. She said, *It's like chess.* I said, *Yeah, it's like watching chess and not knowing what's going on!*

Unsure of what to expect, I watch two groups of women roller skate around what looks like a masking tape track. There is strategy, fine examples of skill on wheels and even lots of hard knocks and spills. What encourages me is that women are central, celebrated and in charge. Self-expression also seems to be encouraged, and I wonder how many of these women had few, if any, other outlets.

Whilst watching women of all ages, shapes, sizes and temperaments, Michelle explains her experience of Newcastle's Same-Sex Marriage Rally earlier that afternoon. Due to an inbox explosion I missed an e-mail alerting me to the rally, and was sitting clearing that very inbox as the rally took place.

Michelle laments that Newcastle's rally attracted 25 people, whilst Lismore had 150 people and the major cities had thousands.

'Is it because Newcastle is closer to Sydney?'

'Nut. Twenty-five people to a rally!? Twenty-four years ago we had a gay nightclub in town that would get 3–400 people every week. You couldn't get that now, and there are more gays and lesbians than twenty-four years ago.'

'So what do you think has changed?'

'It's just a case of 'non-care'. There is not a sense that we're working together for anything.'

Day 176

Monday, 16th August – Newcastle NSW to Bathurst NSW = 323kms

'I've got an idea, jump in the car with me.'

I've just confessed to Simon that I don't have enough photos of Newcastle for my blog and have to get moving in the next few hours if I'm to get to Bathurst before nightfall.

Simon takes me on a lightning quick, 'click and run', Kontiki-like tour of Newcastle's highlights, keeping the engine running as I jump out.

It's strange to think that I might not see Simon, Clark or Ellen again. It surprises me how I fall into these easy, warm relationships with people. After a few days my mind plays tricks on me, assuring me that they are now a part of my everyday life. Then the logistics of the tour rips them away. It feels in my body like I should be seeing them all again in a week, yet my head tells me I'm unlikely to see them again.

With pieces of my body strewn across various communities long behind me, my mind has turned its attention to Bathurst.

Admittedly I know nothing about Bathurst except for two things: *Outlink* was launched there, and there is a big car race there that Peter Brock seemed to win every year at one stage.

Just over a decade since it was launched 4th May 1999 at Charles Sturt University, Bathurst, I was adamant that I would return to the site of *Outlink's* launch. Had it not been for *Outlink*, this tour might never have happened.

I remember Peter Brock because my mother used to work as a production manager for a company that made the custom-made car seats that went into his cars. I still recall my mother coming home one day to tell me he was 'the most arrogant prick' she'd met. A year or two later she came home having had a photo with him on the factory floor and all was forgotten. She seemed annoyed when, as a young boy who retained 'too much', I recalled her first impression.

In any case, *Outlink* and brumm-brumm cars was all I knew about Bathurst.

Many would tell me how Bathurst, about 3 hours drive west of Sydney through the Blue Mountains, is fortunate because it has a tertiary institution: Charles Sturt University. As a rule, the presence of a university is thought by many to increase the likelihood of open, visible LGBT life. For example, the University of South Australia's Whyalla campus is thought to do just that in South Australia's 'Iron Triangle'.

Soon after arriving in Bathurst I head to the local soup kitchen run by the Bathurst Men's Shed. A member of the local LGBT social group, Western Area Gay and Lesbian Service (WAGALS) had invited me to come and say hi. It's safe to say that with the weather forecast predicting a temperature drop below zero, it's freezing. I huddle with three LGBT locals and enjoy a beef stew and a cuppa. My WAGALS contacts joke that they're trying to make the Soup Kitchen nights entirely LGBT.

When I asked one, local teacher Carly, how she thinks LGBT students experience her school, she gives an example of a female couple.

'It's hard to say because a lot of them are hidden I guess. We do have a young lesbian couple, about Year 10, they've decided that they want to show their affection publicly. There has been a bit of teacher backlash. There is this unspoken personal space rule. There's nothing written down. There is kind of a rule that each student must be 30cm away from other students, so technically that's true. These girls are being threatened with suspension if it continues. It's difficult because there is no policy there.'

Me: 'What happens when a heterosexual couple are publicly affectionate?'

'Teachers just walk past.'

I ask how students react to the young lesbian couple.

'I hear kids saying, *Miss, miss, those girls are kissing over there.* I say, *Well they're not kissing you so move on or don't look.*'

Being relatively new to the school and on contract, Carly is wary of rocking the boat too much.

'I've never spoken to the Principal or Deputy about it so I don't know whether I'm allowed to talk about it. At the moment because I'm not permanent I kind of figure once I'm in a school and settled and there for a long time, then I'll come out. I think it's more concern that they are going to be victimised and bullied I think. Because just speaking to my students, the general feeling I get is that they are not accepting of gay people.'

Carly wants to get some clarity.

'Just more acceptance and consistency. If the rule is no public affection, then that's the rule. But if it's OK for all straight kids to hold hands, then it should be the same for the gay kids. Teachers have a big influence in these kids' lives and they should put aside their own personal beliefs and teach kids. Even if they don't accept they should be teaching acceptance. I don't know, is that unreasonable?'

Day 177

Tuesday, 17th August – Bathurst NSW

If Newcastle felt like a week of missed connections, Bathurst saw some LGBT planets aligning. One example is a bi-monthly Bathurst Youth Network meeting which just happens to be this week; a one in 8 possibility.

I've attended countless meetings like this in a former life as a youth worker. I feel at home, right down to the polite, slightly nervous introductions and the uncomfortable process of getting someone to volunteer to be the minute taker. Little does he know what he's in for.

I am asked to talk about the tour.

' … looking at life for lesbian, gay, bisexual and transgender young people in regional, rural and remote Australia. Try saying that five times quickly.'

The audience laughs, and the minute taker chimes in:

'Well can you say that again one more time slowly so I can get it all down?'

After the meeting I'm taken aside by a youth worker who could have been a lumberjack. Steve and his colleagues work to support local 'disengaged' young people. Steve is very concerned about a young man he is working with and wants advice.

After grabbing a cuppa and a seat away from people, I settle in to see what I can do. Steve seems conflicted.

'I'm from Tassie and I'm ex-army, so … I grew up and homosexuality was illegal or it was a mental health issue. I left Tassie and I went into the army and of course there are no gays in the army. And then I went to Sydney and that was the first time I knew about gay people. Gee, I must sound really naïve.'

After some reassurance Steve continued.

'In Tassie there was no grey. It was black and white about gays.'

Many people would give Steve little time, but I could tell by how this man mountain clasps his hands, leans forward and anxiously looks at me that a great deal is possible.

His time in Sydney changed his life dramatically.

'The blinkers came off in Sydney. I thought, *Wow, there's a lot of Asians here and a lot of gays here.*'

Then tragedy struck. Steve's wife and kids were killed in a car accident. He vowed to be a different man.

'I realised I was not happy and that I had to change everything.'

Recently his work with a young gay man has triggered his own process of reflection. This young man was seen by the Principal of his school with another male student.

'He was sitting on the boy's lap and kissing him.'

As a result of bullying, this young man had to leave school and start attending TAFE. Whilst this ended the bullying, it hasn't helped with his home situation.

'He is getting kicked out of home. He gets a lot of grief from his brothers about his size and his weight, about not eating. His two brothers are probably like me.'

Steve explains he tried once to broach the subject of the lap-kissing incident. The young man quickly became uncomfortable and tried to change the subject.

'I took it really hard. I thought I'd upset him so I shut up and I thought I should never talk about it again.'

I talk to Steve about how he tried to talk to his client and he admits that he was so nervous that it might have come out like an incoherent, barely supportive monologue.

Me: 'Rather than avoiding it, what would happen if you took a different angle?'

'Like what?'

Me: 'What if you were open and transparent about your limitations and lack of experience, as you have been with me? What about if you set yourself apart from all the other lumberjacks in his life by saying some supportive things about being gay?'

Within 15 to 20 minutes Steve is a changed man.

'I'd avoided it because I thought I'd blown it, so I moved as far away from it as I could. I just got so wound up because I was worried so much about being PC that I forgot to be real.'

I wonder how many people would have seen Steve and thought, 'Redneck lumberjack'. Now he's sitting with me, looking into my eyes and quiet. Steve struggles to hold back a few tears of relief.

'I feel like a weight has come off. I feel lighter, almost like I want to ring this guy and see him straight away. Thanks so much.'

No Steve, thank you.

Day 178

Wednesday, 18th August – Bathurst NSW

'Oh shit!'

I found out the hard way that there is a Panorama Motel and also a Panorama Hotel in Bathurst. I had turned up at the Panorama Motel for the fourth of five NSWTF book readings. With the reading starting at 4.45pm, I arrived around 4.15pm.

At 4.30pm the Panorama Motel staff finally told me they had no event for teachers booked. I'd been assured by the Bathurst organiser that a gathering of teachers at the Panorama Hotel was already organised.

The receptionist said that if they said Panorama Hotel, then maybe they meant a hotel up Mt Panorama? With rain falling outside, time ticking and Bathurst peak hour building I chanced it and raced like Peter Brock up Mt Panorama, completing a 10-minute drive in a little under 10 minutes.

When the receptionist up on Mt Panorama looked at me blankly I got that familiar sick feeling of 'Oh shit'.

I finally find the right room downstairs. Tucked away in a secluded room are 7 earnest looking people who I assume must be teachers. The time is 5.15pm, 30 minutes after my expected start.

The gathering of teachers is actually a NSWTF meeting and they're still talking business as I sit to stop my head spinning from all the rush of confusion and adrenaline. Eventually I'm acknowledged by the organiser.

I realise now that this won't be anything like my book readings in Lismore, Sydney and Newcastle.

With the order of business wrapping up and me to be announced people are starting to shift in their seats and look at their watches. Before I know what's happening I'm seated before the waiting group not knowing what's expected of me. It's clear that this would not be the typical 90-minute *Beyond 'That's So Gay'* extravaganza.

Me: 'You've all been meeting for a while now. Before I start, would you like 5 or so minutes to grab a drink, check phones and go to the toilet?'

Nods come quickly. The suggestion is clearly appreciated. I confirm with the organiser that this would not be just a book gathering. With everyone seated again I do what I was taught during my time working across Victoria and Tasmania for Kids Help Line – if in doubt, ask the group for their expectations.

One older woman scoffs and rolls her eyes when I suggest I'd only be 10–15 minutes and I'm transported back to any number of staff-rooms over the last 12–13 years. Ladies and gentleman we have an involuntary audience, fasten your seatbelts.

Keeping it low-key, I explain the context for me sitting before them, namely my 38-week tour and my association with the NSWTF. They observably relax.

One senior teacher at a local high school talks about how two gay young men are faring very differently – one is incredibly popular, a sports captain with 'no-one' caring, the other is struggling with a number of other issues, especially with his family, is 'an emo' and being gay seems to be icing on the cake for bullies.

'They used to be friends growing up, but now that's changed. They couldn't be more different. The one who's doing well won't associate with the other one.'

Day 179

Twenty10's Sydney Louis and I are in good spirits for a day of meetings. Given that Twenty10 are looking to come to work in Bathurst later this year, Sydney Louis saw my Bathurst leg as a great opportunity to 'piggy back' and has secured a meeting with the local *headspace* office.

Tiffany from *headspace* is so excited about Sydney Louis and I being in town that she has actually come in on her day off. Although Tiffany sees it differently, a lack of room means we are fortunate to sit down for a cuppa in a kitchen rather than in a consulting room or office.

'Bathurst is big enough but small enough for everyone to know everybody else's issues.'

As for LGBT life, there is still a way to go.

'The over 18s are covered because Bathurst is a university town. It's the under 18 LGBT people that are not well-covered. The stigma is still there. Bathurst is still redneck.'

Not that there are not possibilities. Tiffany said that if an LGBT young people's group was started here, then they'd 'probably do it quietly at first …'

As a service, Bathurst *headspace* has considered what they could do to increase their LGBT-friendliness. Tiffany recalls a service discussion about putting a rainbow flag in the waiting room.

'Some of the clinicians said, *Well is it just tokenistic, will it really make a difference?* I said, *It can't bloody hurt.* The first day it went up the receptionist said there was one young person who said, *I want to thank you for showing your support for people like me.*'

Post-cuppa, Sydney Louis and I drive to the outskirts of Bathurst to *Outlink's* birthplace, Charles Sturt University's Bathurst campus. We are due to meet members of the Queer Collective (QC).

According to an organiser of the QC, Wade, the university remains an LGBT haven of sorts in Bathurst.

'A big issue here in Bathurst for LGBT people is employment. Being employed and being queer. The university employs queer people and if you can't get work with the university you'd struggle a bit. The number of people who are queer who rely on the uni for their employment is really high.

'It's a social group that is built around queer people being able to get together and it's a little bit of political action. It's about being around like-minded individuals who understand the issues, who you don't have to explain things to, and just being involved.'

'LGBT groups for young people say a similar thing across the country. Can you tell me about the political component? Everyone's definition of 'political' is different.

'It's about visibility on campus. That's the basic thing that happens. Our annual Queer Week is a big part of it ...'

Wade speaks quietly, yet with a passion that draws Sydney Louis and I in.

'Just being involved, that means a lot to me. I'm proud of myself for coming out. I have a little brother who is the least queer-phobic person and that has a lot to do with his interactions with me. How he talks to his friends and other people is reflected in that. I've also had friends come out to me and I've felt proud that they would come out to me. QC gives a sense of community and trying to form a community has been important to me.'

For Wade coming out is bigger than his own experience.

'I think the more of us that are out and visible, it's an education for people about what queer looks like. I think we should be proud there are so many of us, and different kinds of people who aren't afraid to stand up and be counted.'

Despite a recent dip in numbers and energy, the QC remains a haven for many who don't feel safe and supported 'in town'.

'There are mainly issues in town, but most people don't go into town anymore. I think in Bathurst a big thing about your experience depends on your ability to pass, whether people think you're queer or not, and how queer. I've done fine because I pass, but people who don't pass probably wouldn't get work.'

Day 180

Friday, 20ᵗʰ August – Bathurst NSW

I'm standing in the foyer of the Orange Civic Theatre, and I'm having regrets. There are high school students everywhere and a local production of stageplay *Rent* is about to commence. It could be any regional theatre, except that it's appropriately been constructed with materials of all shades of orange.

I first heard about this production of *Rent* from Rich, a local health educator with Kite Street Community Centre in Orange, about 45 minutes' drive north-west from Bathurst. To get to Orange you drive through landscapes that look like early Australian landscape oil paintings: rolling hills, simple fencing and a palette of greens and browns. Rich works out of the small yet majestic King George V Memorial Hospital.

Rich explained that there were going to be 520 students from local schools attending and that at the end they wanted someone to get up and speak about homophobia. As is my approach I said 'Yes' without knowing what I would do or what I'd say.

Once Sydney Louis hits town I rope him in to get up with me and talk about the great work that Twenty10 does with young people.

Meeting with Rich and some of his colleagues at Kite Street, I hear about a gay couple who recently broke up at a local secondary school.

'They said about WAGALS, *Look it's mostly for people in their 40s*. They were trying to set up a group for young people. They've now gone their separate ways because they've had a big blue and it's now folded, but they reckon there were more gay young kids. They were saying off the top of their head that there were at least 20 other young gay guys who they know of – guys that would probably be uncomfortable with identifying as gay.'

Rich finds a significant amount of his time is spent dealing with an adult LGBT community.

'We get a lot of people moving out from Sydney, some of it's work. It's an easier lifestyle. Bathurst is a growing population. We've got a lot of employment.'

If you pass that is?

There is also said to be a high number of men who have sex with men who don't necessarily identify with the LGBT community.

'There are some closeted guys who use beats and bash the openly gay guys. For example there was one [who bashed someone] trying to take the focus off himself when he was in front of his mates. I saw him a few months later and asked him why he did it. He said, *He gives the rest of us a bad name. You and I are discreet.* I said to him, *Well I had my reasons [for being discreet] but I didn't go around bashing guys.*'

Sharing his own journey of coming out whilst in a managing role in a local timber mill, Rich now feels strongly about getting the message to guys when they are younger.

So, back to *Rent.* Having agreed to speak to 520 students at the end of the performance, I have to think about what the content of the show is. An ex-boyfriend dragged me to *Rent* when it first hit Melbourne, telling me it was the hit of New York. Not a show kind of a guy, I went along and it's safe to say I couldn't remember a thing about it. I shared this with Sydney Louis.

Me: 'If I recall correctly it has a token gay, a token Asian, a token lesbian, a token everything really.'

With about 7.5 minutes to play with I decide that I'll only try and focus on three things. I'd been told to expect loud homophobic reactions to men kissing, but this doesn't eventuate, so I search hard in the second half for what to do. Sydney Louis helps clarify at intermission.

'Hi I'm Dan and this is Sydney Louis. You've all been sitting for a while so the first thing I'd like you to do is to stand up.' The audience stood. 'And shake it out.'

There's lots of laughing as Sydney Louis and I shake it out onstage. The audience shake it out too.

'Now did anyone notice any same-sex kissing in the show? You might have noticed that in the show people who were gay, lesbian, bi, trans, were all accepted for who they are. I've spent the last 6 months driving around country Australia talking to schools and students about what it's like at their school. What I'd love you to do is to talk to the person beside you or the people around you about if it's OK at your school to be gay, lesbian, bi, trans, whatever.'

After a few minutes I ask for a show of hands. Most students think it's OK at their school, less don't know or say it depends and less still believe it isn't OK.

'What you have all said is what I've found as I've driven around the country. A lot of people thought that because I'm an openly gay man in a truck that I might be bashed, killed or have my tyres slashed. But in most places most people say it's OK. What young people are saying is that the most important thing to them is to be able to be themselves and to have people they can talk to. In NSW, lots of young people talk to Twenty 10.'

Sydney Louis jumps in and gives his Twenty10 spiel.

Afterwards, the lead actor comes up and shakes my hand.

'I wish you'd come to speak at my school in my country town.'

After the show we have some photos taken with the cast, although my new future husband, a strapping local actor, stays backstage and doesn't join in.

I'm invited by the lead actor to come back for their next production in Orange.

Me: 'What's it going to be?'

'I actually don't know, but it's gonna be GREAT!'

Day 181

Saturday, 21ˢᵗ August – Bathurst NSW to Canberra ACT = 296kms

I'd confessed to one of my contacts for Canberra that I was looking forward to going to the National Tally Room on Saturday 21ˢᵗ August. Originally due to arrive on Sunday 22ⁿᵈ August, I decided that attending the National Tally Room won over a Saturday night in Bathurst. I figured that I was unlikely to be in my nation's capital for Election Night ever again.

There was perhaps no-one better to go with than my friend Jaiden. I'd met Jaiden at a national leadership gathering, the 6ᵗʰ National Johnson & Johnson New Leaders Forum, on the outskirts of Sydney in 1998. One hundred 'young leaders' from across Australia came together for four days. I spent most of the time hiding in the corner, given that most of the people there were sickeningly successful small business owners (in IT) or young executives from companies like BHP or IBM. As a volunteer with a gay and lesbian youth group and a severe introvert, I wondered how I snuck in.

I took the approach, much as I do now, of only speaking when I was spoken to. If asked I would explain to people my support of a group of gay and lesbian young people in Geelong and my hope to improve their everyday lives in local schools. I was honest that I didn't know how it would happen.

On the final day in the final session, 'Young Leaders' were invited to stand and reflect on their four days, what they learnt and what they intended to do. Loathing public speaking because it drew attention to myself, I sat listening to young leader after young leader stand and share. I was clear that I was not going to stand. It didn't help that I was feeling emotional after an exhausting program of presentations, discussions and self-reflection.

Then John, one of the oldest of the young leaders rose and started to speak. I looked forward to what he had to say after a discussion we'd had two days before. Between sessions I had been sitting on the floor by a window soaking up the warmth of the afternoon sun. Alone. Happily.

John would come and sit on the floor with me. Slightly annoyed that my solitude was broken, I eventually relaxed and began talking about my work in Geelong. John sat and listened, yet an unexpected thing happened. Slowly people sat down and listened in on our discussion. Before long a significant group of young leaders were sitting listening to me as I talked about my hopes to work in Geelong schools and why.

Now in the final session John began. He said how much he appreciated the opportunity to attend the leadership gathering and thanked everyone who had shared their reflections.

'But I'm interested in hearing from someone who hasn't shared yet. I talked to this young man the other day and since then I haven't been able to stop thinking about what he said. I think he is going to do great things and I'm interested in what he has to say.'

I watched John and, like everyone else , was wondering who he was talking about. After all, everyone else had stood and talked about themselves.

'And that person is ...' He turned to look at me and hence focused the attention of 99 young leaders on me. 'Daniel.'

Damn you. For the record I stood and spoke, yet I couldn't tell you what I said. Whether it was good or bad I'll never know. I suspect it would have been somewhere in between. I remember sitting a little stunned and receiving a round of applause.

Before getting on the bus for the long drive back to Sydney airport John approached me and gave me a handwritten note. Paraphrased it went something like this:

'Dear Daniel, I believe that you are doing a very special thing. One day you will be a leader of 100s of people.'

I never saw or heard from John again, yet I've never forgotten his belief in me, an intensely shy, awkward and self-doubting young man.

Another person who showed faith in me at that leadership gathering was Jaiden. Jaiden was a breath of fresh air because of his powerhouse intellect and self-deprecating humour. I liked how he said that if institutions were not working that they should be destroyed and rebuilt, as well as how he regularly referred to 'evil' people. I laughed a lot in his company.

Involved in student politics during many stints at university, Jaiden, a serial collector of degrees, became involved with the Australian Labor Party after the demise of the Australian Democrats, whom he was asked to represent as a senate candidate for Western Australia.

Today, in Canberra, whilst I looked for sausage sizzles at local primary schools, even though I'd completed a postal vote earlier, Jaiden handed out 'How To Vote' cards in the bellwether seat of Eden-Monaro. Then, instead of attending the victory party of the candidate whose seat he helped retain, I convince Jaiden to queue for one hour and five minutes on a wintery Canberra night to get into the Tally Room.

Once inside, one of Jaiden's friends, a Tally Room regular, explains that tonight the National Tally Room lacks the atmosphere of 2007. I get the impression that everyone is looking through their fingers at the results, wanting to know yet not wanting to know.

I speak with JOY94.9FM for their Federal Election broadcast, but I'm not sure I contribute much. However, I do decide that the National Tally Room is where I want to meet the man of my dreams, such is the disproportionate number of attractive men who give the impression of great intellect.

My Facebook status update tonight is: 'hot nerd burgers'.

Day 182

Sunday, 22ⁿᵈ August – Canberra ACT

With the election result well and truly still in the balance, I find myself in another group fitness class. I'm always interested in seeing who turns up to exercise on a Sunday morning, particularly in winter. It's safe to say that I notice the men in the room first and occasionally my female peers.

Late in the class I look sideways in the mirror to check out my technique during some lunges when I think I see someone familiar. Quite quickly I realise that I'm watching the head of Lifeline doing an impressive set of lunges.

I met Jen when I traveled to Canberra in 2008. I was working in the violence against women sector as the Victorian White Ribbon Coordinator. That visit I also got to shake Kevin Rudd's hand and talk about my work. For the record he looked like he needed to catch up on sleep and get some sun. He did compliment me on my Berlin t-shirt that I pulled over a business shirt to signal my distaste for formalities.

As I walked out of the class I decided to say hi.

Me: 'This might seem strange, but you work for Lifeline, right?'

'Yes. I thought I recognised your face.'

Me: 'Yes we met through White Ribbon.'

'That's it! Well actually – oh have you heard the news?'

I shook my head.

'I guess I can say because they announced it two weeks ago. I'm leaving Lifeline and will be the CEO of beyondblue.'

Me: 'Congratulations.'

'You're in Canberra now?'

Me: 'No actually, I'm based in Melbourne. I'm here because …' I give Jen the usual spiel, but I won't make you read it all over again.

'How interesting,' she said. 'Well I start January 4th so we need to have a coffee.'

I knew I dragged my sorry self out of bed on a Sunday morning for some reason.

Day 183

Monday, 23rd August – Canberra ACT

On a cold morning in Canberra I sit for a hot chocolate with Grant to discuss his work with AIDS Action Council (AAC).

'I've gone from being a participant in a youth group to running a youth group to being a guest speaker,' he says, beaming with pride.

A few years back Grant had been a part of a fledgling network called the Youth Sexual and Gender Diversity Network.

Now heading out to LGBT youth groups to do talks on things like sexual health, Grant admits that groups can have a really varied dynamic, and for white, middle class, private school attending LGBT young people, this can be a shock to the system.

'For some young people, going to the groups can be a bit confronting. Some young people who go there are open about living with violence, being former sex workers, not all of them, but it's much more confronting. That's one of the limitations of the group these days. The youth centres are not like the ones on *Home & Away* where kids just go to hang out.'

A theme through my discussion with Grant is 'engagement' of the Canberra LGBT population.

'Based on stats, we have 12,000 LGBT people in the ACT. On the ACT mailing list we have 2000 people. Twenty young people access each of the Bit Bent LGBT youth groups. There are 600 people who go to Canberra's gay nightclub, Cube, on any one night. My question is, where are the rest of these people? I found the idea that you wouldn't want to get involved with all the LGBT events, venues and activities quite strange, but most guys don't.'

One of the groups that Grant thinks is not being engaged is the young professional set.

'Like a group for young professionals for guys in their 20s who would never access a youth centre.'

One area where AAC is making headway is with schools. Workshops with teachers and workers with young people have happened in the past.

'We do deal with issues of *faggot* and *that's so gay*. We've found that teachers and youth workers tend to throw their hands in the air saying, *It's too hard. What can we do about it? It's too difficult.* Some say, *How can we do anything about it when people who are out and proud are saying it?* Well, my issue is the little guy in the corner whose identity is being used and he's not OK with it.'

And it seems in Canberra it might be better to live up to stereotypes.

'There do actually tend to be the guys that fit the stereotypes. They do theatre, they're not afraid to be fashionable, they do dance, they're in classrooms where it is more conducive to being themselves. Whereas the boofy rugby player or the weedy little guy in the Chem class I think tend to have bigger problems with it all.'

Day 184

Tuesday, 24th August – Canberra ACT

I've been very quiet about my birthday today, only mentioning it to Jaiden, who as an introvert can understand my desire to have a no fuss day to myself. Today I'm trying my best to have a rare 'day off'. I've taken myself out to lunch at a deserted pancake restaurant, downstairs in Canberra's CBD.

I've only been able to go out to lunch because of the generosity of Alice Springs host, Daniel. A few weeks away he'd e-mailed.

'Hi Daniel, I would really really love to shout you lunch for your Birthday if that is OK. Can you email me your bank details so I can put some money in your account? Don't say no either.'

The amount transferred would normally keep me going for a week.

After a lazy day with a long lunch, surfing the internet at the National Library and then gym, I arrive home for dinner with my Canberra hosts, the sister and brother-in-law of Jodie on the Gold Coast.

What I forget is that I mentioned to Jodie in passing that I'd be in Canberra for the Federal Election and my birthday. Not one to make a fuss, I hadn't mentioned my birthday to my hosts. A delightfully entertaining, progressive and welcoming couple, I'd decided that all I wanted to do was sit with them and have an everyday meal, and that their company would be the perfect way to spend my birthday evening.

After dinner as I sit and watch a current affairs program with them, Jodie's sister appears with a small cake.

'We weren't sure if it was today. Happy birthday!'

How lucky am I?

Day 185

Wednesday, 25th August

'My first 6 months in Canberra seemed very different to Sydney to me. There's no Oxford Street, there's no gay community. It seemed very loose to me.'

Evan, from local LGBT glossy magazine, *FUSE*, and I are having a morning cuppa at a café called Milk & Honey in Canberra's CBD. Like many things in Canberra it's modern, yet with a take on décor from the 60s and 70s. It's half full, which makes for a good interview atmosphere.

'It's actually not different to Sydney, it's just a lot smaller. I think that most people are out in the suburbs, having homes and doing lawns and that kind of thing. Whereas in Sydney it just seems that Oxford Street is where everyone is. Plus there's a real public service mentality here. Sydney is very edgy because you can lose your job at any moment so you have to be the best and that shows. In Canberra, because it's a public service mentality you just have to turn up to work and you won't lose your job, which translates to life. I don't wanna trash Canberra, but … It makes for a very serene city, but you only have to be a little bit edgy to be the next best thing.'

'Canberra's very different in that it doesn't have that gym culture. There is a general amount of fatter men in Canberra, they just seem not to care.'

An ex-navy officer from regional New South Wales, Evan decided *FUSE* might be a way to 'fuse' this 'loose' group together. Not that *FUSE* readers want Canberra's non-gym culture in their publications.

'People don't read it, they just want to see cute boys on the cover.'

Day 186

Thursday, 26ᵗʰ August – Canberra ACT

'I'm not exactly sure who you are or what you're doing.'

'Well that makes two of us,' I thought with a chuckle.

I've met Gayle at Tilley's Café, regarded by most LGBT locals as a gathering hot spot. A researcher and health educator, Gayle sits down and wants answers.

It's not uncommon for me to have people give me the 'who the fuck are you and what makes you think you can do this?' approach. I often sense it's part territorial and part ego. It's something that is partly understandable; after all to them I could be anybody. Typically I wait for the initial storm to subside. It comes from a place of good intent.

Gayle attempts to take charge.

'Well let me explain what it is that I'm doing and …'

Although very happy for someone to take charge during my cuppa chats across the country, I feel a need to explain the context of me sitting in front of Gayle. It's important that she's clear why I'm taking notes and for what purpose. And so the verbal arm wrestle begins: Gayle wants to start, I want to set the context so that she can talk until she's hoarse if she wants.

The context of my project completed, Gayle then begins.

'Well as I said I still think everything I was going to say is really relevant to everything you are doing with your work.'

We talk about Gayle's research, the barriers she's faced in doing educational research in this area and how her findings echo everyone else's.

'There is an occasional teacher that can be helpful and LGBT-friendly which is in line with the research. But most LGBT young people didn't know that they could talk to anyone or think they could talk to anyone. One boy had a teacher, he had thought the world of her, it was his favourite subject. She always said, *Come and talk to me about anything.* So he decided to tell her. Her response was, *Why don't you just try to be like the other boys?* He just shut down. He thought all the teachers were going to be like that.'

Given her longevity and experience, Gayle is in a position to assess how schools are faring.

'The evidence 10 years ago said these young people were experiencing abuse and harassment and they still are.'

To many, my strategy to challenge homophobia one cuppa at a time was thought to be reserved only for the staunchest of my opponents. Just as a cuppa and a willingness to listen could open an unlikely dialogue, so too a pair of hot beverages could do the same with a reluctantly trusting ally.

Admittedly this particular occasion required a second round of cuppas for us both: coffee for Gayle; an English breakfast with a side of full cream milk for me.

Day 187

Friday, 27ᵗʰ August – Canberra ACT

'It's primarily a social group but also a support network. You have a get together once a month, a sort of 4–5 hour get together, very informal. About two weeks after that we'll have a café night. It's inclusive rather than exclusive. It's about acceptance and support (and includes their friends and families). It's not very political; we have another group that is more that side of things. They are about trying to change the world, we're about providing a space for people to be themselves.'

Andrea is new to the Canberra Transgender Network (CTN).

I mention that there is some talk of there being different ideas in the trans community about what political action should be taken.

Me: 'What are your views on that?'

'I think the trans community is more fragmented than the gay community. I've had gay and lesbian friends all my life and it seems that the issues they have are less complex than transgender issues. I've met 20 transgender people and come up with 21 different stories. Of the gay people I've met there seems to be a similarity between the stories of gay people and the experiences. And it's for that reason that it's so hard to get political and social acceptance and recognition.'

Not that Andrea is shying away from this.

'That's part of the reason I've become involved politically, to try and give a voice to those who can't speak for themselves. The incidence of transgender people losing friends and family is higher than with gay people in my experience. The general community knows what it is to be gay but they don't know what it is to be transgender or gender diverse. I mean we can't even decide on the terms!'

Even Andrea's e-mail signature demonstrates her commitment to this idea:

When we speak we are afraid our words will not be heard or welcomed.
But when we are silent, we are still afraid.
So it is better to speak. ~ Audre Lorde ~

The issue for Andrea is clear: trans visibility.

'It comes down to a lack of acceptance of anyone who is perceived to be different in the community. In order to be different in this world you have to be extremely confident, because if you're not confident, you get picked on. Many people are just not confident enough to go out and be who they want to be. Until someone is visible and stands up, we remain stigmatised and marginalised. Is it too much to ask for acceptance and diversity? Shit, what are we, human beings or not?'

When I asked Andrea what might help CTN members in the next 6 months, as a way to get practical and less utopian, Andrea is initially stumped.

'What most of our members want is acceptance of friends, family and society and that's not gonna happen in 6 months.'

Yet talking some more Andrea would identify better funding for mental health services and more transgender-friendly workplaces to battle high levels of unemployment as two ideas.

Andrea agrees to posing this question of 'in the next 3–6 months' to the CTN e-mail list and beyond. The first response comes in only two hours later.

'Well, I am accepted at work without condition. I am accepted by my friends without condition. Most of my family accept me without condition. I cannot say at any point in my transition – apart from my doctor who I viewed as a challenge – have I experienced transphobia. Maybe I am blind to it or just have had a better reception than I expected myself. I count myself lucky in this respect.

'What needs to happen and what I want to happen, is to not be so caught up in the endless loop that I have created between examining myself and questioning myself. It is a bad habit that has been developed from a life time of self-doubt, denial and covering up.

'It's not about what I want or who I am any more, it's about just finally accepting me for who I am and getting on with day to day tasks and not distracting myself by getting all introspective. It is a bad habit and one which is hard to break.

'So, the thing which will make the biggest difference in my life in the next 3 to 6 months is to just get on with life and achieve all those things that I know I can and to stop hiding from reality and making excuses.'

Day 188

I'm excited to be attending a launch of the latest instalment of a group fitness class. I book in Bruce for a service and check-up early so I can make the mid-morning start time. I want to make sure Bruce is fighting fit for our trek to Broken Hill in a few days.

Earlier this week Grant explained that the group fitness room, the biggest I'd seen, used to be an indoor swimming pool. This makes sense. Grant told me that our instructor for our class was the daughter of the man who is responsible for bringing those classes to Australia from New Zealand.

Excited enough by this, I was then invited by 'the daughter' to come to the launch for instructors. I'd always heard of these events because you get aerobics instructors from all over in the one place. I figured that couldn't be a bad thing, but also wanted to see how I compared to their fitness levels.

I walk through the gym to find a place to stretch out when I spy a familiar face: Matt. In Rodney Croome's launch speech for *Outlink* in Bathurst, Matt was the subject.

'But beyond all this the project aims to allow young lesbian, gay and bisexual people and the communities in which they live to benefit from and enjoy that sense of integrity, of place and of belonging which my friend Matt so misses, and which ultimately is so important for our happiness.'

Matt, who now lives in Melbourne, is in Canberra and has what I want: his boyfriend is an instructor and is attending the launch. One down, many thankfully to go. For the record I fall in love three times during the class and keep up.

After showering and chatting with some of the instructors, Matt checks in.

'We're all going to lunch. You should join us.'

I think for a moment, then realise one of the instructors that was talking to me in the change rooms has come up because he knows Matt.

'Adam's coming, aren't you Adam?'

'I'm in,' I say.

At lunch Matt is keen to hear what I've been finding, and signs of progress since we met during our *Outlink* days. I'm still thinking about progress and how there can be hiccups. A few days earlier a youth worker,

Donna, talked about starting their own support group for LGBT young people.

'The other kids are getting better, but it has been a long road. They used to be, *that night is Fag Night* and so they knew kids who were turning up early were coming for the group. But it was really slyly saying things and bullying and obviously we picked up on that, so then they were waiting out the front for them to arrive early, out of sight, then we found out about it.'

I said that other organisations have been reluctant to talk about doing what they have.

Me: 'What would you say to them?'

'I think it's a total cop out if people say, *We're not a gay and lesbian organisation so we can't do the work.* I personally think it's everyone's job. You don't have to be gay or lesbian to understand the issues.'

Day 189

Sunday, 29th August – Canberra ACT

It was another case of thinking I'd seen someone familiar as I sat with Jaiden and awaited the start of the AIDS Fundraiser Trivia Night last night.

Me: 'Hmmm, he has that Berlin look I like. He almost looks familiar.'

'Who?' Jaiden asked.

Me: 'That guy over there in the purple Adidas jacket with the 70s porn star mo. It's almost as if I've seen him in Berlin. I have this thing where I go to Berlin and think I see people from Melbourne and I'm here and I see people from Berlin.'

'It's just your mind and wishful thinking.'

Needing to powder my nose, I realise I have to walk past his table. I have been looking his way and I expect a night of slightly uncomfortable looks and nothing more. As I walked past, he jumps up and corners me.

'Hi Daniel, my housemate knows you and I know all about your work.'

Leroy goes on to explain that he is studying his Graduate Diploma in Education and wonders if I have time before I leave to meet.

'Great', I thought. Wary of mixing business with pleasure I watched as Leroy became strictly professional. Exchanging numbers to coordinate our schedules he checked my surname.

'It's Wittenhaus right?'

'Almost, it's Witthaus. Sprichst du Deutsch? [German: Do you speak German?].'

'Natürlich, ich habe für Sieben Jahre in Berlin gelebt [German: Naturally, I lived in Berlin for 7 years]. I used to work in the Heile Welt.'

The Heile Welt was one of my favourite bars when I lived in Berlin in 2006–7 and 2009. A quick perusal of my diary confirmed it: he'd served me a number of times at the Heile Welt and I'd announced to my then-flatmate that he was my future husband.

Yet before I could meet my ex-future husband for a cuppa there was a trivia night. Leroy's team was penalised heavily for using their smartphones to Google answers, so my team leapt to second place in the end. One point separated 1st and 2nd.

I mused on how you could ensure SmartPhone Trivia Night Integrity in a room full of gay men with smartphones, given that most of them were actually paying more attention to Grindr (an application which allows you to find other gay men in your vicinity using GPS) than they were the trivia questions or Google. It was this smartphone focus that later led to my leaving gay nightclub, Cube, soon after my second drink. Well, that and an approach by a straight girl.

'I want you to come and dance,' she said from suddenly right beside me.

'No,' I said. 'That's OK, I'm happy standing here.'

'I've been watching you, really, come and dance.'

Me: 'I'm finishing my drink, I might come in a song or two.'

Not.

Finally I headed out, curious about why I was singled out. Nervously she danced and looked at me.

'You're straight, aren't you? I've been watching you.'

I stopped dancing and looked at her. Seriously? Here? Months on the road and one of my few chances to be thrown to the homosexuals and I'm mistaken as straight.

'No,' I said. 'I'm very gay ...'

'Are you sure you're gay?'

Me: 'Yes, very sure I'm very gay.'

'Well you're hot. Why aren't you picking up?'

I wish that she could tell me the answer to that question.

Me: 'It just doesn't happen like that. And I'm going home soon anyways.'

I thanked her and walked out of the nightclub through a sea of men looking at their smartphones.

*

This afternoon Leroy and I end a few hours of cuppas and talk about our work, our lives and our love affair with Berlin. Leroy lets me know that during these few hours he's been focused on something very different to mobile technology.

'I haven't been able to stop staring at that bottom lip of yours.'

Day 190

Monday, 30th August – Canberra, ACT to Wilcannia NSW = 932kms

I leave early for my destination, only stopping 400kms later for fuel and a new mobile phone. Last night my mobile decided it was no longer going to switch on. Truth be told it had been suddenly switching itself off for the last month or so; I'm only thankful it never happened during a radio interview or important phone call.

I took a chance driving so far without a mobile phone, however a fully serviced Bruce did not let me down. I realise that this is the last major drive I'll be doing for the tour; after this drive west to Broken Hill, the longest drives will be 2–3 hours at most.

Whereas driving east in Queensland I went from red dirt to brown dust, driving north then west along the Barrier Highway I go from green rolling hills, through brown dust before finding myself with orange and red dirt once more.

When I arrive in Wilcannia on a warm evening, I get a brief inkling into life there. No radio and no mobile reception.

Finding my hosts, Elaine and Sal, might be harder than I thought. Elaine had flagged finding her without mobile reception in an e-mail.

'There are no street signs, but as you come into town, you will see the school on your left. Turn right into the street with the school at the left corner and the motel on the right corner and follow that street until you see two big water towers. Then stop and beep your horn.'

I do all that and get no response. So I choose the next option.

'Alternately, if your phone is working call me as you come in and I will meet you on the main street so you can follow me home.'

After going to the service station five minutes before it closes I find the only public phone in town and call Elaine.

What follows is a relaxed, warm evening of eating and talking. Not for the first or last time on my tour, I marvel at how people invite me into their home, provide a fantastic meal (pasta with roast pumpkin on this occasion) and quality company that makes traveling 1000s of kilometers less daunting and lonely.

Elaine tells me about her early relationships.

'I went out with guys who went off to boarding school. These guys were gay. I also knew they weren't interested in seeing me or having sex so it was perfect. One wanted to be an actor on *Home & Away*. I should have known.'

At this stage Sal joins in.

'Well my boyfriend was a Michael Jackson impersonator. I should have known. A really convincing Michael Jackson impersonator. He had the whole dance routine to *Smooth Criminal* down.'

I ask what brought Elaine to teaching.

'One of the lecturers told me I shouldn't be a teacher because I'm gay. He also told the guy who had tattoos he shouldn't be a teacher because he had tattoos. Because I'm stubborn I decided I was going to be. Sometimes people opposing me is the thing that gets me through. Teaching is the thing that 'makes a difference'. Doing something to make it better and teaching is something I can do for 12 hours a day.'

In Australia, remote communities are almost dying in the hope that young, vibrant and visionary teachers like Elaine will teach in their schools.

'I guess that's the good thing about being in such a dysfunctional school. You can only make things better ...'

Not that Elaine knew where she was being posted according to Sal.

'You didn't know where it was. She had to Google it and I thought, *Oh no, where is she going?*

'I was targeted hard and I thought if I didn't go that they could miss out on someone. I didn't want the kids to miss out on an English teacher. And the Principal said it had been three years. So that did it for me. I decided to try it out for 12 months. No-one was twisting my arm to do this.'

Sal had different ideas.

'I decided I wasn't going to go. Then I felt like shit. I went through a week where I thought I was the worst girlfriend in the world. The reputation of the place preceded it.'

A few years on Elaine is out at school, and now that Sal has moved to town, they are known throughout the very small community. Whilst they are largely left alone, and slowly gaining respect and trust, there are still major obstacles.

'Most students think that it's wrong to be gay. For example one said that he'd kill Sal, swears at me and throws stuff at me. But that's not the worst. Then it's white cunt or fat fuck. It's a point of weakness they can exploit. I do have lessons where for an hour I'm sworn at. It hurts more when you have to put up with kids and then go into the staffroom and put up with it from another staff member. It gets to you.'

But slowly Elaine is making a difference, in ways that can only happen over an almost painfully long time. Recently Elaine showed a Powerpoint slideshow about the same-sex marriage debate. The response from students was simple:

'*Why can't you just get married? Really? Why not?* They just assumed that you should be able to.'

Day 191

Tuesday, 31ˢᵗ August – Wilcannia NSW to Broken Hill NSW = 196kms

One sleep in, one late breakfast with Sal and two hours drive later, I reach Broken Hill. Along with Kalgoorlie and Mt Isa, the remote former mining town is one of the places I was warned about.

I soon make my way to local RSL, The Musician's Club. It's the biggest venue in town, although its size is not the reason I'm here. In a room towards the back I'm due to have my fifth and final NSWTF event.

'I thought there would be more people,' remarked one teacher.

Although poorly attended, I stick with my policy of pushing ahead. The group of a half dozen is still three times bigger than my Darwin book reading.

At times like this I remember the words of a dear friend and training guru from Tasmania, Nairn Walker. I met Nairn at the same leadership gathering where I met Jaiden from Canberra. One time I talked to her about a training session I ran with three people in rural Victoria.

'Daniel, I've trained rooms with three people for three days. Then people get to know you and your work. I've been back to the same places and now I'm training 300 people.'

Elaine and Sal have told me this RSL is one of the best feeds in town, so we have the roast special that is on offer. Not a teacher, Sal talks about her own experiences in challenging homophobia in rural NSW.

'I was part of a local queer group. I had a problem with being on panels. There were questions. And so many people had horror stories and [there were] psychos and I thought, *I'm not the best person to do this.* My family was fine, I don't come from a religious family. I wasn't gonna get smited from above. Maybe I'm not the best role model. The worst that I got was, *This makes me uncomfortable because at some stage I'll have to talk to people about it and explain it.*'

There was one opportunity for that local queer group to go to a local school.

To her surprise, Sal was taken aback when the Year 10 health class was full of 'a very big group of baby dykes'.

'It kind of backfired because they said, *We know it's OK. Mostly the issue is that it has become 'so cool' that all these non-gay people are pretending to be so they can hang out with us and they end up being try hards.*'

Day 192

Wednesday, 1ˢᵗ September – Broken Hill NSW

In Broken Hill, Bob explains there has been an informal social grading system ever since the mines were around.

'A Graders are born and bred local. B Graders are from away but basically grew up here, or married in. C Graders? You basically just came into town.' Like many places I've been to this year, locals immediately ask where you are from. In Western Australia it was almost a hopeful anxious question, 'You're from WA, yes?'

Yet like so many systems and quirks, this grading system was anything but a playful icebreaker. Its history is in protectionism. Bob, a former miner, explains.

'Broken Hill culture was built from across the road [a former mine site]. That's where it started, right there. It was tough. You hear stories of strikes going for three months and people standing by their mates. It's a Labor stronghold because it's about unions and standing by your mates. That's the fabric of this town. Broken Hill has a strong history. The union, the mines. The grading system was about people coming in from out of town. They were coming to take away local jobs. It was simple, if you weren't local, you didn't get a job. It's about looking after your own.'

This was a time unlike today, where mines in WA and QLD are more than happy to take outsiders on, such is the lack of people willing to work in the industry.

Bob now works across a vast amount of NSW around Student Welfare with the Department of Education.

'We're not dense in terms of student population but we do have distance.'

Being LGB or T doesn't seem to be coming up across his region. Yet Bob is working mostly with Principals and Deputies. Perception of 'priorities' might also be at work.

'The everyday demand is huge. Delivering content, managing student behaviour, day-to-day welfare of kids is a huge thing. Teachers feel flat out all the time and the demand that they're put under, well.'

Yet in terms of curriculum and supports, Bob is like so many others in regional and rural Australia: he suspects it could be OK, assumes that there is enough being done and is hopeful of how it would go if someone came out as LGB or T.

'Tolerance. Equity is obviously a priority in NSW with Equal Opportunity. Each student has a right to an education regardless. And obviously there's all these things in place to assist their needs. I'd imagine there'd be something in the health and physical education curriculum. If an issue came up we'd address it.'

Day 193

Thursday, 2nd September – Broken Hill NSW

'If you want to go do tertiary stuff then you have to leave Broken Hill. Which is not a bad thing. It's easy to get very comfortable. I know, I came here as a teacher 30 years ago.'

I jumped at this opportunity.

'So you're not an A Grader?'

That kind of talk, I'm told, will make people believe I'm a local. It helps break the ice. Vic, a local youth worker, had been very vague and evasive in the phone call to set up this cuppa. So I'm surprised to meet a man who has considerable energy and personality to burn.

We sit in Vic's sunlit office, out the back of a pre-fabricated building that would have been thrown together about the same time he settled here. It looked uncannily like an over-sized toilet block with its holey bricks, usually designed to encourage ventilation. A fenced off junkyard next door, with a long-abandoned truck and caravan, is a reminder of a time gone by.

Vic paints a picture of a homophobic environment in local schools. 'That's so gay' is commonplace in Broken Hill too.

'I'd say amongst young people there's what I'd call *soft discrimination*. A couple of young people might be sitting around and they use *that's so gay*. I don't think it's a good thing. A lot of young people are using the word gay. It might be just a perception on my part but it's used in a negative way. It's not quite as hard as the word *poofta* or *faggot*, not as harsh but it's still a problem. It's not a good indicator of tolerance and inclusion and that concerns me. And it's particularly evident in high school students.'

Vic does attempt to challenge it, but realises it's not always straightforward.

'You'd be battling to call it vilification. It's not quite shaming, but it's a put down. It's like the other day with a few young guys here I said to them, *In NSW vilification is illegal so just be careful with how far you go*. They were bandying it about quite recklessly.'

According to Vic, 'soft discrimination' has to be challenged.

'What was it with one of the great philosophers? He said, *If you control the language, you control the thoughts and if you control the thoughts, you control the people.* That's why it's so dangerous. By not challenging it, from there it's a springboard to other inappropriate stuff. It's setting a platform up.'

It was only then that Vic asks if I'd found it anywhere else.

'So it's not peculiar to Broken Hill?'

No.

'I've really noticed it in the last two years, it's really been over the top. Generally high schools avoid the issue. It's a hands off situation. Teachers have fairly strict boundaries around what they can say. And if students were going to want to talk to a teacher about sexual stuff then it would have to be with a counsellor. In that case it would have to be with a parent's knowledge and permission.'

Despite this VIC, like others, still believes Broken Hill in general is tolerant. Not that there aren't apparent limits.

'I think that Broken Hill is a harsh environment if you step outside of what's acceptable sexually. People aren't backwards in coming forward in calling people a slut or something else. Generally in Broken Hill gay people have been fairly accepted. When people come out loud and proud then it's a different story.'

Day 194

Friday, 3ʳᵈ September – Broken Hill NSW

'We're a shrinking community. We're in a holding pattern of about 20,000 with an ageing population. Tourism has taken over from mining as the major industry in town. An example is how many art galleries we have in town.'

Vic scratches his head about this, as does another local who says, 'I don't understand it, but someone must be buying all that art'.

I myself go looking for art in Broken Hill, yet not to buy it. In Sydney I had met a young gay artist, Martin. From Berlin, Martin had entered an Outback Open Art Prize Competition. He had wowed me and others with his profession: drawing snail penises for the NSW Museum.

Residing in Sydney, Martin had to make a mad dash to Broken Hill, having already lived there for a period, to 'save' his painting. Those moving the painting had slipped while hanging it and ripped the canvas. Broken Hill is a *very* long train ride, after which Martin quickly patched up his painting and jumped straight back onto the train back to Sydney.

I find the large oil painting and see that he has managed to capture beauty in the bleakness of the landscape. By far the most well-known artist for capturing beauty, colour and movement in the local landscapes is Pro Hart. This name brought to mind an iconic image of my teenage years: spaghetti, red wine, eggs and other food staples thrown onto a carpet to make artwork for a television commercial.

I arrive at Pro Hart's art gallery, north up the hill in Broken Hill, to meet his son, John, and his partner of 8 years, Chris. John is clear that Broken Hill had changed dramatically.

'I had a pretty tough time. Broken Hill was full of rednecks, ex-miners. You couldn't walk down the street without having someone yelling, *Hey you fuckin poofta.*'

It didn't help that John's parents were part of the Assemblies of God.

'You're behind the eight ball because you have, you know, *Sinner, no salvation until you die.* I don't think that's a healthy way for a kid to grow up.'

Now deceased, his dad's fame and eccentricities cast a large shadow over him.

'There was 'This Is Your Life'. He'd drive around town in the Rolls Royce. I didn't want to. I think when you're young you want conformity.'

Being gay in Broken Hill 20–25 years ago seemed hidden.

'Everyone here was pretty much in the closet. You'd have the dinner parties in homes and be totally outrageous, but keep it low-key everywhere else.'

Then John came out.

'I came out of the closet so fast that everyone got hit by the shrapnel. Because my father was so famous I probably copped a lot more because I was so visible. I fell in love. That was the only reason I came out. That was before the whole AIDS thing happened. That was terrible when it all broke loose. I had a partner say to me about the 80s, *It was just becoming trendy to be gay and then the whole AIDS thing hit.*'

It turned out to be more than just your average hindrance to broader acceptance. For John, there is no question that it was a call to arms. Volunteering with friends, John recalls looking after AIDS patients when there was still community hysteria and misunderstanding.

'All those poor bastards who were abandoned by their families. There was one guy where they were leaving food outside the door. You wouldn't treat a dog like that.'

At this point John has to stop, overcome momentarily by the memory. John, Chris and I sit in silence.

'Yeah. I'll never forget it.'

I put down my pen and take the time to look around their makeshift sitting room; the living quarters of the large gallery is being overhauled.

When he starts talking again, John tells me what helped him heal his relationship with Broken Hill and reconcile his experiences was he and Chris moving back to care for his then-dying father. Now they're not moving.

'Broken Hill had changed. I'd changed. But because the mines have closed down and a lot of the rednecks had moved away. People who are here want to be here.'

This is certainly my impression talking to locals, LGBT and otherwise. Nobody gives me the impression they are trapped here. Still, the bigger cities seem to call LGBT locals, or at least the Gs.

'Most of the gay guys tend to move to Adelaide.'

Still healing, John is trying to integrate the new Broken Hill and the new John.

'I've been here 10 years and not heard of anyone having any issues. Fuck, just in the space of 20 years!? Fuck we've moved on here.'

Day 195

Saturday, 4th September – Broken Hill NSW

I've anticipated this moment since sitting at Broome's Cable Beach with Andrew: finally seeing Argent Street and 'that pub'. I tell myself there is a chance that when I do, I might work out how the Priscilla moment shaped Andrew's life and his journey to embracing 'gay' as his identity.

I arrive early evening at 'that pub', Broken Hill's Palace, or Mario's Palace as it's known to the locals. It dominates the corner of Argent and Sulphide Streets with its three storeys and distinctive two-pronged roof. No longer in the hands of Mario's family, a group of locals has bought the local institution and is slowly encouraging the old girl back to her glory days.

You can tell instantly that Mario's is something from another time; it's not what it once was, yet this is part of its charm. The first thing I notice in the bar area is the atmosphere. As I look around there's an air of class, from regal red carpet to beer steins of all sorts on wooden pelmets.

I walk into the foyer, boasting three levels of stairs against walls with colourful murals that leave you dizzy. This is an example of why their business card boasts: 'Where everything is a little bit different'. This place was obviously built with 'out of the ordinary' the goal. Mario was visionary, and quirky at that. Rumour has it that there were once tunnels from the mines straight to the pub's underbelly.

I steal a moment on the pub's grand balcony with the sun dropping slowly. As I overlook Argent Street I feel overwhelmed. Broken Hill was one of those places I was told not to go. I'm surprised to be greeted in this moment by virtual silence, save for the occasional quiet hum of a solitary car driving up the town's main drag. In the calm quiet I wonder whether Broken Hill is that different from anywhere else in regional, rural and remote Australia.

I'm here to have a drink with, arguably, Australia's most famous photographer, Robin Sellick. Robin is a minor local celebrity, as much of a celebrity as you could actually be in Broken Hill, easily talking with any number of locals.

Robin, like other gay men I spoke to in town, feels like he shouldn't be here.

'I said I'd never come back.'

And he could be forgiven for not ever coming back. At 14 years of age Robin picked up a camera and never looked back. At 20 he left Broken Hill for Adelaide, for many a reason, not the least of which was his sexual identity. Interestingly Broken Hill, according to locals, has a closer affinity with Adelaide than Sydney given that the former is five hours drive away and not 13.

'The first thing is that it's Sydney which thinks it's the centre of the universe.'

It was winning a significant photography award that encouraged Robin to use that money and 'go for it'. The goal: the USA. Once in New York, he made his goal to 'meet as many photographers as possible and learn' just as much. After learning a great deal Robin found himself without money, yet he knew he wanted to work with Annie Leibovitz.

Back in Australia Robin's time in New York, persistence and research paid off. He consistently 'sent stuff' until finally he was given the chance of an interview to work for Annie. Knowing that it takes someone dying for a position to come up Robin took a chance: he sold everything he owned and got himself to New York. As he touched down he had $US1000 to his name.

And the rest is history. Celebrities, parties, money, firstly in the US and then in Sydney. Many good times were had with many people we'd all know. Robin told me several stories that I can't repeat, although I'd love to share them. If ever you meet him, ask him about the relationship between a space shuttle and a horse's arse.

Twenty years after leaving Broken Hill and vowing never to return, Robin found himself back and not fully understanding how and why. Yet back on home turf, much of what had been swirling since his departure suddenly made sense. This is a theme of so many LGBT people, particularly gay men, I have spoken to throughout regional and rural Australia: a reluctant homecoming yielding so much more than they could ever have imagined.

For Robin, this manifests itself as an invigoration of his ideas about Australian photography.

'I'm trying to create an Australian style of photography. Every country has a language. We have Australian cinema, architecture, music. Well what's Australian photography?'

Too often Robin believes Australian photographers merely attempt to copy the style of photos they have seen in Europe or in the US. Long frustrated by this, Robin is now putting his money where his mouth is. Next year he's releasing a book of photos of Broken Hill locals in their everyday settings, matched with some landscapes. And there is good reason for Broken Hill being the location. As Robin suggests, Australia could be shaped by all things Broken Hill.

'I think Australia is becoming more and more like Broken Hill everyday. Look at the issues we are facing right now: water management, a better deal from mining, etc. These are all things that Australia could learn from Broken Hill.'

Day 196

Sunday, 5ᵗʰ September – Broken Hill NSW

'Twenty years ago men went to the mines and then the pub at night. Women didn't work, were barefoot, pregnant, all of that. Now it's different. There are same-sex teachers in relationships that are well known. Ten years ago it wouldn't have existed just because of the nature of the community.'

Dorothy had alerted me to changes, for the better, in Broken Hill. I'm not leaving Broken Hill feeling despondent whatsoever.

Rather, I'm reminded of how small the world is. On Friday as I was wrapping up my cuppa with John and Chris, I asked Chris more about his background.

'So where are you from?'

'Numurkah in Victoria, nobody knows it, it's OK.'

'I actually do know it. It's not far from Shepparton. One of my best friends is from Numurkah and I went to his wedding there. You might know him, it's such a small place.'

And it turns out he certainly did.

Not only that, Facebook reminded me of how close to home I really was; some 8 hours drive.

'Hey mate, I was thinking about you yesterday on my drive to work. I was thinking that you were out there somewhere in OZ doing some seriously great work and I hoped you were loving being out on the road. It's tough being away for so long but what an adventure. Can't wait to hear all about it over a cuppa when you get back. Safe travels ...'

Day 197

Monday, 6ᵗʰ September – Broken Hill NSW to Mildura VIC = 297kms

'Nope, sorry, Humpty was sold and now lives in Queensland.'

I stare at the middle aged woman at Mildura's Tourist Information Centre for a while not knowing what to say. Perhaps I'd passed Humpty Dumpty by on my travels in the Sunshine State? When I open my mouth again to ask the question, she's quick and clinical.

'No I don't know where in Queensland.'

I arrived in Mildura hoping to retrace my childhood steps, of which I remember two very clearly. The first is a tourist attraction where my older brother, older sister and myself played amongst things like a giant dinosaur, upside down boot and the old woman's shoe. I'm told that many children were placed on Humpty Dumpty's shoe for photographs. The reason I remember it so vividly is that after this happy snap was taken, my family walked to the car and teased that they would go to the sultana factory without me. It's safe to say I was very unhappy and may or may not have thrown a tantrum.

'You said there was a second thing,' the woman said. 'What was it?'

Me: 'OK, so maybe you can still visit the sultana factory?'

'Not allowed for health and safety reasons. The Sunbeam Factory closed to the public a while ago. But now they have a shop in town? I can mark it on a map if you like?'

Oh the days when I could run through all those sultanas and cough and sneeze away, reaching in to grab them out.

Although not immediately successful, I'm excited to be once again in my home state of Victoria. After 28 weeks on the road, some 7 months, I find myself on the home stretch after covering South Australia, Western Australia, the Northern Territory, Queensland, the Australian Capital Territory and, now, New South Wales.

With only 3 hours to drive from Broken Hill, I set out early and find myself crossing the Murray River into Victoria sooner than I expect – even including a stop to finish up some fruit before a quarantine point. It might have been the very early morning, it might have been moving on from yet another warm, hospitable host or maybe it was getting back into Victoria, but I feel emotional. I hear on the news that a member of 1970s sensation Electric Light Orchestra (ELO) has been killed in a freakish accident by a stray hay bale as he was driving by a paddock. When they play a song in tribute – a song that whisks me back to my childhood – I start shedding tears as the first line plays.

'Hello. How are you?'

Day 198

Tuesday, 7ᵗʰ September – Mildura VIC

'Anita, I was told you would be a great person to talk to, given your great work as a local Principal and now working across the region.'

Cue a modest giggle on the other end of the phone. Yet flattery would not get me anywhere when I floated the idea of us talking about LGBT young people in local schools and challenging homophobia. Anita currently works across the Sunraysia region, which includes Mildura.

'I'd like to help you but my project doesn't take in that particular group. I'm sorry, but ...'

Me: 'And what particular group does your project cover?'

Even though I knew the answer, I asked. Her response?

'Well my project looks at young people disengaged from the education system and ...'

Breathe Daniel. It's a reality that people don't necessarily know. So breathe.

Me: 'Well research evidence shows that same-sex-attracted young people are overrepresented in that particular group.'

Yet it still wasn't biting.

'Well I don't know that research evidence and I ...'

OK, we can solve that.

Me: 'Well I'm happy to come right now and place that research evidence on your desk to consider.'

And so one day later I am sitting having a cuppa with Anita at an art gallery posing as a café, or vice versa. After a reluctant, defensive start, it turns into a pleasant, informative conversation. Anita believes student welfare staff in schools are responding, given her experiences as Principal in one of the, according to locals, 'roughest' schools in Mildura.

'Over the years I've found it's much more likely that gay students would discuss it with student welfare staff. They'd go because they were teased, put under the spotlight a bit. But usually it was associated with other issues. It was never simple. Life isn't that simple.'

Using 'that's so gay' and 'faggot' happens in the Sunraysia region too.

'There seems to be a groundswell over the years of young people using them as 'power buttons', whether it's accurate labeling or inaccurate. In the 15 years I was Principal I saw a big, big change in people's preparedness to talk about homosexuality, but there is still a lot of work to be done. So I guess each generation does its bit to move things on.'

Without going into great detail, Anita and I discuss a number of ways to get LGBT young people onto the agenda locally, regionally and at a state level. Yet like myself, Anita is limited in her project.

'I don't even have money to buy paperclips. All I have is my mouth and my keyboard and that's about it. Ideally I'd like to see a vision for young people. Regardless of their issues, let's get them to the best place possible. The people in this town are aware of the financial benefit for this town if we get these kids engaged.'

However talking to locals, there isn't a great deal for disengaged LGBT young people in the Sunraysia region.

'The main sources of help and support are the well-being staff, and part of that would be the help lines. I'm not sure what's available in Mildura.'

I leave pleasantly surprised that Anita's initial time budget of 30 minutes blew out to closer to 70 minutes. Yet I hadn't accounted for this with the parking meter. I get back to Bruce to find another tour first: a parking ticket.

Day 199

Wednesday, 8th September – Mildura VIC

'There are no support mechanisms for young gay and lesbian people in Mildura.'

'Why not?' I ask.

'Because the people who hold the power and the money for services are heterosexual. So it's not a priority for them. The people who create the programs and have the funding don't even think about them. It's not in their paradigm of thinking.'

Therese at Mildura Rural City Youth Services notes there are no openly LGB or T young people.

'Most young people in this city don't want to be publicly identified. In general there's a social reluctance of people being out. I should know. I'm an out lesbian and I moved up 3 years ago from Adelaide to be with my partner. My personal experience is that there is a fair whack of homophobia here. It's kind of like 10 years ago in that there are a lot of couples who are together, who everyone knows are together, but the couples themselves don't say anything.'

Not that Therese takes this approach herself.

'I know that I stick out. I said to my partner, *You need to know that I'm pegged as a lesbian. I've been pegged long ago before I even knew. You are immediately going to be pegged.* We've been out and proud for 3 years. There are a lot of people who are out. But they're discreetly open. People know that they're lesbians, but there's no gay pride marches, no gay bars and no support organisations.'

For Therese, homophobia is more subtle.

'My partner ... she came out late in life ... hasn't been touched by that hatred that can be spat at you. There's a lot of people in Mildura who are homophobic who do their best to hide it. There is low exposure to alternative lifestyles here so it's inevitable that you're going to come across people that will discriminate.'

Those locals hiding homophobic attitudes don't seem to always be successful in doing so.

'There's a lot of passive discrimination. They don't want to be seen by other people as homophobic and then their attitudes seep out over time. And they think that I'm stupid and don't realise. I've been on the outer my whole life. So I know when people are putting me on the outer, even if they are being nice to my face.'

'Some people would say that things are better these days. What do you think?'

'You forget the awkwardness, the intensity of all that once you've been accepted by family, friends, work colleagues, etc. When you're young and you don't have that bag of tricks of experiences, it can be very confronting.'

Therese notices that being gay isn't that acceptable.

'I ask, *How would you feel if your daughter came home and said she was a lesbian?* A lot of people say they don't care if you're gay but once it's a member of family then they have to face up to it and it's not about the social mask they put on anymore.'

Not that Mildura doesn't have its good points.

'Coming from Whyalla I kind of knew what to expect, but I've been quite surprised. Mildura is extremely multicultural. It's very dynamic in that sense. I've been very accepted by my partner's family, her siblings, her children.'

Still Mildura, like Broken Hill, is torn between its assumed capital and its practical capital.

'In some ways I think that Mildura is estranged from Melbourne because it's closer to Adelaide. We're like a stepsister because we get all our funding from Melbourne, but when people go to capital cities they'll go to Adelaide because it's only 4 hours drive and Melbourne is 5 or 6 and a lot more traffic. A lot of the time we're told we have to do things the Victorian way even though it's not what people want.'

Day 200

'We'd have a trailer with a closet on the back.'

Half a dozen gay and bisexual men roar with laughter. I'm in the lounge room of a local gay man, Oscar, who heads up the local gay and lesbian support group, and someone suggested a way that they could raise awareness about LGBT people during the Harvest Festival Parade, the name the locals call their annual mainstream Mardi Gras.

Oscar has, at very short notice, gathered locals and generously opened up his home, in a quiet street on the outskirts of Mildura. Cuppas and nibbles, and for others wine, are in plentiful supply.

For members like Oscar, it's about getting a message out to local young people.

'That's why I maintain my involvement in the gay group because I do it in the hope that it will make a difference. We didn't have mobiles and internet and phone lines and organisations but now they do and kids are still topping themselves. We have to stop people topping themselves. How do we get the message out to young people that it's OK?'

Jeff is one man who came out in his 20s because he didn't think it was OK. Part of the reason was the hotel he was managing according to Oscar.

'For a time he ran the roughest pub in town.'

Unlike stories in Bathurst, Jeff feels that 'passing' as relatively heterosexual was a barrier for him growing up.

'Passing can be a negative. If you're out and camp you're OK. I actually surprised people when I came out.'

Slowly male patrons found out the guy running the pub was gay.

'Guys would say, *I've never had a beer poured for me by a gay man before.* Some guys liked coming up to shake my hand hard. It got back to me that they did it to see if I got a hard on because I've touched another man's hand.'

I laugh. It's safe to say I encounter many heterosexual men, and others seemingly so, who like to use meeting me as an opportunity to work through their homophobia. I've lost count of the number who want to shake my hand firmly or hug me, in what I've sensed is a daring, brazen challenge they have set themselves. Up there with skydiving and the like, they can say they have survived an encounter with a gay man, heterosexuality intact.

Jeff says his dad took a while to digest the news when he came out. 'When I came out dad didn't say anything. Until one day we were walking through the paddock. He said, *I went to a reunion. I met this woman from Perth called Sally and she has a gay son.* That was the icebreaker.'

Oscar's parents were not so easy to appease. Enter Oscar's son. An apparently confident, attractive young man, Nick is a security guard at a Brisbane gay bar. When in Brisbane, Nick takes Oscar to that bar and has to stop Oscar from hitting men who try to flirt with Nick.

When Nick was younger there was a dinner uniting Oscar's family, especially his opinionated mother where Nick was not present. The next dinner Oscar demanded that Nick come along to prevent him enduring another ear-bashing.

'I said, *You're coming to dinner. I've copped an earful from your fucking grandmother so you're coming to dinner so it doesn't happen again.* He said, *Dad, I've got some things I need to say to grandma and I don't want you butting in.*'

Dinner was said to be civil until Oscar's mother made a couple of comments.

'Nick said, *Grandma, I have something to say to you. You'd better sit down.* Fuck he paid out on her. *Dad's gay, get the fuck over it.* And that's what needed to happen. My 14-year-old son had to get stuck into her.'

Day 201

Friday, 10ᵗʰ September – Mildura VIC

If I wasn't successful at finding Humpty Dumpty, I'm successful in finding the next best thing.

My hosts in Mildura, gay couple Sam and Matt, have finished early and we are all sprawled out over two large chocolate-coloured couches. Sam is curious about how my week has gone.

'So have you done everything you needed to? Was there anyone you still haven't spoken to or anything you haven't seen?'

I recount my story of arriving in Mildura and being quickly dismissed by an efficient, less than sympathetic tourist information centre attendant. At this point Matt turns from watching a US reality show and seems interested.

'That's funny. Do you know my dad was actually the one that built that brick wall that Humpty was sitting on.'

Day 202

'I wasn't game to come out in Swan Hill. Thirty years ago if I'd come out as gay I would have been killed. So I did what was expected of me and got married and had kids.'

Oscar couldn't imagine coming out to his family and friends when he grew up in nearby Swan Hill. Standing with the door of my faithful truck, Bruce, open, I again found myself torn. Once more I was preparing to jump in and drive off to another location just as I felt I was starting to get to know someone and get a deeper understanding of their experience.

With this and the hope of progress in mind I drive about 2½ hours south-east down the Murray River to get to Swan Hill. I pass every so often through smaller towns that are, or at threat of, being engulfed by flooded rivers. After months of driving through western and northern Australia I'm not used to anything other than dry riverbeds. Now I drive over bridges where water is level with the bridge and along roads where water flirts with overflowing them.

It's in Swan Hill beside the uncharacteristically full Murray River that I meet with a blast from my past. In May 2000 I was invited for a series of 'Up North' professional development sessions with local teachers and health professionals.

As I sit on the riverside decking with Wendy, I remember encountering her for the first time and what passed from my lips.

A female teacher had started to dominate a group discussion and was crossing from the professional into the personal. I waited for her to take a breath.

'With all due respect this is not about you, it's about local young people.'

Semi-stunned, both Wendy and I looked at each other. Had I been too blunt?

The answer to that question came from Wendy becoming a devotee to the *Pride & Prejudice* educational program. Wendy would attend the very first *Pride & Prejudice* Facilitator Training that rounded out the VicHealth-funded project. I recall this training so well because it took place on Monday 10ᵗʰ September and Tuesday 11ᵗʰ September 2001. I woke up the next day and my day off was spent in front of the television absorbing the events of September 11.

Last time I was here two incidents stood out. The first was a local gay restaurant owner who floated the idea of a gay pride march down Swan Hill's main street. Wendy explained.

'He had a restaurant and he wanted to do a gay pride march. It was astounding. He was run out of town by the Christians. No, that's not right, it was the Catholics. He was so brave and he was run out of town. His restaurant completely closed down. The local minister was on the news saying, *We don't want those people here*. It was really terrible. It was pretty nasty.'

I recall sitting with that man's mother back in May 2000 as she told of the impact of the Christian runout on the family and her son's business. Defiantly she had told me she wasn't going to leave, because that would be too easy, and it was her home.

The other incident that stood out was a story about a local student I was told in a workshop. Luke was at an inter-school sports carnival between a government and Catholic school. No-one knows much more than the fact a group of young men attacked Luke because he was thought to be gay. At the peak of the attack the young men were said to be kicking him on the ground. Had he not been wearing a helmet during the attack, said the ambulance and police officers who attended after, Luke would have been killed. Luke's family had to move him to another town for his safety. The young men? No-one spoke of Luke's attackers. They stayed in town with no known consequences.

At the time Luke's mother told me he had to live and attend school alone in Bendigo. She and everyone else thought this was a great outcome.

Ten years on I ask Wendy what life is like now in Swan Hill.

'It's alright, just as long as you don't say it, speak it, or stand up for it. I think it's the same in many country towns. It's like in the US military, *Don't Ask, Don't Tell.*'

Wendy believes that being discreetly open doesn't translate to school life.

'I suspect that if a kid was to come out that nothing overtly violent would happen to him but their lives would be made so miserable that they would leave or commit suicide. Life would be relentless and merciless with the other kids. It's hard enough as it is. I don't think there's any difference in how they treat the gay kids now than they did 10 years ago when I met you.'

Wendy believes there are gender differences.

'We had two girls, they identified themselves as lesbian, it was admittedly only to a few friends, but the boys, never at all. Not when they're at school because it's not safe. I live in a town where if anyone comes out, it will be long after they've gone, or if they do it's when they're comfortable coming back. Some of them feel comfortable coming back.'

Doing her best, Wendy let's her students know that homophobia is not OK.

'There are three rules in my class that have always been that way. No racism, no sexism and no homophobia. And the fourth is treat others how you'd like to be treated, which is always with respect. The fifth is don't speak when I am, but that's a different story.'

Day 203

Sunday, 12th September – Swan Hill VIC to Geelong VIC = 373kms

I'm somewhere between Castlemaine and Kyneton, shortly after filling Bruce at a small petrol station on Castlemaine's outskirts.

It's approaching nightfall and I've pulled over to take a phone call from the CEO of a country Victorian organisation.

'I need to use you as a sounding board,' she says.

'Sure, shoot.'

It turns out that there is a large amount of money that will be dedicated to supporting LGBT young people in two Victorian country areas. Her organisation will be one of the funded areas, and she's asking my advice on the second.

'It has to be Geelong.' I reply. 'They have supported this work since 1994 without any state government support, before it was OK, and they were the first local government in Australia to do so. Plus they have a well-connected and resourced youth sector which can be a compare and contrast with your region. People might say I'm biased, but objectively they are the ones.'

'Are you sure? Would they be even interested?'

'Call up the City of Greater Geelong's Youth Services and talk to David. Say I recommended you both talk. He'll be very happy you called him.'

By coincidence I'm driving towards Geelong. Almost 200 days since I left her safe arms I'll return for the briefest of pitstops.

As soon as Bruce is in my mother's driveway, she is up and excitedly waiting to hold me again.

'I just like to touch you and know that you're here and OK.'

It's like I've never been away at all.

Day 204

Monday, 13th September – Geelong VIC to Ballarat VIC = 86kms

'Well I'm fuckin' set, aren't I?!'

My sister, Helene, was recounting her feelings when she realised her lecturer at university was LGBT-friendly. Her lecturer in Community Services, Malcolm, had used examples of LGBT people and their struggle for equal rights during some of her classes.

'I'd heard him say a few things about homophobia here and there, so I just knew. I decided a few weeks before that I was using you for my big assignment.'

I found that out on a Saturday night in Canberra. Moments before the commencement of the AIDS Fundraiser Trivia Night, Helene called to ask some questions of clarification. She laughed that calling her little brother was 'research'. I laughed because my sister was doing a PowerPoint presentation about me on a Saturday night!

From Helene's account, the class was impressed by her presentation on a challenging homophobia project. Referring to me only as 'Daniel', Helene says her classmates were amazed by what they were hearing. At the end Malcolm congratulated her on the thoroughness of her presentation.

'Thanks. I had to ring him to find out a few things, but the rest I found on the internet.'

Malcolm was impressed.

'Wow Helene. That's impressive to actually call him.'

The class murmured, nodded and agreed. Bursting, Helene finally let the cat out of the bag. Being my sister, she chose to sing it.

'He ain't heavy, he's my brotherrrrrrrrr.'

Now, a few weeks later I'm sitting in a tearoom with Malcolm.

I jump straight in and ask him why he's so comfortable and confident in talking about LGBT people and their campaigns for equal rights during his classes.

'My brother's gay,' he says. 'He's about 10 years older than me. He came out when he was a teenager. And he talked about the gay campaign group ACT-UP, so that's how I know about that.'

Me: 'For the sake of others who would wonder how it fits, how does it fit for you?'

'In the early units we run sociology and community development. What we include in that is we talk about the UN Charter of Human Rights. We talk about genocide and different kinds of discrimination. People must work to make sure they are not abusing people's human rights and matching that with the standards in their own places. I include gays and lesbians who were murdered in the Holocaust. There's also a unit called 'Systems and Advocacy' which includes things like gay rights. I always talk about ACT-UP in the 80s and marriage equality as a current example.'

Understandably sometimes the course contact can hit close to home.

'We warn people that a lot of the material covered can be very confronting and for people with issues that are unresolved, then they need to consider that.'

My sister, Helene, has come back to study as a mother returning to work. Yet this is much more than just retraining. And that she was doing so in Ballarat has even more significance than most would realise.

Growing up, my siblings and I, along with my mother, her twin sister and her children, would make the drive most weekends from Geelong to Ballarat. Our reason for doing so was to visit my grandmother, my mum's mum, Muriel Estelle Duffin.

Muriel resided for most of my childhood in a mental institution called Lakeside Hospital. Although the family doesn't know quite what was wrong, it's safe to say it was schizophrenia and bipolar depression along with a touch of pyromania and kleptomania. There is no doubt that these weekly drives impacted on our childhood, yet nothing compared with how it impacted on my mother and her siblings.

It's funny to me now, that my sister and I have not really discussed what these trips to Lakeside Hospital, now a housing development, meant to us. I find it remarkable that I somehow enjoyed the trips to the eerie majestic old stone building with the huge iron doors. It meant family time and seeing 'Big

Nanna', named for her size and how it was relative to her own mother, 'Little Nanna'. I also experienced 'fetching' Big Nanna with fascination.

My mother recalls taking other family members to Lakeside Hospital only to find them vowing never to return. For me, fellow patients of Big Nanna clutching at me and saying that I was their grandson or son was amusing and interesting. My mother still occasionally, and unnecessarily, worries that she has scarred me for life.

Yet it's only been this year that I've realised how deeply these visits affected my sister. After a volunteer placement at a Geelong organisation working with people struggling to maintain good mental health, Helene was moved. Seeing first-hand that few people worked for significant stints in such organisations, Helene knew what she wanted to do.

'They're just like my grandmother.'

For Helene there's a very personal reason to come back to study, even though it was a challenge after leaving school disengaged and disinterested, then after three children.

Like her brother, personal experience has drawn her to her work. Now it's important that real life is reflected in her studies. Hearing about LGBT people makes sense to Helene, just as it makes sense to Malcolm to include them. Yet during my cuppa with him, Malcolm has cause to reflect.

'That's me. I know what I do in my classrooms, but I don't know if other teachers are giving those examples, and how they're teaching it. I think maybe some kind of professional development for teachers should be on offer. It probably needs to be a conscious issue of TAFEs to make sure that teachers are having a discussion about *Are we having these conversations? What do you do? How do you do it?*'

Day 205

Tuesday, 14th September – Ballarat VIC

'Zaque was started 8 years ago. It was worker driven. There were two separate age groups at that stage. As far as I know that only lasted a little while, I don't think it had the numbers, before it was given the heave ho. And then it started again 6 years ago. And it's evolved into the awesome program that it is now.'

On a sporadically drizzly day in Ballarat I sit for a cuppa with 'Karl' who heads up Zaque, the local LGBT young people's group. He explains that the model is simple yet effective.

'We hold weekly meetings. We have a regular attendance of 12–15 young people. One week is our social activities, the other is our community development week where we work on community awareness projects. We held an event for the International Day Against Homophobia (IDAHO) earlier in the year, we had local sport clubs, members of Council. It was good because it got the kids out of their comfort zone, like with the sports people and the high professional council members, which helps break down those stereotypes, for both the Zaque guys and the guys that attended. Last night for example we talked about World AIDS Day. We're gonna try and turn the town hall red which I'm excited about. And it all comes from the young people.'

Like many other LGBT projects, Zaque's online community is larger.

'Zaque has 130 on Facebook, 170 on MySpace and there's the small group of people that keep in contact via e-mail because they're not comfortable coming out yet.'

Our attention turns to the use of 'gay' amongst young people.

'It's not tolerated in our drop-in space for young people, but it's everywhere. If I quiz them on it they'll be like, *That's shit* and so I question them and they'll say, *No I didn't say that.* I don't know if people understand what they're saying almost. Young people will say it and mean *That's so dumb* or *lame.*'

Me: 'Well we know *that's so gay* contributes to negativity in the LGBT-climate, so what is life like for local LGBT young people?'

'Isolating; depressive; homophobic; intolerant. It's definitely moving forward, but it's not moving forward at a pace that I'd like. There are still young people here that are abused and harassed at school and on the street.'

The list goes on. As a local born and bred, Karl can talk about changes in Ballarat.

'When I went to school you just beat the shit out of the gay kids without asking. Of course now they have their bullying policies, which are good. But then a lot of schools will deal with the bullying but not the homophobia. There is a difference.'

There are plenty of stories that are as difficult to hear in Ballarat as anywhere else in regional Australia, yet there are good stories as well.

'The Zaque kids are so strong. I look at some of them and wish I had their strength when I was their age. They're out at school and they put up with shit and deal with it in such a mature way. It's great. I'm proud of where they're at at the moment. I look at where they've come to in the last 18 months and it's amazing.'

Day 206

Wednesday, 15th September – Ballarat VIC

OK, so a blog crisis is averted. I am relieved.

Aside from one requested amendment, where I forgot to change a name when uploading the Gold Coast blog, my blogging each week to capture my local challenging homophobia and LGBT story collection has gone without incident. That is, up until the last day or so.

In a flurry of emails, three people from one regional network ask for their sections to be altered or amended. One says that he could lose his job for my re-telling a *very* de-identified story – offered freely and enthusiastically as I wrote at the time - about a local school, one says that she was not expecting to be quoted and another wants to be removed completely because two other people have been upset.

I sigh, clarify and then go about amending the blog as quickly as possible, internet access-willing.

Tonight I've received e-mails to confirm that all is well once again.

The two affected people in the network have admitted that there was an honest misunderstanding, thanked me for my prompt action and wished me well for the rest of the tour. One admitted that they hadn't been feeling themselves lately and possibly over-reacted.

Although I was shaken at first by the initial ferocity of the e-mail storm, I do have to chuckle that people implied that my weekly blog was widely read.

'Someone other than my mother is reading it?'

Day 207

Thursday, 16th September – Ballarat VIC

'We have some young people who are out and they're obviously saying it's a safe place to be. Other students are even being encouraged by LGBT students to come to the school. I don't think they'd see themselves as being labeled or picked on, but I don't exactly ask them or say, *How has your day been?*'

In contrast with other schools, Phoebe tells me LGBT students don't just rely on one teacher for support.

'If I think of the gay students I know they all have a significant person in the school who they can go to. That can be quite diverse. It can be any number of people, not necessarily the English teacher. It could be the woman running the second hand book shop.'

Examples of LGBT friendliness at her school are numerous.

'We've had male students take male partners to Valedictory Dinners. And we don't cancel, postpone or prevent. There are no judgments passed on who you are with, you can bring a date that is female or male. We also have a few parents who are now in gay relationships and they're quite open about it and coming in to support their kids.'

Me: 'I'm sure anyone reading about this school will be wishing they could come here.'

'Well it's not utopia.'

Even so, there are many similarities between this Ballarat school and others across regional, rural and remote Australia.

'I'd say our girls are really out there compared to our boys here. Our boys probably come out later, the Year 11 or 12 mark. Our girls are probably the Year 9 and 10 mark. The girls are fairly dramatic and swapsy amongst their group … whereas the boys not so much. I think [the boys'] relationships tend to be more outside of school. I think they're probably more stable. They kind of hold off a bit longer in making it public knowledge. They more come out to one or two people whereas the girls come out to everyone.'

Day 208

On an overcast morning on the outskirts of Ballarat I'm sharing a green tea with Olly, a local private school teacher on maternity leave. We're sitting on stools at the bench in her kitchen, and I feel immediately like I'm catching up with an old friend.

Early in her teaching career Olly had decided she wanted to teach in remote communities in WA and the Northern Territory. It's clear that working remotely has impacted on her, and shapes the way she sees the world and her work.

Given our shared experiences, I decide that this cuppa is one where I'll put down the pen and enjoy. And so our interview instead becomes a conversation.

I'm interested in hearing about Olly's experiences of her former, recent, school given the stories I had heard over the years. One of those was the PhD student who re-evaluated *Pride & Prejudice* last year. His thesis supervisor had actually looked at levels of homophobia amongst staff and students at said school a few years ago and found it couldn't be any worse. Olly confirms that it was all, unfortunately, true.

'Every single sentence has *that's gay* in it. I had it banned from my classroom. They actually got used to it, every student knew. But it's absolutely rife, it didn't do much.'

Unlike male staff members, the female staff at the school are proactive. 'All the women are supportive of something being done.'

A number of times Olly comes back to my national tour, seemingly overwhelmed at the logistics and the potential impact.

'Look,' I say, 'you're right, it feels huge to me sometimes, but it's the everyday conversations as a result of the tour that will lead to the biggest change. People often think it's about doing something extraordinary, but it's more about what we do with the people around us. For example, you can think about your classroom ban on *that's so gay*. If nothing else, it's one dissident voice in a sea of homophobia. I've spoken to enough young people to know that can be an oasis in an educational desert.'

Before I leave, Olly loads me up with gunpowder green tea. I'd been fascinated by her special kettle that has a green tea button which ensures the water is heated to exactly 80 degrees. Olly had explained how this means the green tea is not burnt and won't have that bitter taste.

'You know how you get green tea that …'

Me: 'No way, where it has that burnt taste?'

'Exactly, that's because the water is too hot. I bet this tea tastes soft and rounded.'

For the record it did.

Day 209

Saturday, 18th September – Ballarat VIC to Geelong VIC = 86kms

It's a cold morning as I drive back from Ballarat to Geelong, although not as cold as it can be in this neck of the woods.

For the last five years I have been waking early on cold winter mornings to drive to Ballarat Grammar for an annual presentation to Year 9 students. Like other elite schools, Ballarat Grammar sees Year 9 as a pivotal moment in a student's academic life. Given brain development and hormone surges, Year 9 is seen to be a time for less focus on the academics and more on emerging independence, relationships and community engagement.

Arriving at 8.45am each year having braved black ice and fog as thick as soup, I stand before 150 students to start a 90-minute workshop that draws on such things as Kids Help Line, Who Wants To Be A Millionaire, The Simpsons and Challenging Homophobia 101.

Last year I fielded questions from students and encouraged them to generate even more to discuss with their teachers and each other. These questions included:

'When did you find out/realise you were gay? How old were you? How did you know?'

'What was the reaction of your parents, friends?'

'How often have you lost friends because you have told them you are gay?'

'Is it difficult being gay? What is it like?'

'Do you have a boyfriend? Do you live together?'

'Why do gay people not understand sport?'

'Are you offended by some people's homophobic views?'

'Do you ever wish you weren't gay?'

'Do people ever tease you when you are giving talks at school?'

'What should you say to a friend if they tell you they are gay?'

In the lead-up to my Ballarat week I failed to account for Ballarat Grammar starting their school holidays one week earlier than government schools, and hence I missed a chance to have a cuppa with teaching head Lisa, who has done so much for her students and their LGBT awareness over the years.

Bugger.

Day 210

Sunday, 19th September – Geelong VIC

Making sure I have weekend pitstops has provided a sense of routine and familiarity that I have craved all year, although it hasn't solved everything. I still have this sense that I'm disconnected.

I've finished a meal of takeaway fish and chips with my mother, her twin sister, my cousin and his wife. My cousin and his wife have just returned from a few weeks in Japan. Normally fish and chips is one time where I feel most at home and connected to my family.

As they excitedly recount tales and do the modern day equivalent of slideshow night, I couldn't be further away in my mind. With 7 weeks to go of my tour, I can't absorb any of my cousin and his wife's anecdotes. I'm too absorbed in finding a way to get to the finish line.

Day 211

Monday, 20th September – Geelong VIC to Colac VIC = 77kms

'Awwwwwwww. Really?!'

I'm sitting having lunch with Warrnambool's YUMCHA group (Youth United Making Changes against Homophobic Attitudes). The YUMCHAians are in Colac for the day as part of school holiday activities. I've just mentioned that my first boyfriend actually came from Colac. I explain that we used to take it in turns catching the train between Colac and my hometown of Geelong each weekend for stolen moments.

Soon after turning 18 – back in the times before the internet – I was flicking through Melbourne's *Herald Sun*. Each week I looked at a section in the classifieds titled 'Seeks Same'. I almost dropped the paper when I saw an ad for an 18-year-old guy in Geelong seeking the same. Jake lied about being from Geelong, he was from Colac (and being 18, he was 17), yet we ended up meeting and became boyfriends.

Jake was gobsmacked by the number of guys in Colac and Geelong who left messages on the telephone service attached to his ad in the classifieds. He says that I got the nod because I left two messages. I'd called back because I thought my first message was not comprehensive enough. For once my teenage awkwardness got me over the line in affairs of the heart.

It was with fondness that I returned to Colac in the years after Jake and I were no longer together, to support local LGBT young people who had no other option than to access the Geelong-based support project, GASP!. A few years later I would speak with whole year levels at local schools delivering the *Pride & Prejudice* program

As we start eating I'm keen to hear more about the background of the young people in YUMCHA.

Me: 'So is everyone born and bred in Warrnambool?'

A young woman with exceptionally bright hair pipes up.

'I'm from Laidley, it's like forever outside of Brisbane.'

Me: 'I actually was in Laidley for two nights when I was in Brisbane. Mr Gay Queensland comes from Laidley and I was invited to come over to stay there by his family.'

She was gobsmacked.

'You know Laidley!? Oh my god!'

Day 212

Tuesday, 21ˢᵗ September – Colac VIC to Warrnambool VIC = 76kms

'YUMCHA is probably perceived as a gay group, but it's not. We don't discuss anyone's sexuality. I don't even know members' sexuality, nor is it anyone's business.'

Jackie tells me that YUMCHA is based on a Gay-Straight Alliance (GSA), a US model gaining popularity in Australia, where the focus of any grouping or project is challenging homophobia, rather than the support of LGBT young people.

What does reassure the YUMCHAians is what they can do to challenge homophobia locally. Rose lists examples.

'We've had YUMCHA wristbands, 5 or 6 local newspaper articles, no homophobia at all youth events pushed, a short film and we've gone around businesses to put rainbow stickers up to show their local support. We'd ask for the manager or owner and explain what we were doing. It was really good. There were a couple who said they would and still haven't put it up. There were a couple of flat out 'No's. But the real story for them is the mostly positive reaction.'

It's clear that Jackie and the YUMCHA participants get along like a house on fire.

'I talk to them like they're adults. More-so like a Mother Hen! In a funny way, they know I care about them. I also drummed into them that I am not a counsellor. If they want one they can go upstairs.'

The last time I was in Warrnambool was in February as I drove from Geelong to Mt Gambier to commence my tour. Before that the last time I was here were the pair of times I was here to visit my Big Nanna, Muriel, in her final months; she was moved here from Ballarat and quickly diagnosed with cervical cancer. Warrnambool is as cold and windy as I remember.

Brophy Family & Youth Services in Warrnambool is an impressive building that houses a range of youth and community organisations. 'Upstairs' is the local *headspace* office. The opening of the building could very well go down in LGBT history. The visiting Australian Governor-General attended and met some young people from YUMCHA.

'She came to open the building and met some of the YUMCHA crew and was so impressed that she wore her rainbow wristband for the next 3 days of her tour of Warrnambool.'

Jackie has had to re-evaluate her beliefs about how much homophobia young people are experiencing.

'Before I started this job I thought that they did have it better these days because of the role models, the media, the internet. But in fact I find they've got it just as hard, if not harder because of the technology. They can't always escape it. In my day if I was bullied in high school at least I knew once I got out of that environment, I knew I was safe. Kids these days can have it 24/7.

'One young man recently said he was terrified of his parents finding out because his mother is always talking about when he gets married. His father openly ridicules anything gay or gay-friendly on the TV.'

What helps Jackie is that she is not alone in wanting to make a local difference. In contrast to most other regional and rural areas, Warrnambool has a local adult LGBT community that is directly supporting local LGBT young people financially.

'I've been involved with the Warrnambool Gay & Lesbian Party Network, I've lived in a regional area and I know what it's like to not have opportunities to meet and gather with peers. Older, stable poofs and dykes who are settled and financially stable know that and have the time and money to put in to make these events happen.'

Not that it's just local adult LGBT people.

'I go to the footy club every Friday night to do the meat tray raffles. Yes I do,' she laughs. 'And each week they ask me how YUMCHA is going – the success stories, any problems, things they can help with, donations they can make. These are old cockies, potato farmers and the like. They are absolutely horrified that any child should be kicked out of home for any reason because they love their children and grandchildren.'

Day 213

Wednesday, 22nd September – Warrnambool VIC

'I'm not going 38 weeks without sex! Can I take my partner?'

Seated in a Youth Café in Warrnambool, I encourage a group of local teachers, health professionals and homophobia-curious others to consider the first thing that would pop into their head if I told them they were going on my tour tomorrow. It provokes a great deal of energy and discussion.

'If it was all being paid for I'd say, *Beauty, pub crawl!*'

'I'd want to take my kids.'

'Is it already organised?'

'I don't want to go to the schools. Can someone else go to the schools?'

I'm glad to have an audience. Way back in the first week of my 38-week adventure, I had the manager of Brophy Family & Youth Services attending my Geelong workshop. She persuaded me to head to Warrnambool on the other side of my tour.

Originally not on my itinerary, I decided to venture to south-west Victoria during a natural downtime in the tour – school holidays. Hence any attempts to engage local schools and teachers was going to be a challenge.

Now that they are here it's fortunate that I have them talking, because the local newspaper arrives to do an interview and photo of the afternoon. I enjoy this brief interview, yet have my attention diverted by the reporter's colleague. I can honestly say I have never met a more alluring, cheeky and flirtatious photographer. Was I not about to commence this school holidays professional development, I'd ask him out 'for coffee'.

I tear my attention away from him and back to the group. One teacher talks about her school's readiness.

'Many of our staff don't believe gay students exist. They just don't believe in it. It doesn't exist, it can't exist.'

Her colleague sees a diversity double standard.

'If a teacher in a classroom situation overheard a student saying something to an Indigenous or Asian student, they'd crack down on it. Even girls in trade classes if they get a hard time. But you hear, *faggot, that's gay, suck my dick*, shit like that, because it's OK. They say, *We have a policy*. They are so used to saying that at our school that they don't even know if there is a policy, where it is, if it exists.'

Some schools are said to be fearful of repercussions from parents.

'They look at all the problems rather than the problem of young people being vilified for being gay. They would be worried about students going back and saying, *We've talked about gay shit in class*. That they would be concerned and pull them out. They wouldn't, but that's the fear.'

During a break one student welfare teacher laments the school holiday-related numbers.

'I thought there would be a room full of school staff ready to go help counteract the homophobia that is so absolutely rampant in south-west Victoria.'

There are many other questions and comments and it's a great session, but when it's over, the photographer, of course, is nowhere to be seen.

Day 214

Thursday, 23rd September – Warrnambool VIC

I update my Facebook status this morning.

'Daniel Witthaus ... finds himself in a unique situation: at 9.15am this morning he'll be talking on *two* radio stations simultaneously about Beyond 'That's So Gay': The National Regional Tour of Australia 2010 ... Wonders which one mum will listen to, Freshly Doug (www.joy.org.au/listenlive) or ABC West (www.abc.net.au)?

My pre-recorded interview with ABC West was unexpectedly enjoyable. Like most things in life, media folk are varied. Finding a journalist who I feel immediately comfortable with is rare.

The interview was recorded about a week ago when I was in Ballarat. I arrived to find a man who felt more like an eccentric, intellectual uncle. I was ushered into his studio late morning and found him perusing the daily papers with his glasses on the end of his nose. Immediately I felt comfortable, and what followed was a warm exchange. He asked me what I'd found on my tour so far, and as I explained, I was a little surprised, because it was the first time I felt really clear about it myself. I began to realise how close we were to the end and how it was all beginning to come together.

I asked him if he had any idea when our interview would go to air.

'Yes we do. We'll play it next Thursday morning at 9:15.'

I chuckled. I knew, like each and every Thursday morning, I'd be talking with LGBT media mover and shaker, Doug Pollard, for his *Freshly Doug* radio program. As I've travelled across the country it has provided a small dose of consistency.

Doug's producer rings me up just after 9am, Eastern Standard Time. I'm put on hold and some camp song is played before Doug talks to me to kick off his three-hour program.

This particular Thursday morning, after updating my Facebook profile, I sit in Bruce and listen to Anita Ward's version of *Ring My Bell*.

Day 215

Friday, 24ᵗʰ September – Warrnambool VIC

I finish my week at the end of the Great Ocean Road by hearing more about YUMCHA's Jackie. It took an invite to PRIDE March as a chaperone with YUMCHA for her to decide how much she wanted the role.

'I was invited to talk to YUMCHA four years ago. I was very open about my sexuality at work. I was asked because I grew up in a regional area, and to talk about my story of growing up gay in the country. And plus I wrote a gay and lesbian soap opera called Gaybours, basically my thoughts on being out and what worked for me. I have about 60 episodes written.'

'I remember being at PRIDE March and thinking, *This would be the best job in the world, God I'd do this for free.* Don't tell anyone I said that,' she laughed. 'I hadn't wanted anything so much in my life. I lusted after this job.'

When the former YUMCHA project worker left and asked Jackie to apply, she did. Receiving the news she'd been successful was a big moment.

'I think I burst my manager's ear drum because I screamed.'

I put it to Rose that it's rare for any LGBT project worker, especially in regional, rural and remote Australia, to see this work as 'just a job'.

'I agree. I grew up in Ballarat and went to high school up until Year 11. As far as my sexuality was concerned, I didn't know what the words were but I knew I felt different. I knew I was attracted to women, I fantasised about living in a relationship with a woman, but I had no [gay] peers. I knew no-one, I knew no gay people. The only gay people I knew were two old gay guys who ran the local restaurant and basically they were the joke of the town. People said that they used to have orgies up there and [they] were ridiculed.'

Jackie describes a leaning towards the non-conventional, which led her to work in a trade.

'I did a non-traditional program that was an all-female class. We learnt a lot of trades, that's how I became a horticulturalist. I used to climb 100ft pine trees around Lake Wendouree with chainsaws, knives and secateurs. I was terrified of heights but I had to do it. I was in an all-female class and I had to prove something to them, and myself I guess.'

Before long Jackie proved herself, becoming the first woman in Victoria to receive a qualification to allow her to work around power lines. Yet over time her job affected her personally.

301

'The amount of times we'd be up 80 feet and start the chainsaw. You'd start the chainsaw and there would be a family of possums and you were destroying their home. I had to get out of it because it went against everything I stood for. And I like a bit of safety.'

I'm saying goodbye to Jackie over a late lunch. We're joined by Jackie's partner and one of their best female friends, and I admit I'm delighting in the company of women who are not overly concerned, apologetic or delicate about being women who love women. I'm excited to learn their best friend had been a former Youth Director with the Old (Sydney Gay & Lesbian) Mardi Gras and on a committee that produced 'Not Without My Doona' a key document in creating Sydney's Twenty10. I read that document in the first months on the job at GASP! Geelong in 1996.

As we wait for our Thai I realise that I've started to miss my lesbian friends. And so yet again I leave wishing I could stay a little longer.

Maybe Jackie feels the same way as she embraces me goodbye.

'I think I've developed a man crush.'

Day 216

Saturday, 25th September – Warrnambool VIC to Melbourne VIC = 265kms

Today I'm at a pub with a friend, The Bear, to continue an annual tradition of watching the AFL Grand Final. We've decided to watch from the half-full DT's, known for being a gay version of your local pub and being a few doors down from Molly Meldrum's. He doesn't make an appearance today, given he's at the MCG watching his beloved Saints, however he is known to drop in from time to time.

The Bear and I watch a dramatic game unfold. He talks of his plans to join the defence force next year. I smile, remembering this was something he talked about a decade or so before.

Today's Grand Final pits Molly's Saints against the Collingwood Magpies. The commentators have made a big deal of the fact that it is the 20th anniversary of Collingwood winning the 1990 AFL Grand Final.

Talking to Warrnambool's Jackie about football led me to hearing about that day 20 years ago. Like so many women in regional and rural areas, sport, and in particular women's AFL football, proved to be an important avenue for coming out.

'I loved footy as a kid and was pissed off I couldn't play. I didn't even know there was a Ballarat footy team.'

I asked her to elaborate on the appeal of footy to women who love women.

'It's not girly, it's not netball, it's not heterosexual. 50–75% of the women were lesbian or bisexual. It's rugged, it's masculine. I guess it's what attracts the inner dyke. Even though there are some stereotypes, I do believe some stereotypes are true. We have to send very clear signals to other people that we are what we are.'

Being here watching the Grand Final, after having met Jackie earlier this week, seems almost prophetic. Twenty years ago when Collingwood won the 1990 AFL Grand Final, Jackie had her first kiss with a woman.

'I met women from other footy teams, especially in Melbourne, so I started spending a lot of time in Melbourne and led a double life. Almost 20 years ago to the day, when Collingwood was in the Grand Final, a few of the girls and I went out to celebrate because they were Collingwood supporters like me. One woman I didn't even know was a lesbian, because she had kids, but apparently she fancied me. I was at the bar and turned and she kissed me. I got tangled up in a bar stool and fell into the ashtray. It was the most wonderful time of my life.'

Day 217

Sunday, 26ᵗʰ September – Melbourne VIC to Geelong VIC = 76kms

Coming to Kath's home feels different.

Her father Len had recently passed away after a long battle with cancer. His wife Mary had lost a similar long battle not long before. So here I am at the home that Len and Mary built together at around about the same time they were helping the local church get built down the road. Kath's youngest daughter, the youngest of ten, lets me in and tells me that Kath shouldn't be too far away.

I thank the atheist deities that I'm close enough to see Kath at this time, and not across the other side of the country.

As I wait I make myself a cuppa in anticipation of her arrival and think about what I'm going to say. The large kitchen is filled with memories of three generations – photos, books, random things made in art class in primary school.

Kath used to be my former manager at Kids Help Line, where we spent a few years training teachers and health professionals across regional and rural Victoria and Tasmania. I've no doubt that what I learnt during those years through the wise guidance of Kath was significant in me being able to undertake this tour, although she's more modest about it.

Indeed it was Kath, now a trusted mentor and friend, who challenged me at the beginning of 2009 when I was fighting a nagging feeling that I could be doing something more. She was aware that my work in male family violence, a seemingly never-ending quest to get my first book published, and projects in international LGBT education could continue for the next few years.

'Look Dan, you had an impressive 2007 and 2008. For anyone to repeat that in 2009 would be enough. But you're not anyone. You would never be satisfied with repeating a year.'

Ouch. That hurt. It also frightened me. Kath continued.

'What's something big? It's gotta be big. Come on.'

I knew it right away. I dreaded it. The rest can be explained by my tour launch speech in Geelong.

'In Warsaw,' I said, 'I had been asked to guest present and facilitate a worldwide meeting with expert academics and practitioners from every corner of the globe. During a break I was asked about my impressions of Australia, whether it was homophobic, and what national project I would do if I had the chance and the unlimited resources. Instinctively without much thought I said, *I'd jump in a truck, drive around the country talking to LGBT people about their lives and share the strategies and resources that have worked over the last 10 years.* Fortunately or unfortunately depending on your point of view, this idea has come back to haunt me time and again.'

Kath arrives back and announces the news.

'It looks like the funeral will be Wednesday or Thursday. Come on Dan, let's go for a coffee down the river. I need to talk to someone who isn't family.'

Day 218

Monday, 27th September – Geelong VIC to Apollo Bay VIC = 113kms

The Barman and I sit at a picnic table on Lorne's foreshore. There are not the kinds of crowds you expect for this time of year – we even get a carpark for Bruce – yet it's still pretty busy thanks to school holidays.

Yes, that's right. The (Brisbane) Barman is here with me in Victoria.

When he first suggested it, I was reluctant and defensive. I put him off until I realised he was serious about taking a holiday with me during school holidays.

'Look, I've made ridiculous amounts in tips in the last few months. I have been working and not going out or spending anything. I need a break, you need a break and I couldn't think of anywhere else I'd want to be than with you.'

I picked The Barman up in Bruce at the airport and we started on our way after a quick cuppa with my mum and her twin sister. I was incredibly nervous about how it would be, yet I shouldn't have been. He is as relaxed, engaging and sexy as ever.

I munch on my sausage roll, taking swigs of strawberry flavoured milk every so often. The Barman flashes his cheeky smile as he watches the white, equally cheeky cockatoos loitering for scraps.

I needed this, yet would never have suggested it.

Day 219

Tuesday, 28th September – Apollo Bay VIC (day trip to Port Campbell = 96kms)

Another holiday lunchtime, another picnic table, although this time there are no cute cockatoos, only seagulls that won't take 'shoo' for an answer. We munch quietly on our homemade sangas, and I'm reminded of how well The Barman and I do comfortable silences.

'That's a husband right there,' I tell myself, not for the first time.

Our base for the week is one of two cottages set in a fern gully at the end of a long, windy Barham River Road. The longer you drive, the deeper you head into the rainforests of the Otway Ranges. The bonus is that halfway to the cottage you are out of mobile range. It's just The Barman and I, uninterrupted.

Last night after I'd cooked him dinner we combined our powers, especially The Barman's as a country boy, to light the fire. One bout of snuggling later his eyes were hanging out of his head. I planned to work on my blog and agreed to tuck him in. I jumped in behind him and something about all the warmth, a day of his easygoing charm and my arms locking him tightly saw me fall sleep before he did.

I wake up a few hours later in the same position, my arm screaming with pins and needles. It's morning.

We drive down to see what's left of the Twelve Apostles, then find a seat by a little bay on Port Campbell's foreshore.

When I'm not shooing seagulls or sneaking looks at The Barman, I'm still daydreaming about his daydream – that he'll win '30 million bucks in the lotto' and start an LGBT community centre in Brisbane.

'Would you move to Brisbane if I gave you an entire floor?'

Day 220

Wednesday, 29ᵗʰ September – Apollo Bay VIC (plus dash to Melbourne and back = 374 km roundtrip)

It's been an exhausting day, so I'm relieved to arrive back at the cottage. Two wines later with the fire roaring, The Barman and I are watching *Rockwiz* with delight. The green tartan-print chairs are deep, so there is enough room for both of us to sit. After today all I feel like doing is holding him tightly from behind.

First thing this morning, after a long hug and a smooch, I drive for a few hours to Melbourne to attend the funeral for Kath's dad. I sit with my former Kids Help Line colleagues and we listen to the family pay their respects to Len Ralph.

If ever I lose both my parents I could only hope that I would handle it the way Kath has, with grace, perspective and lots of loving laughter. She giggles when talking about how the local church ladies, all the height of Oompaloompas, demanded that they cater for the wake. We sit with a cuppa, homemade scones, small squares of slices, and handmade sausage rolls, all from recipes generations old. I'm grateful for the efforts of this small group of community-minded women.

Before I leave to make my way back to Apollo Bay Kath asks if I could come to her car. She'd bought me a present. With ten children, five siblings, a life and a funeral, it's a measure of this woman that she even gave a passing thought to me. From the back of her car she passes me a magic pen, named as such because it records people's voices as you take notes. Given all of my conversations and note taking, for Kath it's a no-brainer that I should have this pen.

Yet it's not the magic pen, it's the thought behind it. Kath explains that the delicate cloth bag that she's placed the pen in is one of Len's. As a family who took in international students before it was the *in thing* or lucrative, Len had collected all manner of mementos from around the world.

'He would have loved for you to have it. Geez you do such good work Dan.'

Just when I thought he couldn't get any closer, The Barman sighs and shifts backwards. I hold him as tightly as I can.

Day 221

Thursday, 30th September – Apollo Bay VIC

If ever you are going to fall for someone, walking through the lush, rain-soaked rainforest in the Otway with umbrellas will pretty much seal the deal. It's our last full day together, which seems pretty cruel. The Barman and I fit so well together. He looks so huggable in his khaki green army jumper.

I've noticed that as the year has rolled on, I find it harder and harder to connect with people. Sure I can have a genuine, cuppa-inspired deep and meaningful, but beyond that I just find myself wandering about feeling like I'm watching life and not participating. The Barman has a way of looking at me that makes me uncomfortable. He locks his eyes on mine and waits, not becoming distracted as I fidget or try to deflect his gaze. He seems to observe and sense what is going on for me. On the one hand that is reassuring; on the other it's unsettling, given life is about to take him away again.

'What are you thinking?'

'Lots of things Chipmunk …'

Day 222

Friday, 1ˢᵗ October – Apollo Bay VIC to Geelong VIC = 113kms

There's ample parking but I'm not going to use it. The driveway of Geelong's Avalon Airport is full of speed bumps, which means it either keeps you unnecessarily delayed from getting to the terminal or, in this case, prolongs the inevitable goodbye.

'You don't have to come in,' The Barman says. 'It's OK.'

Me: 'I'd like to. Are you sure that's what you want?'

The Barman gives a small nod. I know not to push it and instead respect it.

He was so cute this morning, telling me that he wanted to skip having a shower.

'It maximises our snuggle time and I can shower when I get home.'

The Barman drops his bag on the footpath and comes in for what we know will be our last embrace. He's as nervous as at our first hug. He keeps his gaze downwards and looks sheepishly up at me one final time.

'Catch ya Handsome.'

Day 223

Saturday, 2ⁿᵈ October – Geelong VIC

The AFL Grand Final between the Saints and the Magpies was drawn last Saturday, so I'm watching the Grand Final repeat with my mum on her big screen. I'm hoping the Saints will pull it out, however I have a feeling that they missed their chance last weekend when they staged a remarkable comeback.

At the same time I'm completing a job application for a position with the Victorian Equal Opportunity & Human Rights Commission (VEOHRC). Now that I have six weeks of my tour left, my attention is turning more and more to what I'll be doing after.

Sure, people encourage me to relax and recuperate, but that's hard after not working for 8 months – and counting – and spending all my savings on a social change project. I'll file that post-tour break under 'I Wish'.

Day 224

Sunday, 3rd October – Geelong VIC to Shepparton VIC = 251 kms

'Make mine a raspberry and lemonade,' I say, and laugh.

I've arrived at Shepparton's GV Hotel for a catch-up with Ro, a force of nature for all things good in the north-east of Victoria. I find her sitting in the larger of two rooms for drinking and dining. She's snagged us a booth in a prime corner position.

Ro is another person I first met during my *Outlink* days. Like myself, Ro had been asked by Rodney to be on *Outlink's* Management Committee of LGBT young people and service providers. Keen to have representation from every state and territory, as well as gender balance, Ro and I represented Victoria.

The original *Outlink* class of April 2000 has gone on to many a great and varied thing, and Ro's story has been impressive professionally and personally.

Ro has grown Shepparton's Uniting Care-Cutting Edge (UCCE) from a one-woman position into a remarkable organisation that rightfully describes itself as 'a frontline rural support agency, working with marginalised communities of disadvantage in the North-East of Victoria'. A regular for years in chairing such peak youth organisations as the Youth Affairs Council of Victoria (YACVic) and state government committees in employment and training, Ro only just recently retired as the chair of Victoria's Ministerial Advisory Committee for LGBT Health. Personally, Ro has also built a home for her partner and her daughter.

In the years following the *Outlink* project, it was Ro who helped navigate it through waters of broken funding promises and a need to re-strategise. It was UCCE that auspiced *Outlink* when the Australian Human Rights Commission wanted to pass it to a regional organisation.

When I needed a means of driving around the country for my tour, it was UCCE who provided a nominal lease on the vehicle now known as Bruce Ford. It was UCCE who also auspiced the *Beyond 'That's So Gay'* tour so that individuals could make tax deductible donations to put diesel into a thirsty Bruce. And it's been UCCE staff who have supported me remotely over the duration of the tour whenever I had questions about my vehicle or matters of donations.

If touching down at my mum's in Geelong felt like I was coming home, touching down in Shepparton feels like touching down in my professional home.

Day 225

Monday, 4th October – Shepparton VIC

'I wasn't bothered when he came out as gay. I was more shocked when he came out and told me he smoked. Just think, all those times I needed a smoke and he had them hidden all that time.'

It's just after 7:30pm on a Monday night and a handful of parents, including one nicotine-friendly mother, are sitting around in a small carpeted hall on an array of couches and chairs. Tonight is the monthly Parents and Friends of Lesbians and Gays (PFLAG) meeting for Greater Shepparton. It'd be fair to say that those gathered could have been parents from anywhere in Australia.

I'm lucky enough to sit down for a cuppa with a tireless, no-nonsense PFLAG mum, Phyllis, who's been instrumental in seeing PFLAG through its first year. Her road to PFLAG started when her own son, Alan, came out to her and her husband, Bob.

'We handled it pretty well when we found out that he was gay. He had just finished uni. I'd come home from tenpin bowling on a Wednesday night. He said, *One of my friend's has committed suicide.* I said, *Did you tell your dad?* and he hadn't. I went and got Bob and Bob said, *Your friend wasn't gay, was he?* And it turned out he was. It was pretty horrifying. There was a group of maybe 2 or 3 young guys who had committed suicide. We took him the next day to a family counsellor.'

Soon after, Bob needed answers.

'Alan told his dad he was gay on a Saturday night. I'd gone out. I know now why Bob did stay home, because it was his way of finding out. He just came out and asked Alan. Bob is the sort of person who digs to find an answer, he's a tradesman. He wouldn't have been satisfied unless he found out. And he knew if he did confront Alan that he would find out and perhaps that's why he wanted to do it without me there. When I came home Bob said, *Alan's got something to tell you*, and Alan said, *I'm gay.* I said, *OK.* It was really horrible. Alan cried. I've never seen him cry so hard. I guess it would have been a huge relief to him.'

Phyllis pauses.

'I suppose I felt isolated. To stay involved I joined the local gay group, GV Pride, as a secretive member. Then Alan's partner mentioned about PFLAG. I said, *Couldn't we do something here, even if it was meeting as a group to have a cup of coffee?*

A roadtrip to PFLAG Melbourne and a local newspaper article later, and PFLAG was up and running.

'I think we've helped a lot of people. I really think we've made a difference. I just wished there'd been a PFLAG when Alan came out and I would have been there quick smart.'

To celebrate their first anniversary, the group called Shelley Argent, PFLAG stalwart and celebrity. It was Shelley who encouraged Phyllis to tell one of her best friends about Alan. Like many parents of LGBT young people, Phyllis and Bob had differing views on who to tell, when and if at all. Phyllis felt the strain of having only Bob, Alan and GV Pride to talk to about it.

'I've always wanted to talk to someone outside that circle. Shelley said, *I think it's time you talked to someone else.* So I told my girlfriend. She said she had thought Alan was gay. I asked her why and she said, *I don't know, it's just a feeling I had.* It was such a relief. I didn't have to hide. Before, she and I used to talk about our kids, but then I stopped. Now we can talk about our kids again.'

Day 226

Tuesday, 5ᵗʰ October – Shepparton VIC

'I don't think I have to go to the meetings, but Phyllis gets me at a weak moment.'

Whereas Phyllis can at times be reluctant to talk to others about her son, Lydia isn't at all. Over a cuppa in the board room of the UCCE offices she opens up.

'I call a spade a spade. I'm a shit-stirring bitch.'

Lydia actively lets people know about her son, Colin.

'I get so annoyed when people start with all that. They ask if Colin has a girlfriend. I say, *He's got Matt. Who's Matt? Oh, you didn't know Colin was gay?* Then later this woman said, *Oh wouldn't it be awful if you lived up the road from a gay person.* I thought, *Eventually it'll click in with her.*'

Colin had not come out to Lydia until he was 26 years old.

'I did ask him when he was 19, and he said *Definitely not* …

Then a family joke turned a little more serious.

'He'd been out and I asked, *Did you meet a nice young lady?* I used to say that as a joke to all my boys. This time it backfired because we were sitting at the table and he said, *Mum, I don't like girls. Mum, I'm gay.* I thought, *Right.* That's got to click in with the brain, doesn't it? So we sat and talked about his life. I said, *Why didn't you tell me? You could have written me a letter, or said, Mum, sit down, I've got something to tell you.* Colin said, *I thought you might throw me out. I don't want you to see me any differently.* I said, *Stand up. No, I don't see you any differently.*'

Not that Lydia didn't question it all at first.

'You go through a lot of guilt at first, like, *What did I do wrong?* I didn't do anything wrong, it's just one of those things. As a child he basically did all the same things, climbed trees, broke his arm.'

Lydia's hope is that Colin will not be treated differently.

'It doesn't worry me, but it worries me that they'll treat Colin differently. We had family members where it was expected that he would go around and tell them he's gay, and I said, *Why? When did Colin's brother come around and tell you he was heterosexual?* Colin's brother, Jamie, won't put up with any shit from the family. He has said, if Colin and Matt aren't invited to things, then he's not going. And I said, *If you're not going, I'm not going.* So basically if they're not invited, it's not a family thing to us.'

Not that Lydia is expecting a change anytime soon.

'Everyone does know everyone else's business. But no-one is going to come up and say anything to my face. They might say it to each other, but not to me. It would be a bit rude. Everyone tells me down in Melbourne it's completely accepted; but then it's not completely rejected here … Matt lost all his friends when he came out. He had to start from scratch basically. Colin didn't have that many to start with. I don't think Shepparton is gonna change much.'

Still Lydia is happy with her family.

'I have two grandchildren, two grand step children and two grand-dogs. I don't think it's really such a big deal. I think *What's the fuss?*'

Day 227

Wednesday, 6th October – Shepparton VIC

Just as in Warrnambool, Shepparton locals have many and varied responses
when I ask them how they'd go if they were about to head out on a 38-week
challenging homophobia tour.

'I'd go but I don't want to drive, or worry about the accommodation.
And I must have a hair dryer.'

'Would be fun, but I'd be worried about the possible violence.'

'I'd be worried about leaving the kids behind, otherwise there would be a
lot of, *Are we there yet?*'

Thanks to the tireless efforts of UCCE's Diversity facilitator, Damien, I
find myself training, at short notice, 13 local teachers, health professionals and
homophobia-curious others. Not only that, Damien insisted they all pay for
attending, meaning that I've raised enough money to pay for Bruce and I to
sail to and from the Apple Isle on the *Spirit of Tasmania*.

During an afternoon break I accept an invitation from one man to join
him on a couch near one of the few windows in the ageing carpeted hall.

'How did you find Broken Hill? I'm the Secretary of a national Rolls
Royce club. We're all going to drive up there from around the country.'

Me: 'Wow, have I got a contact for you.'

I told him he had to talk to John, the son of Rolls Royce-loving Pro Hart.

Me: 'Make sure you tell him that you did this training and that I suggested
you make contact. Be sure to let him know of your roots too, and how it's
close to his partner, Chris', hometown of Numurkah.'

By the time we finish the workshop the sunshine has disappeared from
the corner windows and it is raining. No matter. To end I ask everyone to talk
about what they'd be taking away from our meeting. Every single one of them
mentions something that they'll do differently the very next day they go to
work.

Day 228

Thursday, 7ᵗʰ October – Shepparton VIC

Damien is roaring with laughter.

'Oh my God Dan, you have to see this.'

A dog has stolen my thunder in the *Shepparton News*. News of my visit to Shepparton has hit the broader public. Whilst I'm pictured standing awkwardly under a blossoming tree, below is a picture of some adorable puppy licking his lips, with a fluffy duckling in the foreground. Alas, not many Shepparton folk will be reading about challenging homophobia.

I need a laugh. I've logged onto Facebook to find invites to 3 different campaigns to raise awareness about 'a recent spate of gay teen suicides in the US'. I'm asked to wear purple, to give a damn, to tell people it gets better, to say no to bullying and so on. In a way I applaud the energy and motivation, yet I can't help but feel deflated that a familiar pattern is repeating itself – 5 or 6 awareness campaigns competing against each other for attention and people's time and energy. Given I head up a statewide campaign for men to get involved in the prevention of male family violence, I know only too well the 'campaign fatigue' in the broader community.

'God what one's that? There are so many different coloured ribbons.'

People regularly speak to me of the challenge to keep up with such campaigns and admit to just giving up trying.

Not that this is a reason to stop, but after over 33 weeks of talking to people in regional, rural and remote Australia, everyone is clear: they are over awareness-raising campaigns.

They just want to be told what to do. But not in a few years when educational utopia hits. Not when legislation is finally changed. Not when all the homophobes die out or are finally drowned out by an LGBT-friendly majority. They want to know what they can do *now*.

In 1998 I was speaking to the head of a peak young people's organisation. 'What will you do in 6 months Daniel when everyone has moved on? This is a fad. Things are better these days.'

When I decided to undertake this tour last year, I was asked, 'Do you really need to do a national challenging homophobia tour? Maybe in the bush, but really things are so much better these days. We have x, y and z.' Some also implied that I was looking for homophobia where there was none (interestingly this comment was leveled at me by people who didn't work with young people, nor in schools). Some thought maybe I had nothing better to do with my time.

Many of those same people are now shocked and appalled that young LGBT people might want to end their lives. As I hit the home straight of my tour I'm getting clearer and clearer: there has never been a better time to be LGBT and young in Australia. Yet until they are linked in with new and improved supports, have internet access with privacy and no restrictions, come out to supportive people and develop their self-confidence, young people today are still reporting the same level of abuse, harassment and discrimination that they did a decade ago.

*

It was in the late 1990s when I met Tim, who has since moved up to a property outside of Shepparton with his partner, Andrew. Andrew was the boss of my then-boyfriend, and invited us as a couple to watch a new series – *Queer As Folk* – from the UK. With an excited gaggle of gays we all sat and watched all six episodes back-to-back, with people dropping off one by one as the gay marathon wore us down.

Tim and I have crossed paths professionally and personally many times over the years, so it's with some excitement that I meet him for a cuppa. He's glowing from his life in rural Victoria.

'We've just converted an old primary school. You have to come and stay.'

Day 229

Friday, 8th October – Shepparton VIC

With the end of the tour drawing near there has been an increasing amount of questioning around what I'll be doing 'after'. In Shepparton I have even more reason to reflect when I attend a cancer charity fundraiser screening of *Eat, Pray, Love*. As Julia Roberts' character concluded her 'year' of self-discovery, I too consider what I've discovered myself whilst undertaking a year of uncovering more about LGBT life in contemporary Australia. When Julia's handsome partner bursts into a flood of tears when his son leaves for home, I too start crying, although I'm not quite sure why.

In some ways it's been a week of pondering the end. Shepparton is where I had picked up Bruce in February, and here I am again. Tonight I'm sharing photos of my tour thus far to local LGBT community members and their families. I show photos from each location and tell stories, whilst at the same feeling some disconnect from them. Have I really been all over the country?

This week I've been hosted by Damien and his partner, Cris, and I couldn't have been more comfortable. Damien and I talked at length in ways I rarely get to do about how LGBT life and work interact, the blurring of the professional and the personal. It's been a blessing and a curse to experience such a satisfying taste of comfort and reflection.

Once again I want to stay longer. Once again I want, at the same time, to take someone with me for companionship.

And it could be that people are now noticing. Seated in a comfortable armchair during a break in my training on Wednesday, I sit and speak briefly with a woman teaching art. She smiles and admits she should be in retirement. She is persistent in quizzing me about what the tour means and what could follow, gently pushing past my attempts to be ambiguous, evasive and low-key.

Later, looking into my eyes, and perhaps staring into my soul, she grabs my hand with both of hers before she leaves for the day. I've had many well wishes, but this was somehow more focused. Smiling warmly but searchingly she offers her final thoughts.

'Good luck with your life.'

'Thanks', I thought. 'I'll be OK, but I'll certainly need it.'

Day 230

Saturday, 9th October – Shepparton VIC to Geelong VIC = 251 kms

One of the attendees of last night's slide night, Leon, discovered I was an avid tennis fan. I got talking to Leon after, particularly appreciative of his mother attending with him. She seemed to enjoy herself.

Leon promptly invited me to a hit of tennis this morning before I leave Shepparton for Geelong. Conveniently his local club is around the corner from Damien's house, with 8 hardcourts in close proximity to a football oval that has more dirt than grass.

We decide to play a match and I'm quickly up 6-0, 5-2 before we really have to get moving. I serve better than I should have; I haven't hit since Al in Perth quickly dispensed with me at his club's hardcourts. Win or lose, it's a joy to run around and hit tennis balls. Although it would have been nice with less wind.

Day 231

Sunday, 10th October
Geelong VIC

I arrive early in the night and head up to the first floor of a local pub on Geelong's Waterfront. One of the new owners has invited me to the first of a new local gay and lesbian night called Klozet.

The place is slow to fill, however it does. Although the bar and stage for two drag shows is inside at the top of a wide set of stairs, most people are heading outside to the deck area. The warmer evenings are coming, although most seem to either be smoking, or wanting to be around the smokers. This is certainly not a poster for a healthy, smoke-free LGBT event.

The last LGBT-produced night I attended would have been around 1997/8. Legends Cabaret Restaurant turned itself into a gay nightclub for a night where you could dance on stage in between drag shows by a classmate of my sister.

As I reminisce, two gay men from that era walk in with some others. Noel and Tony were members of the Geelong PFLAG chapter I started all that time ago. There's a lot to catch up on.

Day 232

Monday, 11th October – Geelong VIC to Shepparton VIC = 251 kms

'Now I have to remember how to be a youth worker again.'
That makes two of us.

Ro reflects on how long it had been since she started at UCCE as a youth worker. She and I have been asked to facilitate UCCE's 'Diversity' program, a support group for LGBT young people, for the first of three hours, something we are both happy to do.

Relaxing on couches and in beanbags in the same, trusty hall I've frequented the last week, each young person tells a different tale about coming to the group.

'I found out through the fish and chip shop. The woman serving saw I had a spray-on tattoo of the gay male symbol and asked me if I knew about Diversity.'

'I knew it was there but I didn't feel comfortable coming because I wasn't comfortable then.'

'Because it's fun. You get to meet nice people and eat lots of food.'

I put to them that some would question the need for Diversity given that things are supposed to be 'better these days'.

'I needed it when I was younger because I didn't know anyone else who was gay. I needed to meet people who were going through similar stuff to me, being gay and in the country. Because not every gay person is going to use the internet. And it's a safe place to be gay, so you're not picked on for being gay.'

I ask them to describe Shepparton for me.

'It's crap. I'm sorry but that's the first thing that comes into my head when you ask that. I think it's a bit of a boring place.'

'I'd say it's a dump. There's nothing much to do. There's shopping and coffee, but that's it.'

They are not that different to LGBT young people from across the country that say they have two options to pass the time: sport and drinking. I know that Shepparton has a strong regional tennis competition having made an annual pilgrimage to the town's Easter Tennis Tournament with my gay doubles partner and lesbian mixed doubles partner for six years. I also know that everyone was more interested in drinking than playing tennis – which incidentally, despite my lack of alcohol consumption, still hasn't helped my playing record here.

One young woman describes how she feels the city and the country differ.

'You have no idea, the city is so different. In the cities it doesn't matter, you can blend in. When I go to Melbourne it's amazing. People dress the way they want and do what they want. They just don't give a shit.'

I press them for the reasons why they love, sometimes albeit begrudgingly, their place and the people around them.

'I don't think it's as bad as people make out ...'

'I can walk down the street here and not get anything. But I was in Melbourne the other day and some guy wound down the window and yelled out, *Faggot!* So there you go, Melbourne is more homophobic than Shepparton.'

Day 233

Tuesday, 12th October – Shepparton VIC to Mirboo North VIC (via Bairnsdale VIC) = 568kms

After a drive from Victoria's north-east to the green, dairy-friendly hills of Gippsland, I find myself in Bairnsdale for the start of my Gippsland week. I've arrived with enough time to find a comfy spot beside the water tower that dominates the main shopping strip. One brief radio interview by mobile later, I'm ahead of schedule for my first meeting in eastern Victoria.

'I hope you don't mind but I've ordered lunch for us. I'm sorry that it's only a few plates of sandwiches though.'

Only? I'm sure I'll clean off a plate of sandwiches on my own. This is the equivalent of the red carpet being rolled out and I'm going to savour it.

I arrive at a local college for a cuppa with student welfare coordinator Sandy, who contacted me in the weeks before. Ahead of time Sandy called me and I encouraged her to invite other staff if she thought they'd be interested.

When I arrive, rather than a 30–40 minute conversation, I find an impromptu training session with a small group of local teachers and health professionals.

I'm especially pleased to see Carl, a longtime regional coordinator of local education and youth sector partnerships. He jumped in early and e-mailed me at the start of the tour. Carl, like many of his peers across other Victorian regions has fought hard to keep LGBT young people on the agenda of local schools and organisations.

A decade ago, when I first met him, there was much cause for optimism. There was an unprecedented amount of State Government dollars for LGBT support being thrown around from unlikely corners. Many asked if this was the start of the mainstreaming of all things L, G, B and T. I recall a prominent LGBT worker of the time emoting, 'We are going to be just like drug and alcohol, we're going to be everywhere!'

I was thought to be a bit of a pessimist when at that very time I warned of slippage. Around me I observed a complacency that slowly crept in – there was momentum on the LGBT gravy train and nothing was going to stop it. Therefore many took their eye off the ball. I could continue with the analogy and say many swung thereafter and missed, but that would be overstating it. Most stopped swinging.

'It's gone off the agenda since then. The school used to promote sexual diversity very well, but it seems to have dropped off.'

Not that there weren't signs it needed attention, according to another teacher.

'Years ago we had an all-day training at our school. They said we'd go through all the research evidence about same-sex-attracted young people. Half a dozen people got up and walked out.'

'Well, now no-one is walking out because it's never talked about,' Carl adds.

Day 234

Wednesday, 13th October – Mirboo North VIC

I've woken to a thick fog. I peer out my bedroom window and can just make out a well-used wheelbarrow. Is it just parked there or is it ornamental?

My host, Matt, must have already left, given I look over at the clock to see it's just after 8:00am. To find this place I went on a wild goose chase last night as the sun was going down. Back roads and rolling hills is something that Gippsland does as well as anywhere in the country. Unfortunately my GPS wasn't cooperating. I could have been bush-bashing through paddocks for all it cared.

When I found some mobile coverage I finally called Matt, who guided me safely to his long, landscaped driveway. He and his ageing border collie, Pip, greeted me and brought me in to the warmth of this well-planned brick homestead.

I'm sure I slept so long thanks to food, wine and Matt's company. After a mushroom risotto entrée, I enjoyed a hearty meal of steak and vegetables washed down with a few reds.

With no appointments or interviews until tomorrow and Friday, I decide to have a Big Day In. There is no mobile coverage, which doesn't faze me, however there is wireless internet in abundance.

As Pip and I hang in the slow-to-warm-up kitchen, I look out over the clearing valley and wonder what it would be like to come out in picturesque Mirboo North.

Day 235

Thursday, 14th October – Mirboo North VIC to Traralgon/Rosedale/Morwell/Geelong VIC = 333kms

Often people ask me about a typical day, and Thursday 14th October 2010 is a good example of a *Beyond 'That's So Gay'* Tour day.

7.12am   Awake after having slept in. Forgot to set my alarm because my mobile had no reception at my accommodation the night before. Throw myself through a shower and my things in a bag.

7.29am   Run past my incredibly understanding host, Matt. I pause to hug and thank him, and take up his suggestion to grab a banana for the road.

8.03am   Stop and jump out to take a photo of something resembling a brown coal smoke stack (this for the weekly photo challenge from Sydney Louis, who has enjoyed vicariously travelling through my photos shared online.

8.19am   Arrive in Traralgon earlier than I'd feared, check messages after being out of mobile range for 36 hours. Find a few people got very upset believing I'd 'ignored' them, even though they are aware that sometimes I don't and can't get mobile or internet access.

8.30am   Meet with Eve in a café for a cuppa interview. Eve has another commitment so we both have to get down to business.

9.05am   Pay for hot chocolate with mobile on my shoulder, on hold before a JOY94.9FM interview and saying goodbye to Eve.

9.10am   Commence my weekly 'Freshly Doug' JOY94.9FM interview. Unfortunately Doug is on leave due to a death in the family, yet I have a light, relaxed and fun interview with his stand-in.

9.19am   Conclude JOY FM interview and receive a few texts about the interview. I think it went well.

9.26am   Arrive at McDonalds to use their wi-fi to check for any e-mail emergencies and to update my Facebook status (which communicates to my mother that I am still alive).

9.50am   Start the drive to Rosedale.

10.25am   Arrive in Rosedale and meet Jo in the Rosedale bakery. I decide it's been too long since I've had a coffee scroll.

11.45am   Bid Jo goodbye, only to find out a minute later that she has a flat battery.

11.49am   Negotiate the use of a random woman's jumper leads.

11.53am   Bruce jumpstarts Jo's car.

11.54am   Bid Jo goodbye a second time.

12.13pm   Pull over to take a phone call. It's from a Triple J producer who wants to do an interview. We talk about how, where and when. It has to be in the next two hours.

12.45pm   Arrive in Morwell and head to the local *headspace* earlier than my 2.00pm cuppa interview. They agree to let me use an empty office.

1.00pm   Commence Triple J interview.

1.09pm   Conclude Triple J interview.

1.12pm   *headspace* manager asks if we can do the cuppa interview early because something has come up.

1.21pm   Commence cuppa interview with *headspace* manager, local youth worker and LGBT group co-facilitator.

1.47pm   Sigh with relief when some leftover sandwiches from staff training are placed on the table for me to plunder.

2.45pm   Conclude cuppa interview.

2.51pm   Call ABC radio producer about another interview.

2.57pm   Use *headspace's* internet to again check for any e-mail emergencies. Respond to the most urgent in no particular order.

3.41pm   Move Bruce so that I don't get a parking fine.

3.50pm   Hang with the receptionist ahead of the start of *headspace's* Open Day (4–9.00pm) to celebrate Mental Health Week. Get introduced to a male psychologist, female youth worker and male nurse. Hearing about my tour sparks off much interest and ultimately leads to them talking to each other. I strategically disengage and leave them all talking with one another for the first time about sexual diversity and challenging homophobia.

4.00pm   Meet with local LGBT young people and health professionals and others who wander in.

5.45pm   Partake of the BBQ out the front of *headspace*, enjoying hamburgers and sausages in bread.

6.12pm   Talk to the *headspace* manager's son about his recent trip to a remote Indigenous community that I had visited in May.

6.30pm   Enjoy seeing a dance performance by a group of young women and LGBT group co-facilitator. This is followed by a little boy doing an impromptu dance performance that holds the diverse audience's attention for an entire song.

6.40pm   LGBT group co-facilitator informs me his hope to show a TED talk on the big screen will not happen due to technical difficulties. Looks like I'm on.

6.42am   Introduced to gathered audience and talk about the *Beyond That's So Gay'* Tour, plus present an abridged photo journey that I had presented the week before in Shepparton.

7.45pm   Conclude presentation.

7.46pm   Commence my goodbyes.

7.49pm   Talk to a young trans person about their experiences. Meet that young person's partner. They try to convince me that I'm a celebrity and they can't wait to tell all their friends in the US. I try to convince them I'm far from a celebrity.

7.59pm   Sit in Bruce setting the GPS for my mum's.

10.33pm   Arrive at my mum's for hugs, a catch-up and to again check my e-mails.

Day 236

Friday, 15ᵗʰ October – Geelong VIC

I'd looked forward to finally meeting Jack, a local young gay man, who had spoken before me on the ABC's *Bush Telegraph* program back in February. Jack came to the ABC's attention after reading a moving piece he wrote for website Heywire, 'regional youth telling it like it is'. Now Jack is studying community services and co-facilitates Whatever with local youth worker, Moira.

I'd sat yesterday with Jack, Moira and local *headspace* manager, Zoe. Zoe is quite outspoken about the challenges of even providing something like *Whatever* locally.

'*Whatever* is restricted to the Latrobe Valley, not the whole of Gippsland. This is the only area that has a formal project for LGBT young people. There are no generalist youth services and I think that is a real issue. So that makes it really hard for there to be any focus on these issues.'

Me: 'So if there is a lack of generalist youth services, why is *headspace* partnering with a local youth organisation to keep *Whatever* up and running?'

'It's because Moira and I have decided it's important and have lobbied our organisations to do the work. There is no funded LGBT work in this region. We've done that because nobody else is, not because we have particular knowledge and skills.'

Whatever has had success in its short history.

'Having the *Whatever* project for 5 years has really helped. It really has put it on the agenda. It's youth led, youth action. It's the best social work we do, by hanging around and doing nothing. We just barrack from the sidelines. It's a group that they own and they direct. And yes they whinge when nothing happens too. But nothing happens out of that group that we own.'

The results are encouraging.

'We have young people who had dropped out of school and had jobs at Maccas and now they've gone back to uni to do social policy because they want to change the world. Sometimes they know more about stuff than we do.'

Yet Zoe, Moira and Jack don't assume that the 15–20 young people they see each week are representative of all local LGBT young people. Zoe explains.

'The young people that we know are faring well, but what we know is that it's the ones who we don't know who are the marginalised ones. It's not the kids that are out. It's the kids who are sitting in the back of the classroom hearing that Maths is *gay* and that such and such is a *faggot*. Year 8 and year 9 are still some of the harshest places in the world, especially for young men. I bet it's still as shit as anywhere.'

For this reason working schools is a focus.

'We've had good success in some state schools. We haven't had any success with any of the private schools, but then again we haven't tried too hard. I think we've got really good individual advocates in the schools, stickers, brochures, posters.'

Yet Zoe keeps an open mind about how well this works.

'It's all very well to have posters around, but I think that young people are swamped by that visual material. And there's still the fact that anything that you tell them at school they have to report to their parents.'

Zoe suggests that the parent community might not be so receptive.

'I think there's a whole lot of people in the community who don't think it's an issue. In their mind they're not homophobic so they can't understand how anyone could be. You need to loudly shout the messages to drown it all out. If you don't have any personal connection to it, you'd be annoyed how many people say they don't know any gay people.'

Despite the challenges, people like Jack, Moira and Zoe are focusing on what they can do, and doing it well. This clearly excites Zoe.

'We love that shit.'

Day 237

Saturday, 16th October – Geelong VIC

This afternoon I'm writing my Gippsland blog and pondering progress. My visit there reminds me of a common theme in non-metropolitan parts – if you're very lucky there was a local LGBT conversation happening, but it happened so long ago that locals cannot remember what exactly was said or who was involved. Sometimes there are examples where it got exciting there for a while, but now there has been a return to silence. Or maybe there always was silence.

Hence when people ask what I'm trying to do with all my cuppas I tell them I want to start local, everyday conversations where there haven't been any before, or to reinvigorate local, everyday conversations that haven't happened for a while. One gay man driving around the country in a gay truck is about providing an excuse and permission for those conversations to take place. No more, no less.

With a mix of larger and smaller towns, the Gippsland region needs the silence broken as much as anywhere. It very much reminds me of the Gold Coast, what with its axis being one long highway, its reliance on cars to get anywhere and a lack of any real central, focal point for the community. Only Gippsland is colder and with less bling, yet has more country-like landscapes and industry; and no fun parks, with all due respect to Gippsland's Gumbaya Park

Given its vast distances and similarities to the Gold Coast, I wasn't surprised when told that to get to *Whatever* from where I was staying in Mirboo North, a young person would have to catch a bus at midday, wait a few hours and attend *Whatever* from 4.00–9.00pm, and then catch a bus back the next day at midday.

When I met with local regional health chair, Eve, she talked of the barriers of living in smaller pockets of Gippsland.

'I know of 6 or 7 young men who've left town. Yet if you talk to the community, they don't mind lesbians and gays – but they just don't want to see 'em.'

One local young woman recently lost her job at a national supermarket chain.

'She kissed her girlfriend goodbye in a small Gippsland town. She went to work and she lost her job. Like that.' She clicks her fingers.

Although some leave, some stay and fight.

'There was one brave young man. He was at the supermarket and wore nail polish and was really out there. They told him he had to remove his nail polish. He took them on. If the girls were allowed to wear nail polish, then why couldn't he? He won that battle, but eventually he had to leave town.'

Eve remains concerned.

'So it worries me for young people. When's it going to stop? We know there's nothing for young people in these towns. And we think it's appalling and the attitudes are appalling.'

I asked her what she'd say to people who think it's better these days.

'I have people say to me, *But it's OK now, Ellen DeGeneres is openly lesbian.* So what? She's this rich American star and so that makes it OK to be gay here? It doesn't.'

To illustrate her point Eve cited a personal story.

'I went to see a doctor. I told him I was a lesbian and he put his head down and said, *There's nothing I can do to help you with this problem.* Look me in the eye when you talk to me! Because I am who I am, a regional health chair, I could find another doctor. But what about young women, and young men? It's the same as in the big cities, what goes on, but you can get away from it in the cities. In a small town you can't.'

Eve shows concern about the LGBT social opportunities in the region.

'It used to be centred around the pub scene. Now some groups are very private and would meet informally, but you have to be part of that clique. There is a large group of lesbians in their 40s who meet and are quite closeted and don't want anyone from outside. They are just so closeted. They're in relationships. So if you were single and young then you wouldn't be welcome.'

Matt made a good point when he recalled the demise of the local LGBT support group.

'The ones who were most upset at the demise of the network sadly were the most marginalised.'

Day 238

Sunday, 17th October – Geelong VIC to Melbourne VIC = 76kms

I've found two of my best friends from tennis, Matt and Joe, at one of the back tables of Fitzroy café, Arcadia. Joe has always raved about breakfasts here on the weekend and invited Matt and I to celebrate my near return to normality.

I'm told to either order from a wall of carefully chalked blackboards or to just go to a glass cabinet and point at whatever looks appetising. I still just go for bacon and eggs. Matt, one of the fussiest eaters I know, passes and sticks with a cola.

'OMG, so you have to tell us all about it.'

Joe's gregarious exuberance matches his home decorating – Versace cushions and soup terrines – and his playing style: all or nothing. Matt is more interested in salacious details of who I've 'met' on tour.

Me: 'To be honest I am just so sick of myself. I'd much prefer to hear about other people's lives. What's been happening with you guys?'

Day 239

My check-up and clean at the dentist has just turned into a filling for a cavity he's found.

I really don't like my teeth at the best of times, let alone when I have my dentist smiling at me. His smile is too perfect, white and big to be real.

At least I feel comfortable as he goes about his work. I'm unsure of whether it's the anesthetic or my lying flat on my back looking at nothing in particular on the white ceiling, but by the time he's drilling I am close to micro-napping. No grasping the chair arms with cat claws from me.

For some, going to their publisher might also be akin to visiting their dentist. That's my next stop. It takes me a little longer than expected, given that as it approaches school finishing in Melbourne the roads thicken considerably with shuttles on a collection run.

By the time I arrive at the industrial park in the bayside suburb of Cheltenham, I'm overdue for the toilet and run past reception in what must look like a comical dash.

My contact all year, Thea, who has been sending books and educational packages to all corners of Australia, is waiting with a box ready to go after I had my chance to go. She's shorter and warmer in person than I anticipated, given most of our correspondence has been very business-related.

'Elaine said she wanted to say a quick hello.'

Head of the publishing company, Elaine drops down to ask how it's all going.

'You know,' she says. 'I'm glad you insisted on the title of the book and the front cover. I've received lots of positive feedback about it – like two Principals only last week.'

Originally Elaine had wondered if my book should be called 'Affirming Diversity in Australian Classrooms', with a cover that looked like it catered more to a primary school market. I insisted it must be called *Beyond 'That's So Gay'*, and have a cover that reflected the content. A friend would do a cartoon of me in a classroom. The last thing I wanted was for people to think they'd been tricked into buying a book on broader diversity, only to find it was all about challenging homophobia.

'To be honest we've been really surprised by the sales. We have a few copies going out each week. And not just to the same places, it's been all over Australia.'

Day 240

Tuesday, 19ᵗʰ October – Melbourne VIC to Devonport TAS

Whilst the funds raised from my workshop in Shepparton paid for Bruce and me to sail to and from Tasmania, this only extended to a seated berth for me on the *Spirit of Tasmania*. At first I thought it'd be no sweat. Oh how wrong I was.

Only three hours into an expected 14-hour journey and already I would give most things in my possession to lie down comfortably. Instead I shift from one side to the other, depending on how much my hip is cramping. After falling asleep early in a firm, narrow-backed seat, I'm now wide awake at 11:00pm.

I try and do some writing which thankfully tires me quickly under the dim light provided at the end of an adjustable lamp. I go back to sleep.

When I wake around 3am I swap sides in the chair, noticing that fewer people have their lamps on. As I close my eyes again an LGBT report-writing lightbulb goes off. A growing dilemma about how to communicate what I've found is quickly forgotten as I grab my backpack and grab some paper and pen. I know from experience it's good to write things down immediately, rather than leave it to the chance of my memory in the morning.

What follows is page after page of tour observations, themes and ideas for communicating LGBT complexity to a new audience. At first I write 3 pages, then turn off the light, feeling content. But moments later, I again turn on the light for another flurry of writing. I repeat this process four times until I close my notebook and turn off the light two hours later, having stopped at eight pages of writing.

Day 241

'I grew up on a farm just outside of Smithton. Being gay growing up in Tasmania, it's not a very open minded place. There's a really masculine and feminine way to be and nowhere in between. There's no grey area.'

I'm chatting with Neil via Skype, a first for the tour. Until recently he lived in Smithton, a place I hadn't been to, although I knew of it. It's the kind of place that, when mentioned, elicits a host of pre-judgment.

For a variety of reasons Neil felt he didn't fit. There's a reluctant softness in his voice as he explains.

'I didn't fit with the norm, I never have. As a young child I was smart, which was never really looked upon favourably by my peers, and I wasn't a great footy player. Because I was so small. I was better at individual sports than team sports. And I got teased a lot to be honest, about being gay. I didn't really know what it meant.'

Me: 'You really didn't know, or...?'

'OK I knew what it meant, but not what it meant for me. Look, I can have sex with men or women, but it's about who I fall in love with. So therefore I would identify as a gay man.'

Adopted from another country by his family, Neil grew up being one of the few people in Smithton who was not Caucasian.

Me: 'Did racism ever come into play?'

'My parents are very well known. They come from quite good families, so everyone kind of knows. So they know I was adopted and my story. So it was never really an issue. There was one girl in Grade One who made me cry. She called me something like a fucking black abo. I couldn't understand why she said that. *But I'm not Aboriginal!*'

Growing up, Neil describes being in a very religious, heterosexual world.

'Everyone went to church. They did the whole thing that everyone was expected to do down there which is to get married and have kids. I obviously fought with it for a long time. Years. I used to cry about it a lot and ask, *Why?* I told mum and dad I was gay, hung up and then I wouldn't answer their calls for a week, which was big. I usually talk to them every day or else they get anxious. Mum didn't agree with it, because my dad's in the church but said, *I love you anyway*. Dad was like, *That's cool, we still love you*. My dad's really groovy.'

Coming out to his church friends was different.

'They all pretty much disowned me. I tried so many times. The amount of tears that I shed over such a ridiculous thing, which was just me. And now I say, *Why wouldn't God love me if this is who I am?* What got me most was more because I was so open, raw and honest to these people, and I was punished for being honest. That hurt more than anything and to be honest that's why I left the church. Nothing to do with the fact that I was gay. I find the church to be one of the most political places I've ever seen. I'm not saying that negatively, it's more factual. I mean people pretend that everything's perfect when it's not.'

Telling his university friends helped.

'When I told my friend Ernie he said I was camp as a row of tents and he didn't care and that he loved me.'

Yet ultimately Neil needed to get away from Smithton.

'If I do go to church it's with my parents, with my granddad because they asked me. And I don't feel like I'm going to be struck by lightning when I go inside.'

Neil might finally be approaching the place he has sought most.

'It's been a long process to be honest. But now it's like, it's me. I'm happy with who I am. There's no internal fight anymore.'

At a recent event in Sydney, Neil thought about his new world, far away from Smithton.

'I was dancing and there were these hot guys dancing next to me and they were like everyone else, looking all straight and hot. Then, the event stopped, they turned to each other and just started kissing. It was one of the hottest things I've ever seen. No-one batted an eyelid and they were in their own little world. That made me go, *That's the part of the world that I want to be a part of.* I want to be loved. It's white picket fence, it's finding a man who'll love me for me being me. And hopefully bring children into the world. I'm a lover not a fighter.'

Day 242

Thursday, 21ˢᵗ October – Launceston TAS

My day is bookended with radio interviews. This morning I had my usual
cross to *Freshly Doug*, during which I talked about Gippsland.

The rest of the day I'm spending with Nairn, her partner Shane and their
toddler, Marley. Nairn is my Launceston host, who I'd met at the same
leadership forum where I'd met Canberra's Jaiden. Nairn had made a name
for herself and set up solid foundations for her role as international training
expert whilst working in a student welfare role.

Tomorrow the family will be heading out on a fortnight-long training trip
to the mainland. They have it down now to a fine art, and relish being able to
go as a family unit.

I'm lucky enough to be using their home as a Tasmanian HQ whenever I
am north. Nairn and Shane have been generous in opening their home to me
for years now, and I've seen their home grow from a simple two bedroom
home into a two-storey, three bedroom dream home with decking, spa bath
and a first floor that opens up onto second-to-none vistas of northern
Tasmania's Tamar Valley.

It's here, lounging on big couches filled with cushions, that Nairn reminds
me of my encounter with one of her friends, 'Bazza', many years before.

Bazza, a teaching colleague of Shane's, had joined Nairn, Shane and
another friend on a weekend to Melbourne to watch a footy match. It was
during a wet winter of 2001, and Nairn suggested we meet after the match at
the bar at their CBD hotel. When she arrived, Nairn was alone – Shane and
Bazza would follow later – and she warned me about what was to come.

'Um, it looks like it's us Daniel Schmaniel. We just learned a lot about
Bazza.'

Bazza had asked what the plan was after the match, and meeting up with
me was acceptable until Bazza found out I was gay. A job hazard when you
do 'gay stuff' and people ask after your work. He was still coming along with
Shane, though, but he wasn't happy about it.

By the time Nairn and I finished one drink, Shane and Bazza had arrived.
Bazza watched from a safe distance as Shane greeted me with a warm hug. A
lifetime of enforced politeness brought him forward to gruffly say *Hi* and
shake my hand. Firmly.

Shane and Bazza pulled up some chairs and soon Nairn, Shane and I were talking about what we'd been up to. We were making the most of the time, as we were lucky to see each other once or twice a year. When Shane, a teacher, asked more about my work, Bazza showed interest.

I asked him how the mandatory anti-homophobia in every Tasmanian school had gone down at his school.

Bazza said the school was yet to follow Department policy.

'My principal says, *There are two things we never talk about in my school: suicide and homosexuality.*'

After a drink and our first interaction Bazza relaxed, and before long we were four people in conversation. Bazza added this personal story to the conversation:

'When I was a kid my dad used to say every Saturday morning without fail, *What should we do today Bazza? Go down to Salamanca and bash some pooftas?*'

Time slipped by and as we all realised it was time to start wrapping up, Bazza sat up with a look that he had something to say.

'Um, well. Look, Dan. I wanna show you what kind of a bloke I am. No, really, I'm a good bloke mate. Wait until you hear this. You too Nairn and Shane. Now you both know that my boy Will, he means the world to me. Right? Right? He's 1 year old and he's everything to me, I'd guard him with my life. Now I admit, I was pretty bloody spooked before, cos' of all that stuff I said about dad. But listen to this. I've met you, and I think you're a good bloke. If Will was here right now, I'd let you hold him. Yeah, really. How good is that? I'd let you hold my son. Can't believe I've said that.'

Nairn laughs, as she does every time she recounts it, and holds her mouth.

'Can you believe how proud he was of himself?'

Day 243

Friday, 22ⁿᵈ October – Launceston TAS

My website is down. Over the course of this roadtrip, I've feared things like a flat tyre, weeks where no-one will speak to me and even something like a broken bone, but not this – this is one of those things that comes out of nowhere. And it's hit me hard.

I'm acutely aware that I have little energy to expend on hiccups, big or small. That this is my weak area – IT and websites – makes it feel even worse. A year's investment of content, written and visual, has evaporated, seemingly like my resilience.

Nairn and Shane are not in the house, so all I've done for the last half an hour is scream 'Fuck!?'

I discovered this morning that my website is inexplicably down and my tour e-mails are no longer working. A friend has generously offered to host the website and e-mails for free with his hosting company. Now said company is uncontactable and I am without a website or e-mails.

I talk to two people. Firstly, the young gay man who, for free and with quiet joy, put together my thatssogay website. Lukas, who I call Cutes because of his impossibly blue eyes and strong dark curls, is calm, understanding and helpful. Secondly, the young gay man who put together my prideandprejudice website in a process that ultimately led to him coming out to me and everyone around him – James, who I call DJ thanks to his burgeoning hobby. James is calm, understanding and helpful. I pity them both.

It doesn't help that I cannot answer all of the questions that Lukas and James have for me. This won't be resolved easily, nor quickly.

Frustration doesn't begin to describe it.

Day 244

Saturday, 23rd October – Launceston TAS

If anyone can distract and cheer me up, it's Glenn. Nairn's local hairdresser, some would think him describing himself as 'camp' would be an understatement. Like one of my best friends from Geelong, he is a wondrous argument that people are born gay.

His fingers full of rings and well-maintained claws, he holds out his hands with limp wrists and laughs wickedly with a relaxed ease. Glenn has a delightful Aussie drawl, dragging out words and raising his highly organised, manicured eyebrows with delight.

Tonight, over some Thai takeaway, Glenn describes going out in Launceston.

'It's not scary in Launceston. I'm there on the dancefloor with all my fag hags. And all their big macho boyfriends stand at the bar. I mean, they wouldn't get on the dancefloor for anyone. But they tell me, *Don't worry, we've got your back.*'

Not that Glenn can't handle himself. Recently at an engagement party outside of Launceston at a football club, he had to deal with a man who seemed to have a problem.

'I was there with a girlfriend. This guy kept looking at me and finally he came up and said, *Are you gay?* Just his tone, it was really low. *Are you gay?* I said, Yes, are you? He then said, *I don't like fags. I'm not one but my cousin is and he got married.* I said, Did you go to the wedding? *Yeah, it was fucking beautiful.* I said, Did your cousin wear a dress? *What do you mean?* Well there's always a bride and a groom. *Nah, nah, my cousin's boyfriend wore one.* He just kept asking personal, probing questions until I finally said, Are you trying to hit on me? *Nah, nah, I'm not.* I said to my friend, Quick, backs to the wall, he's trying to hit on us.'

Glenn is often between Launceston and Devonport, where his partner lives and works. At a town in between, Deloraine, Glenn recently went with his partner for a meal.

'There's a gay couple who own a hotel there, and we didn't go to that hotel, we went to the other one. And we walked in and there are two guys and a girl sitting at the bar. One said, *Look at those dirty fucking faggots. They've got to be gay if ever I've seen 'em'.* It was really horrible. A really nice restaurant if ever you're there. He was beside himself, he'd never experienced that before. He wrote to the local papers about it. I said to him, *I get this everyday!*'

Sunday, 24th October – Launceston TAS to Hobart TAS = 200kms

When I was first volunteering for GASP! in Geelong I became aware of the gay law reform campaign in Tasmania, and one name in particular: Rodney Croome.

My friendship with Rodney grew from a trip to Tasmania in late 2000 where we saw all parts of his home state. I myself was most interested in the north-west, given its bitter homophobic history, explained by Rodney

Croome as *the site of some of the worst homophobia during the long and bitter gay law reform campaign of the 1990s.*

Rodney and I took in Devonport, Penguin, Burnie, as well as Strahan, and it's less visited cousins, Rosebery and Queenstown, with its fascinating museum and unforgiving football oval of stones rather than grass or even dirt!

Sitting in an inner Melbourne café a year before the tour officially kicked off, Rodney sat and absorbed what I had just told him: that I wanted to repeat and expand on his efforts a decade earlier. What I've always admired about the unflappable Rodney is that he can never be rushed. Calm, considered and thoughtful in his wisdom, this time would be no exception. Thus I waited, half anxious and half excited, knowing that what he'd say next would be pivotal. Finally he spoke.

'Are you ready?'

I knew exactly what he meant and slowly nodded, lifting my eyebrows slightly to mock the seriousness of the moment. Despite this, Rodney felt the need to ask me again.

'No Dan. Are you *rreealyy* ready?'

Rodney has a way of stretching 'really' and changing the tone of his voice, a remnant of his relationship with a German man who has an adorable, accented way of saying the same word.

Again I looked deep into Rodney's eagle-like eyes and nodded slowly.

'I am,' I said.

Rodney's eyes dropped to the rustic table, he lifted his eyebrows comically and let out a big sigh. We both half-laughed nervously.

Only Rodney could *rreeaalyy* comprehend what I had planned to do. For a decade, long after it was completed, we had talked over and over again about his experiences with *Outlink*, his observations, the opportunities and the challenges.

Some of our most insightful conversations have happened while walking to the end of his street, which boasts a rivulet, and walking by the Cascade Brewery and up Mt Wellington. It's impossible to walk with Rodney without discovering some new fact, told with a slight breathlessness because we both spend so much time talking. I tease Rodney that he is obsessed with firsts, longests, biggests and the like.

'Did you know, Dan, that the Cascade Brewery is the oldest continuing brewery in Australia? Did you know that Hobart is lucky to have Mt

Wellington? Hobart has the lowest rainfall of any of the capitals, yet our water storage is at the highest capacity. Mt Wellington is high enough to block most of the rainclouds, and our dam is on the other side.'

It's on one of these walks I make a confession to Rodney that I've thought for a decade, without really thinking about it, so to speak, about what could be done to build on his work and what would need to be done to meet what he originally defined as 'an overwhelming, impossible amount of need' in regional, rural and remote Australia.

Only Rodney could have comprehend what would flood my way upon the announcement of what I was doing.

Day 246

Monday, 25th October – Hobart TAS

'I guess I'm fairly lucky that I haven't had a bad experience. I'm fairly aware of my rights in the education department. I know that if someone on the staff were to discriminate against me that I have rights and I know the channels to go through. I am the kind of person who is confident and I don't ever let people know that I'm not.'

Lee takes a tea whilst I opt for a banana smoothie. We're sitting by the window in a known LGBT-friendly café formerly known as *Kaos*.

'I found it easier to be open with kids in high school. In my teaching style I am fairly open in general. My home life is a big part of who I am. Yes they may have a reaction to that, but I just continue on, let them deal with that and then they move on. And I've never been disappointed by that. More often than not there will be kids who say, *Oh my aunty is gay, or my friend is gay*. I think some of them, the staff that is, were shocked by me being out. Students would say things like, *You fat lesbian* and I'd say, *Hey, I'm not fat.*'

Homophobia is just as rampant in Hobart as anywhere else in Australia. 'It's commonplace. *That chair's gay* and all that stuff.'

Letting students know that her sexual identity is not something that can be used as a weapon against her was key.

'One student spray painted something homophobic about me on the side of the gym. All the teachers said, *Don't go out there and look*. Well I made sure everyone knew I was out there having a look and that they knew I wasn't affected. I didn't have a reaction, but the kids did. Because I was out at my school and supported by the parents, the kids then look at any kid who is homophobic and they know it's not OK and they know why.'

'I had respect as a teacher so when kids came out I was thinking, *Shit, are the community going to think that I'm turning kids gay*. But it wasn't like that. They didn't. They were actually really happy that they had an 'expert' in the community,' she laughed.

Being pregnant and then becoming a mother has been more helpful for Lee in coming out to her primary school students than it was for her teacher partner.

'Interestingly her kids know she is in a same-sex relationship, but they just don't understand it. They know she is a mum, but they don't understand that I had the baby. They hate homosexuals because that's what their parents tell them and she doesn't know how to address that in her classroom without getting too much attention herself. Whereas it's easier for me because I had the baby, so they ask me about it. Although they still ask about the dad ...'

Lee reflects on her own experiences versus those of her partner.

'She was ostracised from the word go, so she has those really horrible situations to think about. But I don't have that; I haven't been shaped by those earlier experiences. At her new school she hasn't had a bad experience in a few years, but she's waiting for one.'

Day 247

Tuesday, 26th October – Hobart TAS

'Daniel! That's the beauty of Facebook, I knew your face.'

I'd been wandering towards the school's reception, possibly looking a little bit lost, when Uma jumps seemingly out of nowhere.

I chuckle, because no matter how many times it has happened this year, it still surprises me.

Uma excitedly navigates me through the school grounds, and I tell her *hi* from Rodney's partner, Raf. They all move in the same group fitness class and dinner party circles. Rodney told me they exercise hard and they eat just as hard.

Talking with Uma we move to a classroom where we are quickly joined by a Year 11 and 12 Philosophy class, some other interested students and another teacher. Uma has announced my visit to the entire senior school.

'I got up and told all the Year 11s and 12s and some of the jock group started and I just looked at them and asked, *What's the problem guys?*'

I certainly felt many pairs of eyes on me as I was escorted through crowds of students to this classroom. No doubt it'll be the same on the way out. Having felt the *That's him, that's the gay guy/poof/faggot* vibe before, many of the students are aware of what is going to take place in this classroom. Still, two young men chose independently to come and contribute well. During a break, Uma gushes.

'It's great because they didn't have to come. They're such beautiful boys.'

I talk about my tour, tell a few stories, then ask them if they hear 'that's so gay' and how their teachers handle it – or not.

'All teachers say something when they hear it,' Uma said.

'I've never heard a teacher say anything,' one of the young men said.

'Well [young man] you have not been in one of my classes at the time!'

'Yeah but that's you. We all know you would.'

Day 248

Wednesday, 27ᵗʰ October – Hobart TAS

'I've had speech therapy. I learnt to talk in a Marilyn Munroe whisper, but I fucking refuse to use it.'

Long-time transgender advocate, Martine, explains the restraint she has felt with some organisations that have supported her, one example being her speech therapy.

Recently an insurance company telephone call centre operator didn't believe Martine was Martine.

'They refused to talk to me about my insurance policy because it said I was Ms Delaney and they thought they were talking to a bloke.'

Yet Martine is doing something that most other trans folk don't do – remaining visible.

'Most trannies just want to transition and disappear into the woodwork and live their lives. Very few trannies want to stand up and be noticed.'

Martine has deliberately become 'Martine The Trannie' because she wants to make a difference and be a voice.

'It's a deliberate choice. I'm a media slut basically.'

When Martine was selected to play soccer for the Tasmanian women's soccer team she needed to be open and OK with media intrusion.

'At times it drives you a little batty and it's a pain in the arse but I have a strong belief that a lot of what happens in your life is because of your actions, so there's no point getting pissed off about that.'

That kind of perspective might help when Martine, her same-sex partner and daughter wake up to graffiti and broken glass in, on and around their family home.

Martine believes she is being joined by more and more trans folk as time goes by.

'It's a growing tension. Trans folk around the country are becoming more vocal. How do we get some input into policymaking without riding on the back of LGBT stuff? I must admit I do get a little concerned for bisexual, trans and intersex folk.'

Too often B, T and I get left behind, or as some say, 'that little BIT'.

'Even though they start off with LGBTI, they rapidly break down into the needs of gays and lesbians.'

Not that Martine isn't understanding, yet that has its own threshold.

'In Tasmania services are bound to be an almost generic LGBT service because the numbers aren't there. It's not being negative about the services. Most trans folk end up feeling like, *Oh, they can't offer me very much.* It's not about getting inclusive, it's that they don't get it. For trans folk it's really good to talk to somebody who understands. The reality is that trans stuff is so different to anything else. It really doesn't matter how thoughtful, empathetic, intelligent and sensitive someone is. Most people just don't get it really. They think they do, they get their head around some of it, but ultimately they don't get it. I feel anger and disappointment that there is nothing specific because of the numbers, unless we can increase the number of trannies in Tasmania. The only option is to go to a sexual health clinic, and it's often not about sexual health.'

Day 249

'I think that the North Coast has come a long way. It's got a ways to go, there's still people hiding, but a big percentage of people are now coming out.'

According to Deidre, the head of Working It Out (WIO), statewide peak LGBT support organisation, the northern parts of Tasmania might be improving. We're upstairs at a heritage listed building on the outskirts of Hobart's CBD. It's a long way away from the isolation of the North West.

Magda, WIO worker in the north, is down in Hobart for a few days and explains.

'The people who are coming out in the North West are 30 years older than LGBT people in Launceston. The gay men move out or they hide. We still have people that are the only gay in the village.'

Clarifying what they do and clearing up misconceptions is something WIO is working to address. Deidre is eager to be clear.

'Working It Out targets people who are negotiating their gender and sexual diversity.'

In other words, they service those people who are 'working it out'. Magda is also seeing an increase in training from services like *headspace*. The model to respond is a simple one.

'We give them rainbow stickers, we provide posters and we work through an audit. It's really up to them.'

Given that, like every other LGBT service and project across Australia, WIO is over-capacity, Deidre is mindful of services referring inappropriately.

'Services find out that a client is gay and because they've run out of petrol they call us.'

More recently WIO has had more transgender and intersex people accessing their service than gays, lesbians and bisexuals.

'It's invariably homophobia that impacts on transgender and intersex clients most. It's funny because a lot of the time we hear about how different we all are across the LGBTI communities.'

Not that Working It Out thinks it has gender diversity all worked out.

'That inclusiveness is hard.'

Day 250

I'm having a cuppa and chocolate cake in Launceston *headspace's* upstairs tearoom with Russ (who I've met a number of times over the last decade), Roberta and Judy. Counsellor, Roberta, pushing crumbs around her plate, comments that young men experience homophobia differently.

'Maybe the guys find it harder, mental health wise, because they probably get bullied more for being gay. Gay guys probably cop it worse than lesbians.'

Counsellor, Judy, sees it affecting not just LGBT young people.

'I've certainly had 13–14 year olds who don't identify as gay where other kids have called them gay or faggot and they've been extremely stressed by that. One young man had a group of older guys come up behind him and fake hump him.'

Judy sees a pattern of family rejection locally.

'It's the family reactions. I've had some guys who have had some depression. They've had really negative reactions from family members, like not talking to them for two years. That's a really severe reaction and that's probably more the trend.'

Russ reflects on public displays of same-sex affection.

'I'm thinking even through the Launceston mall. I can't recall seeing a male same-sex couple holding hands.'

'I've seen girls,' adds Roberta, 'but you think, *Are they friends?*'

One of Roberta's clients is having issues going out in public, even without a partner, until recently.

'One young guy had anxiety from walking down the street during the day because he thought people were looking and staring at him because he was gay. The only time he felt safe and confident was at night with his friends. He was one of the ones who had the response of no contact with family members for 3 years after coming out.'

Recently there have been young men receiving counselling where sexual identity has come up as an issue. Roberta recalls:

'He thought I was there to tell him if he was gay or not. I said to him, *That's OK, if you want to talk about it, it's fine.* I had another guy saying in a session that being gay was wrong. I said, *I don't think there's anything wrong with it.*

Now he's opted to see another counsellor to sort through sexuality stuff. He was involved with a church and stuff and was very fired up about it.'

Russ sees the overall impact of homophobia on LGBT young people locally but sees young women as presenting with substance use issues.

'LGBT young people are faring worse, because if you look at the data they are still overrepresented. Mental health, self-harming behaviours, sexual health. I'd find the girls are more involved with substance use.'

I ask about their connection with Working It Out. Judy believes these ties could be strengthened, but to be fair, she missed an introductory session with Working It Out that happened in recent years.

'Personally I don't know about services like Working It Out. If I find a person has a particular set of issues that's when I'd be tending to know about the service. We all have to work harder because young people feel like they have to have it worked out before they walk through their door.'

I leave the meeting and am wished well by the cute, bespectacled receptionist. My smile sours when I get back to Bruce. Thank-you to Launceston parking officers who've given me a parking fine for being 10 minutes over due to the success of this *headspace* visit and the staff's generous expansiveness, and their moist, rich chocolate cake which contributed to my physical expansiveness.

Day 251

Saturday, 30ᵗʰ October – Launceston TAS to Ulverstone TAS = 118kms

This place feels a little too 'posh', as my mum might say, to be having just a hot chocolate. The Greens Education Spokesperson for Tasmania, Paul O'Halloran, has invited me to Lancaster House. The building has dominated this corner of Ulverstone since 1923.

Now renovated, it has floor to ceiling windows to make the most of its proximity to the Leven River. We sit beside the windows on designer, dark chocolate leather chairs. It couldn't be more civilised.

It's hard for me to believe that just over a decade ago, people were arriving to protest gay law reform with placards and pitchforks. Here.

This kind of anti-gay sentiment spurred action, as Rodney wrote in a guest spot on my tour blog:

'The idea for *Outlink* was hatched by then Human Rights Commissioner, Chris Sidoti, after he launched the Working It Out report, a needs analysis for young LGBT people on Tasmania's North West Coast, in Ulverstone in 1998. Ulverstone was the site of some of the worst homophobia during the long and bitter gay law reform campaign of the 1990s. The North West Coast had also seen some tragic gay youth suicides as a result of that homophobia.'

Whilst some young gay men, such as Smithton's Neil have gone from strength to strength, sadly many young men like him in Tasmania's north west don't, according to Paul.

'In Tasmania there are 17 suicides per 100,000 population, and the national average is 8. Obviously there are a lot of young people not feeling OK with who they are.'

*

I delighted this week in watching Rodney anxiously chopping fresh ingredients in readiness for partner Raf's return home from work. As I watched him chopping on a spotless, clear kitchen bench, I recalled how that very bench used to be covered in a logjam of old magazines and current newspapers. Eating used to be functional and quick and Rodney would moan about cleaning, because why would you want to do something you've done before?

Now he chops, cleans and plays house. I think I spied contentment. I'm not sure, but I hope I'm right.

Day 252

Sunday, 31ˢᵗ October – Devonport TAS to Melbourne VIC

I'm thankful that Bass Strait is calmer than the trip over, and infinitely calmer than the sickeningly rough Sea of Marmara on the ferry ride I took back to Istanbul from regional Turkey way back in 2003.

I approach a nameless deck bar and grab a cuppa. As I sit in a booth straight from an 80s Las Vegas casino, I re-learn that black tea doesn't taste the same out of polystyrene – no matter how much sugar you put in it.

After a few sips I smile thinking of how the mythology of the 'cuppa' has grown. Too many times now I've been on the phone to a concerned local who would fret that, as a gay man from the big smoke, I'd be demanding the best coffee in town. After politely listening to them brainstorming options out loud, I'd let them know that I wasn't a coffee drinker and that if they had hot water and a teabag I'd be happy to come to them.

Facebook status update for this day: Daniel Witthaus lands in Victoria … Plans on stayin' a while …

Day 253

Monday, 1ˢᵗ November – Melbourne VIC to Geelong VIC = 76kms

Fuck, I'm lost. I'm stuck in a housing development nightmare somewhere on Melbourne's outskirts.

Normally I'd have GPS – it's one I had on the tour borrowed from the Bear – and I'd be OK, however I just left that at The Bear's mum's house in a suburb that kisses Melbourne's urban fringe. His mum wasn't home, so I just left it inside the garage as per The Bear's instructions.

Given my next fortnight will involve Melbourne, Geelong and Shepparton, I felt it was safe to say goodbye to The Bear's GPS, or Seamus, as he calls it. Obviously I was wrong. Every street is a blur of footpath-less front yards and suburban brick houses mixed with the odd Georgian monstrosity. This won't help me find my way out of this carefully planned maze.

Thankfully I have nowhere in particular to be any time soon.

Haven't I seen that house before?

Day 254

Tuesday, 2ⁿᵈ November – Geelong VIC

Although I hadn't planned it that way, sneaking back into Melbourne the week of the Melbourne Cup was a fortunate time for 're-entry' to the place I've called home for the last 11 years (save a few stints living in Berlin).

This serves to shorten my week considerably (for non-Melbournians, this 'Race that stops a nation' on a Tuesday means that *nobody* does *anything* on the Monday).

I spend most of the day blogging about Tasmania. The good news is that before getting on the Spirit of Tasmania, I receive news from web knights in shining IT armour, James and Lukas, that my e-mails and my website are all back up again.

Although I'll now have to rebuild my website content again, I at least have a skeleton to put some blog meat on bare bones. Someone anonymous has even posted a comment on my reborn thatssogay website, asking when my Tasmania blog will be posted.

As on AFL Grand Final Day, mum offers me scotches and Coke regularly as we sit watching the neddies all afternoon in anticipation of the Cup. Again I politely decline before succumbing to join her in a celebratory drink.

Me: 'I can't tell you how glad I am that this tour week for Melbourne is shortened.'

Mum looks knowing.

We both know I'm never very productive when I smell the finish line.

Day 255

Wednesday, 3rd November – Geelong VIC to Melbourne VIC = 76kms

It would probably surprise most to know that I don't enjoy coming to this building at all. For so many it is a beacon of LGBT research and leadership, yet for me it's somewhere I avoid.

I first came to this building when I made the trek up from Geelong with a GASP! colleague in 1998. We wanted to visit all the gay and lesbian organisations, talk about the challenges we faced, and seek guidance and wisdom about how to respond locally. I began explaining the project, but was quickly cautioned by an LGBT educational mafia heavy.

'Look a lot of people who know what they are doing have worked on ´Catching On´ and that will change everything. It's going to be addressed very soon. It's great you want to do something but quite clearly no school is going to let you through its doors.'

The Catching On resource, an inclusive sexual health curriculum, would come out. Seven years later. Local young people, as I saw it, couldn't wait.

A few years later I joined that same LGBT educational mafia heavy at a statewide forum for teachers and health professionals about supporting LGBT young people in educational settings. Representatives from the Department of Education and the Catholic Education Office joined us on a panel. After I talked about *Pride & Prejudice*, said heavyweight got to her feet.

'Of course we could all do what Daniel does and go into schools, throw hand grenades and leave, but …'

Over the years I've heard similar things have been said by the now head of this organisation in meetings I haven't attended, so I have respectfully declined going to any gatherings unless it's absolutely necessary.

One person who is cooperative and supportive in that organisation is Roz. She has generously organised and promoted *Beyond 'That's So Gay': The Tour Diaries* for the Rainbow Network, a network for those working with LGBT young people across Victoria.

It's a refreshing change to come to this building and genuinely look forward to it. I'm warmly welcomed by Roz and soon a small but committed gathering of teachers, health professionals and homophobia-curious others is seated and ready for two hours of storytelling. I'm humbled that two members of the audience are people I looked up to in the late 1990s as role models of LGBT change.

When I ask what has brought them here today, I'm taken aback when an academic answers my question.

'I came to your book launch in February and, I hate to say it, I remember thinking, *I hope you don't get killed.* I want to know how it all went now that you're back.'

It's easy now to look back on such statements and smile, if not laugh. With virtually the tour complete, those who have followed the tour, even from a distance, can see that I was relatively safe and supported in all parts of Australia. Yet at the start of the year most people had fears, on some level, even if it was that my truck would break down.

Some of their other tour-related thoughts offered were indicative of common questions, concerns or hopes.

'I'd have to prepare myself to hear people's stories.'

'I know it's terrible but I thought, *What will I wear?* because I'm going to so many different climates.'

'I'd wonder how to approach things. Things are going to be different in Toorak compared to Bundaberg.'

'I was just dreaming of Esperance and desert holidays.'

'How could I be passionate, but not go overboard with my message?'

'I'd expect that there would be differences across the states, even the regions.'

'I'm thinking of staying with different people all over the country. I'd just find that exhausting.'

'I'd want to know where to get good coffee, good places to cycle, going jogging and bushwalking. That would be really important for me.'

I spend the last portion of our two hours together previewing some of my findings. These include observations of the LGBT sector, LGBT young people, homophobia more generally in communities, where the future might lie and ongoing challenges.

Before she leaves, one of my former role models, and now friends, makes my day.

'Thanks for everything you've done. It's incredible.'

Day 256

Thursday, 4th November – Melbourne VIC

The last time I was in this lift, with its walls of mirror and Melbourne cityscapes, I was leaving the building after my book launch in February. I'm visiting the JOY94.9FM studios, located in a 'Community Hub' of services set up by the City of Melbourne. In a street of buildings old and new, this art deco building and former home of the Commonwealth Banking Corporation stands out, in a good way. It's hard to fathom that I'm back again on the back end of my tour. As the lift goes upward, the fact that I've made it around the country sinks in.

Rather than do a 'phoner' for my weekly check-in with radio presenter Doug Pollard, he asked me to upgrade my 10–15 minute cross in my Melbourne week to a one-hour discussion as part of *Digging Deeper* segment.

On a journey where so much changes, I craved routine, and, as I've said, this weekly segment was important. Wherever I was and whatever was happening I knew what I'd be doing each Thursday morning.

Before this tour I had only met Doug once or twice very briefly, however now we greet with the warm hug of old friends. Doug is revered, feared and reviled in equal quantities, at times dividing people with his journalistic wrath. Yet there is no doubt that this grandpa-esque bear keeps everyone abreast of anything and everything LGBT across the globe. He also supported my tour before most others did, and was responsible for drawing further attention and support to it. And, say what you like, but apart from my mother, he's the only person who has been calling me each week.

I'm teased quickly about the five song selections I've made to accompany my interview.

'Now, we have often talked with Daniel on the phone as he's been travelling 'round Australia on his *Beyond 'That's So Gay'* tour but today we've got him in the studio and we've got him for a full hour – and he has to go and pick Kermit the Frog – why did you pick that for your first choice, Daniel?'

Me: 'There's something about Kermit the Frog. If you YouTube it you can see him sitting on a log, you know, with the banjo. If you don't melt you have a heart of ice. I've been around the country and when I've selected that song for various radio stations, they've had a very emotive response to it – which has been negative – but afterward, they go: Awww.'

'Yeah, it's amazing isn't it? He's only a scrap of felt with somebody's hand up his backside so to speak.'

I'm surprised that the interview focuses on me for the majority of the hour. Doug is clear about why he is putting me, rather than my tour, under the microscope.

'I want to put things in context 'cos a lot of people have been saying over the weeks and months you've been doing this, *Who is this Daniel Witthaus, where does he come from?* You know, *What's he about*, so let's start back at the beginning.'

Me: 'That's a very good place to start.'

'No, we're not going to do *Sound of Music*. I refuse to have a *Sound of Music* track. Where were you born?'

Our conversation spans my childhood, teenage years and early adulthood. Mentioning my sister's love of singing Elton John's *Daniel* to me leads to a Melbourne gay identity SMS'ing in and offering to invite me to one of his parties next time Elton John is in town.

'Doing things like that must put an enormous strain on any relationship so you're not in a relationship at the moment or you are?'

349

Me: 'Like I tell everybody, I have a boyfriend and he's called the *Beyond That's So Gay'* tour and we've been together for 38 weeks. Once it's over I'm …' I couldn't help cracking up laughing … 'back on the market. But sure, it's been a really difficult one for me.'

'Dare I ask what you're going to do next?'

Me: 'I'm going to have a mid-life crisis.'

Doug laughs, 'You can't afford the Porsche.'

Me: 'I'm not sure how I'd go with the Hawaiian shirt and a man half my age – but anyway, I need routine and the other thing I need to do is, I need to find the first eligible bachelor who walks by me and we're going to snuggle for a considerable period of time.'

On the way out Doug hands me a piece of paper with someone who has SMS'd in to the radio station to say that he would offer himself to be the next eligible bachelor to be snuggled.

I hotfoot it out of JOY and walk briskly to Bruce to both save myself a parking fine and get moving to a presentation I'm giving to some students. Once inside Bruce I become curious and decide to SMS the mystery eligible bachelor. I reach into my back pocket – gone, lost. Must have fallen out.

I chuckle.

'Daniel Witthaus. The story of my life.'

Day 257

Friday, 5th November – Melbourne VIC

No! That's all I need.

Somehow I've lost my parking ticket at Federation Square's carpark. First the number of my mystery bachelor and now this. What next? Unless I can find it, it's the maximum day rate for 90 minutes of parking.

I've just jogged from the Centre for Adult Education on Flinders Lane to jump in Bruce and get moving to make it on time to a workshop I'm running for an elite private school two hours outside of Melbourne.

I'd stayed behind to talk to a young bisexual man who took offence over a questionnaire I started with for his class. The course coordinator had invited me to come do a lunchtime presentation to a group of 'young people disengaged from mainstream education'.

'Why was there no bisexual visibility in that activity?' he demanded. 'It was all about gays and lesbians.'

'If you remember, the instructions were for half of the room to answer questions as a same-sex couple and the other half as an opposite-sex couple. Bisexual people could have been in either side of the room. I purposefully didn't talk about identity, only the relationship.'

'Oh, that's right. Oh, you're right. Sorry. Well let me tell you …'

I decide to bite the bullet and pay the full day rate and get on the road. I even 'Batmanned' Bruce, meaning I backed into the carspace so that I could make a quick getaway, like driving the Batmobile out of the Batcave.

Once on the road I make pretty good time.

I arrive in Mt Macedon and find the winery where the leadership team from one of Melbourne's elite private all-boys schools is gathered. I soon find myself in a high-ceilinged room with exposed beams and plenty of natural light. I'm reminded again that these elite schools really know how to get away and fulfill their professional development calendar.

It goes exceptionally well, so much so that I'm invited to stay for an end-of-day celebratory drink. I'm humbled, given that this is a very private celebration for the retirement of one staff member of some 25 years, and another who is moving his family to China.

'That went *very* well Daniel. If I have anything to do with it, we'll have you at our school at the start of next year,' says the professional development coordinator before throwing back a generous gulp of white wine.

Day 258

Saturday, 6th November – Melbourne VIC to Geelong VIC = 76kms

Just as it was no mistake that I started my tour in my hometown, The City By The Bay, so too it is no mistake that my homecoming is to be in Geelong.

With a follow-up training scheduled, I checked in with Geelong in October, and heard nothing. With each additional week the silence became louder and louder.

I call and discover I've become an afterthought. Any promise of a follow-up training for local teachers, health professionals and homophobia-curious others has just evaporated and I'm now given the impression that I am an unwelcomed annoyance.

'It's been really busy …'

Great. I have deliberately organised nothing for my final week, as advised, out of respect. I recall my scepticism when Geelong's Mayor had talked about my final tour week, in February, offering 'I'm absolutely serious, anything we can do'? Yes, I suspended disbelief.

I'm astonished to hear that 'getting' funding along with another regional Victorian area is the main reason why my homecoming has been an inconvenience and casualty; the same funding I was called about weeks ago, and recommended Geelong for.

I know there is nothing I can really say, other than to congratulate everyone on the funding, to do the radio interview and to accept an offer to present to local LGBT young people in a few weeks.

I write in my journal:

'Officially this is the final week of the tour. Is that it? I guess so. There it is. I guess I know that after something big there is emptiness. There is silence, nothing. And whilst I find that I need this silence and space, I'm also aware that I wanted some celebration. Am I expected to throw my own? No. After this year, I'm not going to throw my own 'I'm home' party. I guess it would have been nice. I would have liked that. And what then of today? Well I was going to clean out Bruce, but I can't be fucked …'

It's official: I'm sulking. I spend most of the day responding to a backlog of e-mails and other messages.

Day 259

Sunday, 7th November – Geelong VIC

I spend an entire afternoon and evening putting up every blog of the tour and re-writing all the different sections of my website.

Facebook comment on my status update:

'I thought you were finished??? come on guy. get it over with. pregnancy dont go this long! and a massive fairy clap for you. you got any idea how much you have achieved? it will hit you when you sit down and take a deep breath and relax. def got a man crush on you …'

Day 260

Monday, 8th November- Geelong VIC

Journal entry: 'Are we there yet?'

Day 261

Tuesday, 9ᵗʰ November – Geelong VIC to Melbourne VIC = 76kms

I meet a few people from the Victorian Equal Opportunity and Human Rights Commission to discuss homophobia in mainstream sport and my recently withdrawn job application.

During my first week in Tasmania I was told about two upcoming educator positions with the organisation; a role I had as a sessional for the last five years. Whilst happy to have the flexibility in the past as I pursued other projects, with the end of the tour approaching I started to panic: what would I do with the rest of my life. In emotional waters that felt more tumultuous than those in Bass Strait, this role felt like a life-raft in the distance.

I swam hard and got the application in. I then thought better of it; my ability to move straight into a Monday to Friday job in the public sector would be lacking in the coming months to say the least.

Yet this realisation, and the life-raft floating away only exacerbated my feeling of being lost at sea.

Day 262

Wednesday, 10ᵗʰ November – Melbourne VIC

I visit the ABC Southbank Studios to talk on Radio National's Bush Telegraph with host Michael Cathcart. I feel like I've come full circle: not only was I here talking with 774 ABC Melbourne's Jon Faine shortly before my tour commenced, so too I was talking with the calmly cheerful Michael during a training break in Geelong. To the credit of his producers, they've tracked me down to find out how everything unfolded.

Michael looks much younger than I expect, yet his calm, wise and reassuring warmth is the same across a faux-wooden ABC studio desk as it is over the phone and across the airwaves.

After, I head up the narrow thoroughfare of Centre Lane to grab some Vietnamese rolls and the best vanilla slice in Melbourne. It's been far too long. I squirrel them away in my backpack, ride down to the banks of the Yarra and get reacquainted with some old gastronomic friends.

Day 263

Thursday, 11ᵗʰ November – Melbourne VIC to Geelong VIC = 76kms

Over 90 minutes I'm on the receiving end of an interview by a freelance journalist who wants to write a feature for a major newspaper. He invites me to his northern suburbs home after his partner comes home and talks about my lunchtime presentation to CAE students a week ago. I leave wanting him to be one of my friends.

I half-chuckle with a tinge of sadness. The feeling of leaving great people behind has been a constant on this prolonged drive. Before I even make it back to Bruce a montage of faces plays out in my mind – an ode to lost potential friends: Lois Lane in Perth, Percy and Steven in Broome, Alice Spring's Daniel, Country Queensland's Jono, Lismore's Marg and the list goes on. Of course the montage spices up with the additions of The Barman and The Dancer. The fact that I know The Dancer won't keep his end of the post-tour bargain makes the memory of The Barman burn that much more.

Day 264

Friday, 12ᵗʰ November – Geelong VIC

I complete my final blog and celebrate with a scotch and Coke. My family are out of town for the weekend due to a country wedding.

Day 265

Saturday, 13th November – Geelong VIC

It's raining cats and dogs, so I spend the day inside doing some final e-mails and making some adjustments to my website.

Facebook post from a Perth woman who saw me in a Body Pump class, yet we never spoke: 'Congratulations Daniel! What an amazing feat; i hope your reflections consist not only of happy memories, but also many important achievements. Wouldn't it be fantastic if you happened to be contemplating doing it all again, to reach some of the folk you missed this time round? One more sunrise and that's it!!'

Day 266

Sunday, 14th November – Geelong VIC

I'm at the second 'Klozet' party, Geelong's new LGBT night, coincidentally the evening of my last tour day. I meet a number of blasts-from-my-past, including a young man I used to drive to Melbourne for under 18 gay and lesbian dance parties – along with a mini-busload of other eager Geelong-based attendees.

I meet a younger gay man, an eligible bachelor, who is insistent on snuggling. I'm taken aback when he tells me he lives with his parents and brother, and that they won't mind me going back to his house. Maybe Geelong has progressed more than I thought.

Facebook comments for the day include:

Congratulations Dan, someone should give you an OAM.

Nought days to go!!! You hero!!

Congratulations Daniel … I bet it's been an amazing adventure.

Have a rest now Daniel.

Congrats reaching your goals! Best wishes THE BEST is yet to come …

My Facebook status update: Day 266+; 0 days to go.

Day 267

Nothing prepared me for the silence.

After 266 days, not counting the non-stop 6 months pre-tour, I found it hard to stop. After a few days in refuge with my mother, she confessed, 'I love you Daniel Edward, but if you don't relax I'm going to strangle you'.

Around this time I walked through my mother's living room and wondered what was on the large, blaring television. A former AFL footballer had completed an 8-day run from Adelaide to Melbourne to raise awareness and money for Breast Cancer. Footage of people joining his journey flashed on his screen and I then stood open-mouthed as he ran into a studio full of cheering people and adulation. Practically speechless, highly emotional and exhausted he sat being interviewed.

The emptiness of my silent homecoming was now filled with envy. He was warmly embraced, welcomed back and thanked. He spoke of how eight days of hearing women's stories had moved him beyond words.

I myself was beyond words. A fully sponsored, highly organised – and not by him – journey of eight days and he was welcomed like this? Eight days of women's stories moved him beyond words?

In the raw aftermath of the tour, and the dark contemplation that the last 18 months of my life might have been a waste of my time, I laid very low at mum's. I did my best to digest what it is I'd done and what it was I discovered. Re-entry to everyday life post-tour was a challenge to say the least. I found it hard to believe that the tour was actually over and that I could relax and stop worrying.

For months I struggled, asking myself over and over if I had just made one of the biggest mistakes of my life. Yes that sounds melodramatic, but the post-tour silence was deafening for this semi-reformed workaholic.

Post-Christmas I was taken in by a generous friend, Rohan, who gave me a roof over my head as I digested it all and took those next logical steps. Whilst I flailed emotionally and socially, I did do what I do best when I'm unsure: I worked. A series of summary reports, media rounds – including one TV appearance where I was assured that my chest hair trended on Twitter and I became the first person on Australian TV to say challenging homophobia was not '6 weeks of anal sex education' – that and developing and delivering workshops for Australian Marriage Equality.

Once the silence was broken, it didn't get quiet again.

Acknowledgments

Beyond Priscilla was as much a rollercoaster as the original drive. After hundreds and hundreds of cuppas I felt a responsibility to share countless yarns that were trusted to me so readily, warmly and with such candidness.

To the many and varied LGBTI organisations, media outlets, projects and community groups, thankyou; for all the supposed agendas and in-fighting, you did a remarkable job of showing me your best, believing in this project and supporting me to splutter around the country. Special mention to Doug Pollard and the *Freshly Doug* team at JOY94.9FM. Another special mention to Paul Hollingworth for his company for the first 8 weeks on the road, and then remote support from Melbourne thereafter.

To those who provided free cuppas, meals and shelter, I am forever indebted. I witnessed the best that country Australia had to offer and only completed my drive because of its generosity. I was sheltered for a staggering 235 of 266 nights on tour, thus saving me in the vicinity of $25-30,000 at the very least. Special thanks to Rohan Randall for post-tour sanctuary.

Motafrenz car club, Deb Holder and Jim Doultre with Matthew Richie kicked off donations through Uniting Care-Cutting Edge (UCCE) Shepparton for fuel, and the generosity thereafter did not wane. For their part, UCCE, especially Ro Allen, let me take my openly gay truck, Bruce, around the country and were never far away, especially Damien Stevens, to provide me with logistical support. Note to Bruce: although incredibly thirsty at times, you *never* let me down *once*.

Thanks to Kenton Penley Miller, Paul Bugeja and Fiona Sawyer who read very early drafts of my manuscript and provided assistance. Thanks to my publisher, Gordon Thompson, for giving me the idea to turn a heavy, stagnant 20 chapters into a lighter, nimble 266 days; for understanding the heart and soul of this rollicking rural rollercoaster and, with Ashley Sievwright and Helen Bell's support, working through my tendency to overwrite and get in the way of the story. Special thanks to Luke Gahan for introducing me to Gordon.

A shout out to the young gay and lesbian Eastern Europeans on that cold, Warsaw afternoon who asked the question that started this crazy adventure. And then to Katherine Cooney, Rodney Croome and Mum for confirming that this drive must happen. Special thanks to Rodney for his pioneering project efforts with *Outlink* and for sharing so much of his experiences, hopes and regrets.

A long and strong bear hug to the men in my life who held on, or at least tried to, as I undertook the endeavours of this drive and this book: Shaun, Chris, Neil, Scott and Sander. Thanks for understanding that I can't sit still.

Finally, special thanks to my family of Mum, Mick and Helene, who never question my need to follow my dreams and adventures; special thanks to Mick for storing my stuff in his garage for a year. To my family, for enduring my long absences, and homophobia because of your youngest son/little brother, all my thanks for loving me more fiercely as a result.

www.ingramcontent.com/pod-product-compliance
Lightning Source LLC
Chambersburg PA
CBHW021133090426
42740CB00008B/771